COVENANT

VOLUME ONE

ONI
PRESS

COVENANT

LYSANDRA VUONG

CREATED BY	BOOK DESIGN BY
LYSANDRA VUONG	**CAREY SOUCY**
LAYOUT	EDITED BY
DESIGNER	**DESIREE RODRIGUEZ**
MIRANDA MUNDT	**& MEGAN BROWN**

PUBLISHED BY ONi-LiON FORGE PUBLISHING GROUP, LLC.

Hunter Gorinson, president & publisher • Sierra Hahn, editor in chief • Troy Look, vp of publishing services • Spencer Simpson, vp of sales • Angie Knowles, director of design & production • Katie Sainz, director of marketing • Jeremy Colfer, director of development Chris Cerasi, managing editor • Bess Pallares, senior editor • Grace Scheipeter, senior editor Karl Bollers, editor • Megan Brown, editor • Gabriel Granillo, editor • Jung Hu Lee, assistant editor • Michael Torma, senior sales manager • Andy McElliott, operations manager • Sarah Rockwell, senior graphic designer • Carey Soucy, senior graphic designer • Winston Gambro, graphic designer • Matt Harding, digital prepress technician • Sara Harding, executive coordinator • Kaia Rokke, marketing & communications coordinator Joe Nozemack, publisher emeritus

ONIPRESS.COM 🅕 FACEBOOK.COM/ONIPRESS
🅧 TWITTER.COM/ONIPRESS 🅞 INSTAGRAM.COM/ONIPRESS

SC ISBN: 978-1-63715-281-2   HC ISBN: 978-1-63715-477-9
eISBN: 978-1-63715-282-9   LCCN: 2023939197   PRINTED IN CHINA

ONI
PRESS

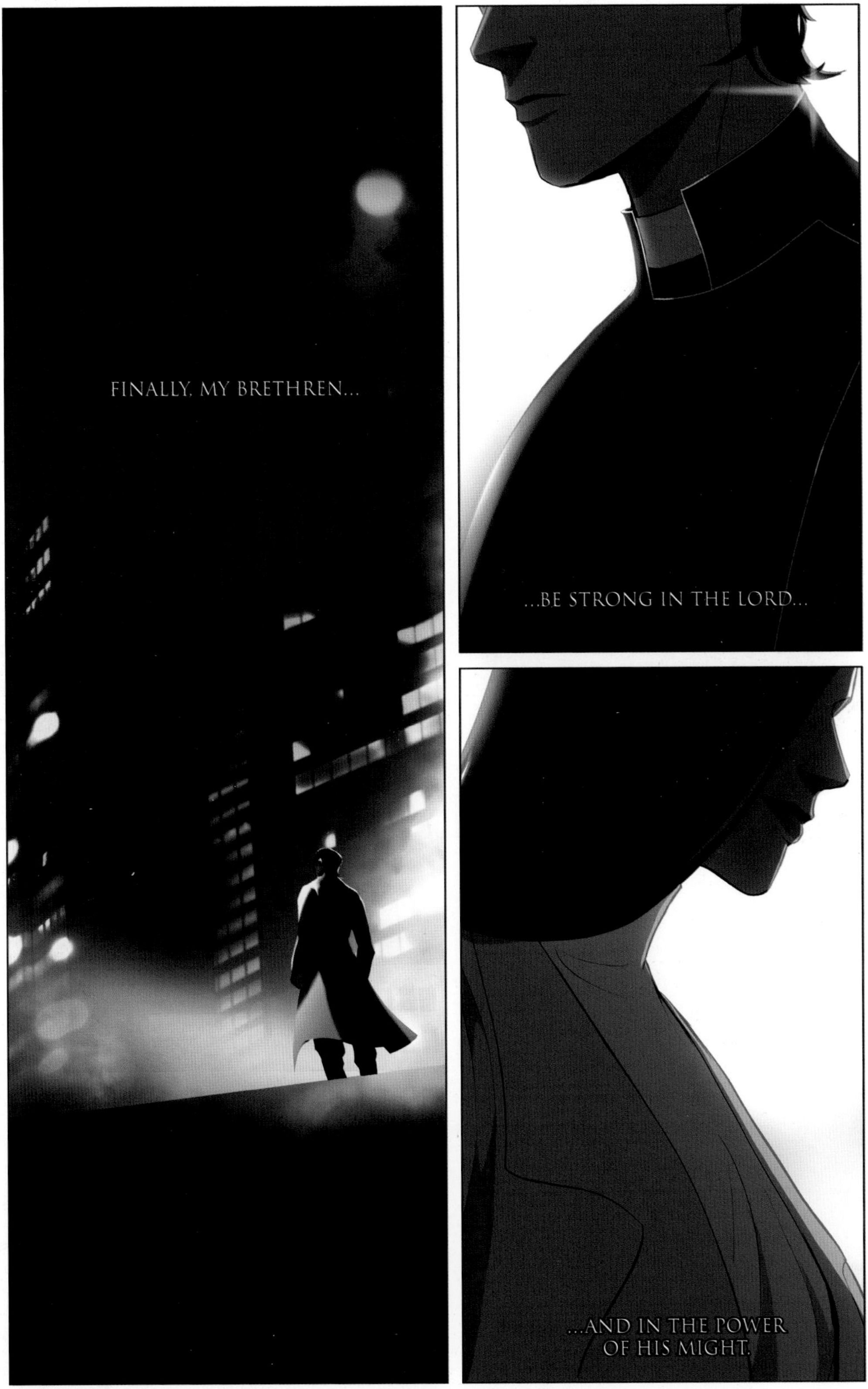
FINALLY, MY BRETHREN...
...BE STRONG IN THE LORD...
...AND IN THE POWER OF HIS MIGHT.

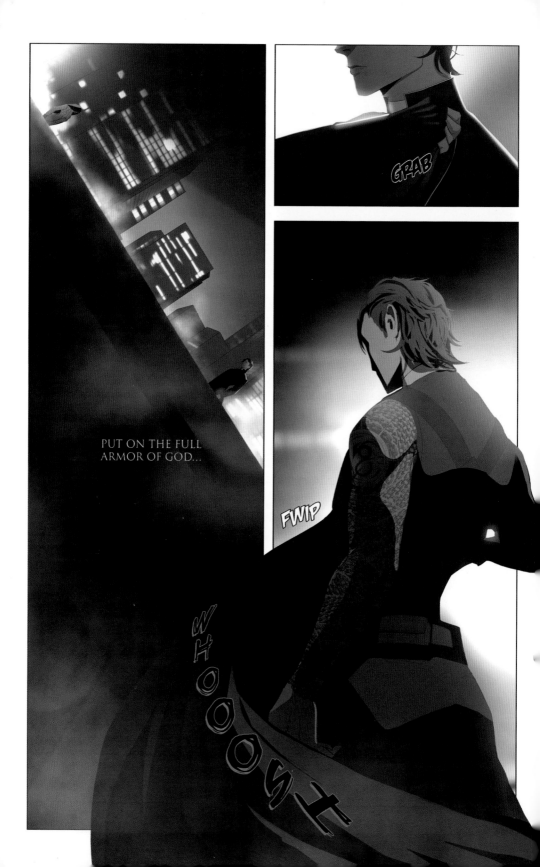

PUT ON THE FULL
ARMOR OF GOD...

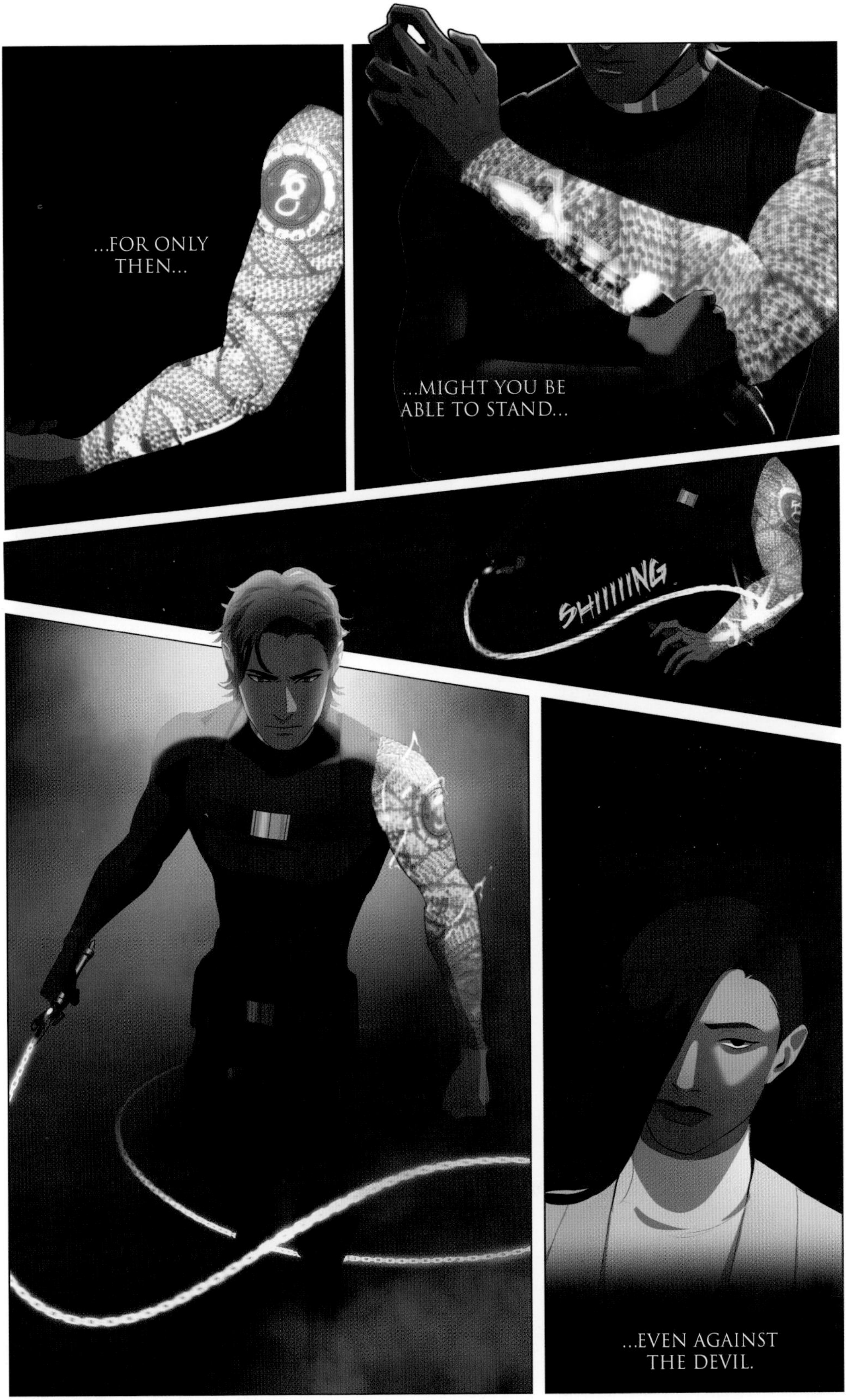
...FOR ONLY THEN...
...MIGHT YOU BE ABLE TO STAND...
SHIIIING
...EVEN AGAINST THE DEVIL.

FOR WE WRESTLE NOT AGAINST FLESH AND BLOOD.
BUT AGAINST PRINCIPALITIES...
CLACK
CLACK
...AGAINST POWERS...
CLACK
...AGAINST RULERS OF DARKNESS...
...AND...
CLACK
...AGAINST PURE WICKEDNESS.

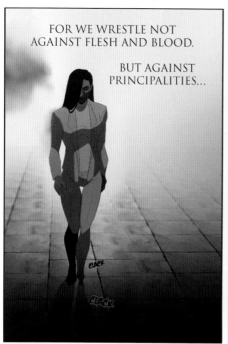

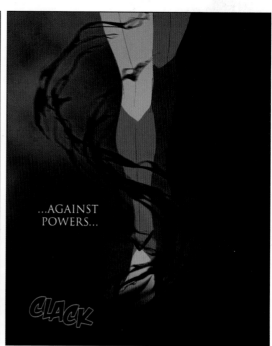

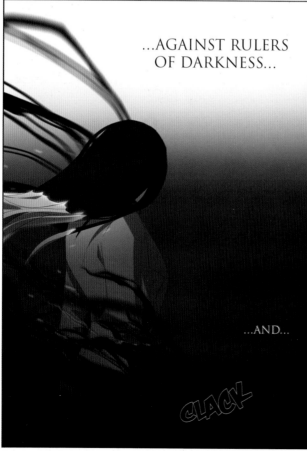

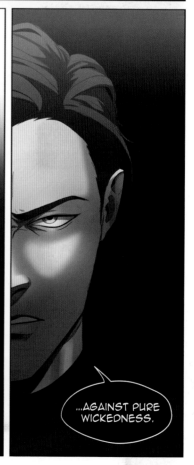

COVENANT

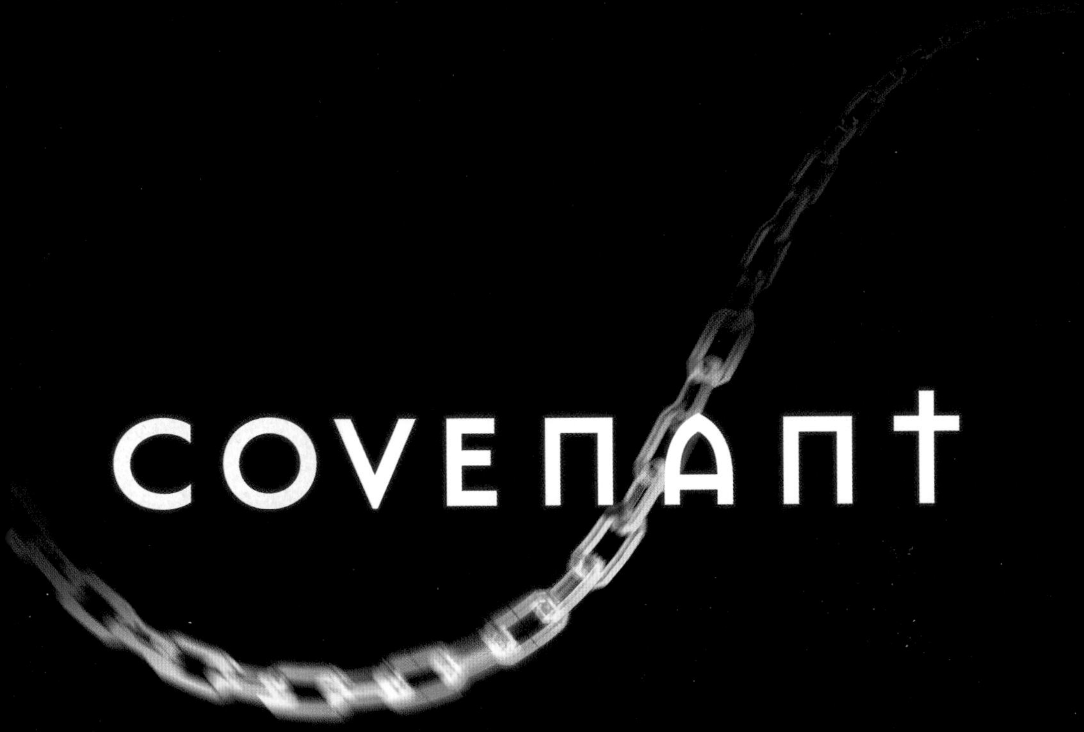

BOOK I

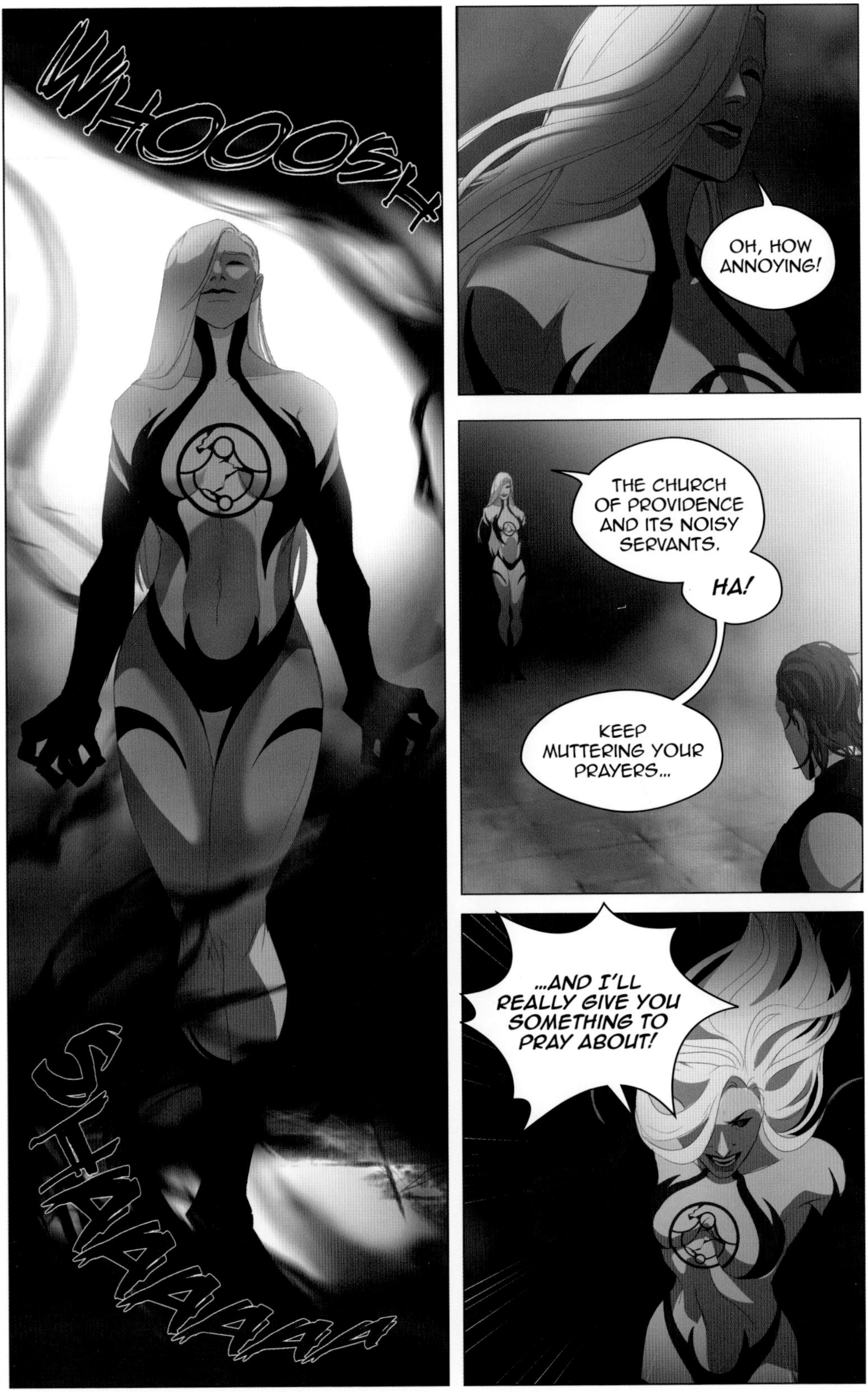
WHOOOOSH
SHAAAAAA
OH, HOW ANNOYING!
THE CHURCH OF PROVIDENCE AND ITS NOISY SERVANTS.
HA!
KEEP MUTTERING YOUR PRAYERS...
...AND I'LL REALLY GIVE YOU SOMETHING TO PRAY ABOUT!

SO THAT WHEN...

SHIIING

FWIP

...THE EVIL DAY COMES...

SHIIING

HA HA HA

DDITION TO A
AKE UP THE SHIELD
FAITH, WITH WHICH YO
CAN EXTINGUISH ALL T
AMING ARROWS OF
ONE. TAK

AND FIRM TH
WITH THE BELT
BUCKLED AROUND
UR WAIST AND TH
EASTPLATE O

YANK

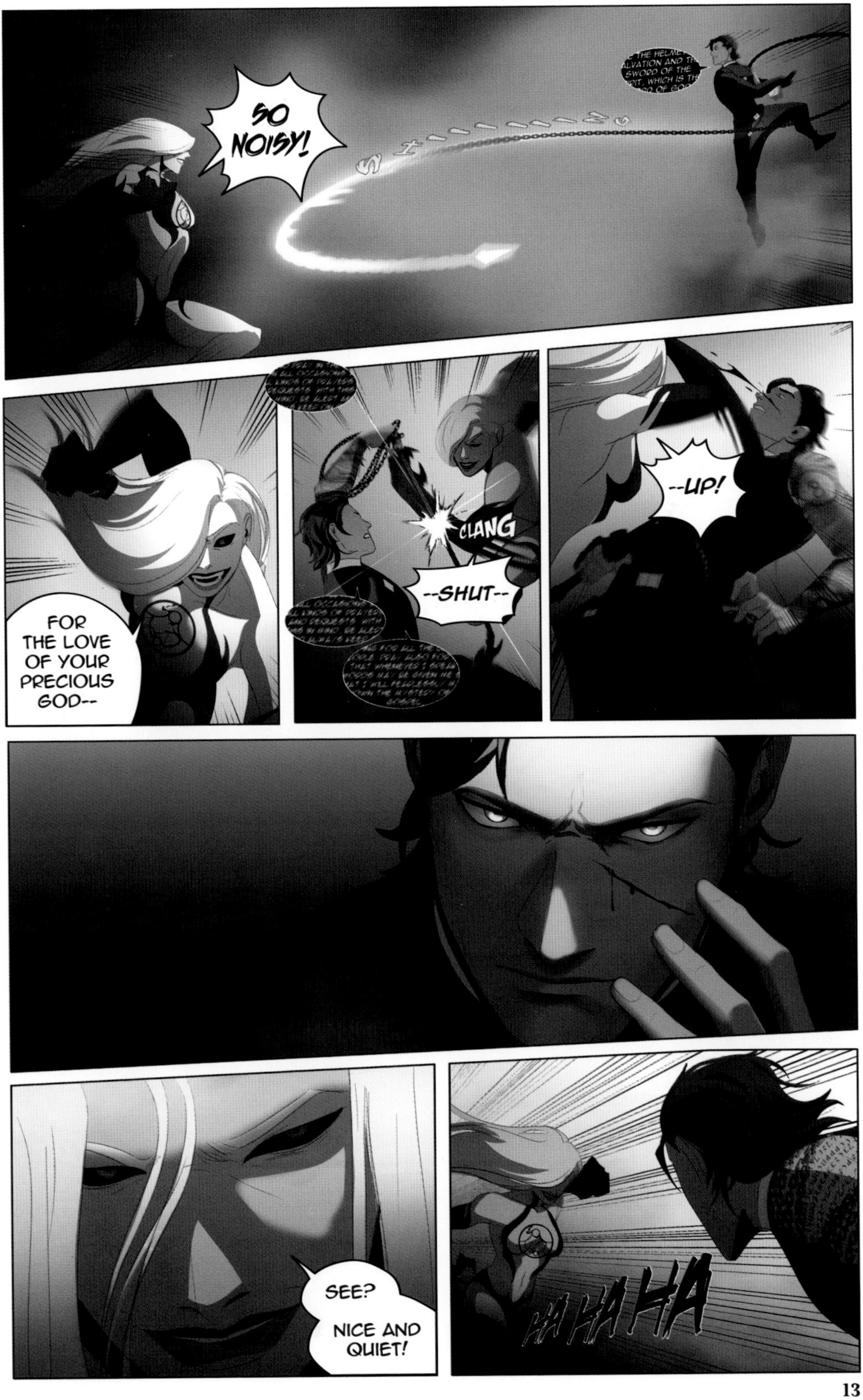
SO NOISY!
FOR THE LOVE OF YOUR PRECIOUS GOD--
CLANG
--SHUT--
--UP!
SEE?
NICE AND QUIET!
HA HA HA HA

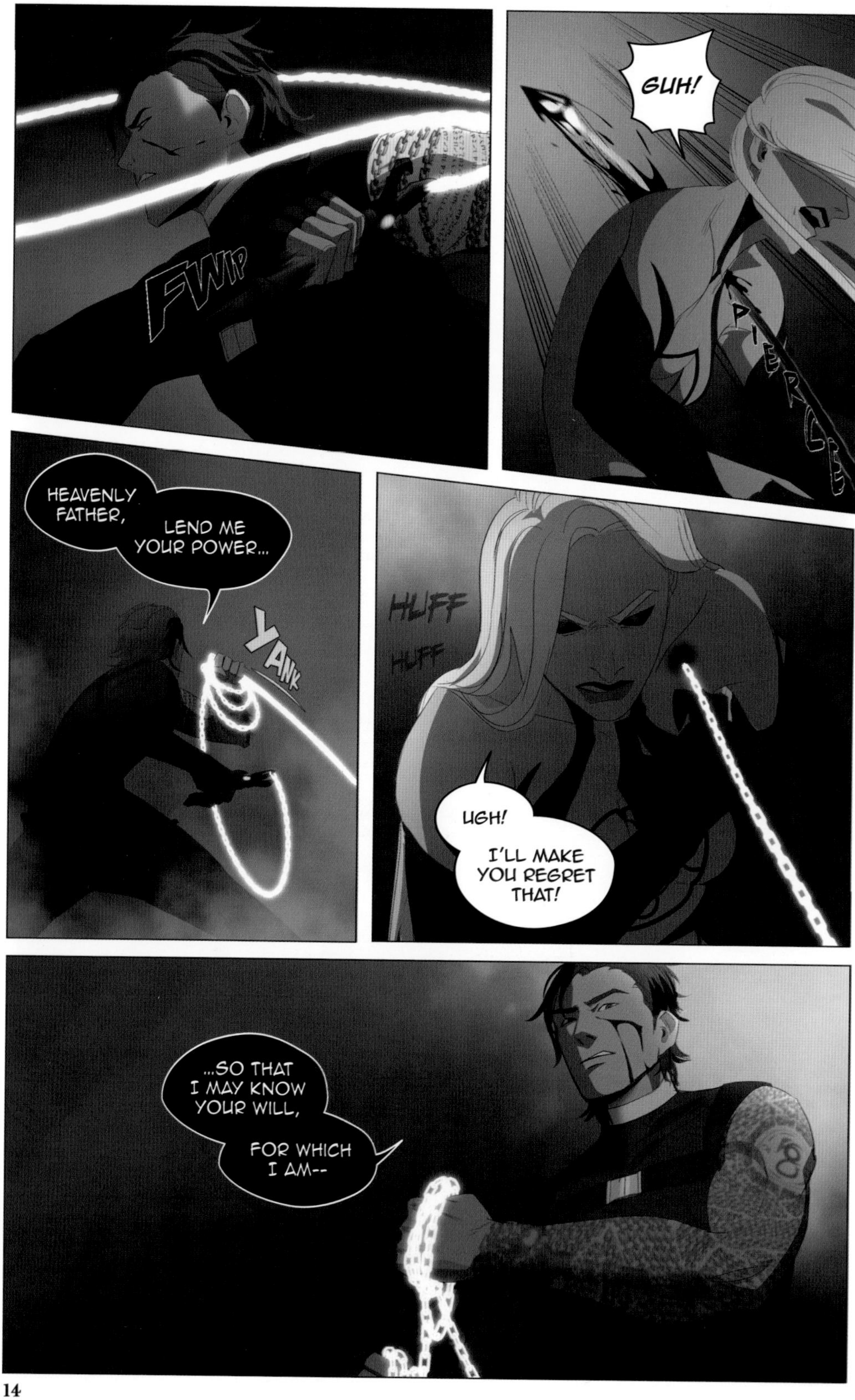

FWIP
GUH!
PIERCE
HEAVENLY FATHER,
LEND ME YOUR POWER...
YANK
HUFF
HUFF
UGH!
I'LL MAKE YOU REGRET THAT!
...SO THAT I MAY KNOW YOUR WILL,
FOR WHICH I AM--

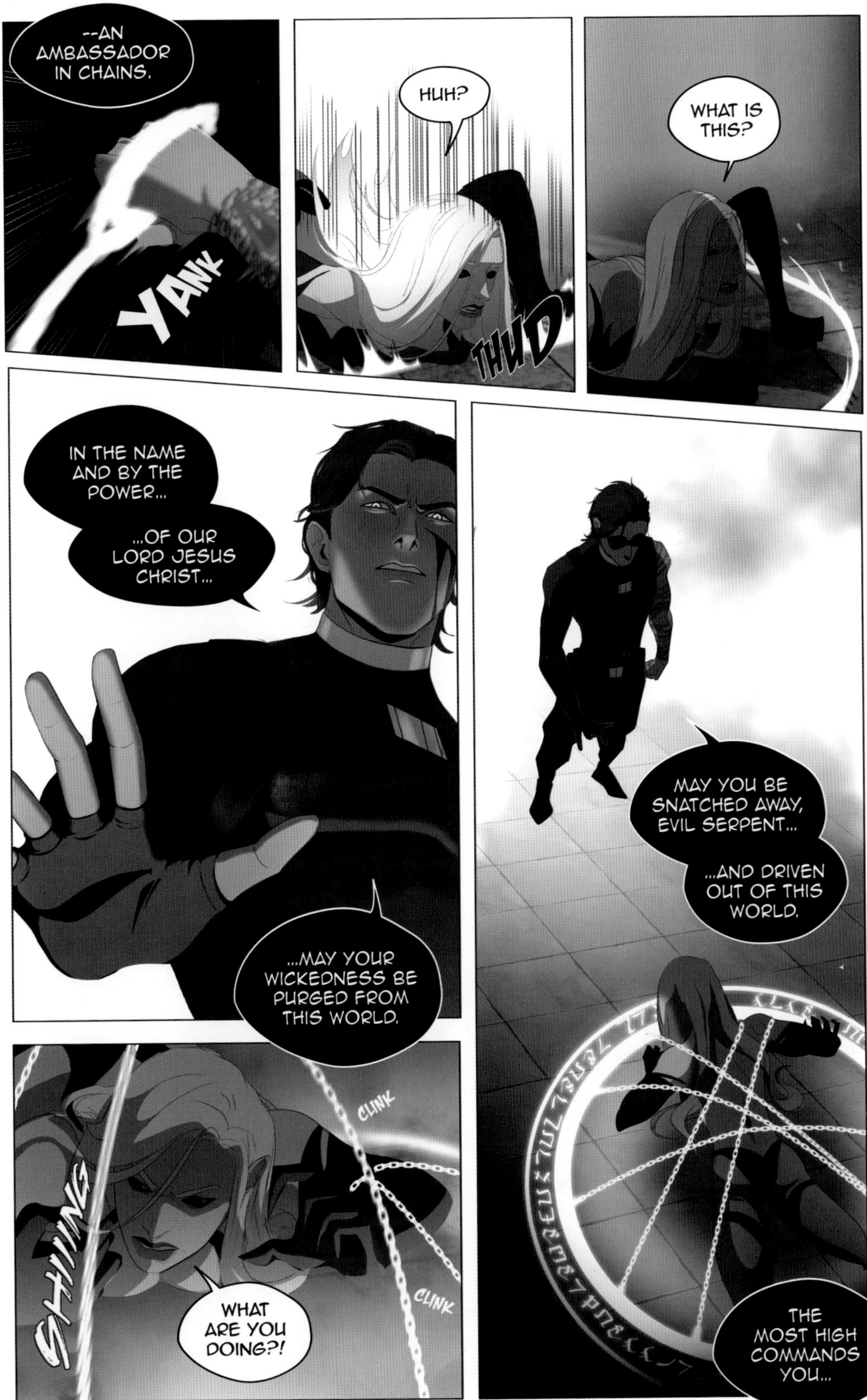
--AN AMBASSADOR IN CHAINS.
YANK
HUH?
THUD
WHAT IS THIS?
IN THE NAME AND BY THE POWER...
...OF OUR LORD JESUS CHRIST...
...MAY YOUR WICKEDNESS BE PURGED FROM THIS WORLD.
MAY YOU BE SNATCHED AWAY, EVIL SERPENT...
...AND DRIVEN OUT OF THIS WORLD.
CLINK
SHIIING
CLINK
WHAT ARE YOU DOING?!
THE MOST HIGH COMMANDS YOU...

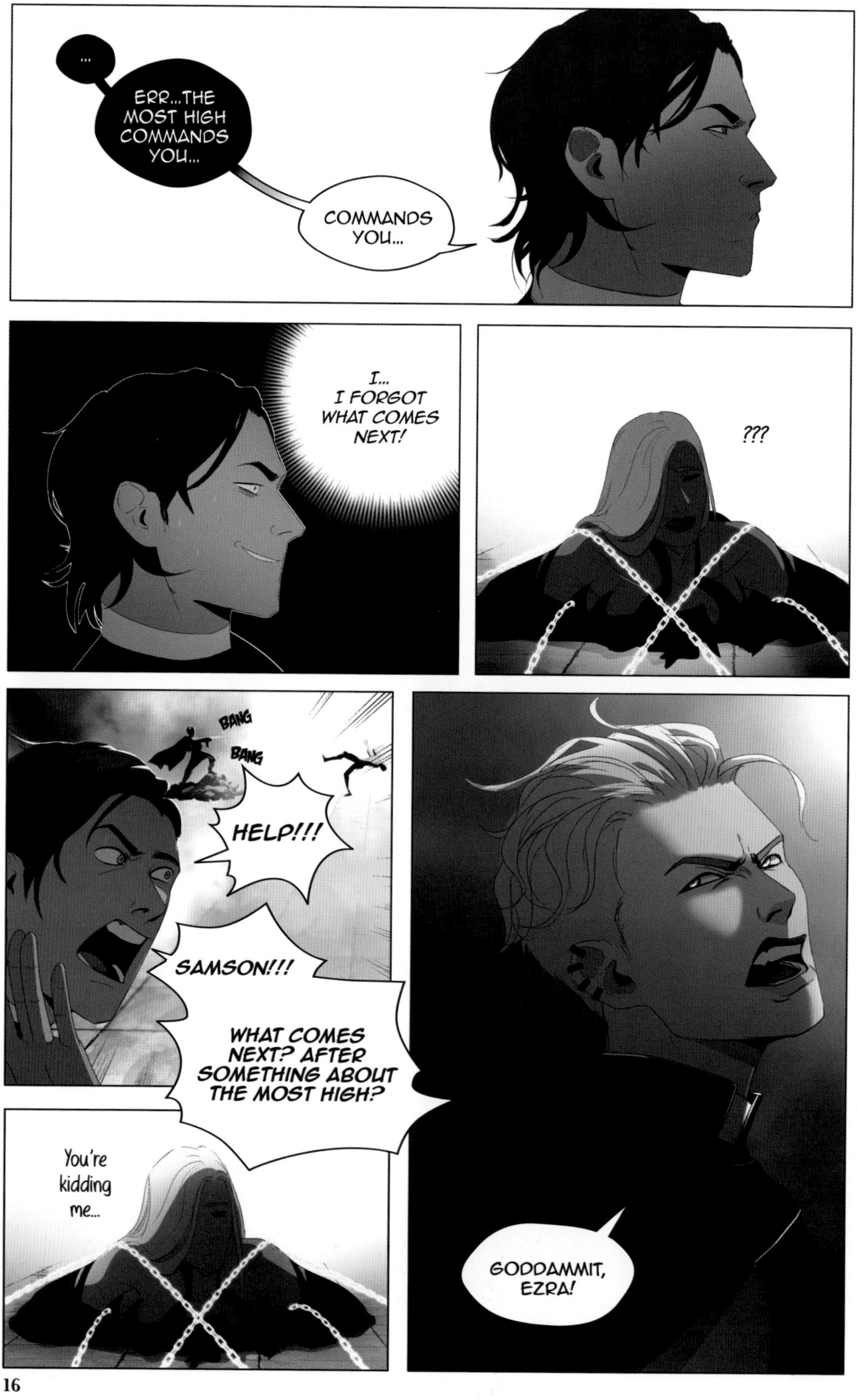
...
ERR...THE MOST HIGH COMMANDS YOU...
COMMANDS YOU...
I... I FORGOT WHAT COMES NEXT!
???
BANG
BANG
HELP!!!
SAMSON!!!
WHAT COMES NEXT? AFTER SOMETHING ABOUT THE MOST HIGH?
You're kidding me...
GODDAMMIT, EZRA!

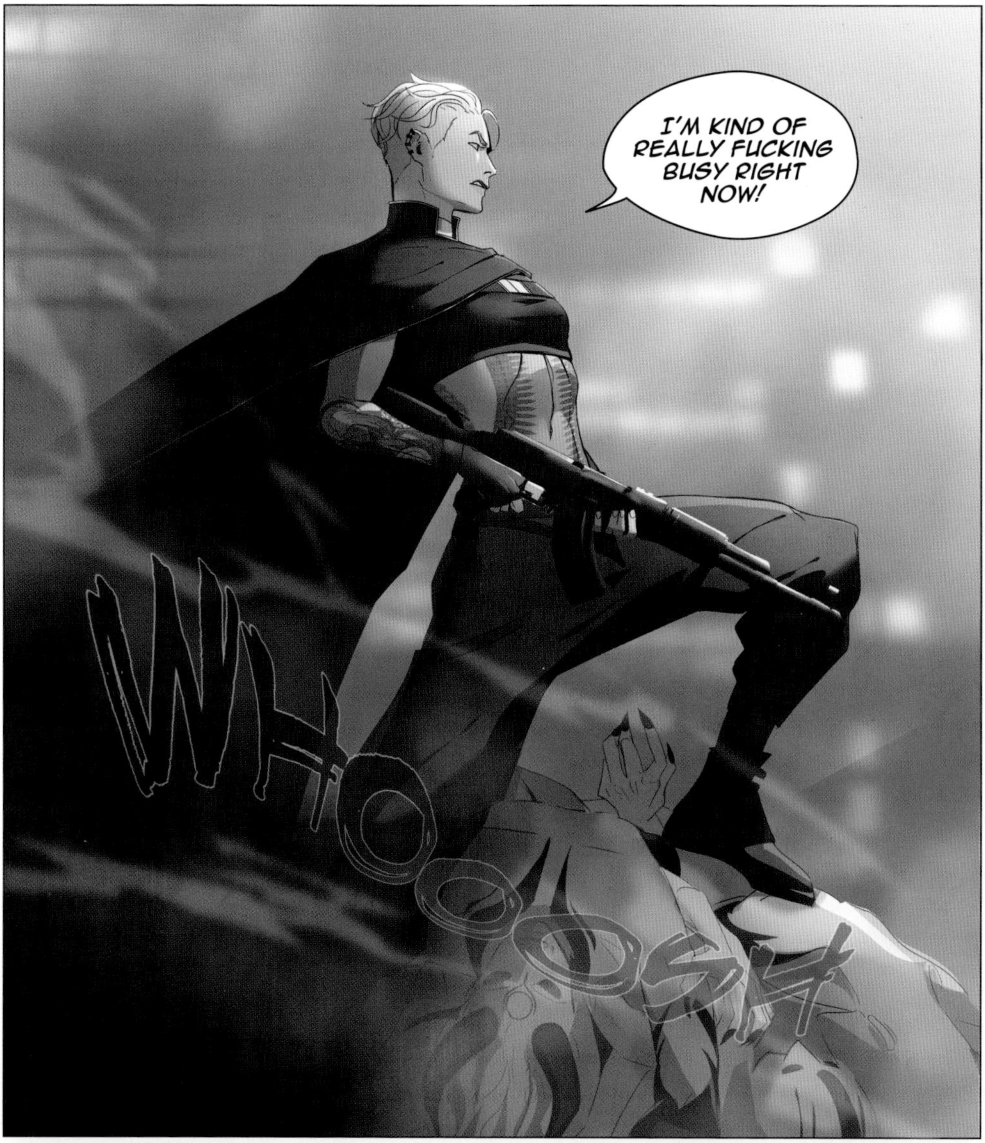
I'M KIND OF REALLY FUCKING BUSY RIGHT NOW!
WHOOOOSH

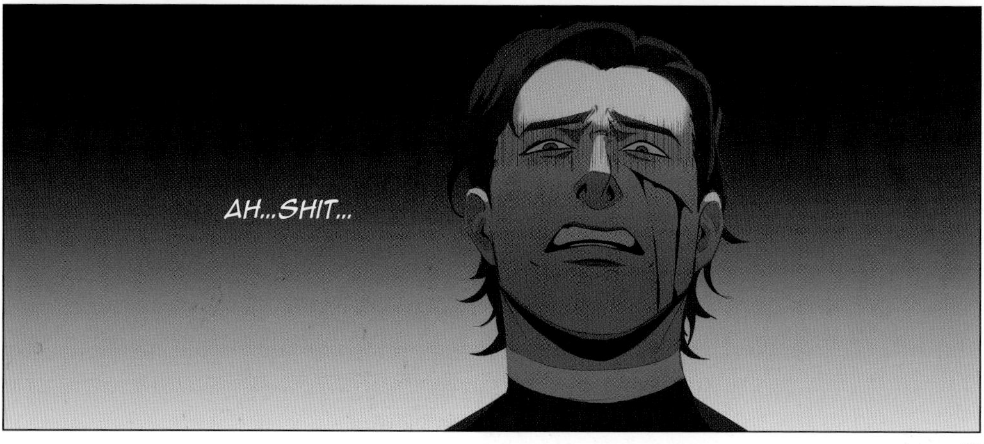
AH...SHIT...

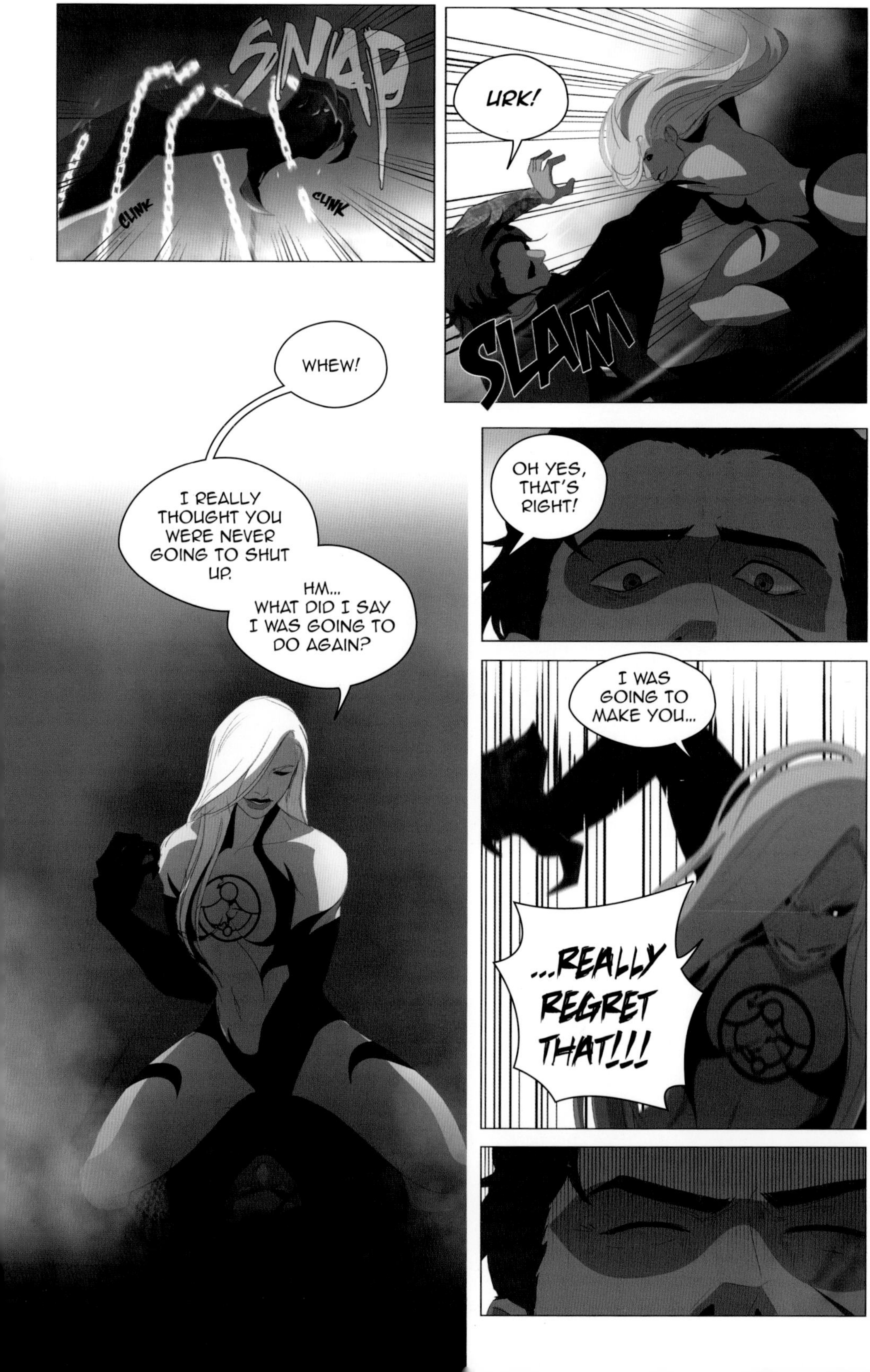
SNAP
CLINK
CLINK
URK!
SLAM
WHEW!
I REALLY THOUGHT YOU WERE NEVER GOING TO SHUT UP.
HM... WHAT DID I SAY I WAS GOING TO DO AGAIN?
OH YES, THAT'S RIGHT!
I WAS GOING TO MAKE YOU...
...REALLY REGRET THAT!!!

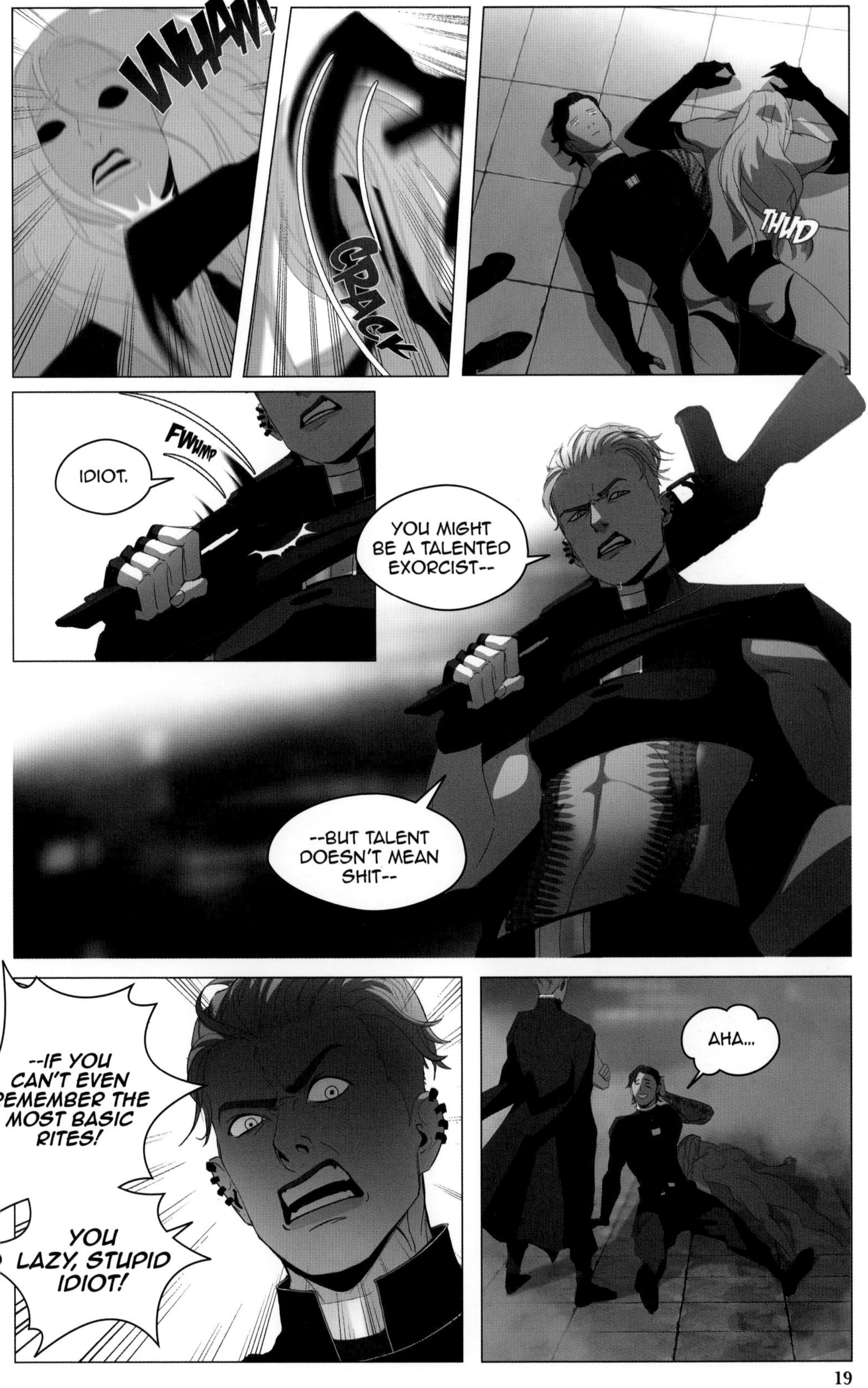
WHAM
CRACK
THUD
FWUMP
IDIOT.
YOU MIGHT BE A TALENTED EXORCIST--
--BUT TALENT DOESN'T MEAN SHIT--
--IF YOU CAN'T EVEN REMEMBER THE MOST BASIC RITES!
YOU LAZY, STUPID IDIOT!
AHA...

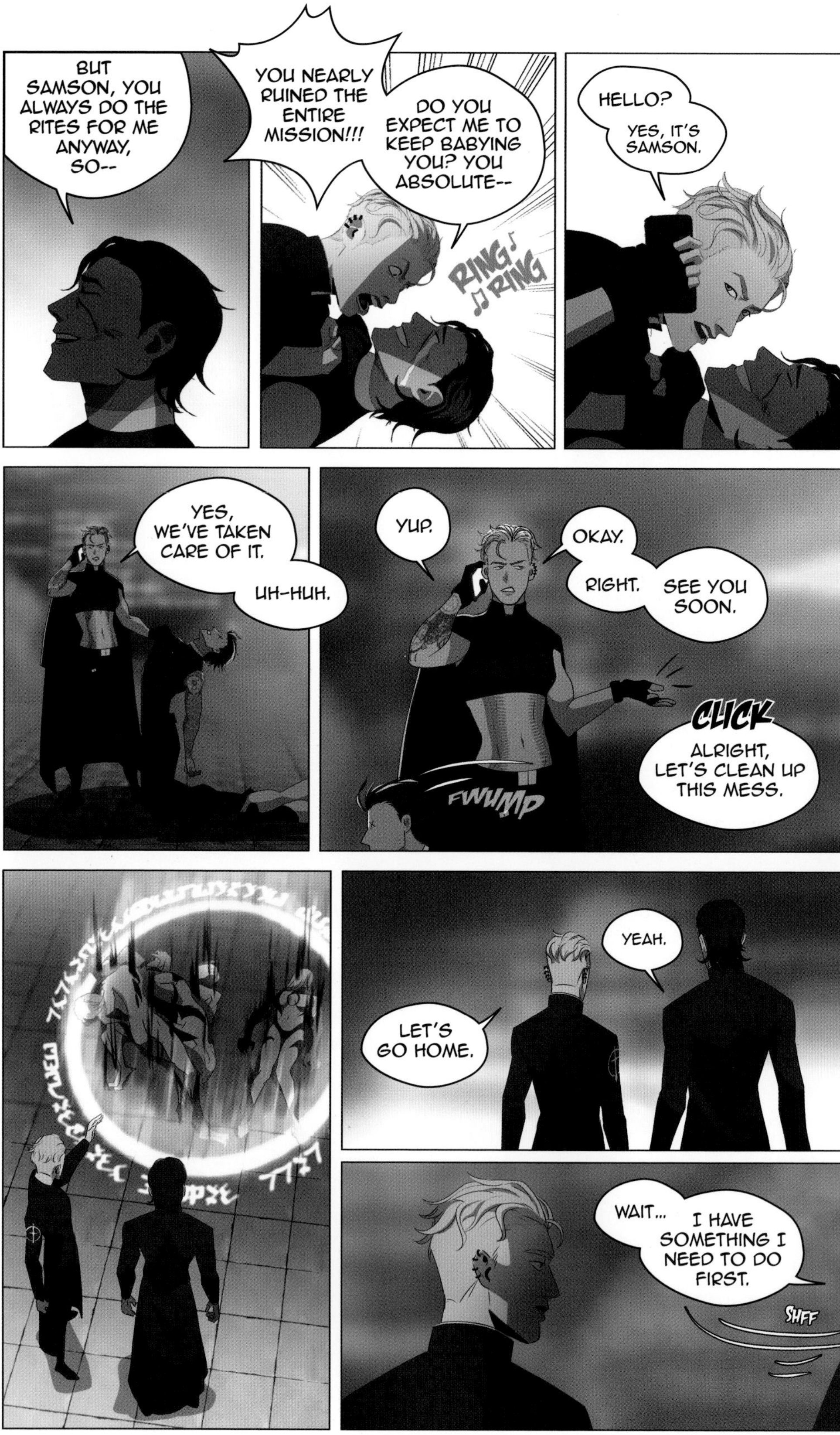
BUT SAMSON, YOU ALWAYS DO THE RITES FOR ME ANYWAY, SO--
YOU NEARLY RUINED THE ENTIRE MISSION!!!
DO YOU EXPECT ME TO KEEP BABYING YOU? YOU ABSOLUTE--
RING♪ ♫RING
HELLO?
YES, IT'S SAMSON.
YES, WE'VE TAKEN CARE OF IT.
UH-HUH.
YUP.
OKAY.
RIGHT.
SEE YOU SOON.
CLICK
ALRIGHT, LET'S CLEAN UP THIS MESS.
FWUMP
YEAH.
LET'S GO HOME.
WAIT...
I HAVE SOMETHING I NEED TO DO FIRST.
SHFF

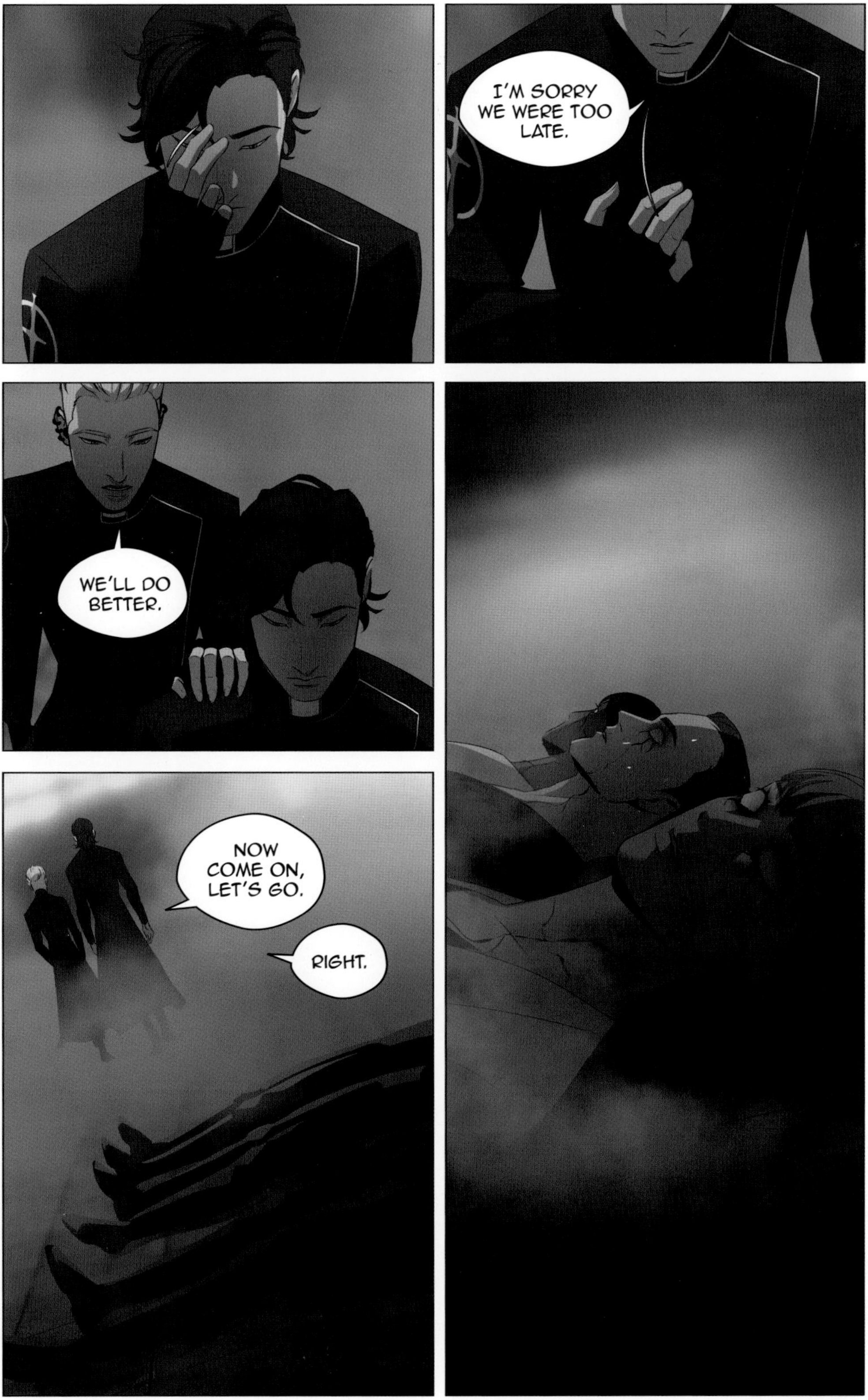
I'M SORRY WE WERE TOO LATE.
WE'LL DO BETTER.
NOW COME ON, LET'S GO.
RIGHT.

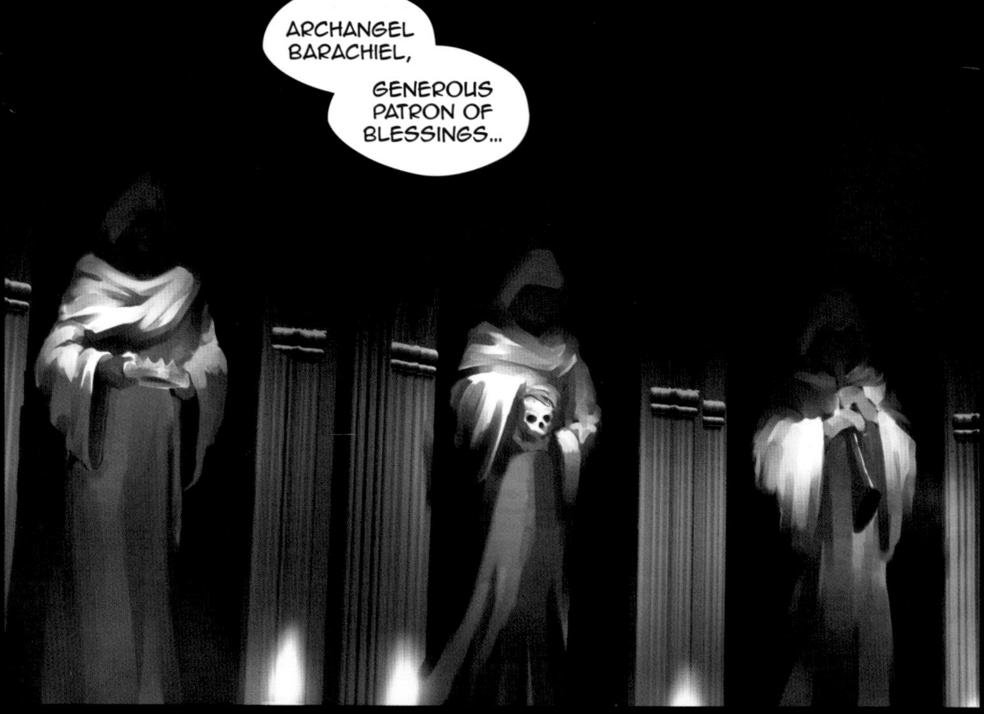
ARCHANGEL BARACHIEL,
GENEROUS PATRON OF BLESSINGS...

BOOK II

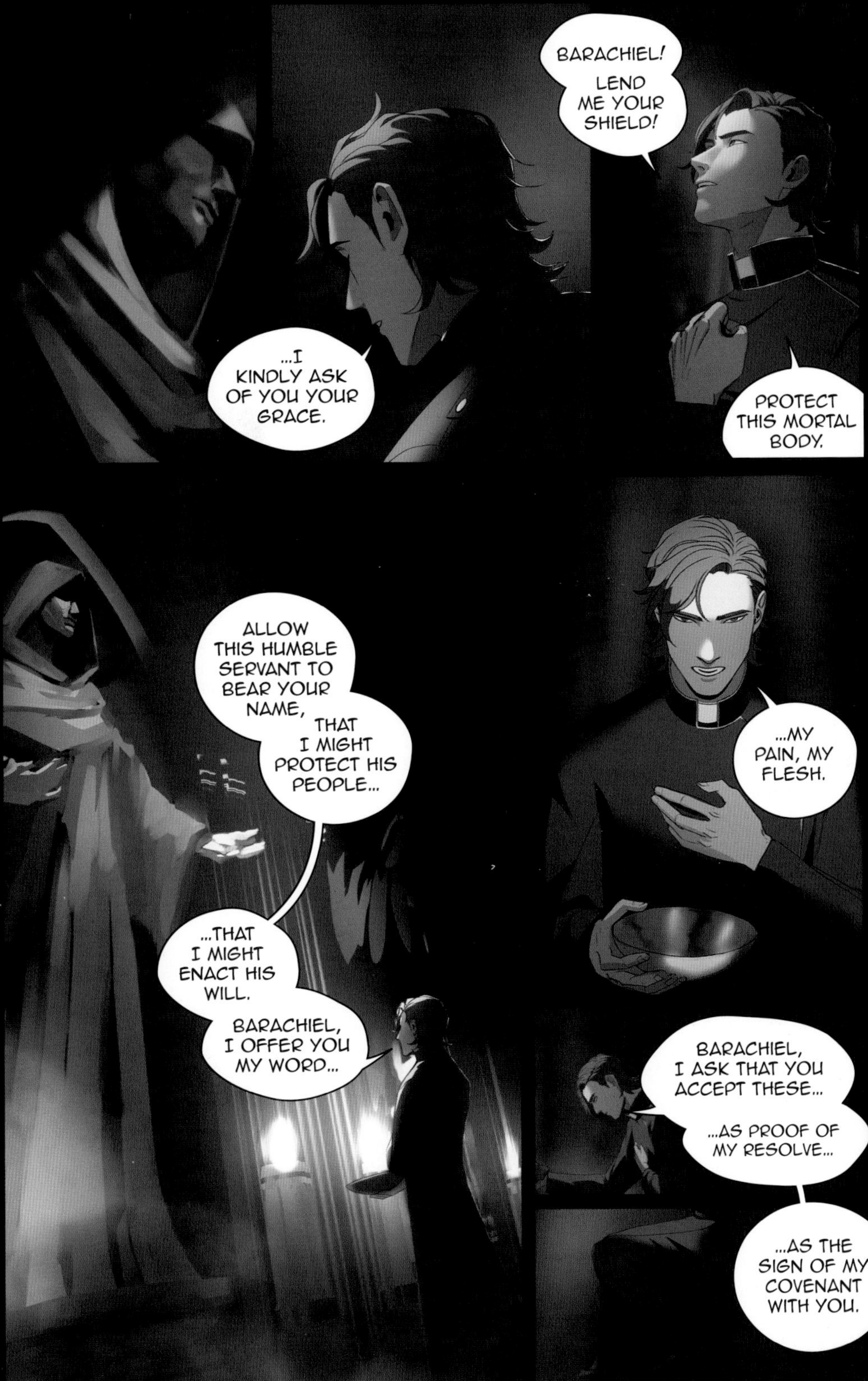
BARACHIEL! LEND ME YOUR SHIELD!
...I KINDLY ASK OF YOU YOUR GRACE.
PROTECT THIS MORTAL BODY.
ALLOW THIS HUMBLE SERVANT TO BEAR YOUR NAME,
THAT I MIGHT PROTECT HIS PEOPLE...
...THAT I MIGHT ENACT HIS WILL.
BARACHIEL, I OFFER YOU MY WORD...
...MY PAIN, MY FLESH.
BARACHIEL, I ASK THAT YOU ACCEPT THESE...
...AS PROOF OF MY RESOLVE...
...AS THE SIGN OF MY COVENANT WITH YOU.

AMEN.
DRIP
DRIP

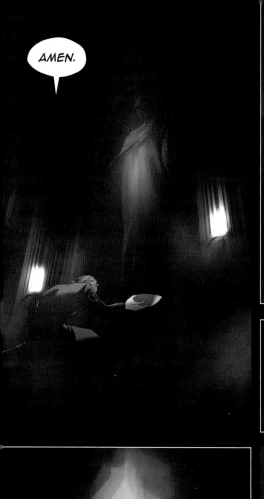

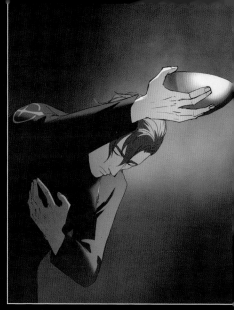

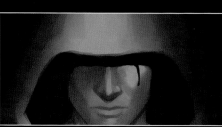

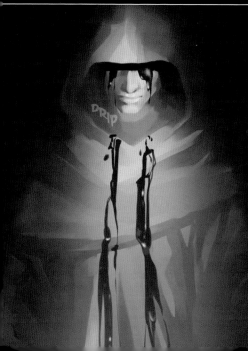

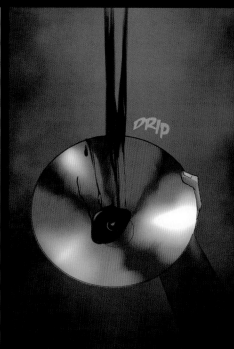

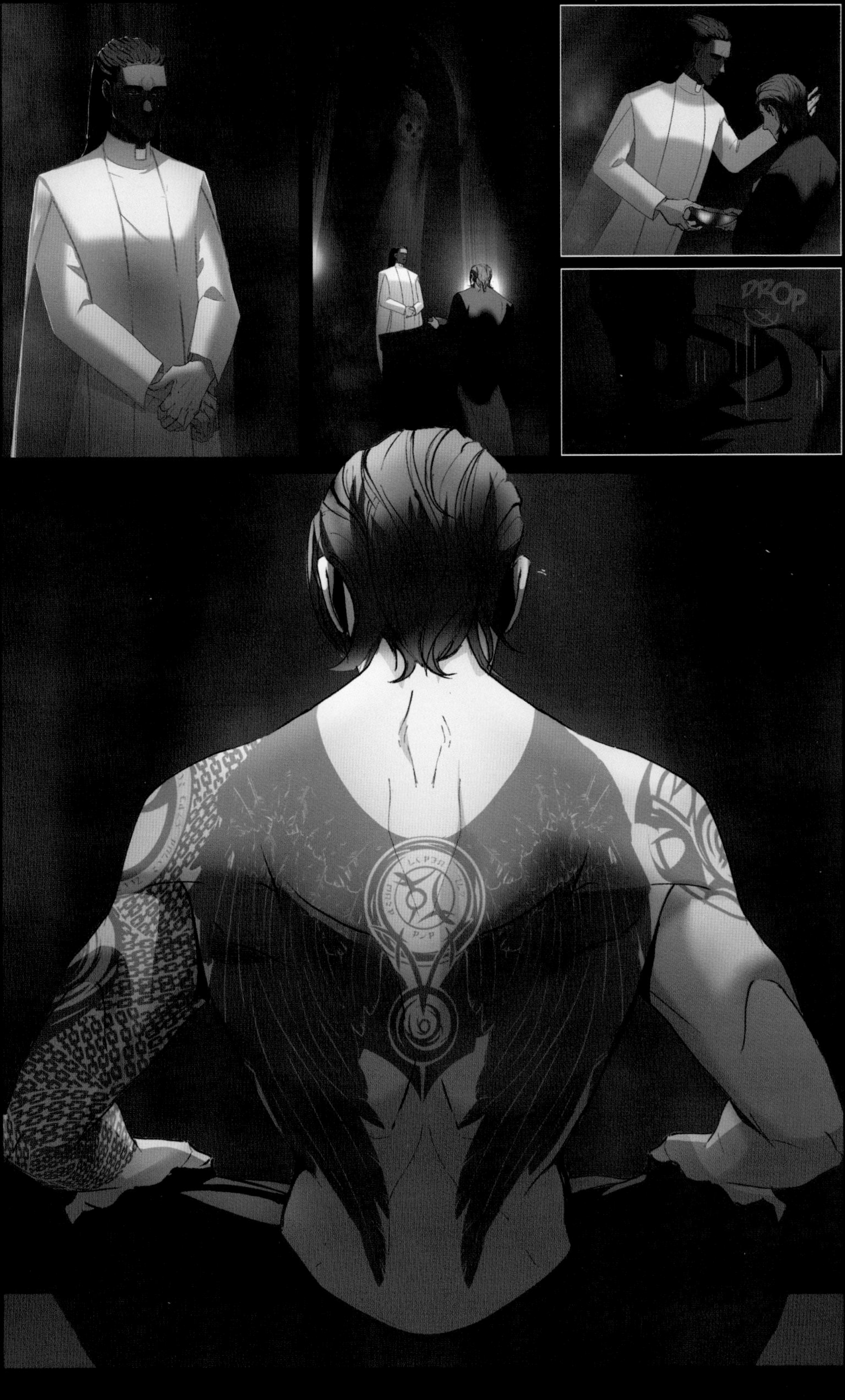
DROP

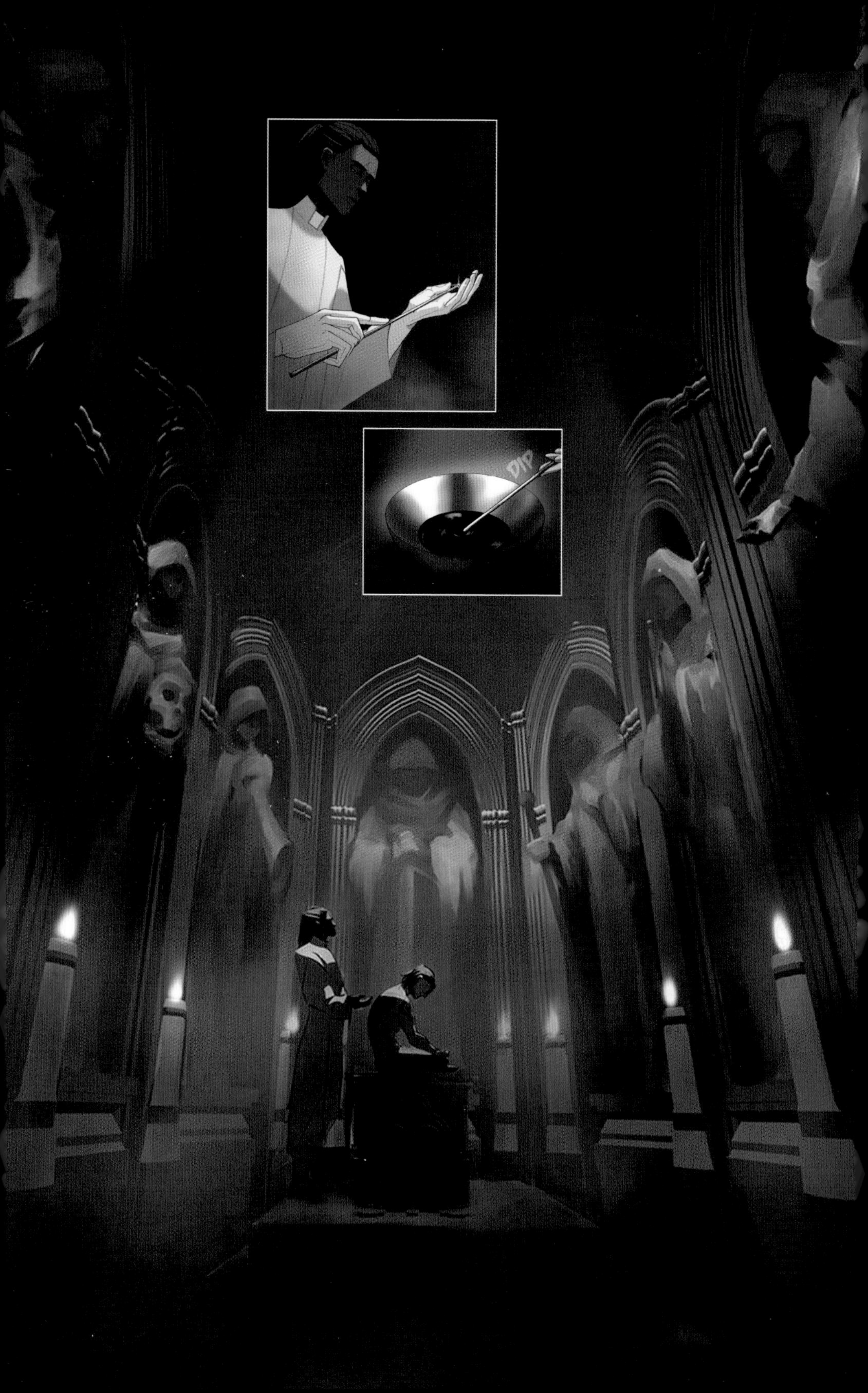
DIP

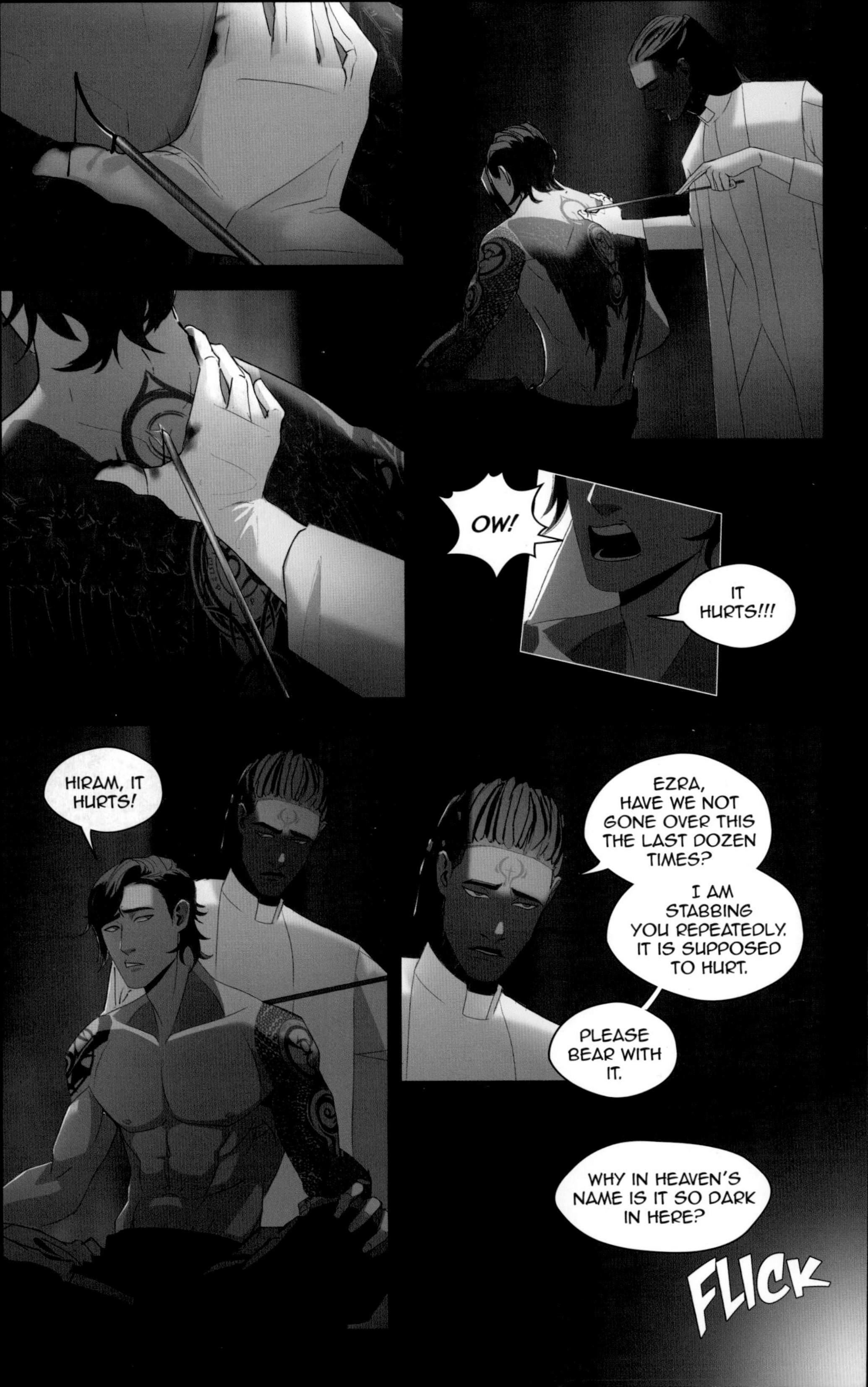
OW!
IT HURTS!!!
HIRAM, IT HURTS!
EZRA, HAVE WE NOT GONE OVER THIS THE LAST DOZEN TIMES?
I AM STABBING YOU REPEATEDLY. IT IS SUPPOSED TO HURT.
PLEASE BEAR WITH IT.
WHY IN HEAVEN'S NAME IS IT SO DARK IN HERE?
FLICK

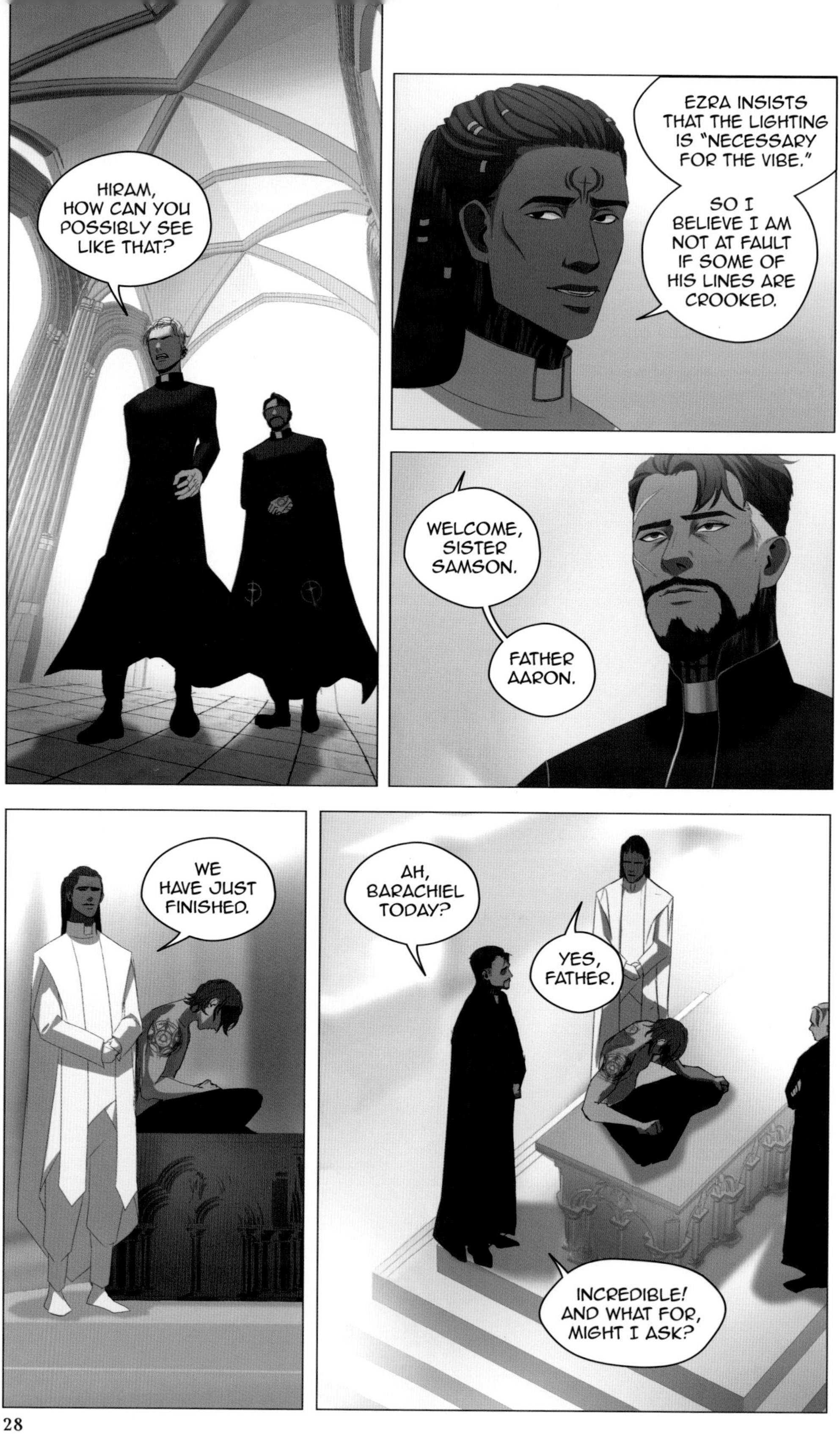
HIRAM, HOW CAN YOU POSSIBLY SEE LIKE THAT?
EZRA INSISTS THAT THE LIGHTING IS "NECESSARY FOR THE VIBE."
SO I BELIEVE I AM NOT AT FAULT IF SOME OF HIS LINES ARE CROOKED.
WELCOME, SISTER SAMSON.
FATHER AARON.
WE HAVE JUST FINISHED.
AH, BARACHIEL TODAY?
YES, FATHER.
INCREDIBLE! AND WHAT FOR, MIGHT I ASK?

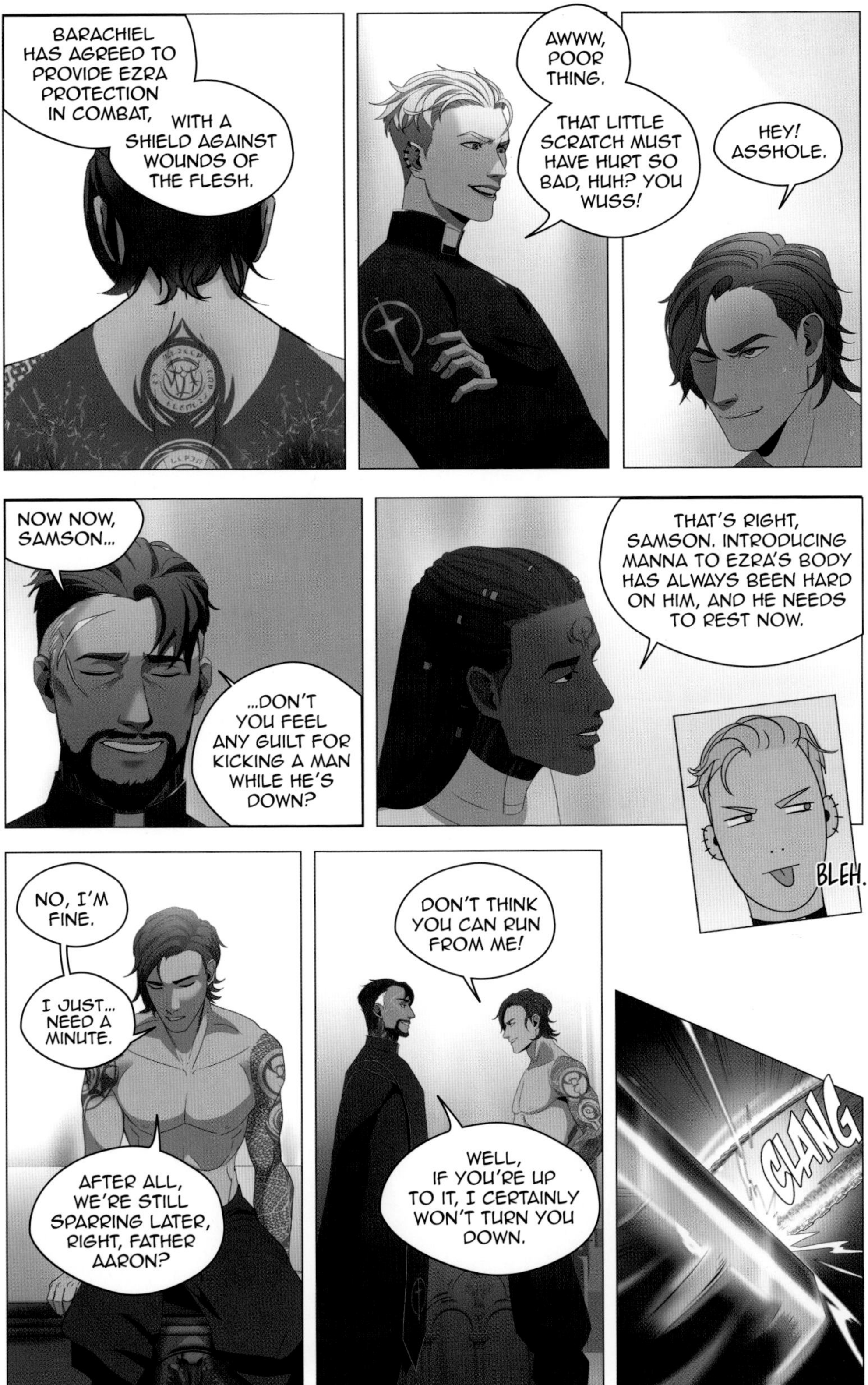
BARACHIEL HAS AGREED TO PROVIDE EZRA PROTECTION IN COMBAT,
WITH A SHIELD AGAINST WOUNDS OF THE FLESH.
AWWW, POOR THING.
THAT LITTLE SCRATCH MUST HAVE HURT SO BAD, HUH? YOU WUSS!
HEY! ASSHOLE.
NOW NOW, SAMSON...
...DON'T YOU FEEL ANY GUILT FOR KICKING A MAN WHILE HE'S DOWN?
THAT'S RIGHT, SAMSON. INTRODUCING MANNA TO EZRA'S BODY HAS ALWAYS BEEN HARD ON HIM, AND HE NEEDS TO REST NOW.
BLEH.
NO, I'M FINE.
I JUST... NEED A MINUTE.
AFTER ALL, WE'RE STILL SPARRING LATER, RIGHT, FATHER AARON?
DON'T THINK YOU CAN RUN FROM ME!
WELL, IF YOU'RE UP TO IT, I CERTAINLY WON'T TURN YOU DOWN.
CLANG

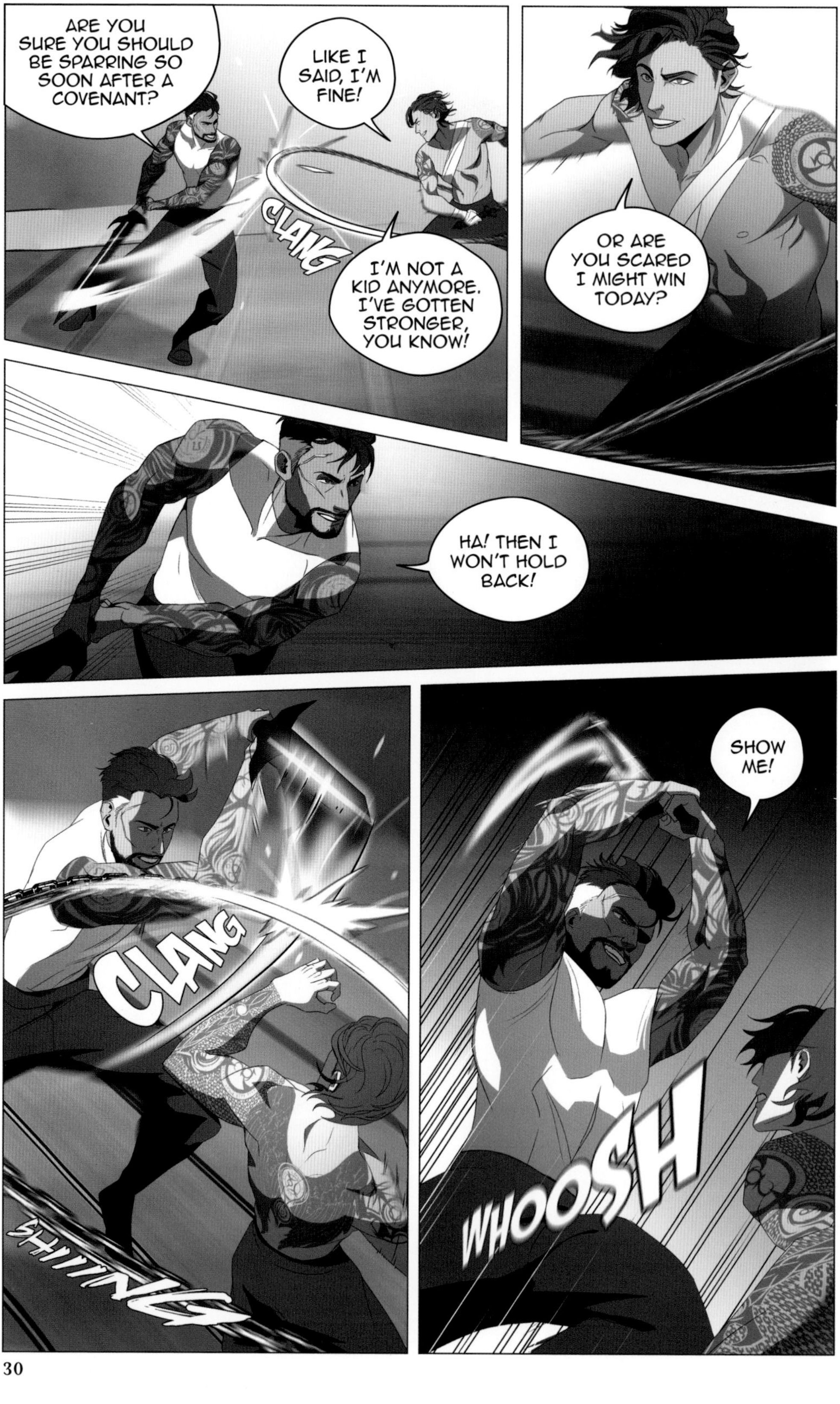
ARE YOU SURE YOU SHOULD BE SPARRING SO SOON AFTER A COVENANT?
LIKE I SAID, I'M FINE!
CLANG
I'M NOT A KID ANYMORE. I'VE GOTTEN STRONGER, YOU KNOW!
OR ARE YOU SCARED I MIGHT WIN TODAY?
HA! THEN I WON'T HOLD BACK!
CLANG
SHIIING
SHOW ME!
WHOOSH

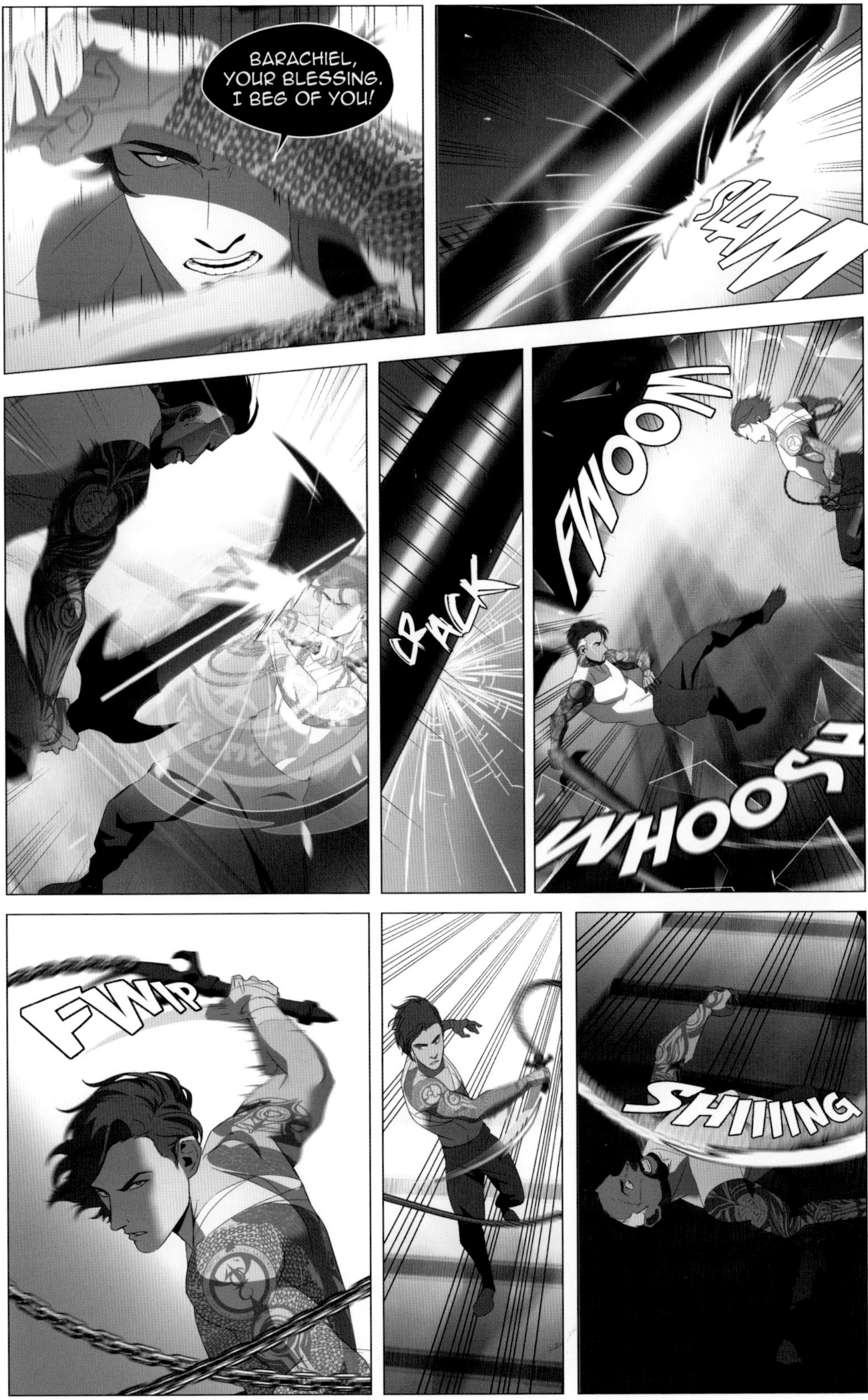
BARACHIEL, YOUR BLESSING. I BEG OF YOU!
SLAM
CRACK
FWOOM
WHOOSH
FWIP
SHIIING

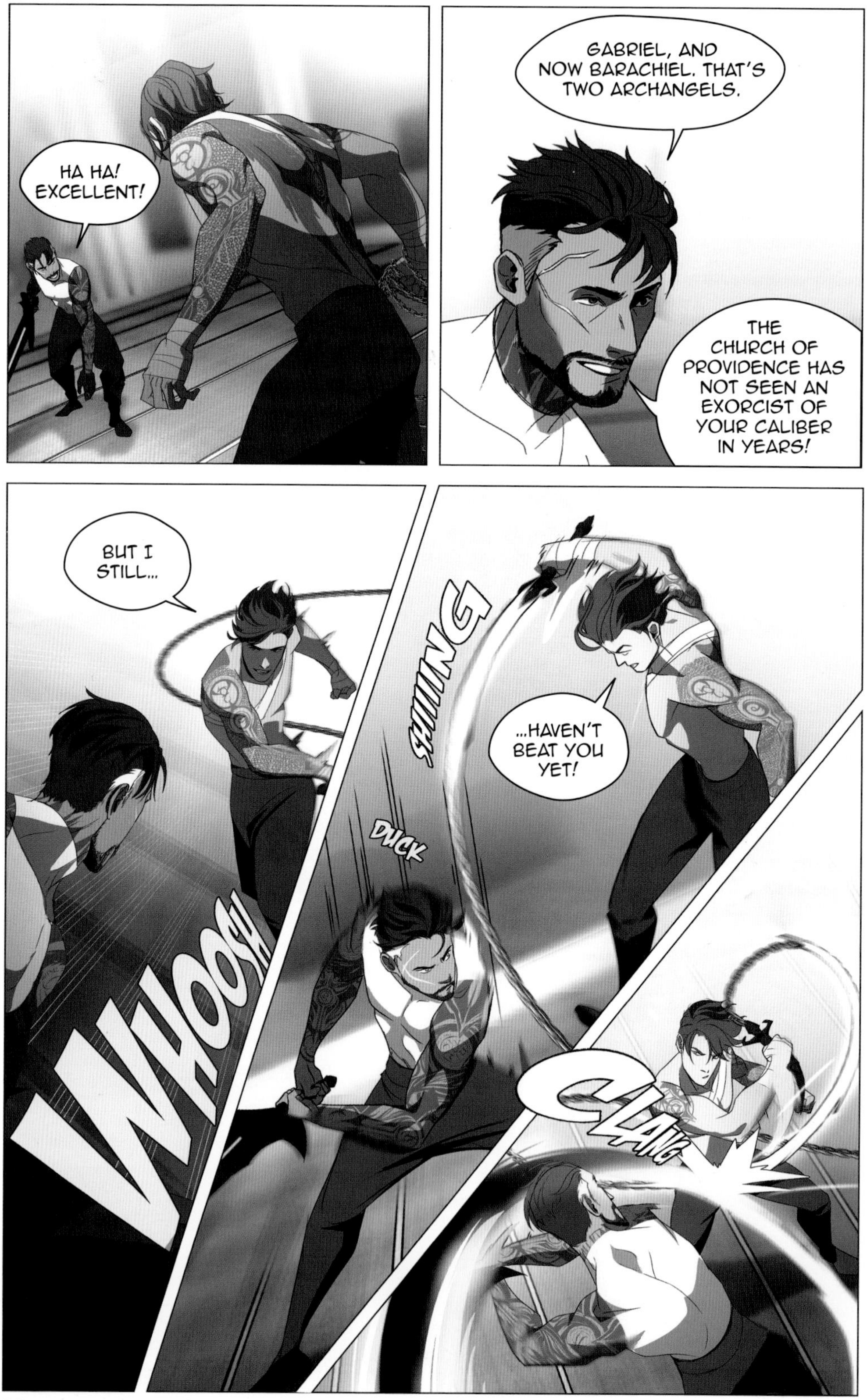
HA HA! EXCELLENT!
GABRIEL, AND NOW BARACHIEL. THAT'S TWO ARCHANGELS.
THE CHURCH OF PROVIDENCE HAS NOT SEEN AN EXORCIST OF YOUR CALIBER IN YEARS!
BUT I STILL...
WHOOSH
SHIIIING
...HAVEN'T BEAT YOU YET!
DUCK
CLANG

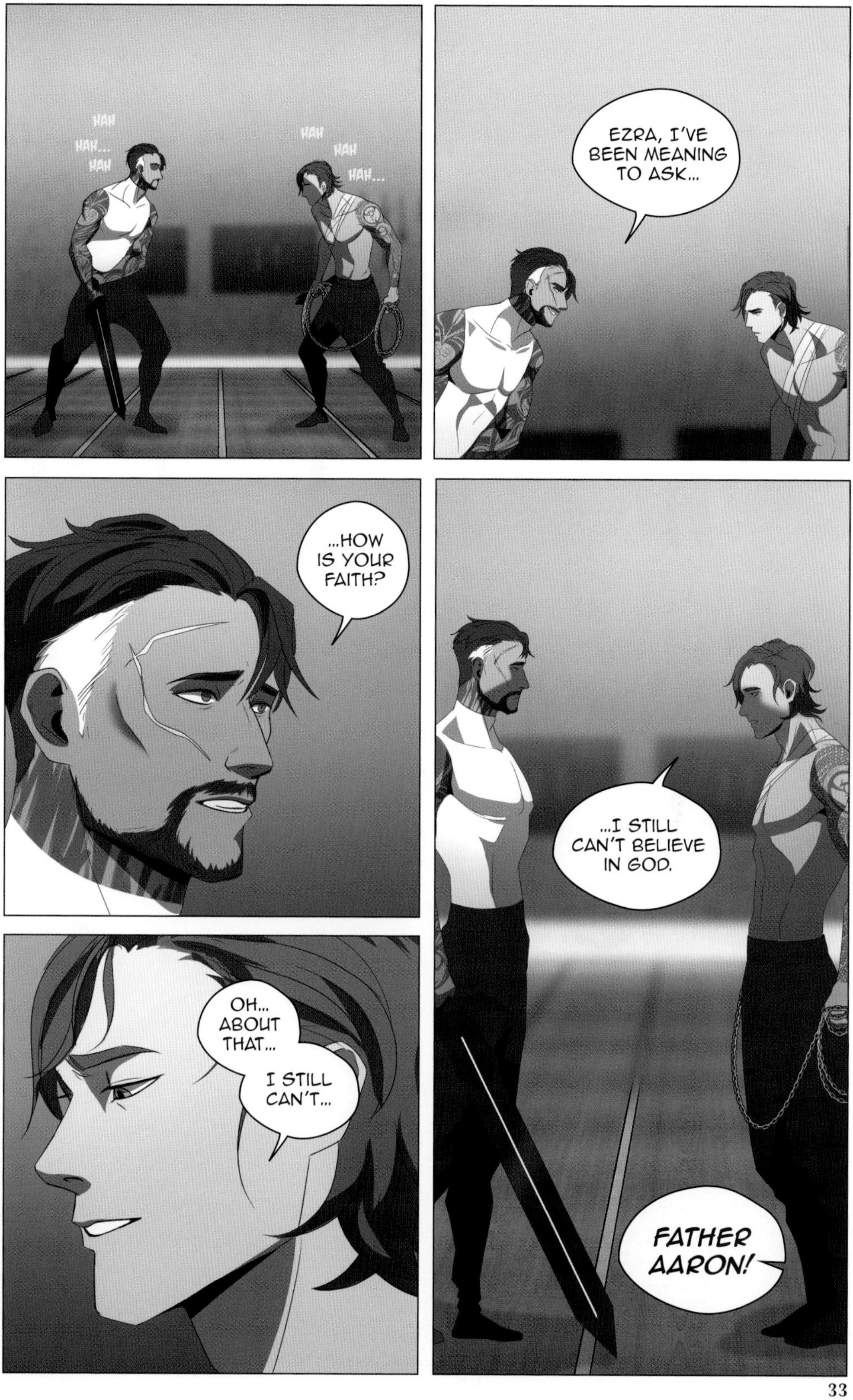
HAH
HAH...
HAH
HAH
HAH
HAH...
EZRA, I'VE BEEN MEANING TO ASK...
...HOW IS YOUR FAITH?
OH... ABOUT THAT...
I STILL CAN'T...
...I STILL CAN'T BELIEVE IN GOD.
FATHER AARON!

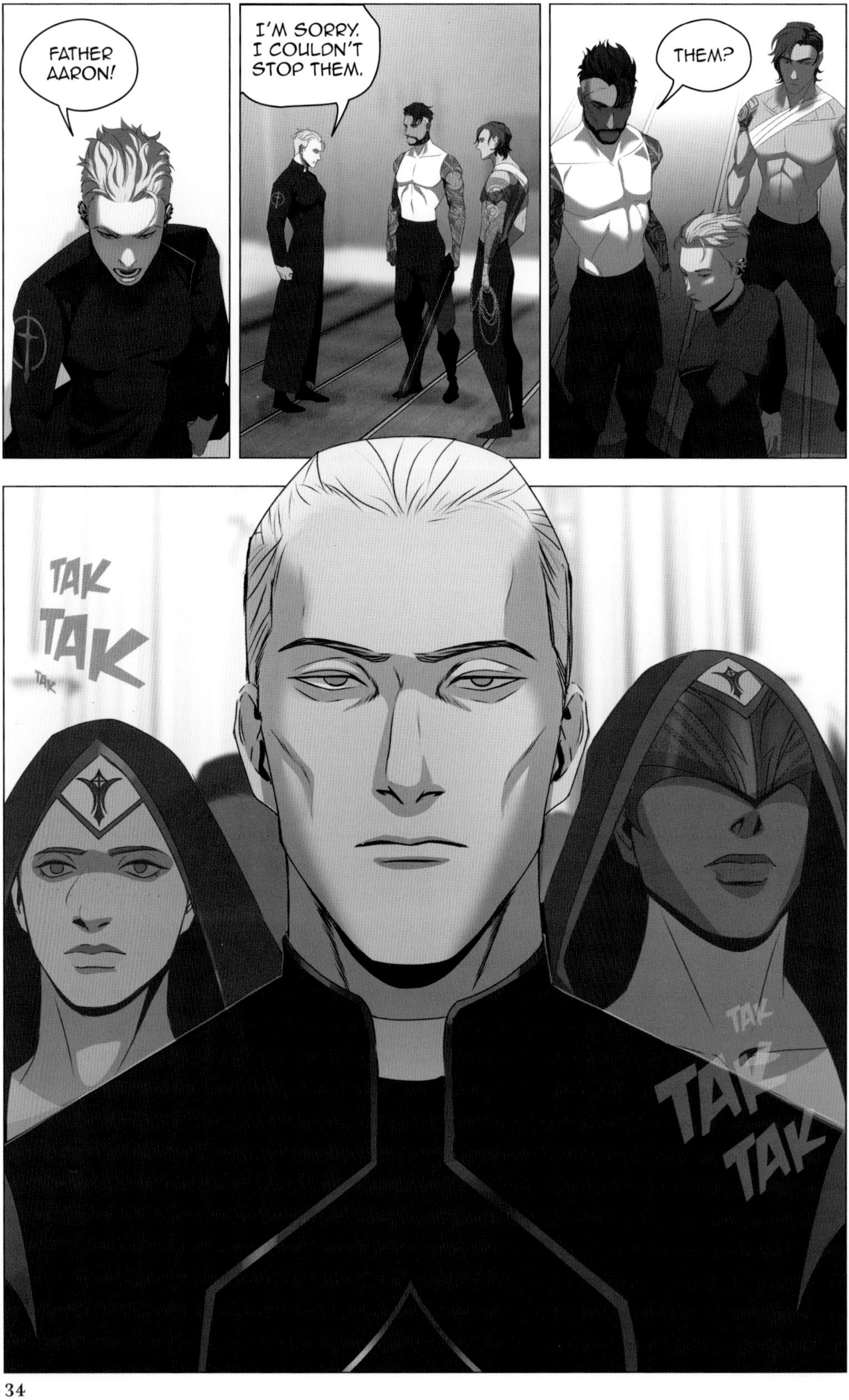
FATHER AARON!
I'M SORRY. I COULDN'T STOP THEM.
THEM?
TAK TAK TAK
TAK TAK TAK

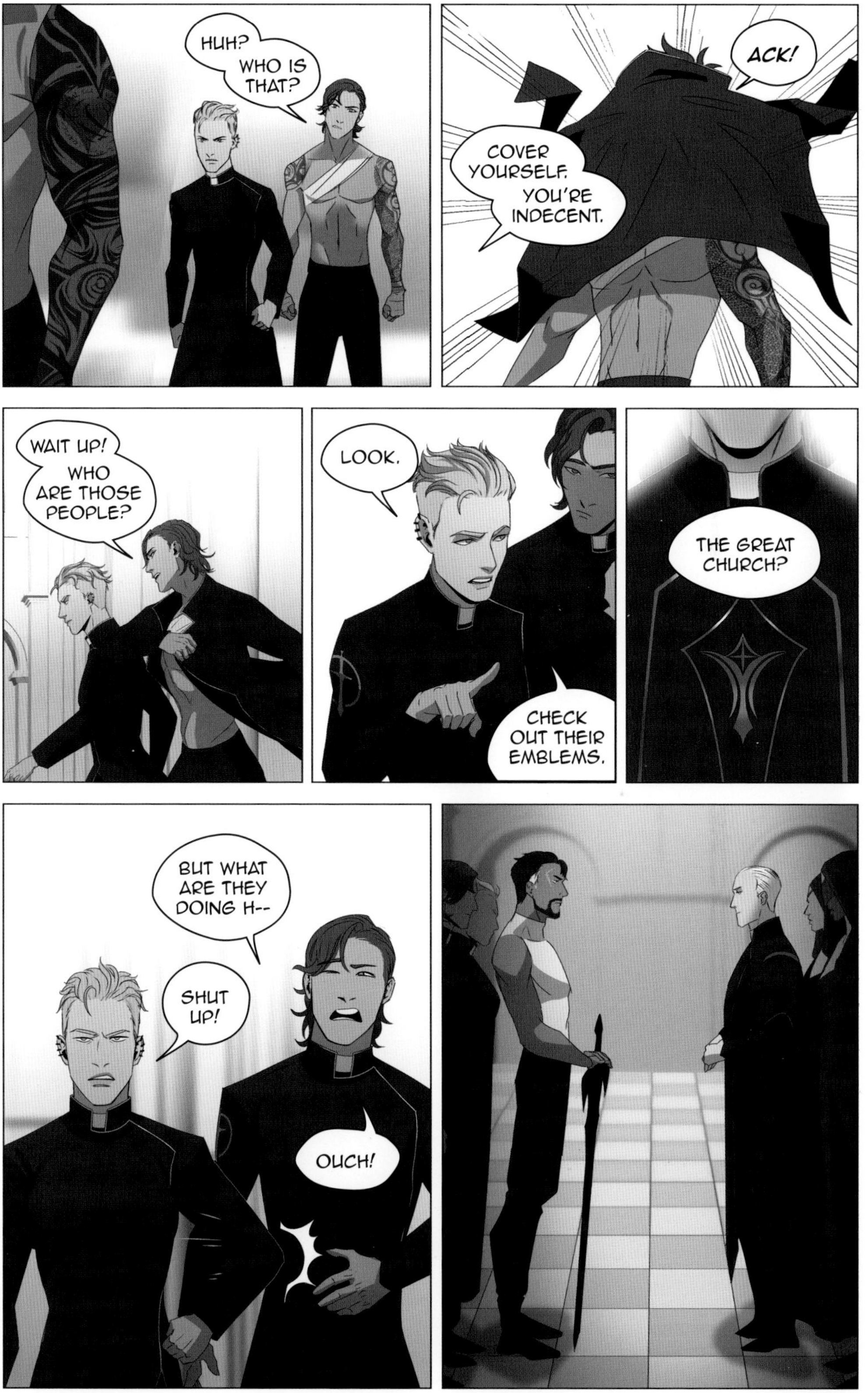
HUH?
WHO IS THAT?
ACK!
COVER YOURSELF. YOU'RE INDECENT.
WAIT UP! WHO ARE THOSE PEOPLE?
LOOK.
CHECK OUT THEIR EMBLEMS.
THE GREAT CHURCH?
BUT WHAT ARE THEY DOING H--
SHUT UP!
OUCH!

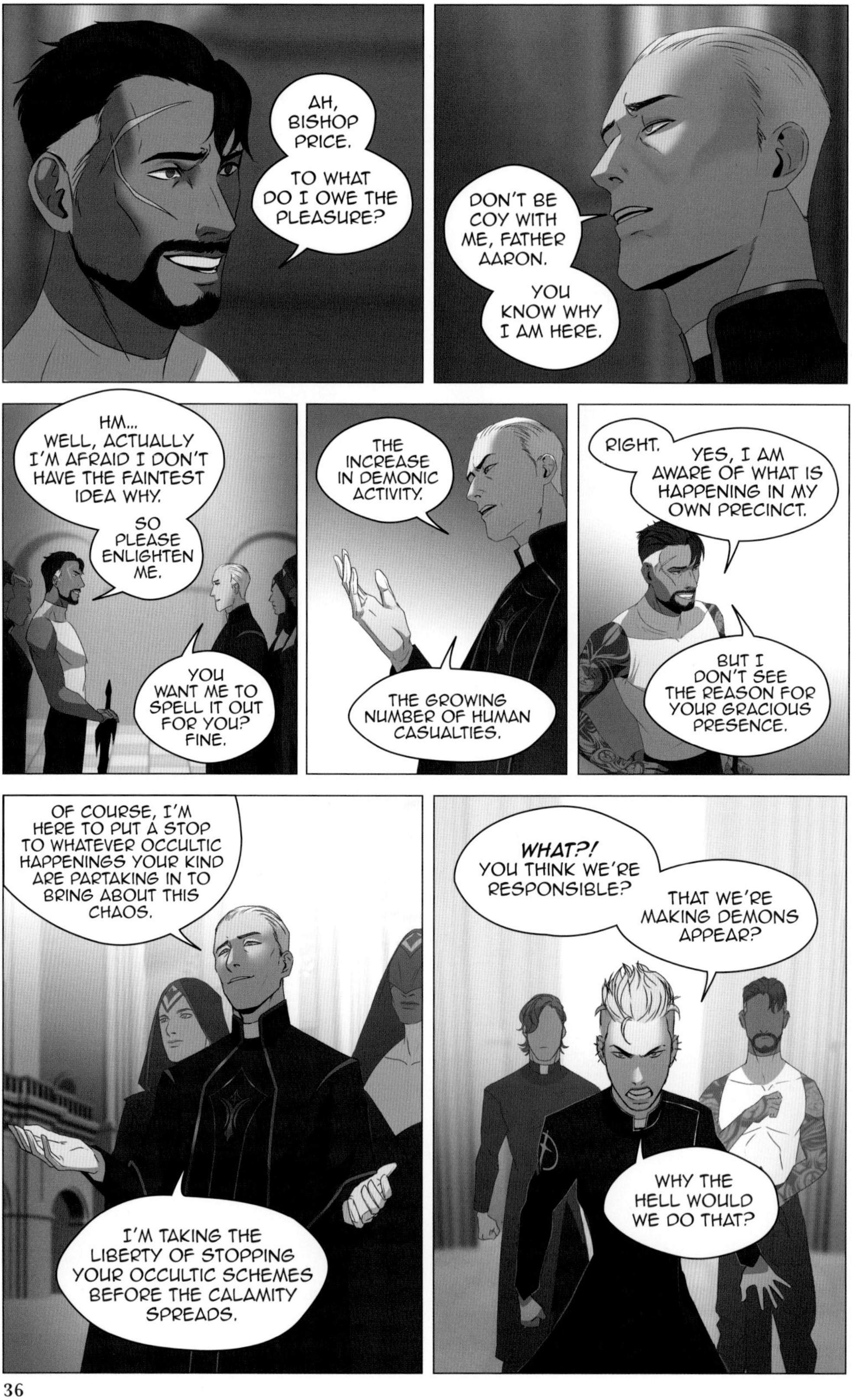
AH, BISHOP PRICE.
TO WHAT DO I OWE THE PLEASURE?
DON'T BE COY WITH ME, FATHER AARON.
YOU KNOW WHY I AM HERE.
HM... WELL, ACTUALLY I'M AFRAID I DON'T HAVE THE FAINTEST IDEA WHY.
SO PLEASE ENLIGHTEN ME.
YOU WANT ME TO SPELL IT OUT FOR YOU? FINE.
THE INCREASE IN DEMONIC ACTIVITY.
THE GROWING NUMBER OF HUMAN CASUALTIES.
RIGHT.
YES, I AM AWARE OF WHAT IS HAPPENING IN MY OWN PRECINCT.
BUT I DON'T SEE THE REASON FOR YOUR GRACIOUS PRESENCE.
OF COURSE, I'M HERE TO PUT A STOP TO WHATEVER OCCULTIC HAPPENINGS YOUR KIND ARE PARTAKING IN TO BRING ABOUT THIS CHAOS.
I'M TAKING THE LIBERTY OF STOPPING YOUR OCCULTIC SCHEMES BEFORE THE CALAMITY SPREADS.
WHAT?! YOU THINK WE'RE RESPONSIBLE?
THAT WE'RE MAKING DEMONS APPEAR?
WHY THE HELL WOULD WE DO THAT?

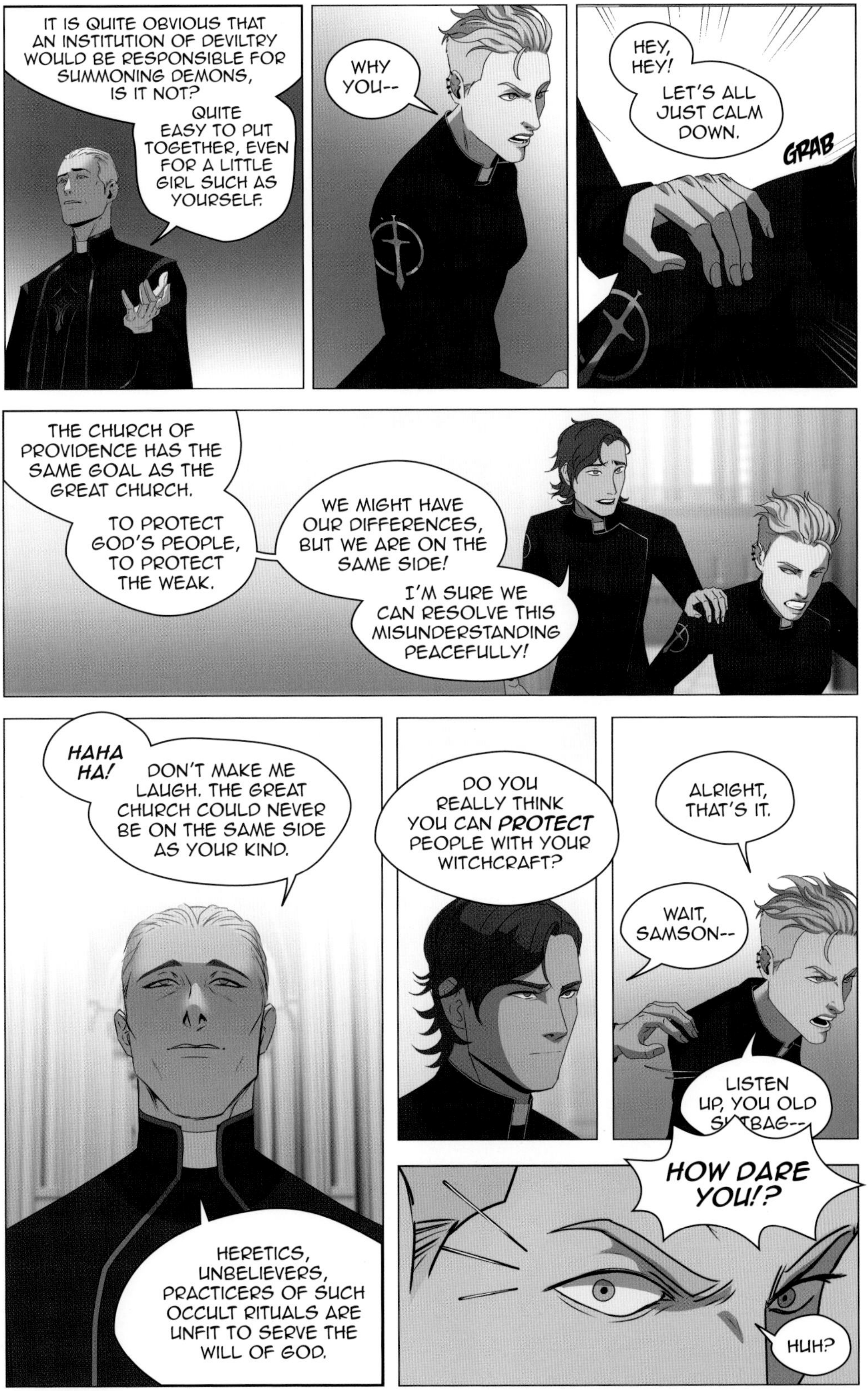
IT IS QUITE OBVIOUS THAT AN INSTITUTION OF DEVILTRY WOULD BE RESPONSIBLE FOR SUMMONING DEMONS, IS IT NOT?
QUITE EASY TO PUT TOGETHER, EVEN FOR A LITTLE GIRL SUCH AS YOURSELF.
WHY YOU--
HEY, HEY!
LET'S ALL JUST CALM DOWN.
GRAB
THE CHURCH OF PROVIDENCE HAS THE SAME GOAL AS THE GREAT CHURCH.
TO PROTECT GOD'S PEOPLE, TO PROTECT THE WEAK.
WE MIGHT HAVE OUR DIFFERENCES, BUT WE ARE ON THE SAME SIDE!
I'M SURE WE CAN RESOLVE THIS MISUNDERSTANDING PEACEFULLY!
HAHA HA!
DON'T MAKE ME LAUGH. THE GREAT CHURCH COULD NEVER BE ON THE SAME SIDE AS YOUR KIND.
HERETICS, UNBELIEVERS, PRACTICERS OF SUCH OCCULT RITUALS ARE UNFIT TO SERVE THE WILL OF GOD.
DO YOU REALLY THINK YOU CAN PROTECT PEOPLE WITH YOUR WITCHCRAFT?
ALRIGHT, THAT'S IT.
WAIT, SAMSON--
LISTEN UP, YOU OLD
HOW DARE YOU!?
HUH?

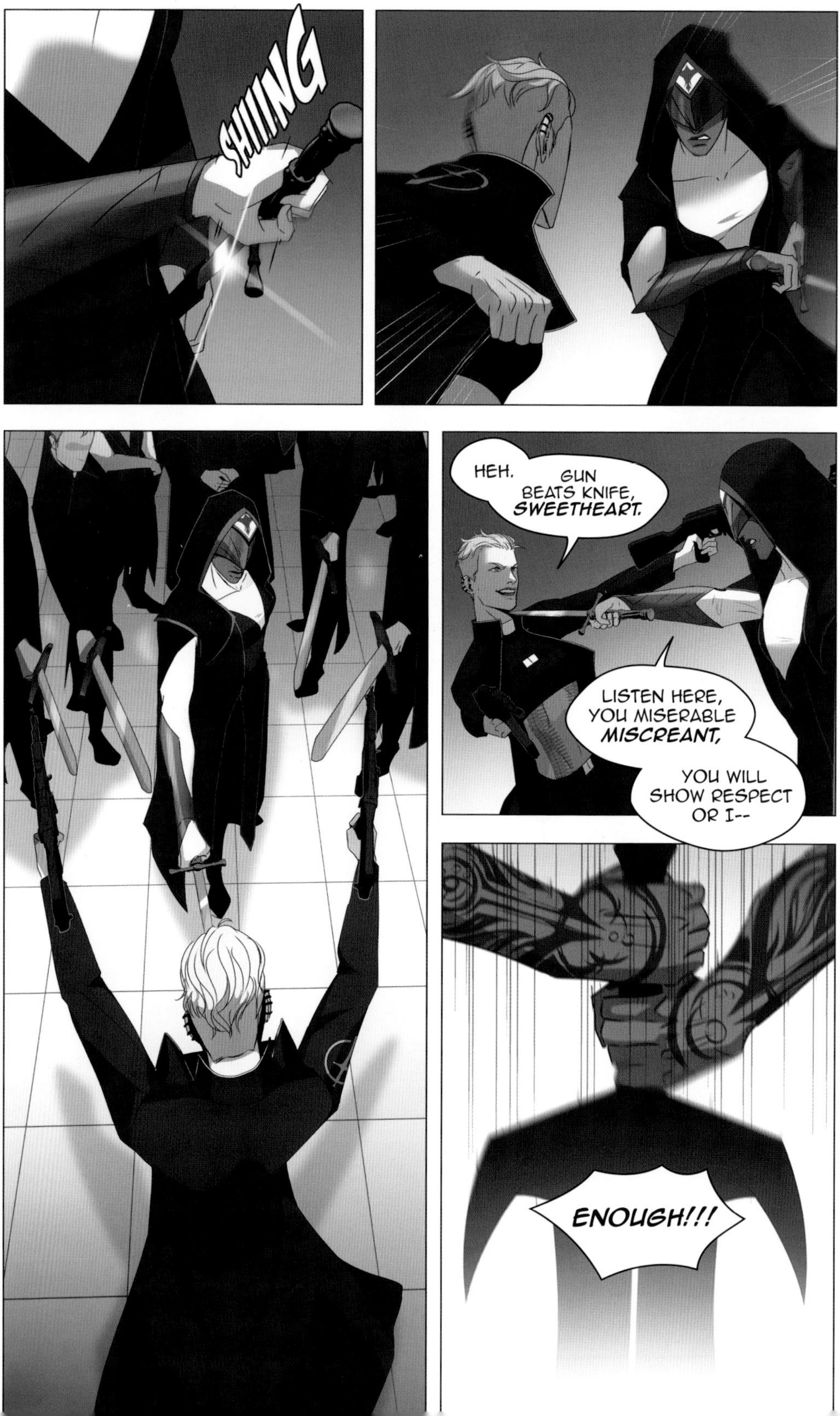
SHIING
HEH. GUN BEATS KNIFE, SWEETHEART.
LISTEN HERE, YOU MISERABLE MISCREANT,
YOU WILL SHOW RESPECT OR I--
ENOUGH!!!

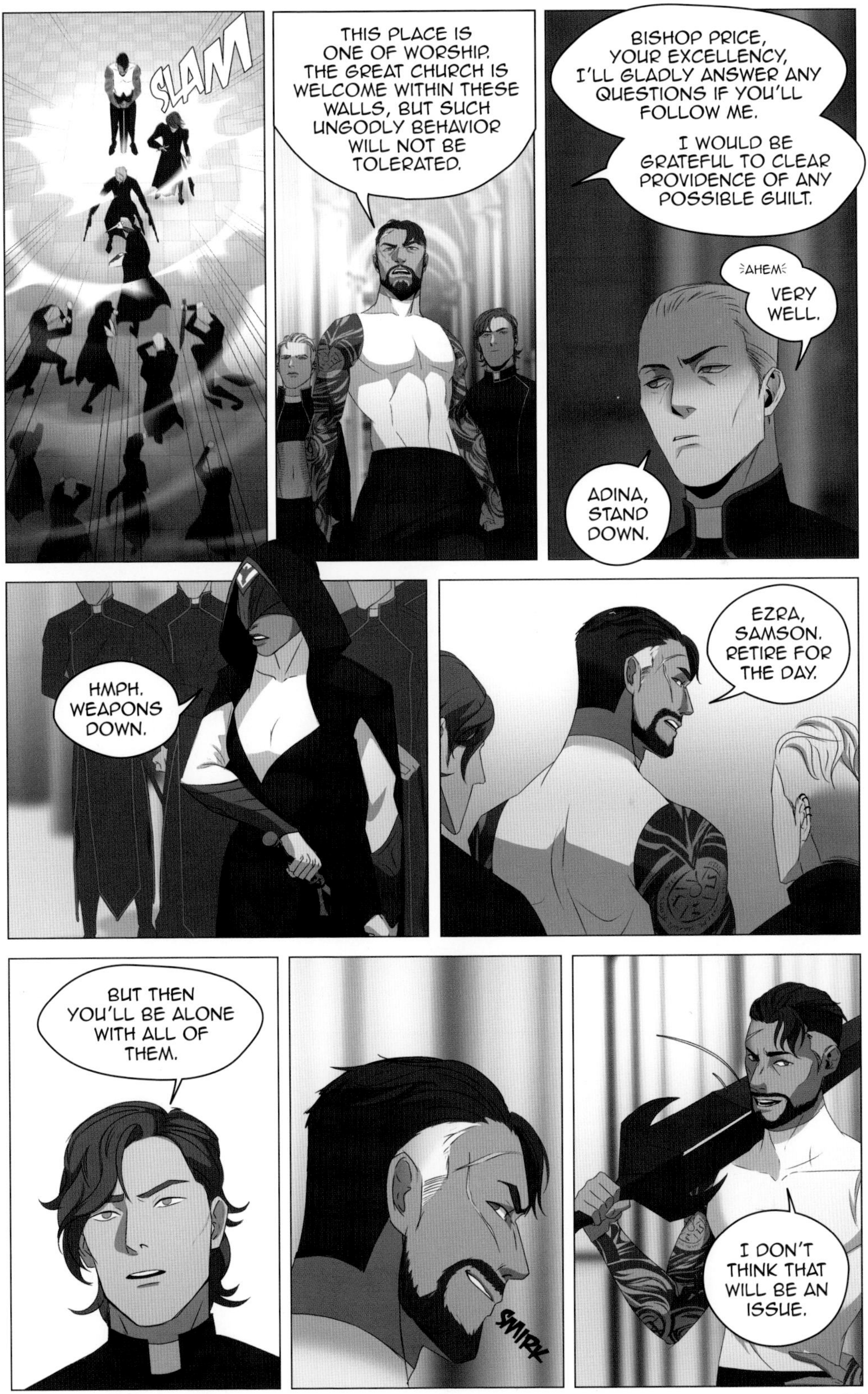
SLAM
THIS PLACE IS ONE OF WORSHIP. THE GREAT CHURCH IS WELCOME WITHIN THESE WALLS, BUT SUCH UNGODLY BEHAVIOR WILL NOT BE TOLERATED.
BISHOP PRICE, YOUR EXCELLENCY, I'LL GLADLY ANSWER ANY QUESTIONS IF YOU'LL FOLLOW ME.
I WOULD BE GRATEFUL TO CLEAR PROVIDENCE OF ANY POSSIBLE GUILT.
AHEM
VERY WELL.
ADINA, STAND DOWN.
HMPH. WEAPONS DOWN.
EZRA, SAMSON. RETIRE FOR THE DAY.
BUT THEN YOU'LL BE ALONE WITH ALL OF THEM.
SMIRK
I DON'T THINK THAT WILL BE AN ISSUE.

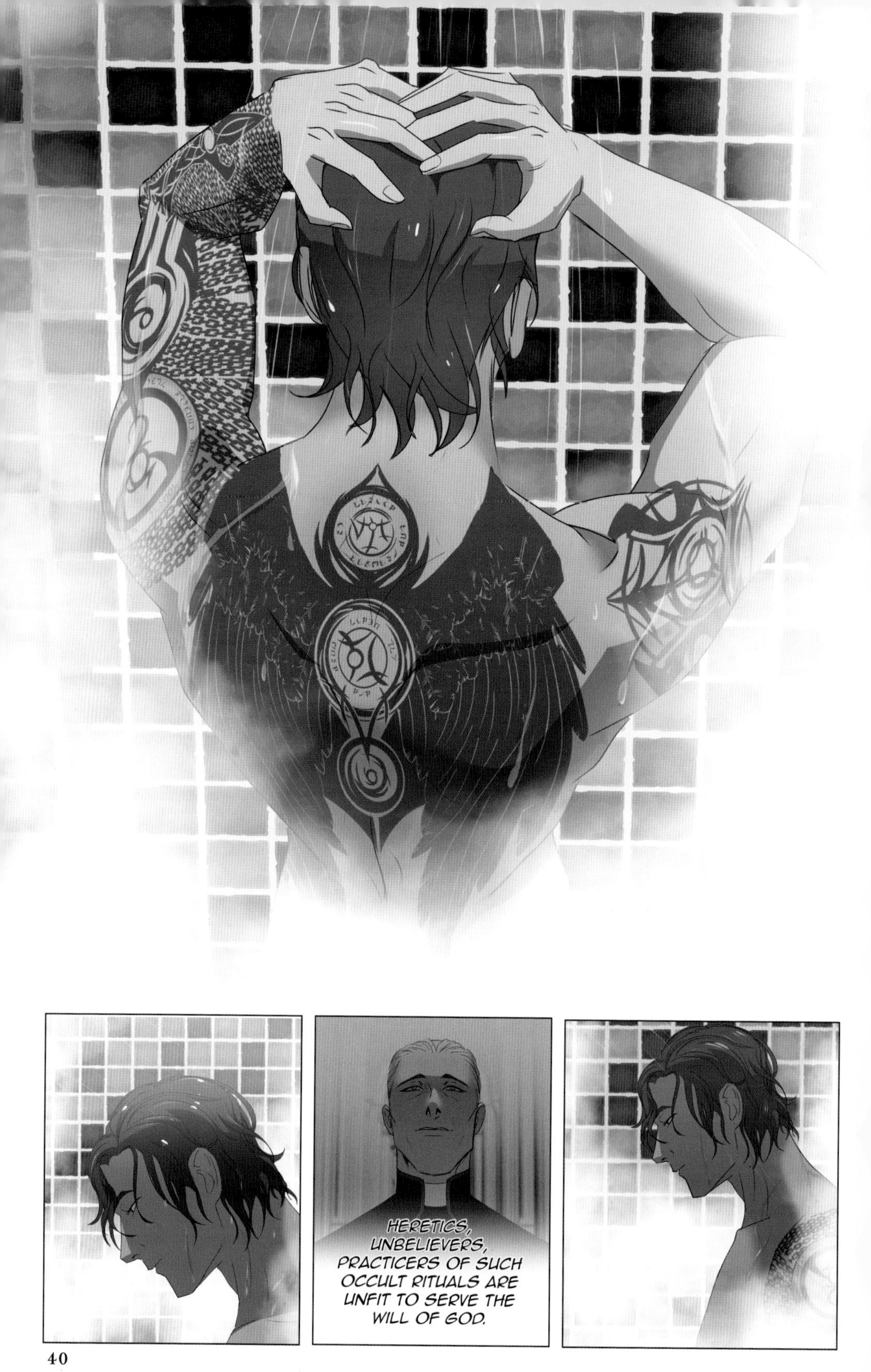
HERETICS, UNBELIEVERS, PRACTICERS OF SUCH OCCULT RITUALS ARE UNFIT TO SERVE THE WILL OF GOD.

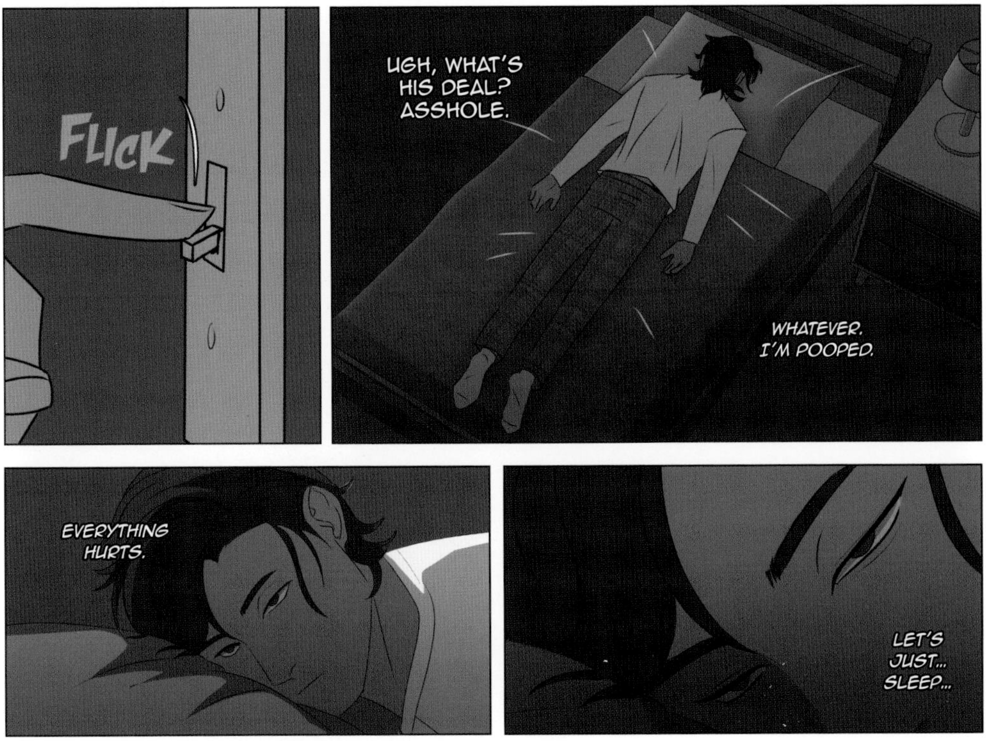
FLICK
UGH, WHAT'S HIS DEAL? ASSHOLE.
WHATEVER. I'M POOPED.
EVERYTHING HURTS.
LET'S JUST... SLEEP...

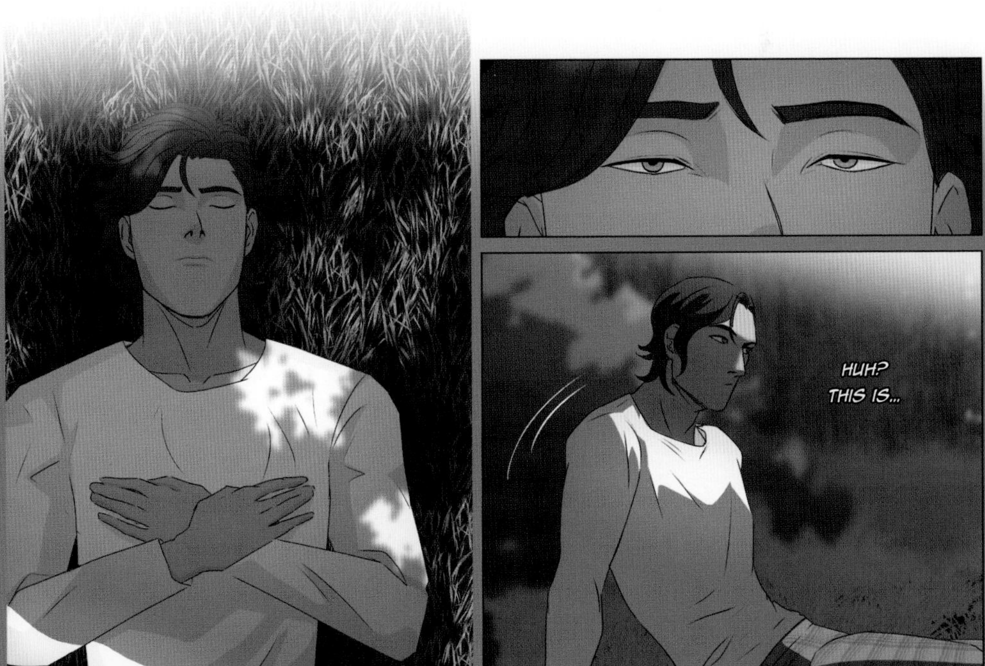
HUH? THIS IS...

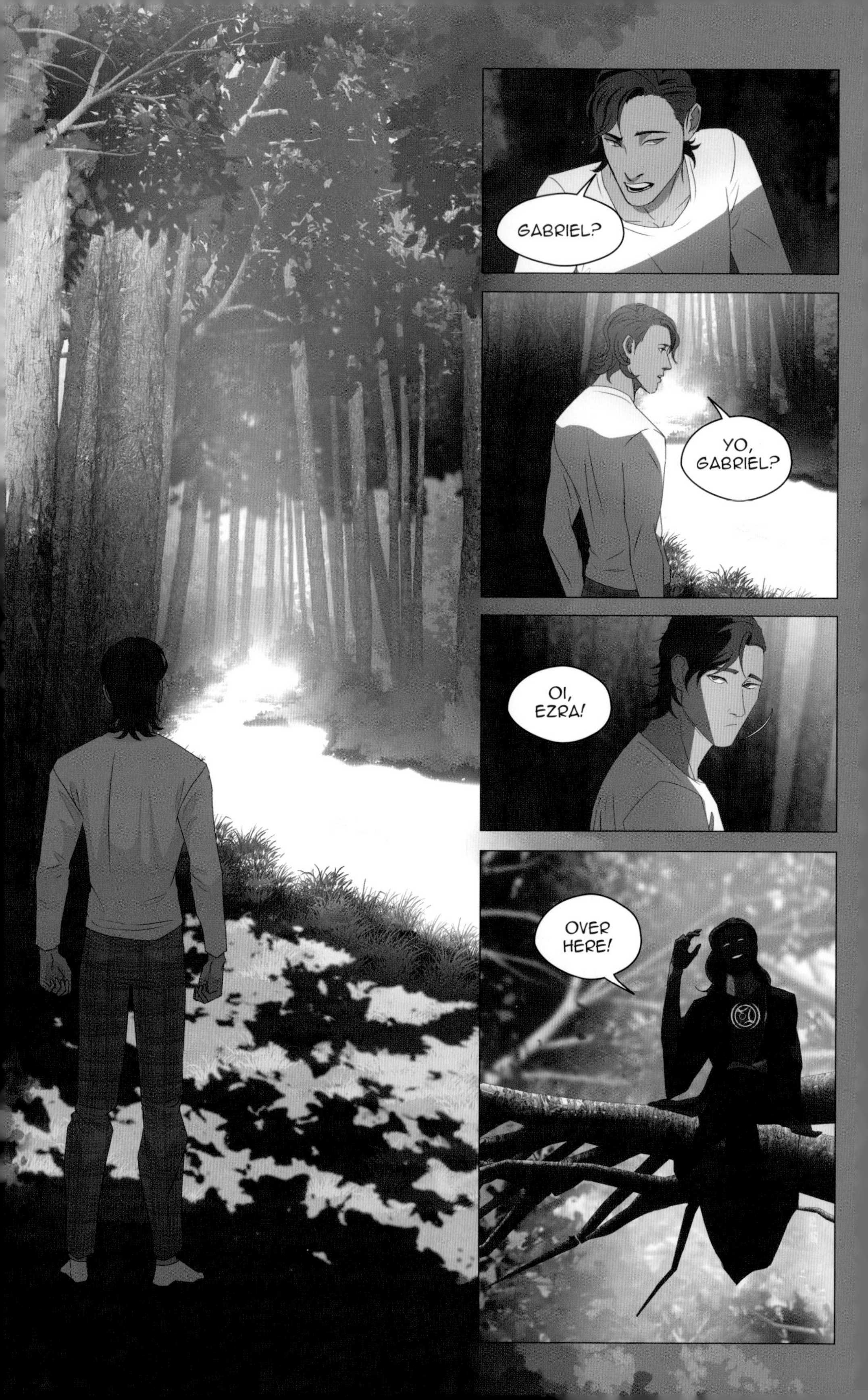
GABRIEL?
YO, GABRIEL?
OI, EZRA!
OVER HERE!

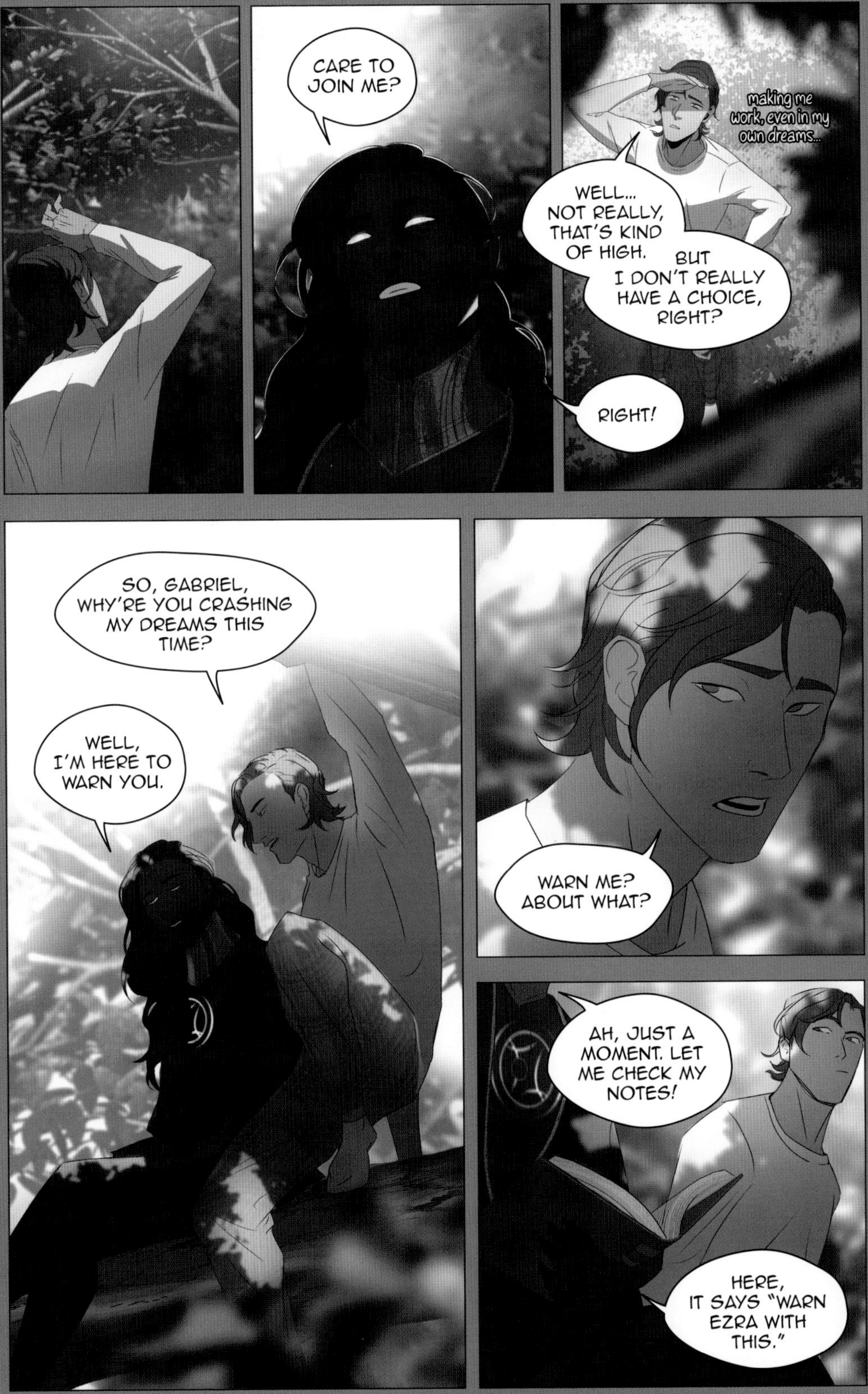
CARE TO JOIN ME?
making me work, even in my own dreams...
WELL... NOT REALLY, THAT'S KIND OF HIGH.
BUT I DON'T REALLY HAVE A CHOICE, RIGHT?
RIGHT!
SO, GABRIEL, WHY'RE YOU CRASHING MY DREAMS THIS TIME?
WELL, I'M HERE TO WARN YOU.
WARN ME? ABOUT WHAT?
AH, JUST A MOMENT. LET ME CHECK MY NOTES!
HERE, IT SAYS "WARN EZRA WITH THIS."

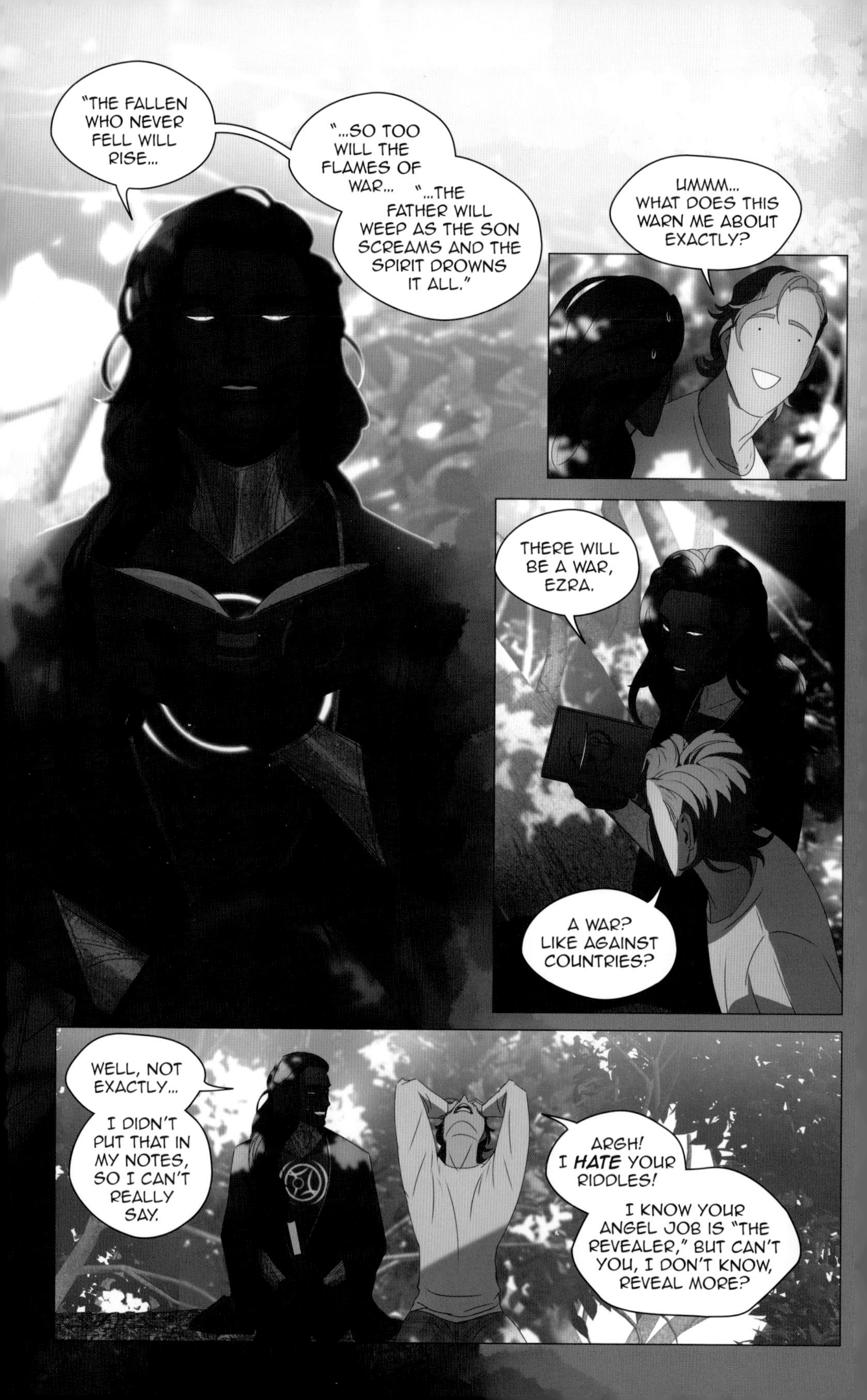
"THE FALLEN WHO NEVER FELL WILL RISE...
"...SO TOO WILL THE FLAMES OF WAR...
"...THE FATHER WILL WEEP AS THE SON SCREAMS AND THE SPIRIT DROWNS IT ALL."
UMMM... WHAT DOES THIS WARN ME ABOUT EXACTLY?
THERE WILL BE A WAR, EZRA.
A WAR? LIKE AGAINST COUNTRIES?
WELL, NOT EXACTLY...
I DIDN'T PUT THAT IN MY NOTES, SO I CAN'T REALLY SAY.
ARGH! I **HATE** YOUR RIDDLES!
I KNOW YOUR ANGEL JOB IS "THE REVEALER," BUT CAN'T YOU, I DON'T KNOW, REVEAL MORE?

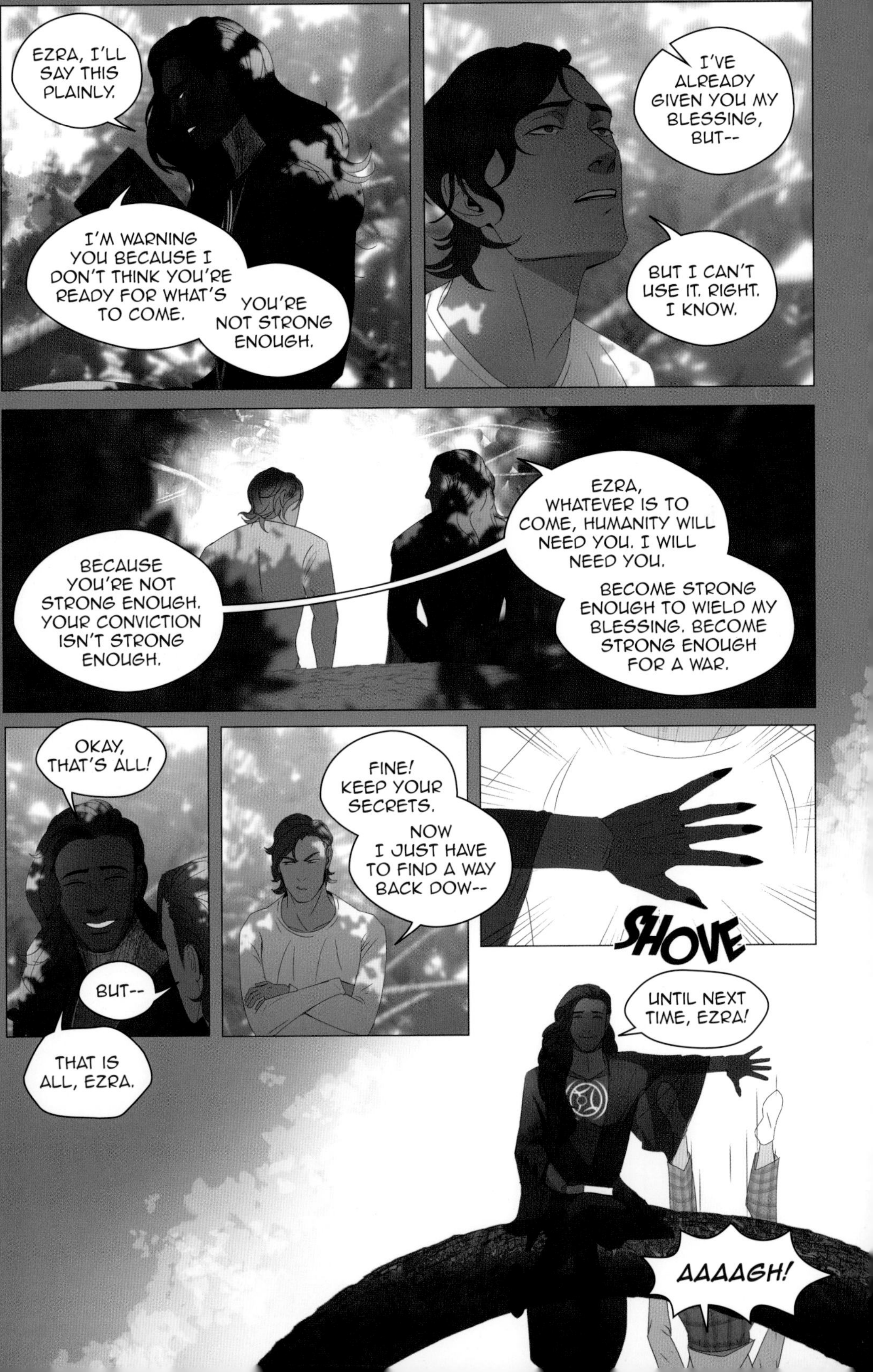
EZRA, I'LL SAY THIS PLAINLY.
I'M WARNING YOU BECAUSE I DON'T THINK YOU'RE READY FOR WHAT'S TO COME.
YOU'RE NOT STRONG ENOUGH.
I'VE ALREADY GIVEN YOU MY BLESSING, BUT--
BUT I CAN'T USE IT. RIGHT. I KNOW.
BECAUSE YOU'RE NOT STRONG ENOUGH. YOUR CONVICTION ISN'T STRONG ENOUGH.
EZRA, WHATEVER IS TO COME, HUMANITY WILL NEED YOU. I WILL NEED YOU.
BECOME STRONG ENOUGH TO WIELD MY BLESSING. BECOME STRONG ENOUGH FOR A WAR.
OKAY, THAT'S ALL!
BUT--
THAT IS ALL, EZRA.
FINE! KEEP YOUR SECRETS.
NOW I JUST HAVE TO FIND A WAY BACK DOW--
SHOVE
UNTIL NEXT TIME, EZRA!
AAAAGH!

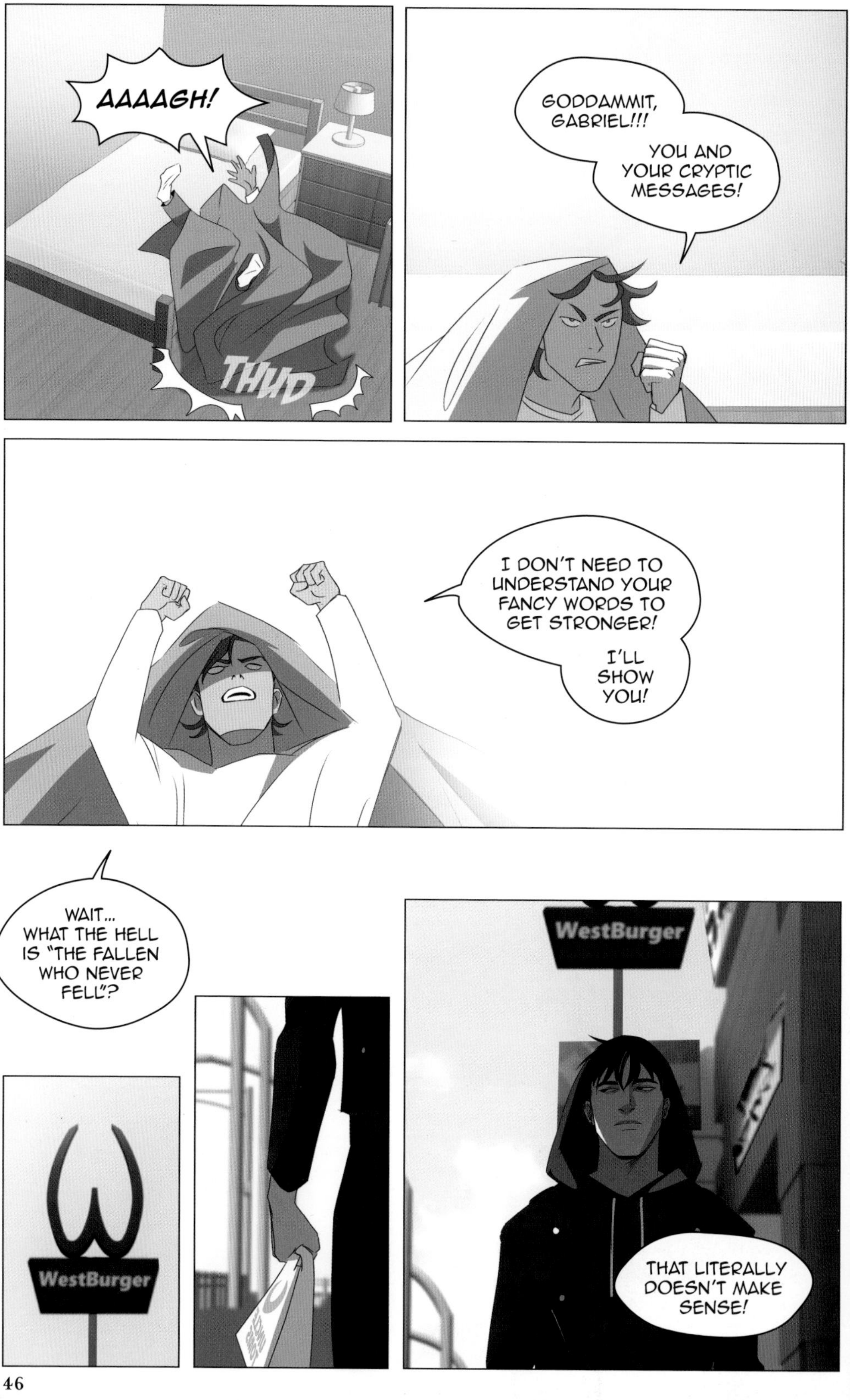
AAAAGH!
THUD
GODDAMMIT, GABRIEL!!!
YOU AND YOUR CRYPTIC MESSAGES!
I DON'T NEED TO UNDERSTAND YOUR FANCY WORDS TO GET STRONGER!
I'LL SHOW YOU!
WAIT... WHAT THE HELL IS "THE FALLEN WHO NEVER FELL"?
WestBurger
WestBurger
THAT LITERALLY DOESN'T MAKE SENSE!

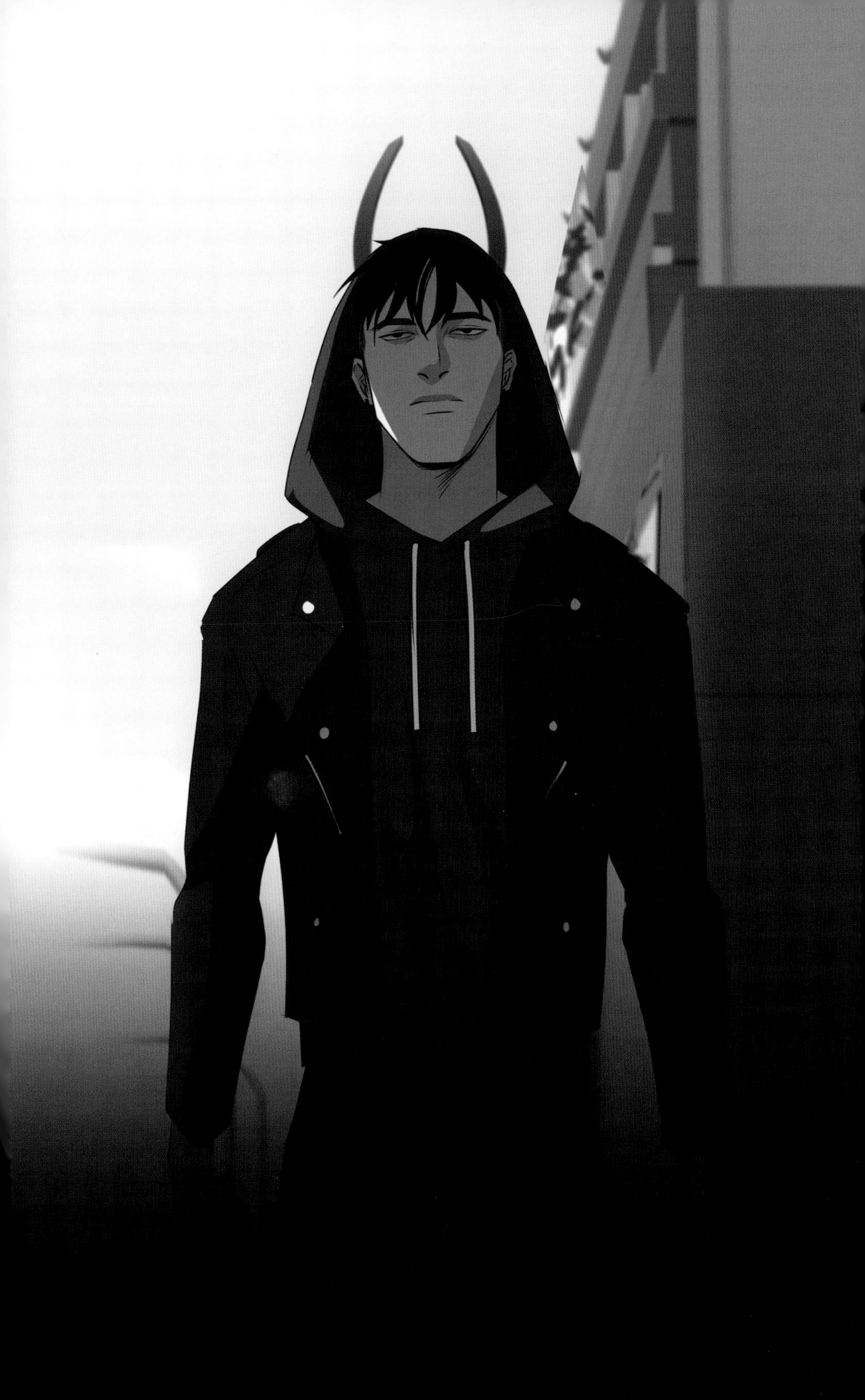

BOOK III

WHERE ARE YOU TAKING ME? WHAT IS YOUR AIM?

MY MEN ARE RIGHT OUTSIDE, SO IF YOU TRY ANYTHING--

FEAR NOT, YOUR EXCELLENCY. I AM ONLY SHOWING YOU THE PROOF THAT YOU SEEK.

I ASSUME YOU ARE UNFAMILIAR WITH HOW THE CHURCH OF PROVIDENCE OPERATES, YES?

HMPH. I KNOW ENOUGH.

SISTER LEAH, WE HAVE GUESTS.

OH? VISITORS?

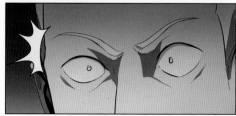

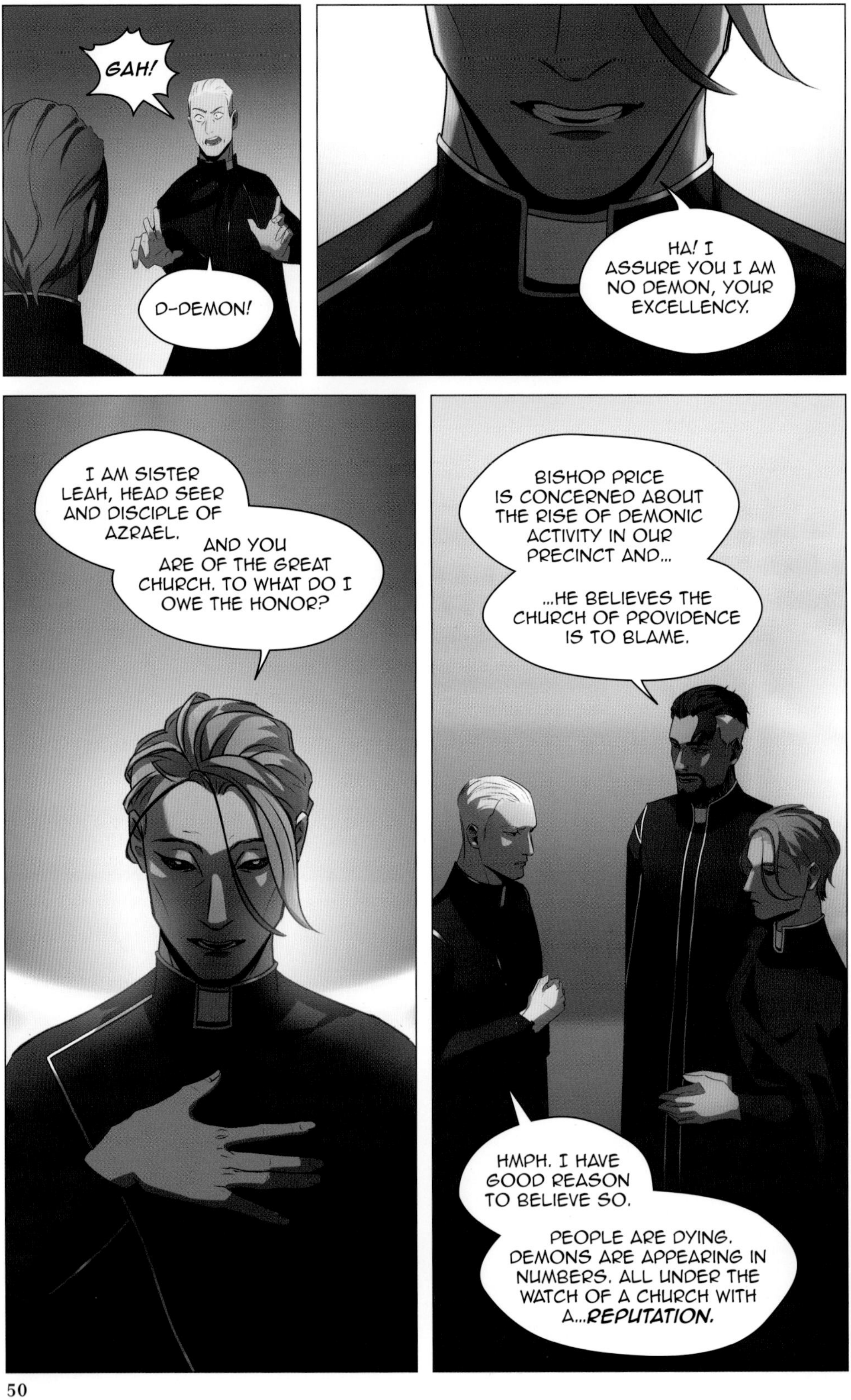

GAH!
D-DEMON!
HA! I ASSURE YOU I AM NO DEMON, YOUR EXCELLENCY.
I AM SISTER LEAH, HEAD SEER AND DISCIPLE OF AZRAEL.
AND YOU ARE OF THE GREAT CHURCH. TO WHAT DO I OWE THE HONOR?
BISHOP PRICE IS CONCERNED ABOUT THE RISE OF DEMONIC ACTIVITY IN OUR PRECINCT AND...
...HE BELIEVES THE CHURCH OF PROVIDENCE IS TO BLAME.
HMPH. I HAVE GOOD REASON TO BELIEVE SO.
PEOPLE ARE DYING. DEMONS ARE APPEARING IN NUMBERS. ALL UNDER THE WATCH OF A CHURCH WITH A...*REPUTATION.*

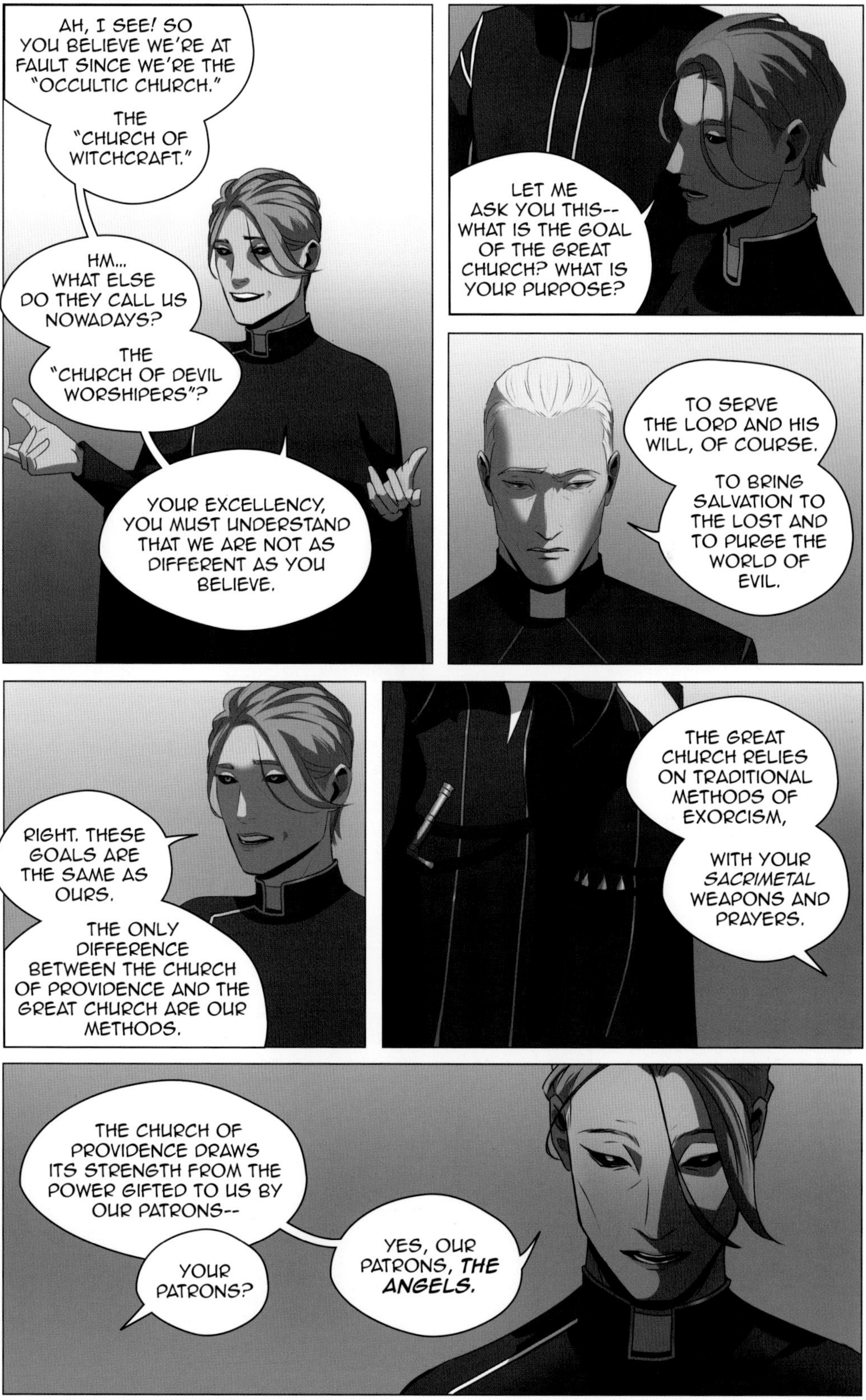
AH, I SEE! SO YOU BELIEVE WE'RE AT FAULT SINCE WE'RE THE "OCCULTIC CHURCH."
THE "CHURCH OF WITCHCRAFT."
HM... WHAT ELSE DO THEY CALL US NOWADAYS?
THE "CHURCH OF DEVIL WORSHIPERS"?
YOUR EXCELLENCY, YOU MUST UNDERSTAND THAT WE ARE NOT AS DIFFERENT AS YOU BELIEVE.
LET ME ASK YOU THIS-- WHAT IS THE GOAL OF THE GREAT CHURCH? WHAT IS YOUR PURPOSE?
TO SERVE THE LORD AND HIS WILL, OF COURSE.
TO BRING SALVATION TO THE LOST AND TO PURGE THE WORLD OF EVIL.
RIGHT. THESE GOALS ARE THE SAME AS OURS.
THE ONLY DIFFERENCE BETWEEN THE CHURCH OF PROVIDENCE AND THE GREAT CHURCH ARE OUR METHODS.
THE GREAT CHURCH RELIES ON TRADITIONAL METHODS OF EXORCISM,
WITH YOUR *SACRIMETAL* WEAPONS AND PRAYERS.
THE CHURCH OF PROVIDENCE DRAWS ITS STRENGTH FROM THE POWER GIFTED TO US BY OUR PATRONS--
YOUR PATRONS?
YES, OUR PATRONS, ***THE ANGELS.***

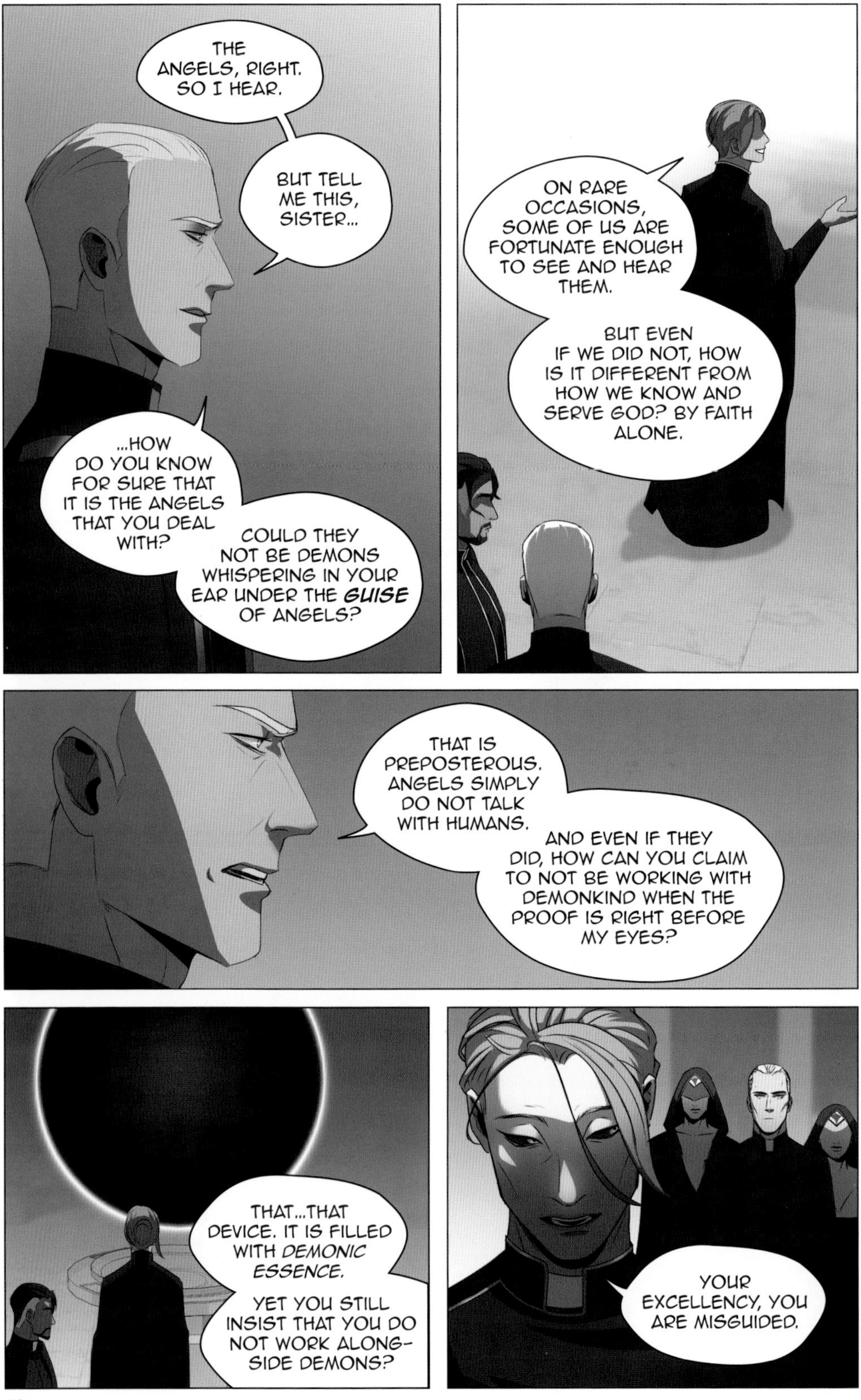
THE ANGELS, RIGHT. SO I HEAR.
BUT TELL ME THIS, SISTER...
...HOW DO YOU KNOW FOR SURE THAT IT IS THE ANGELS THAT YOU DEAL WITH?
COULD THEY NOT BE DEMONS WHISPERING IN YOUR EAR UNDER THE *GUISE* OF ANGELS?
ON RARE OCCASIONS, SOME OF US ARE FORTUNATE ENOUGH TO SEE AND HEAR THEM.
BUT EVEN IF WE DID NOT, HOW IS IT DIFFERENT FROM HOW WE KNOW AND SERVE GOD? BY FAITH ALONE.
THAT IS PREPOSTEROUS. ANGELS SIMPLY DO NOT TALK WITH HUMANS.
AND EVEN IF THEY DID, HOW CAN YOU CLAIM TO NOT BE WORKING WITH DEMONKIND WHEN THE PROOF IS RIGHT BEFORE MY EYES?
THAT...THAT DEVICE. IT IS FILLED WITH *DEMONIC ESSENCE.*
YET YOU STILL INSIST THAT YOU DO NOT WORK ALONG-SIDE DEMONS?
YOUR EXCELLENCY, YOU ARE MISGUIDED.

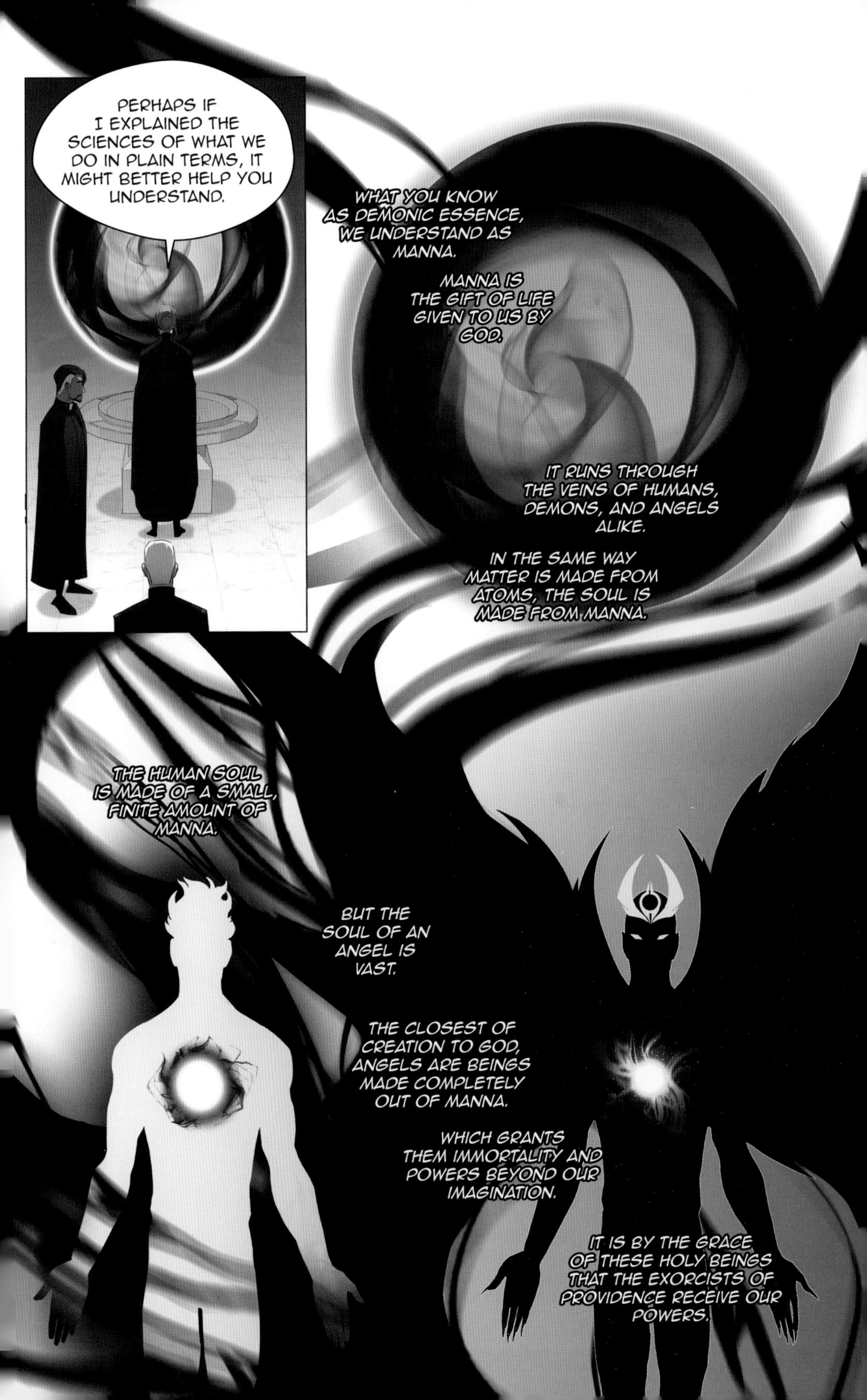

PERHAPS IF I EXPLAINED THE SCIENCES OF WHAT WE DO IN PLAIN TERMS, IT MIGHT BETTER HELP YOU UNDERSTAND.
WHAT YOU KNOW AS DEMONIC ESSENCE, WE UNDERSTAND AS MANNA.
MANNA IS THE GIFT OF LIFE GIVEN TO US BY GOD.
IT RUNS THROUGH THE VEINS OF HUMANS, DEMONS, AND ANGELS ALIKE.
IN THE SAME WAY MATTER IS MADE FROM ATOMS, THE SOUL IS MADE FROM MANNA.
THE HUMAN SOUL IS MADE OF A SMALL, FINITE AMOUNT OF MANNA.
BUT THE SOUL OF AN ANGEL IS VAST.
THE CLOSEST OF CREATION TO GOD, ANGELS ARE BEINGS MADE COMPLETELY OUT OF MANNA.
WHICH GRANTS THEM IMMORTALITY AND POWERS BEYOND OUR IMAGINATION.
IT IS BY THE GRACE OF THESE HOLY BEINGS THAT THE EXORCISTS OF PROVIDENCE RECEIVE OUR POWERS.

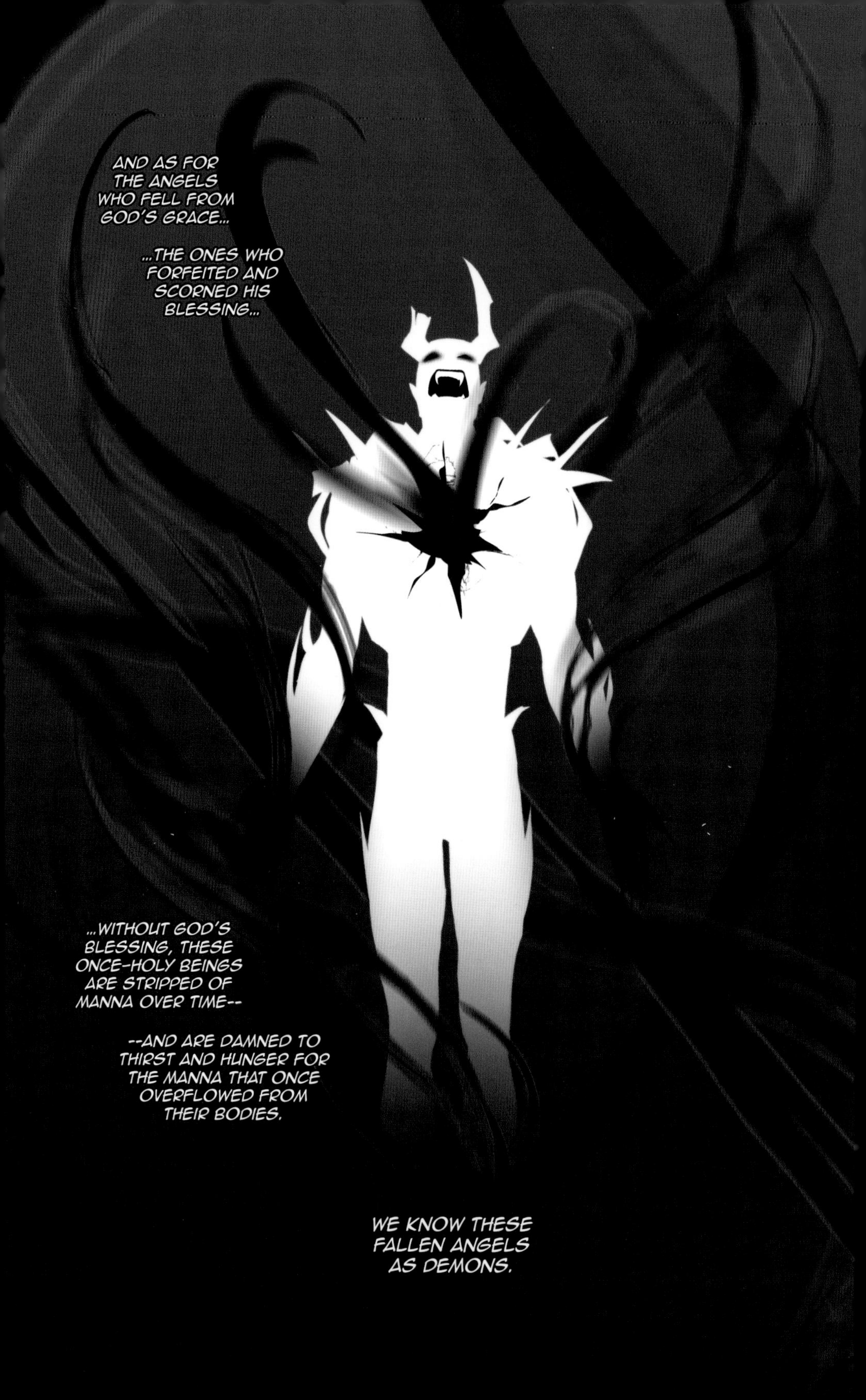
AND AS FOR THE ANGELS WHO FELL FROM GOD'S GRACE...
...THE ONES WHO FORFEITED AND SCORNED HIS BLESSING...
...WITHOUT GOD'S BLESSING, THESE ONCE-HOLY BEINGS ARE STRIPPED OF MANNA OVER TIME--
--AND ARE DAMNED TO THIRST AND HUNGER FOR THE MANNA THAT ONCE OVERFLOWED FROM THEIR BODIES.
WE KNOW THESE FALLEN ANGELS AS DEMONS.

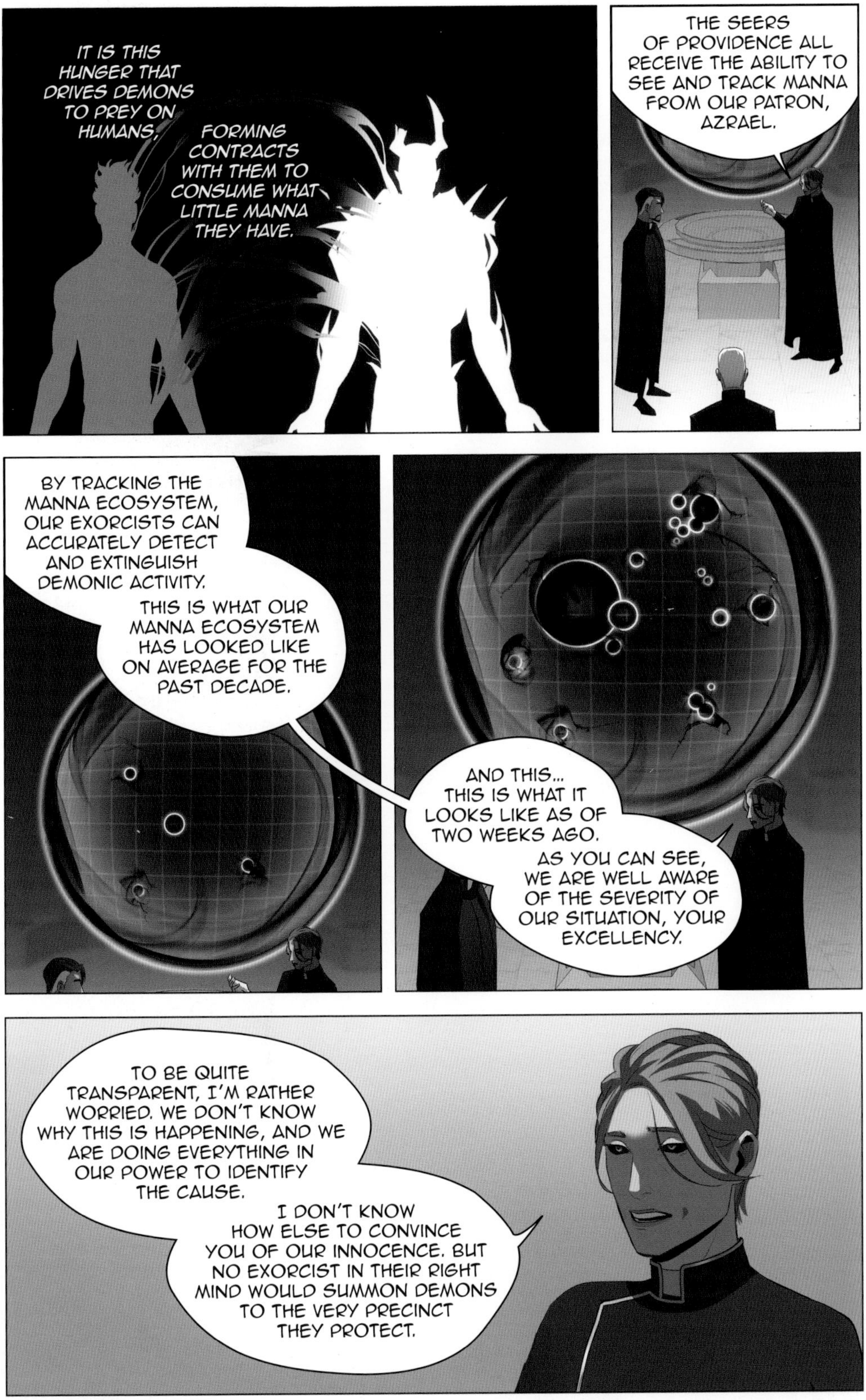
IT IS THIS HUNGER THAT DRIVES DEMONS TO PREY ON HUMANS,
FORMING CONTRACTS WITH THEM TO CONSUME WHAT LITTLE MANNA THEY HAVE.
THE SEERS OF PROVIDENCE ALL RECEIVE THE ABILITY TO SEE AND TRACK MANNA FROM OUR PATRON, AZRAEL.
BY TRACKING THE MANNA ECOSYSTEM, OUR EXORCISTS CAN ACCURATELY DETECT AND EXTINGUISH DEMONIC ACTIVITY.
THIS IS WHAT OUR MANNA ECOSYSTEM HAS LOOKED LIKE ON AVERAGE FOR THE PAST DECADE.
AND THIS... THIS IS WHAT IT LOOKS LIKE AS OF TWO WEEKS AGO.
AS YOU CAN SEE, WE ARE WELL AWARE OF THE SEVERITY OF OUR SITUATION, YOUR EXCELLENCY.
TO BE QUITE TRANSPARENT, I'M RATHER WORRIED. WE DON'T KNOW WHY THIS IS HAPPENING, AND WE ARE DOING EVERYTHING IN OUR POWER TO IDENTIFY THE CAUSE.
I DON'T KNOW HOW ELSE TO CONVINCE YOU OF OUR INNOCENCE. BUT NO EXORCIST IN THEIR RIGHT MIND WOULD SUMMON DEMONS TO THE VERY PRECINCT THEY PROTECT.

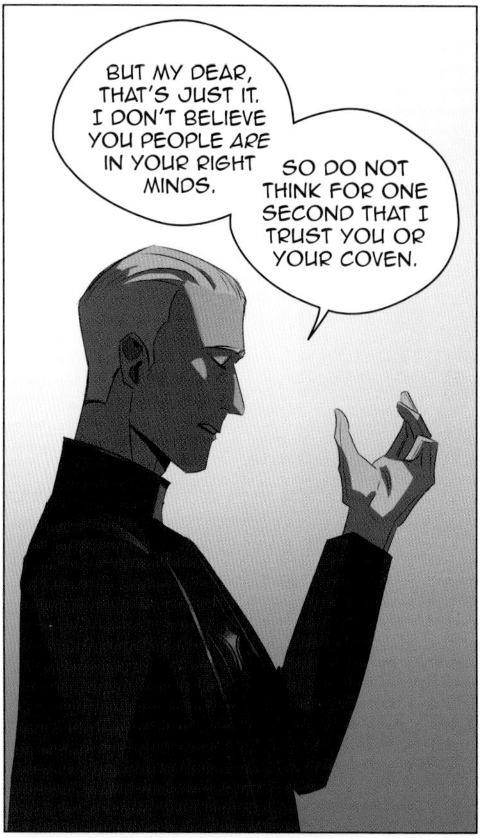
BUT MY DEAR, THAT'S JUST IT. I DON'T BELIEVE YOU PEOPLE ARE IN YOUR RIGHT MINDS.
SO DO NOT THINK FOR ONE SECOND THAT I TRUST YOU OR YOUR COVEN.

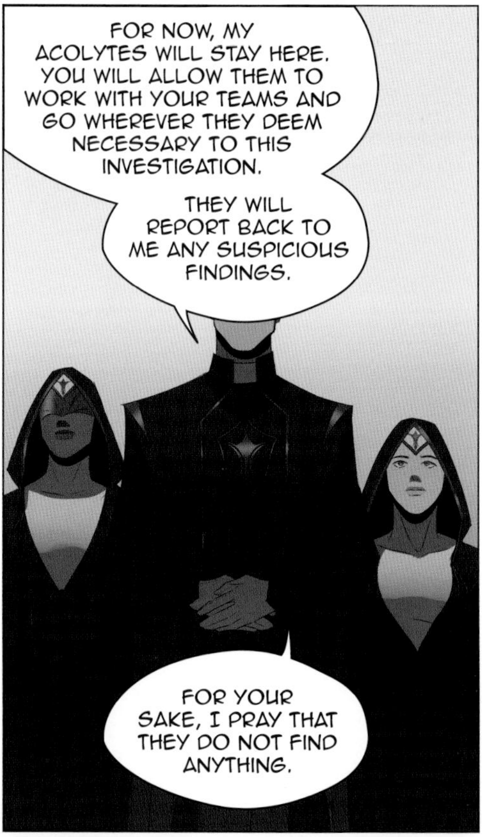
FOR NOW, MY ACOLYTES WILL STAY HERE. YOU WILL ALLOW THEM TO WORK WITH YOUR TEAMS AND GO WHEREVER THEY DEEM NECESSARY TO THIS INVESTIGATION.
THEY WILL REPORT BACK TO ME ANY SUSPICIOUS FINDINGS.
FOR YOUR SAKE, I PRAY THAT THEY DO NOT FIND ANYTHING.

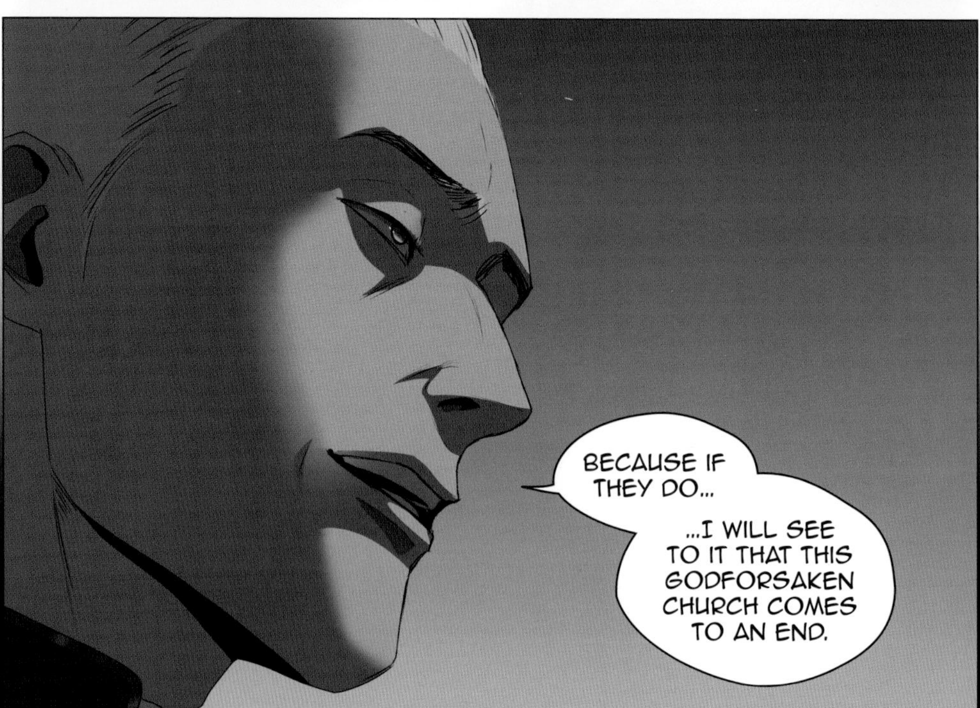
BECAUSE IF THEY DO...
...I WILL SEE TO IT THAT THIS GODFORSAKEN CHURCH COMES TO AN END.

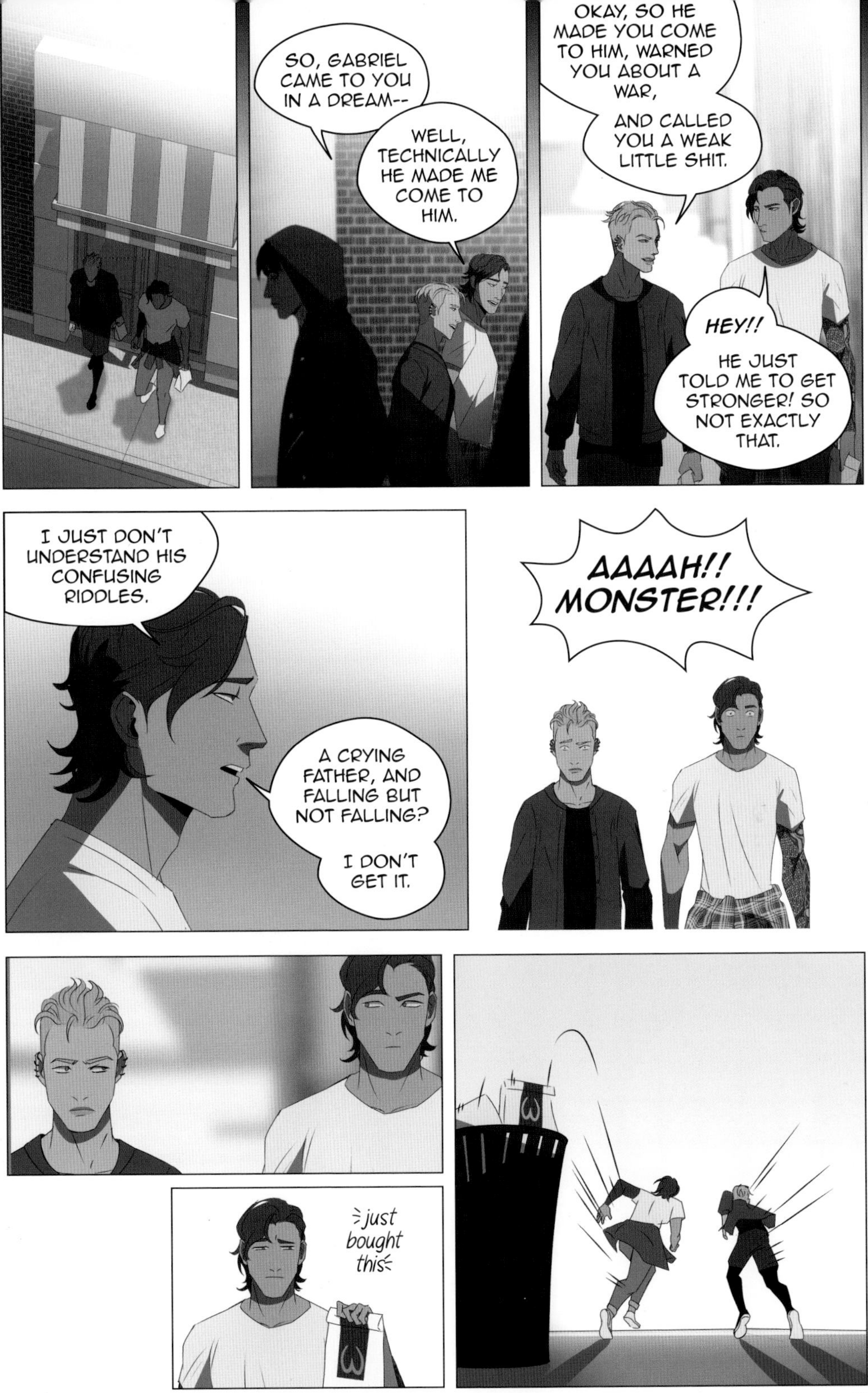
SO, GABRIEL CAME TO YOU IN A DREAM--
WELL, TECHNICALLY HE MADE ME COME TO HIM.
OKAY, SO HE MADE YOU COME TO HIM, WARNED YOU ABOUT A WAR,
AND CALLED YOU A WEAK LITTLE SHIT.
HEY!!
HE JUST TOLD ME TO GET STRONGER! SO NOT EXACTLY THAT.
I JUST DON'T UNDERSTAND HIS CONFUSING RIDDLES.
A CRYING FATHER, AND FALLING BUT NOT FALLING?
I DON'T GET IT.
AAAAH!! MONSTER!!!
just bought this

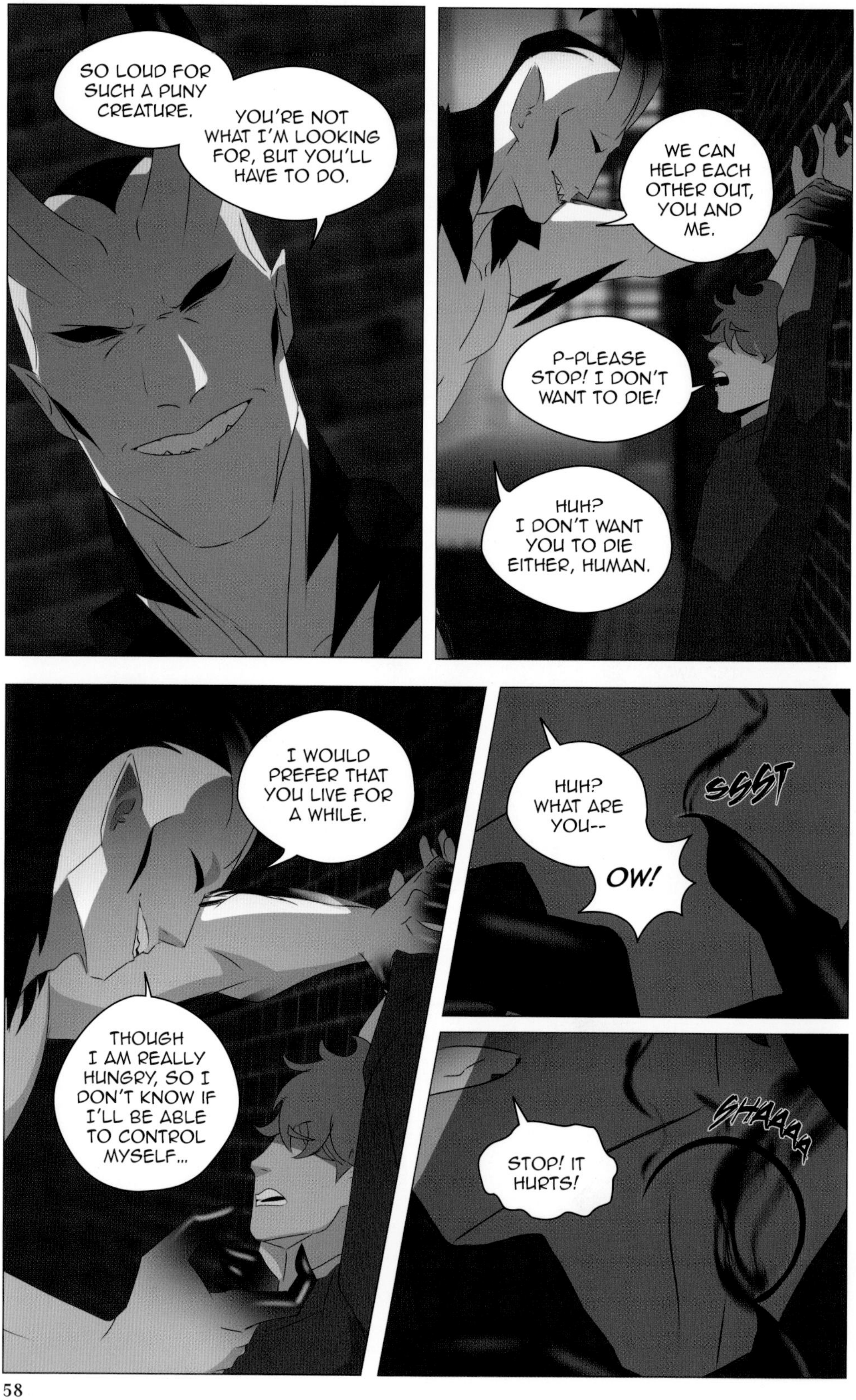
SO LOUD FOR SUCH A PUNY CREATURE.
YOU'RE NOT WHAT I'M LOOKING FOR, BUT YOU'LL HAVE TO DO.
WE CAN HELP EACH OTHER OUT, YOU AND ME.
P-PLEASE STOP! I DON'T WANT TO DIE!
HUH? I DON'T WANT YOU TO DIE EITHER, HUMAN.
I WOULD PREFER THAT YOU LIVE FOR A WHILE.
THOUGH I AM REALLY HUNGRY, SO I DON'T KNOW IF I'LL BE ABLE TO CONTROL MYSELF...
SSST
HUH? WHAT ARE YOU--
OW!
SHAAAA
STOP! IT HURTS!

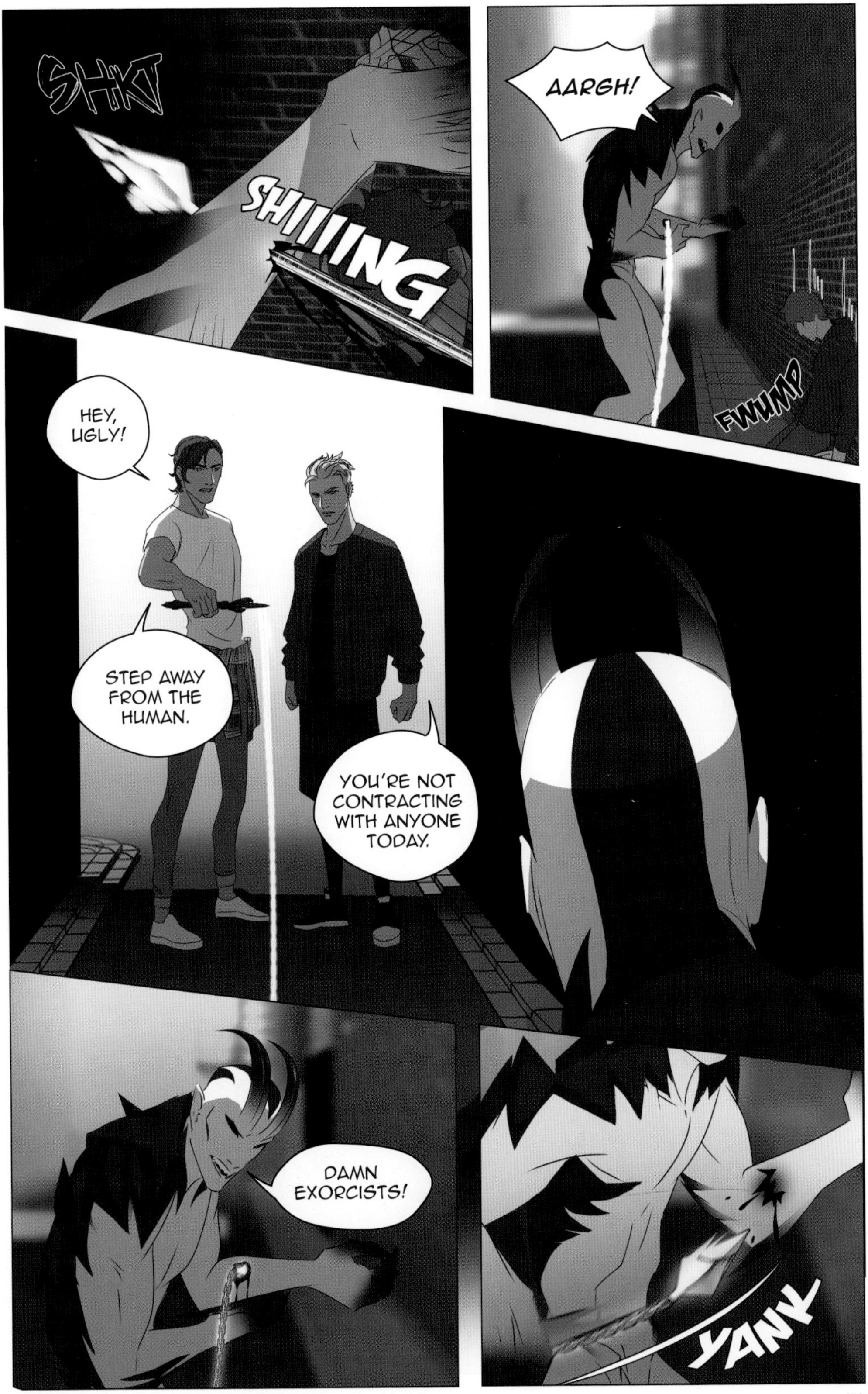
SHKT
SHIIIING
AARGH!
FWUMP
HEY, UGLY!
STEP AWAY FROM THE HUMAN.
YOU'RE NOT CONTRACTING WITH ANYONE TODAY.
DAMN EXORCISTS!
YANK

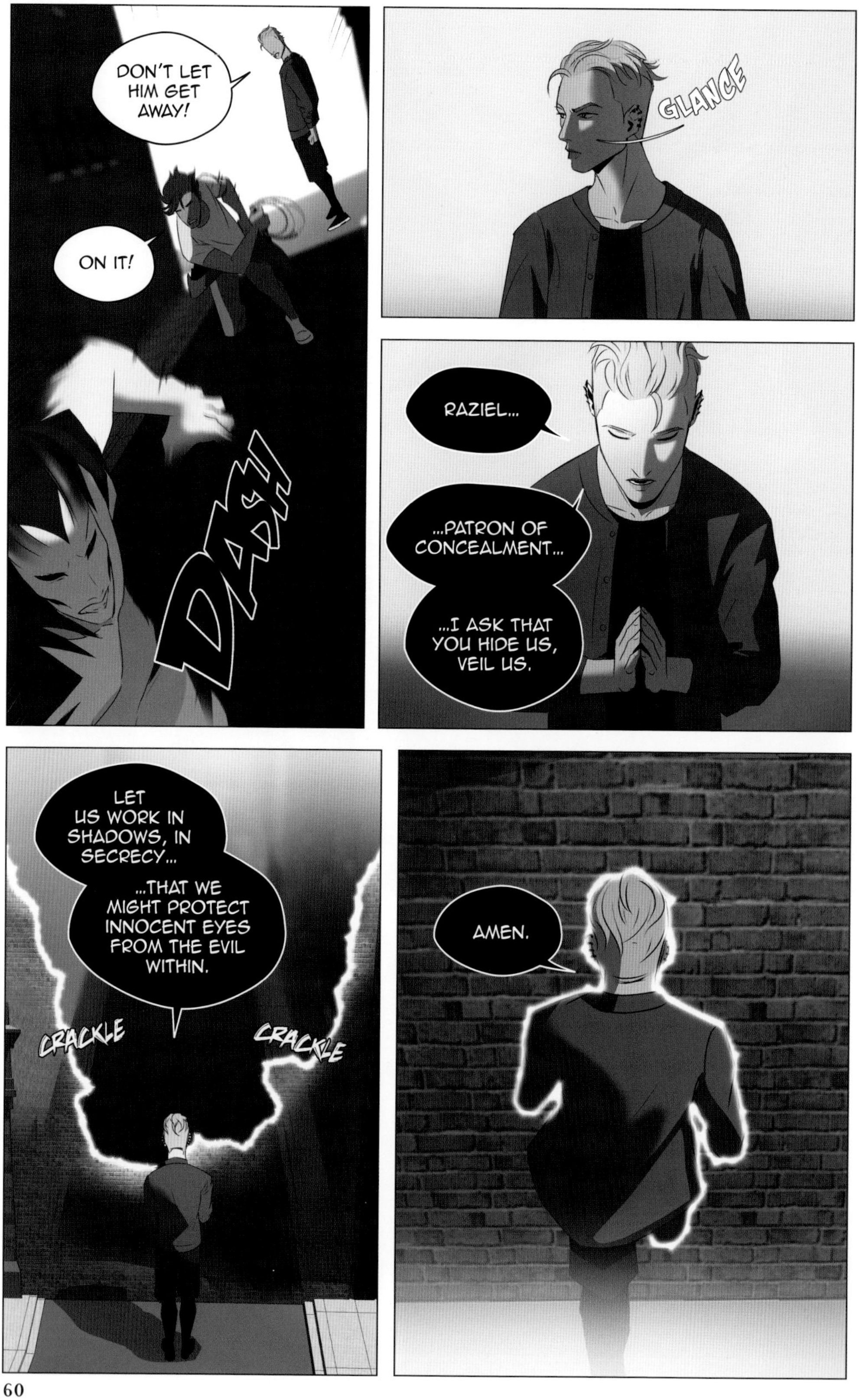
DON'T LET HIM GET AWAY!
ON IT!
DASH
GLANCE
RAZIEL...
...PATRON OF CONCEALMENT...
...I ASK THAT YOU HIDE US, VEIL US.
LET US WORK IN SHADOWS, IN SECRECY...
...THAT WE MIGHT PROTECT INNOCENT EYES FROM THE EVIL WITHIN.
CRACKLE
CRACKLE
AMEN.

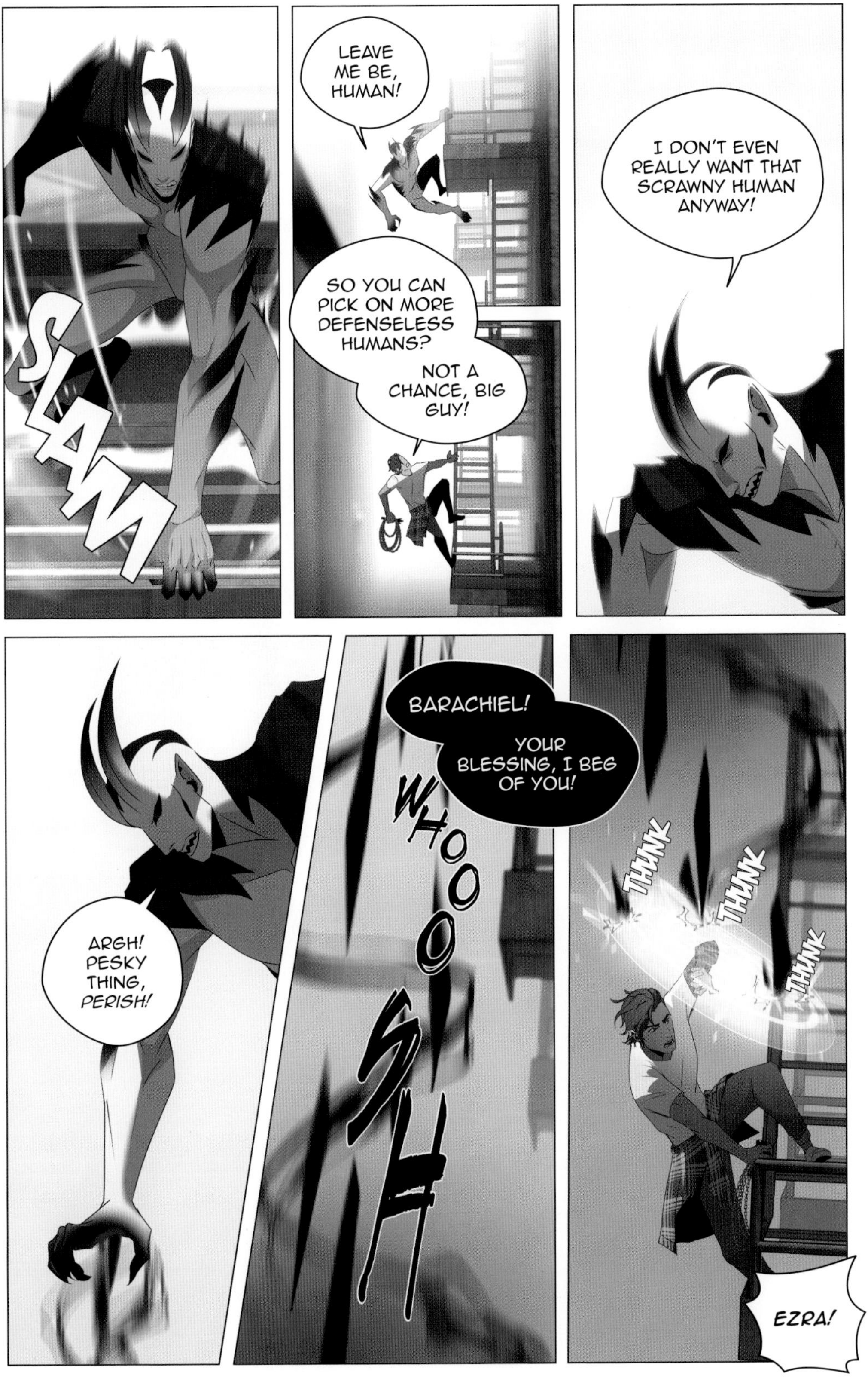
SLAM
LEAVE ME BE, HUMAN!
SO YOU CAN PICK ON MORE DEFENSELESS HUMANS?
NOT A CHANCE, BIG GUY!
I DON'T EVEN REALLY WANT THAT SCRAWNY HUMAN ANYWAY!
ARGH! PESKY THING, PERISH!
WHOOOSH
BARACHIEL!
YOUR BLESSING, I BEG OF YOU!
THUNK
THUNK
THUNK
EZRA!

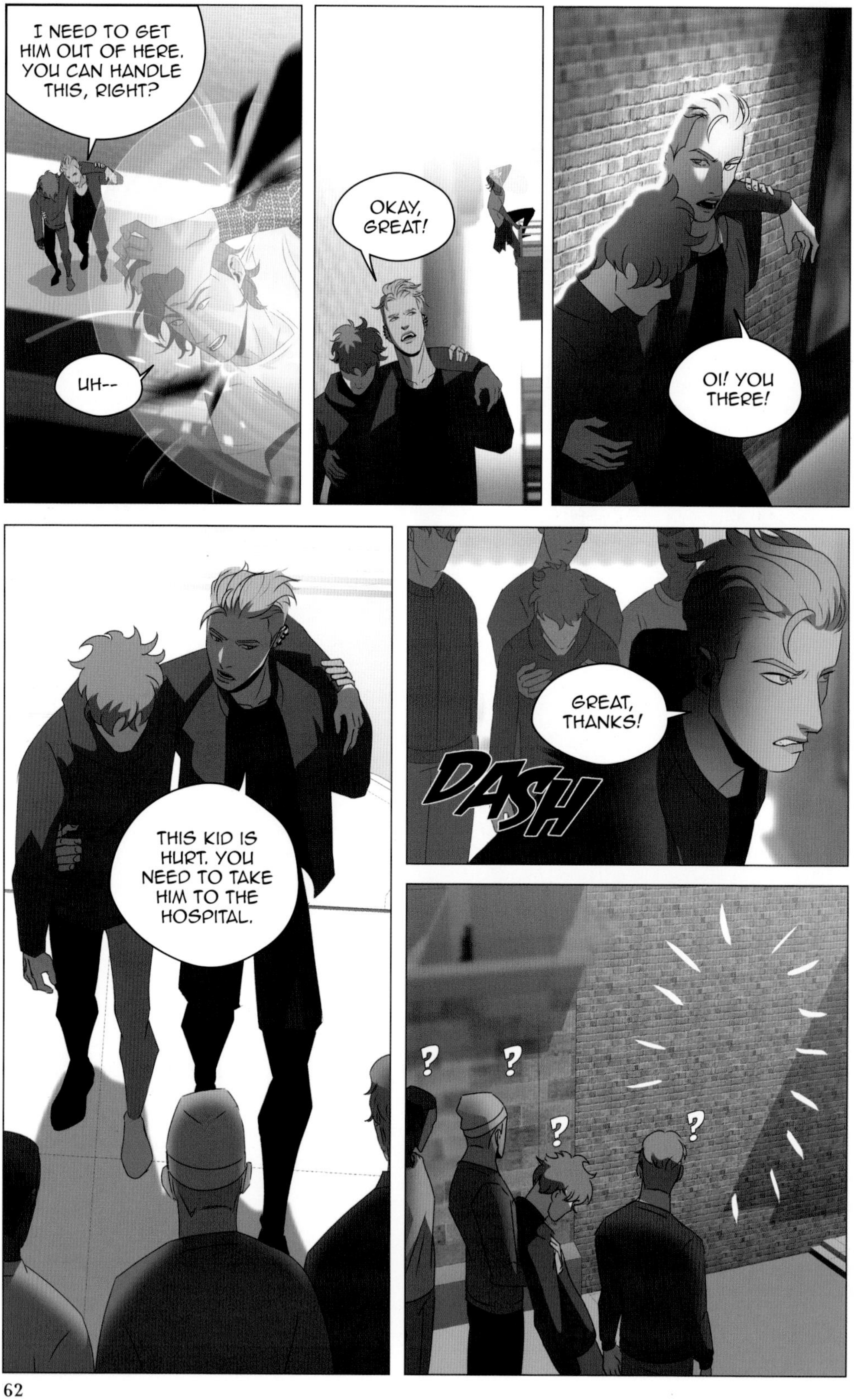
I NEED TO GET HIM OUT OF HERE. YOU CAN HANDLE THIS, RIGHT?
UH--
OKAY, GREAT!
OI! YOU THERE!
THIS KID IS HURT. YOU NEED TO TAKE HIM TO THE HOSPITAL.
GREAT, THANKS!
DASH
?
?
?
?

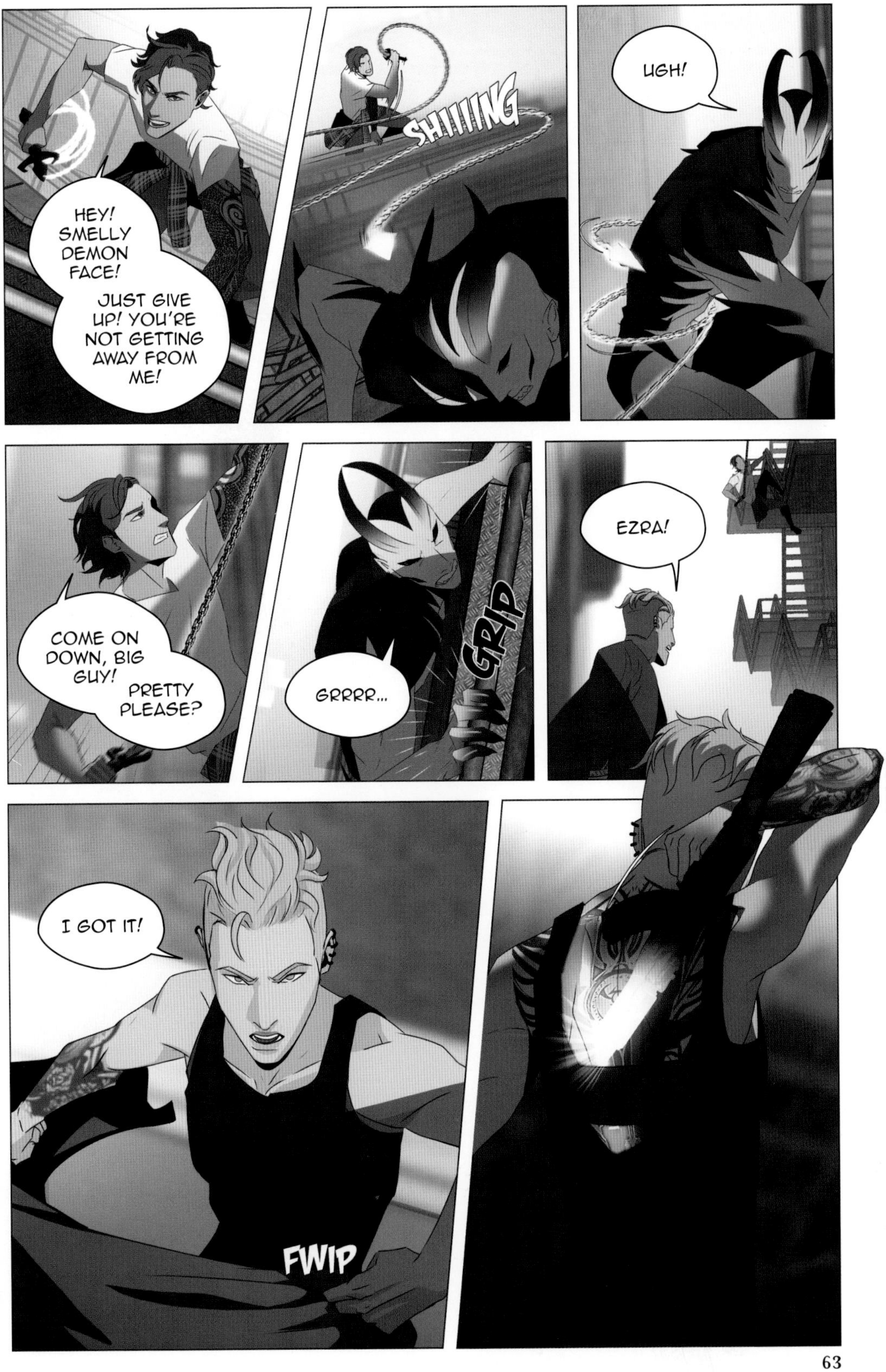
HEY! SMELLY DEMON FACE!
JUST GIVE UP! YOU'RE NOT GETTING AWAY FROM ME!
SHIIIING
UGH!
COME ON DOWN, BIG GUY!
PRETTY PLEASE?
GRRRR...
GRIP
EZRA!
I GOT IT!
FWIP

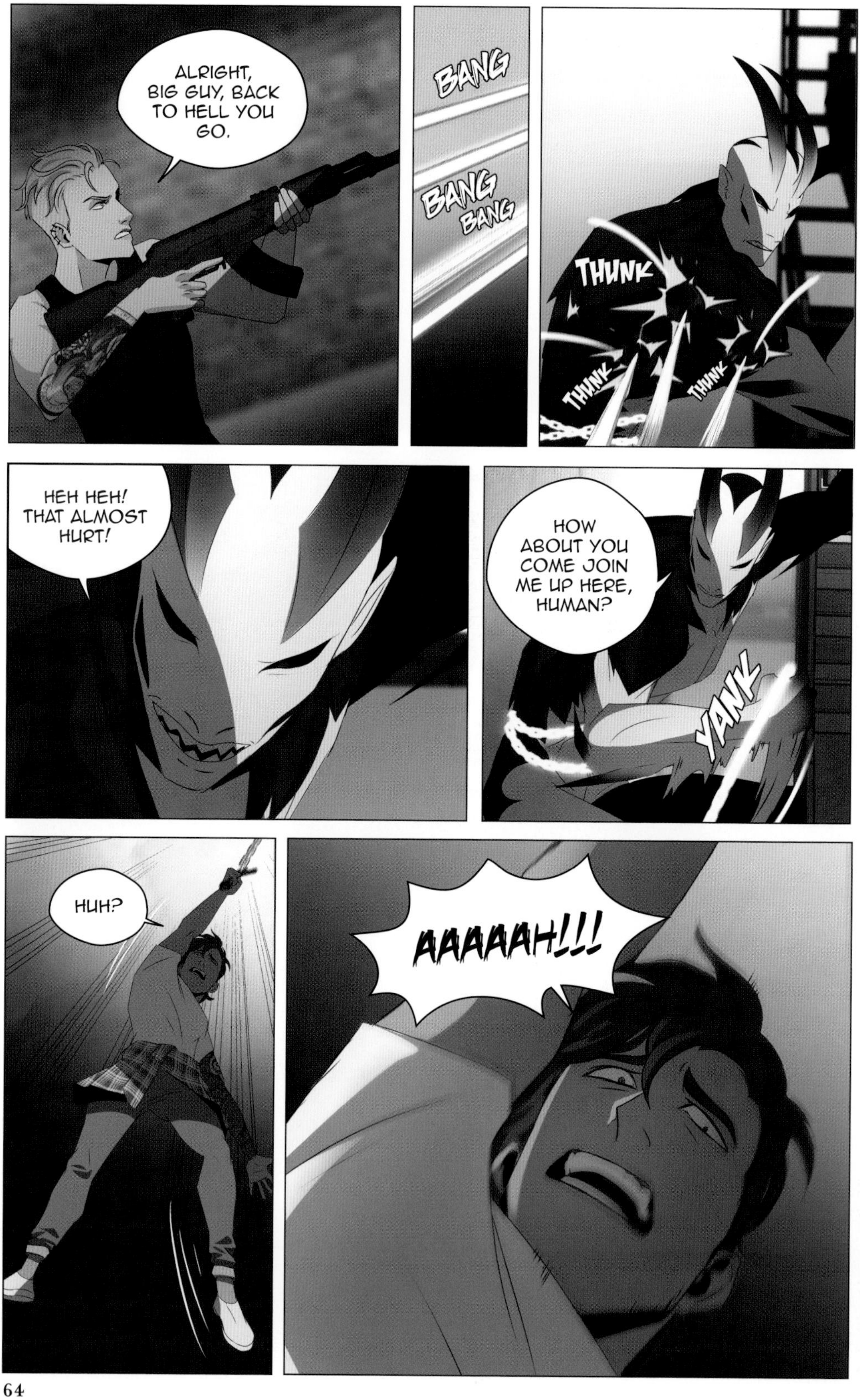
ALRIGHT, BIG GUY, BACK TO HELL YOU GO.
BANG
BANG BANG
THUNK
THUNK
THUNK
HEH HEH! THAT ALMOST HURT!
HOW ABOUT YOU COME JOIN ME UP HERE, HUMAN?
YANK
HUH?
AAAAAH!!!

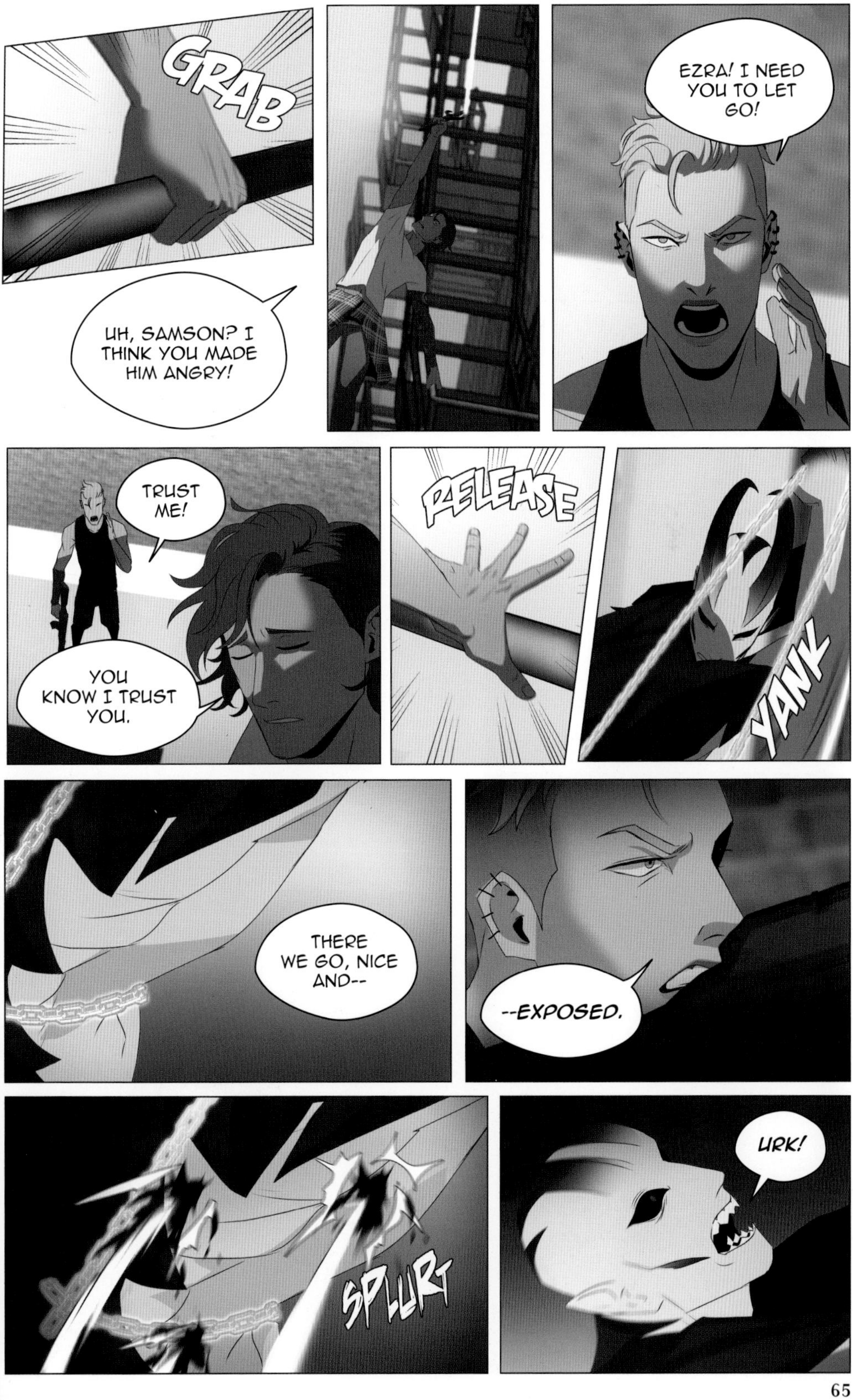
GRAB
UH, SAMSON? I THINK YOU MADE HIM ANGRY!
EZRA! I NEED YOU TO LET GO!
TRUST ME!
YOU KNOW I TRUST YOU.
RELEASE
YANK
THERE WE GO, NICE AND--
--EXPOSED.
SPLURT
URK!

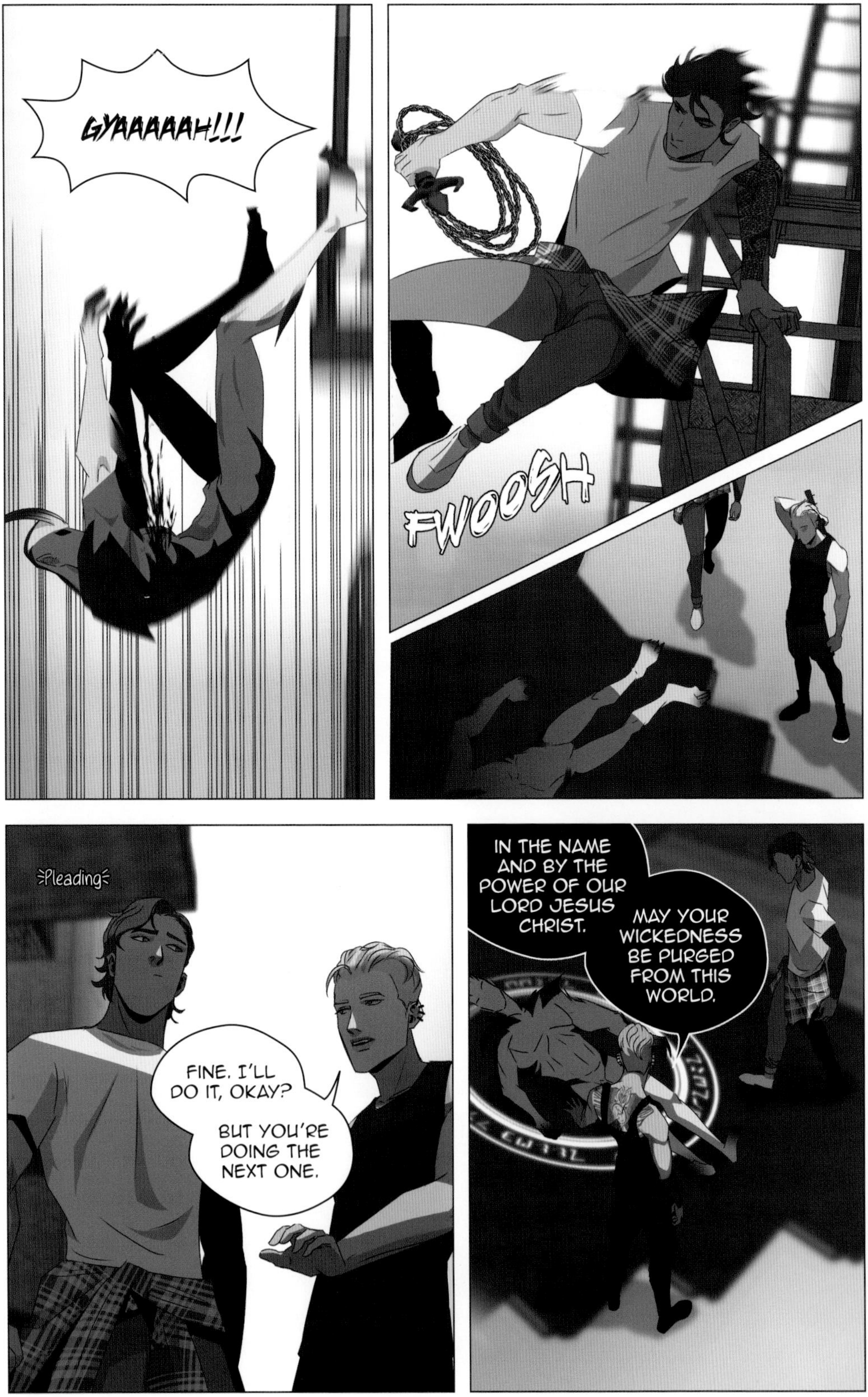
GYAAAAAH!!!
FWOOSH
Pleading
FINE. I'LL DO IT, OKAY?
BUT YOU'RE DOING THE NEXT ONE.
IN THE NAME AND BY THE POWER OF OUR LORD JESUS CHRIST.
MAY YOUR WICKEDNESS BE PURGED FROM THIS WORLD.

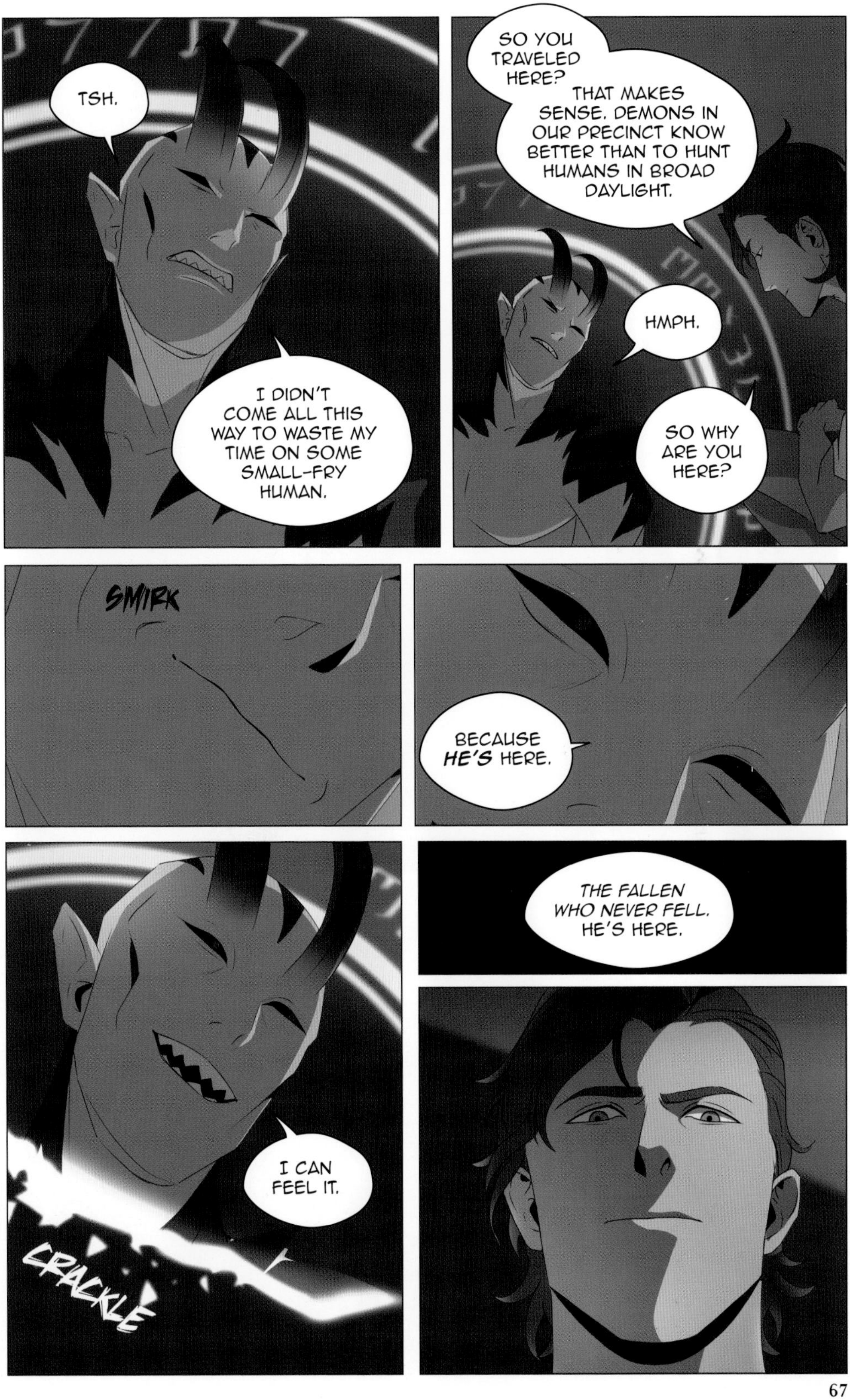
TSH.
I DIDN'T COME ALL THIS WAY TO WASTE MY TIME ON SOME SMALL-FRY HUMAN.
SO YOU TRAVELED HERE?
THAT MAKES SENSE. DEMONS IN OUR PRECINCT KNOW BETTER THAN TO HUNT HUMANS IN BROAD DAYLIGHT.
HMPH.
SO WHY ARE YOU HERE?
SMIRK
BECAUSE HE'S HERE.
I CAN FEEL IT.
CRACKLE
THE FALLEN WHO NEVER FELL. HE'S HERE.

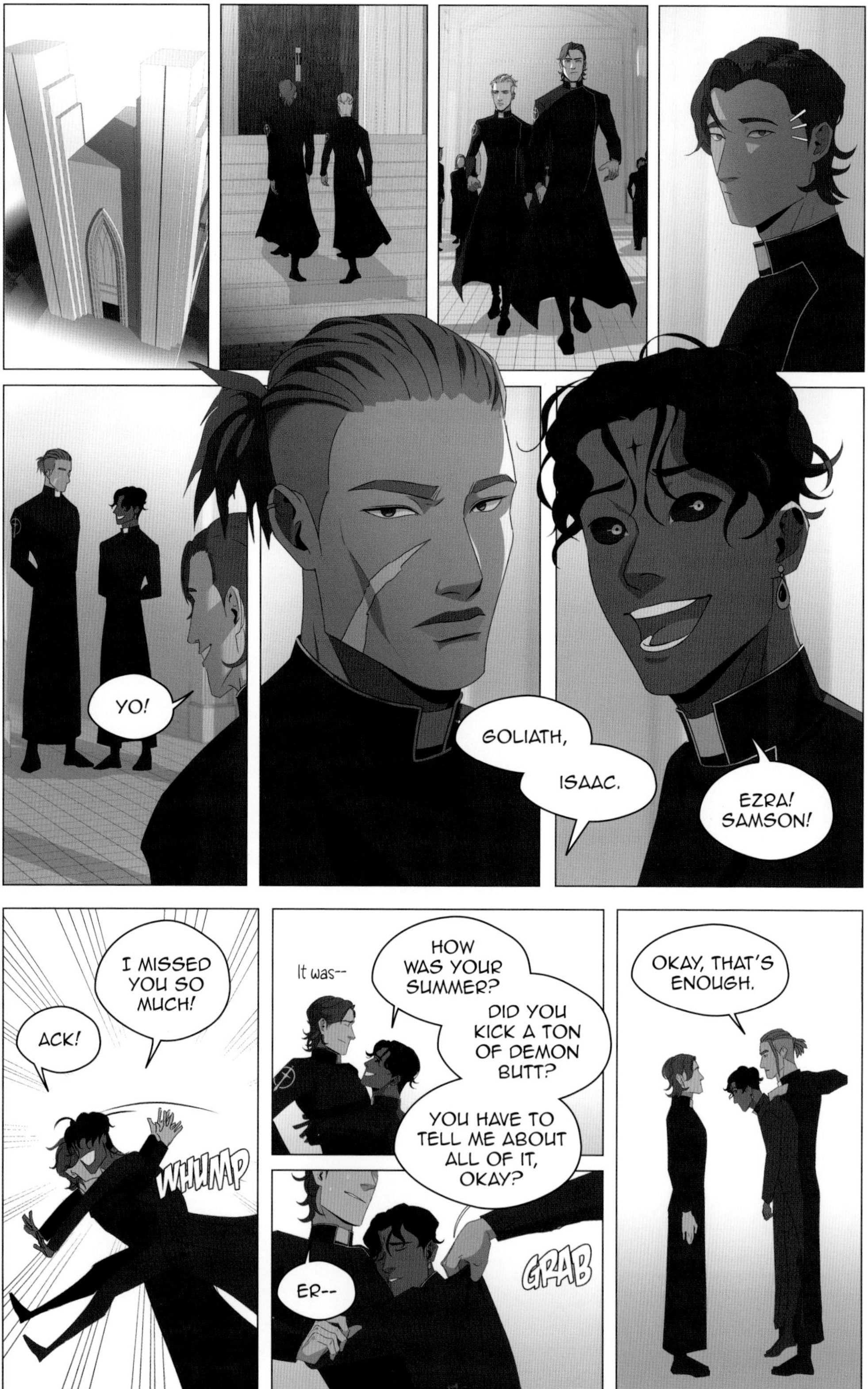
YO!
GOLIATH,
ISAAC.
EZRA!
SAMSON!
I MISSED YOU SO MUCH!
ACK!
WHUMP
It was--
HOW WAS YOUR SUMMER?
DID YOU KICK A TON OF DEMON BUTT?
YOU HAVE TO TELL ME ABOUT ALL OF IT, OKAY?
ER--
GRAB
OKAY, THAT'S ENOUGH.

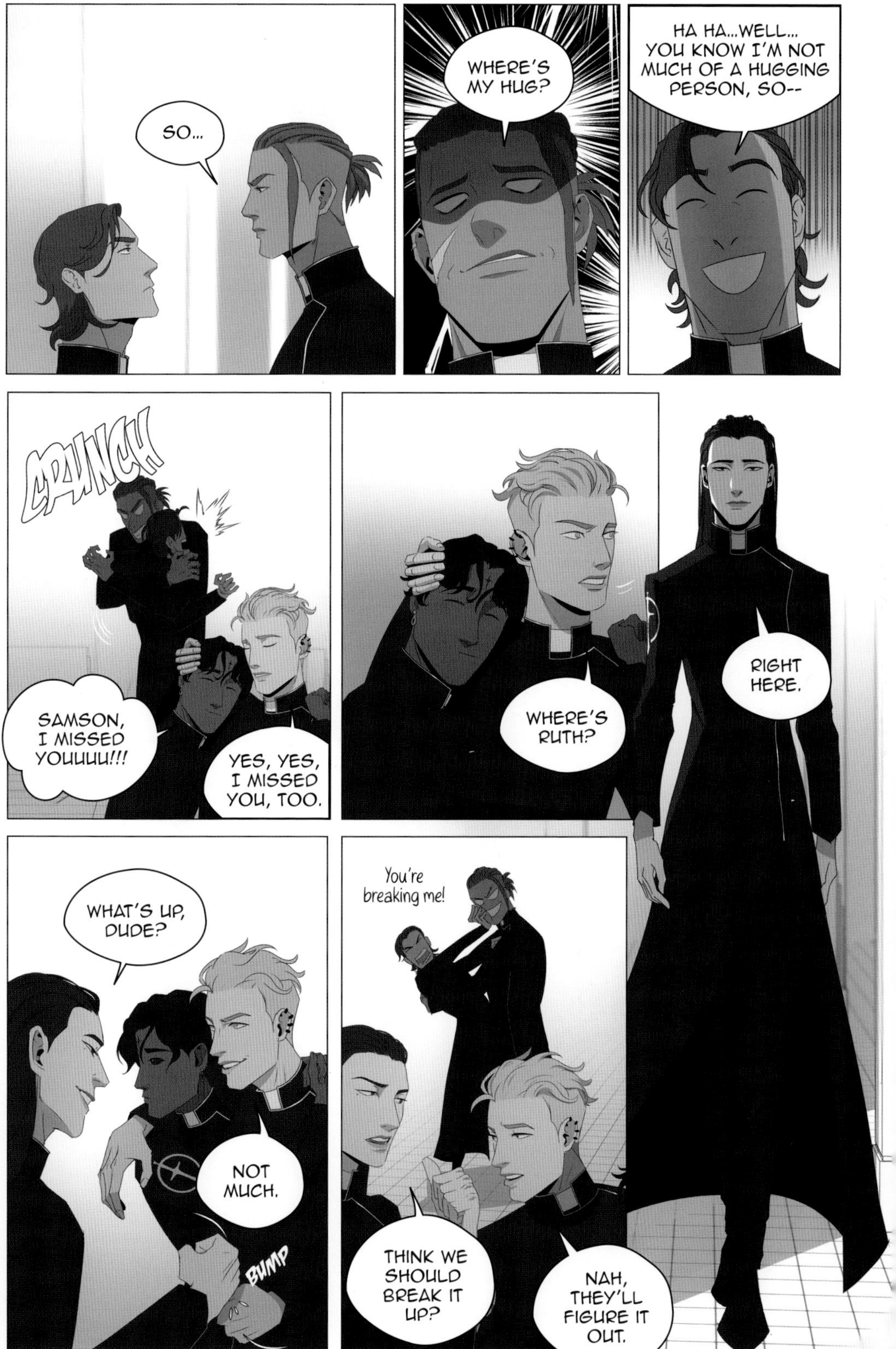
SO...
WHERE'S MY HUG?
HA HA...WELL... YOU KNOW I'M NOT MUCH OF A HUGGING PERSON, SO--
CRUNCH
SAMSON, I MISSED YOUUUU!!!
YES, YES, I MISSED YOU, TOO.
WHERE'S RUTH?
RIGHT HERE.
WHAT'S UP, DUDE?
NOT MUCH.
BUMP
You're breaking me!
THINK WE SHOULD BREAK IT UP?
NAH, THEY'LL FIGURE IT OUT.

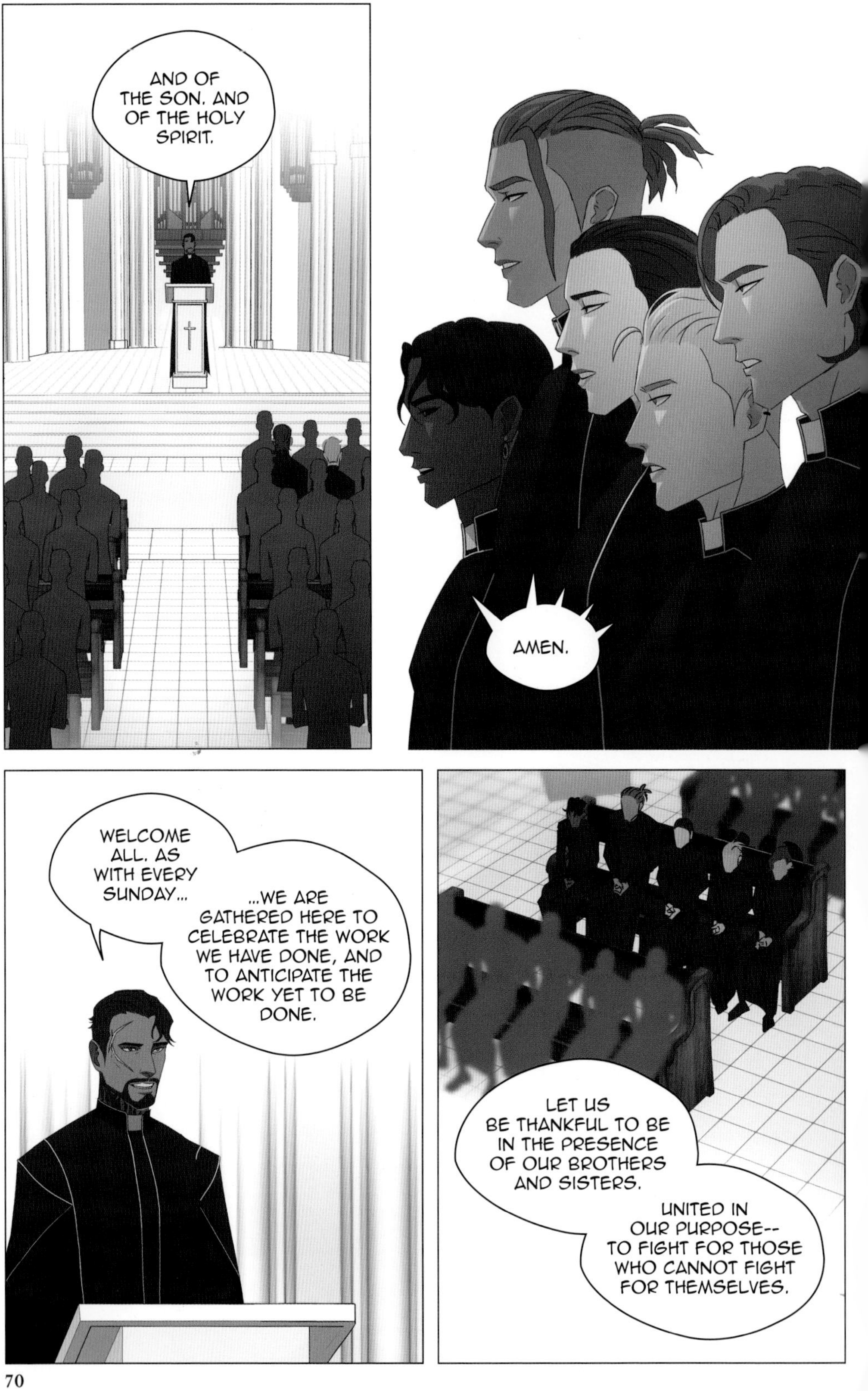
AND OF THE SON. AND OF THE HOLY SPIRIT.
AMEN.
WELCOME ALL. AS WITH EVERY SUNDAY...
...WE ARE GATHERED HERE TO CELEBRATE THE WORK WE HAVE DONE, AND TO ANTICIPATE THE WORK YET TO BE DONE.
LET US BE THANKFUL TO BE IN THE PRESENCE OF OUR BROTHERS AND SISTERS.
UNITED IN OUR PURPOSE-- TO FIGHT FOR THOSE WHO CANNOT FIGHT FOR THEMSELVES.

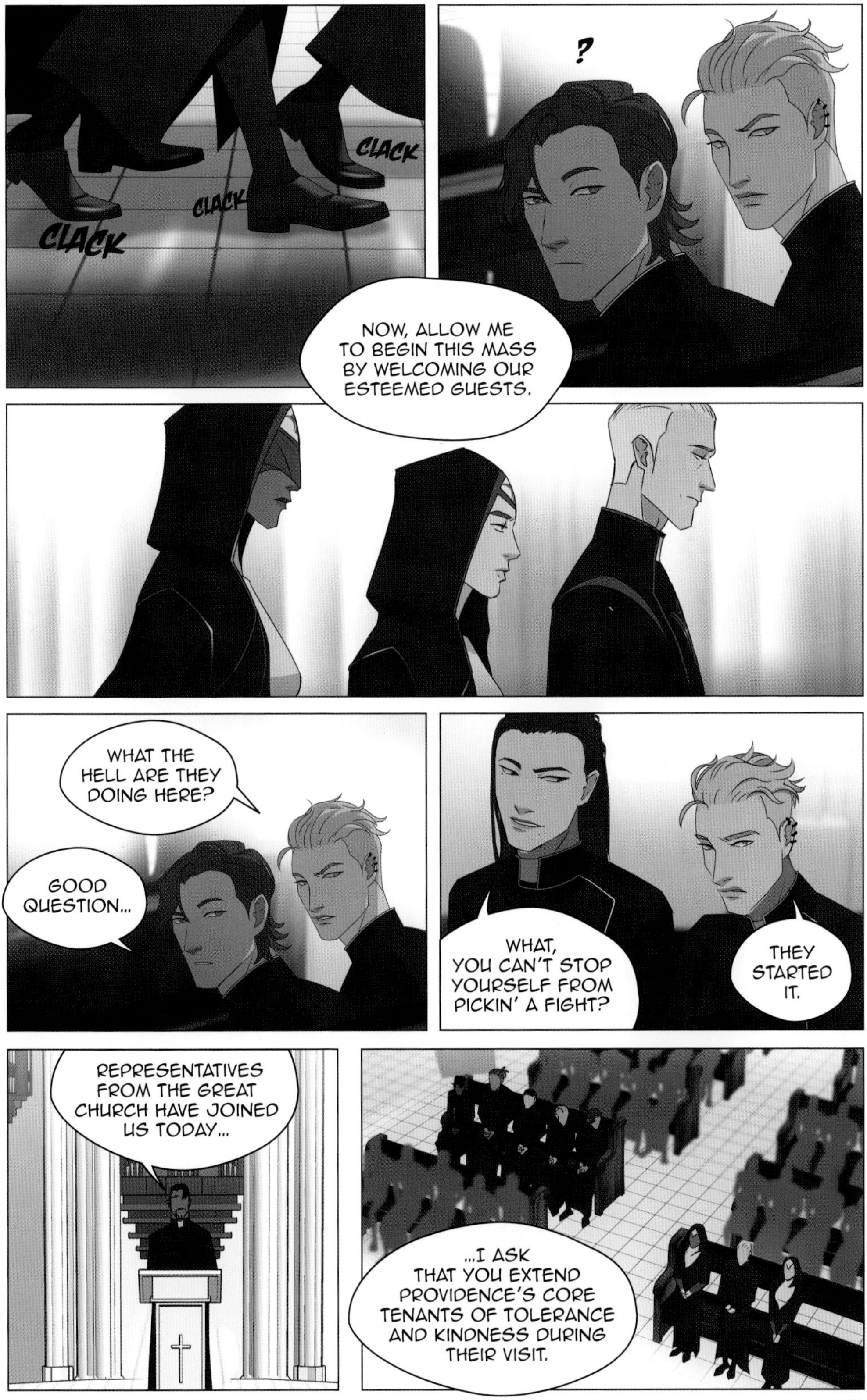
CLACK
CLACK
CLACK
?
NOW, ALLOW ME TO BEGIN THIS MASS BY WELCOMING OUR ESTEEMED GUESTS.
WHAT THE HELL ARE THEY DOING HERE?
GOOD QUESTION...
WHAT, YOU CAN'T STOP YOURSELF FROM PICKIN' A FIGHT?
THEY STARTED IT.
REPRESENTATIVES FROM THE GREAT CHURCH HAVE JOINED US TODAY...
...I ASK THAT YOU EXTEND PROVIDENCE'S CORE TENANTS OF TOLERANCE AND KINDNESS DURING THEIR VISIT.

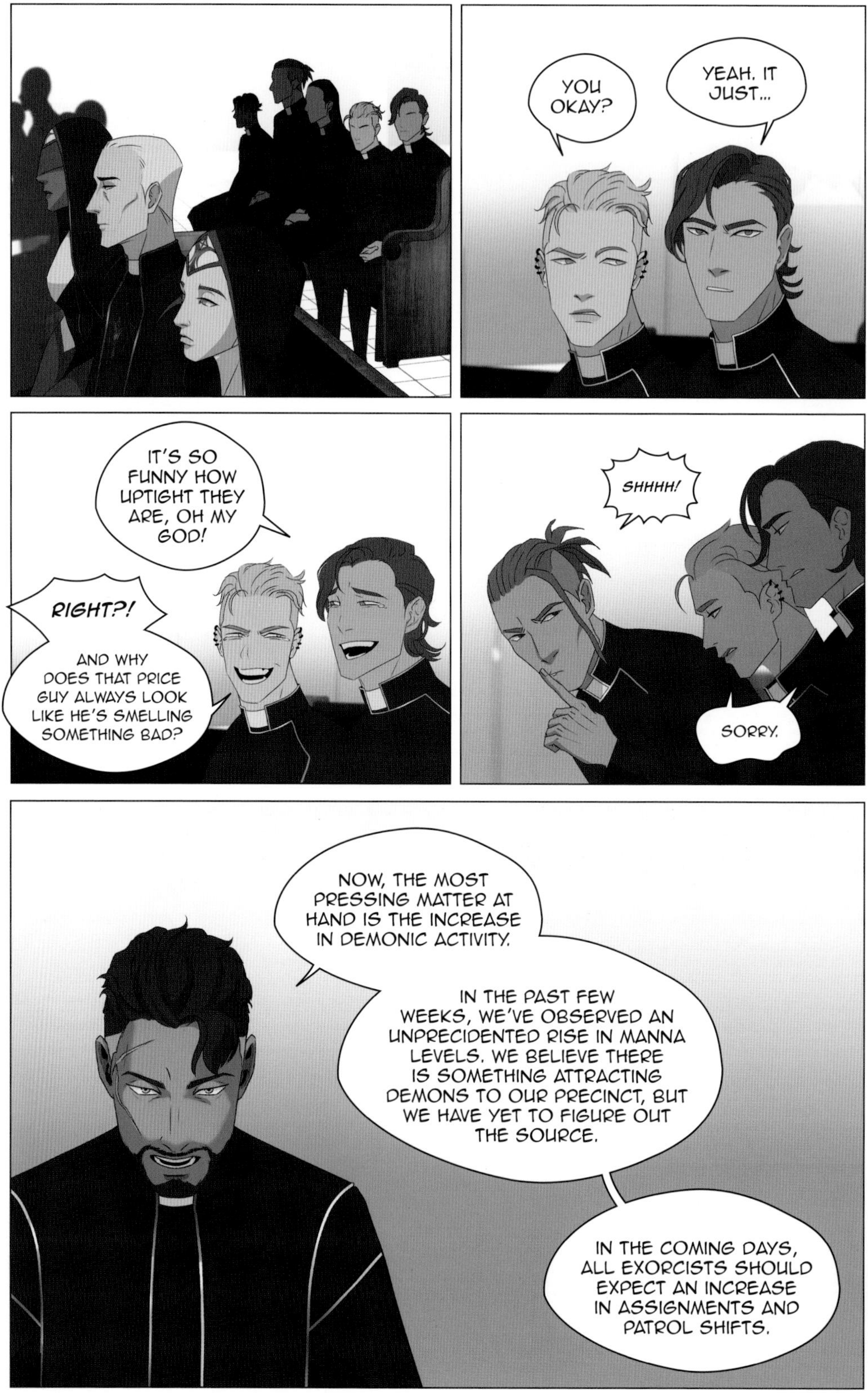
YOU OKAY?
YEAH. IT JUST...
IT'S SO FUNNY HOW UPTIGHT THEY ARE, OH MY GOD!
RIGHT?!
AND WHY DOES THAT PRICE GUY ALWAYS LOOK LIKE HE'S SMELLING SOMETHING BAD?
SHHHH!
SORRY.
NOW, THE MOST PRESSING MATTER AT HAND IS THE INCREASE IN DEMONIC ACTIVITY.
IN THE PAST FEW WEEKS, WE'VE OBSERVED AN UNPRECIDENTED RISE IN MANNA LEVELS. WE BELIEVE THERE IS SOMETHING ATTRACTING DEMONS TO OUR PRECINCT, BUT WE HAVE YET TO FIGURE OUT THE SOURCE.
IN THE COMING DAYS, ALL EXORCISTS SHOULD EXPECT AN INCREASE IN ASSIGNMENTS AND PATROL SHIFTS.

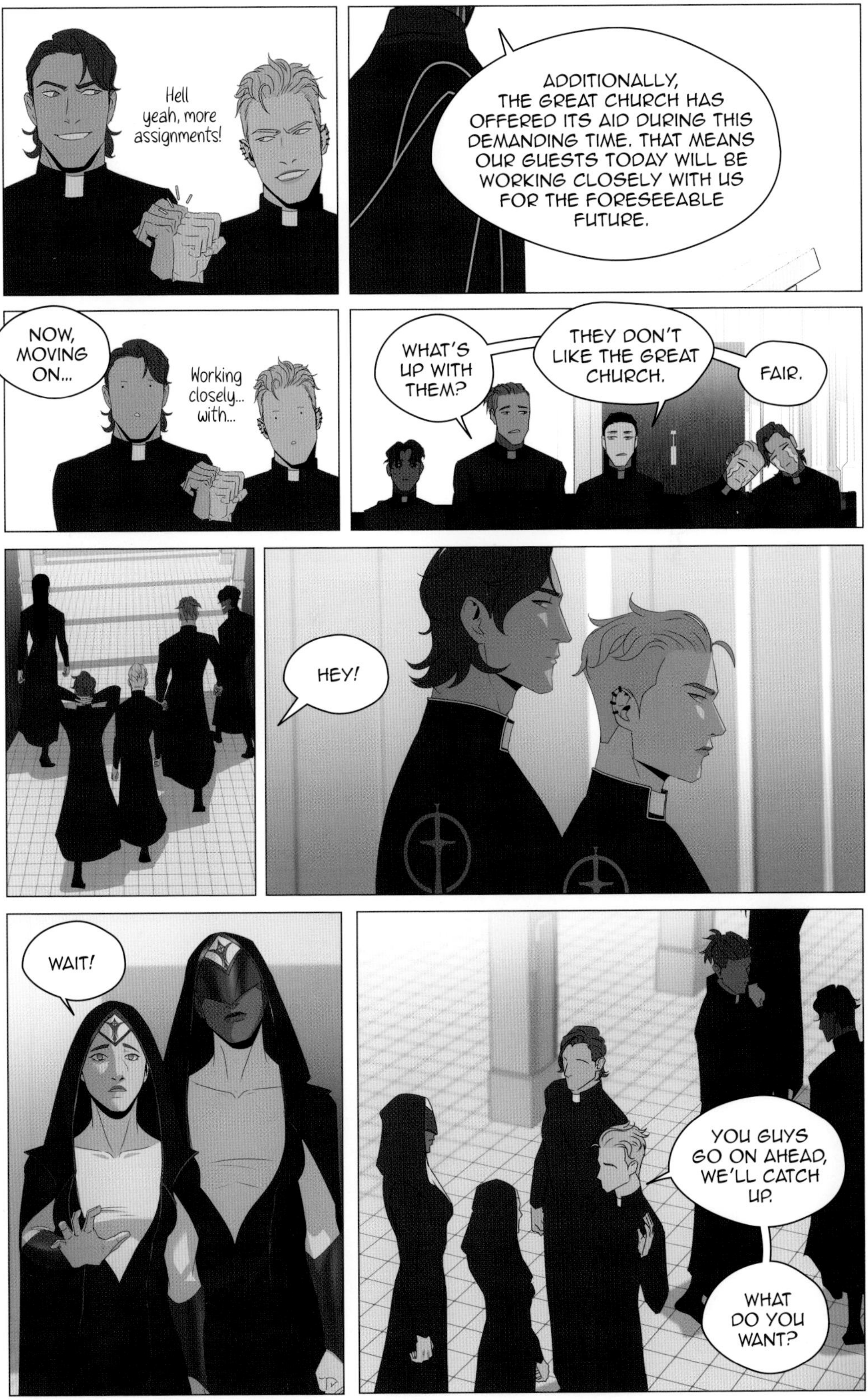
Hell yeah, more assignments!
ADDITIONALLY, THE GREAT CHURCH HAS OFFERED ITS AID DURING THIS DEMANDING TIME. THAT MEANS OUR GUESTS TODAY WILL BE WORKING CLOSELY WITH US FOR THE FORESEEABLE FUTURE.
NOW, MOVING ON...
Working closely... with...
WHAT'S UP WITH THEM?
THEY DON'T LIKE THE GREAT CHURCH.
FAIR.
HEY!
WAIT!
YOU GUYS GO ON AHEAD, WE'LL CATCH UP.
WHAT DO YOU WANT?

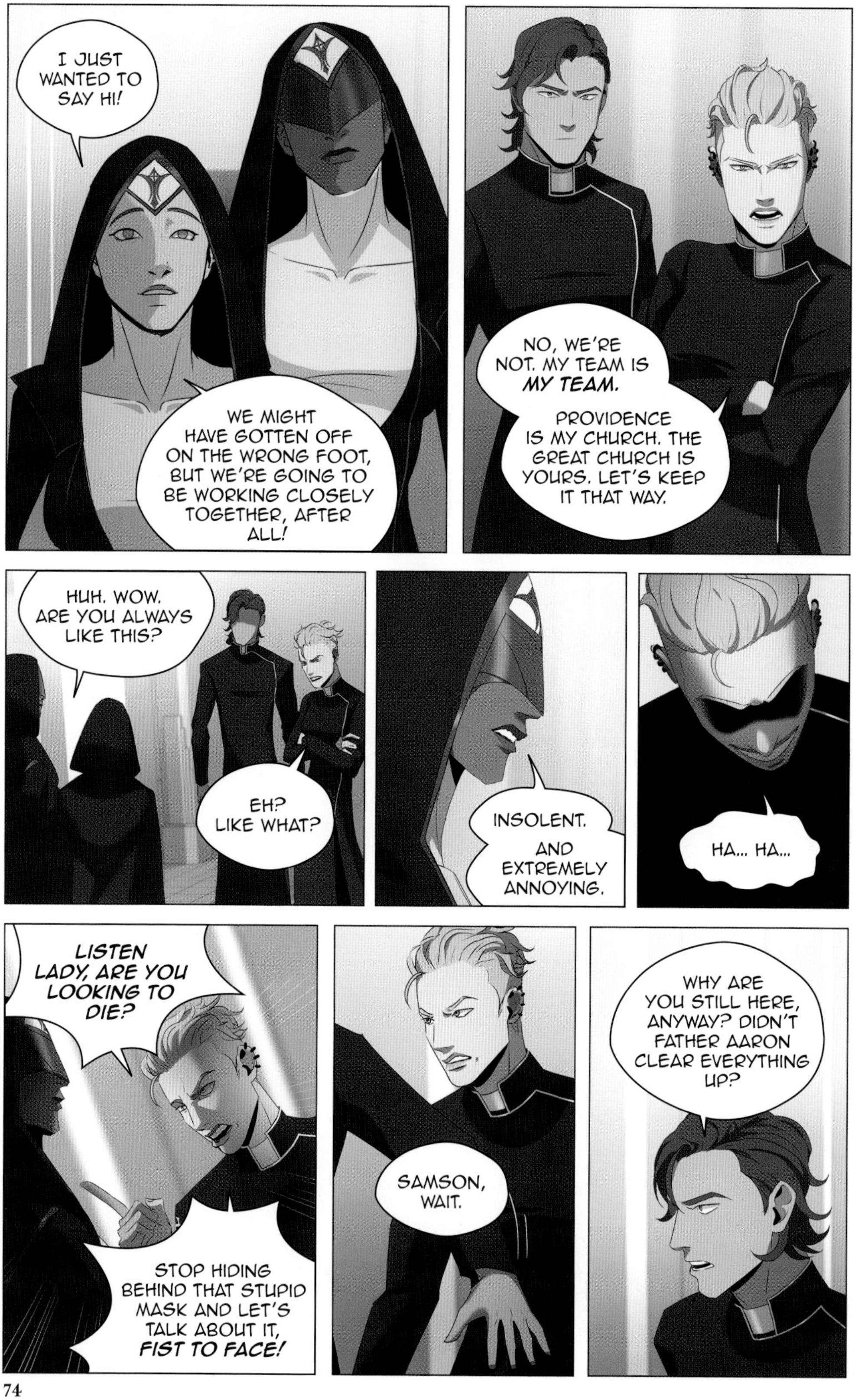
I JUST WANTED TO SAY HI!
WE MIGHT HAVE GOTTEN OFF ON THE WRONG FOOT, BUT WE'RE GOING TO BE WORKING CLOSELY TOGETHER, AFTER ALL!
NO, WE'RE NOT. MY TEAM IS ***MY TEAM.***
PROVIDENCE IS MY CHURCH. THE GREAT CHURCH IS YOURS. LET'S KEEP IT THAT WAY.
HUH. WOW. ARE YOU ALWAYS LIKE THIS?
EH? LIKE WHAT?
INSOLENT.
AND EXTREMELY ANNOYING.
HA... HA...
LISTEN LADY, ARE YOU LOOKING TO DIE?
STOP HIDING BEHIND THAT STUPID MASK AND LET'S TALK ABOUT IT, ***FIST TO FACE!***
SAMSON, WAIT.
WHY ARE YOU STILL HERE, ANYWAY? DIDN'T FATHER AARON CLEAR EVERYTHING UP?

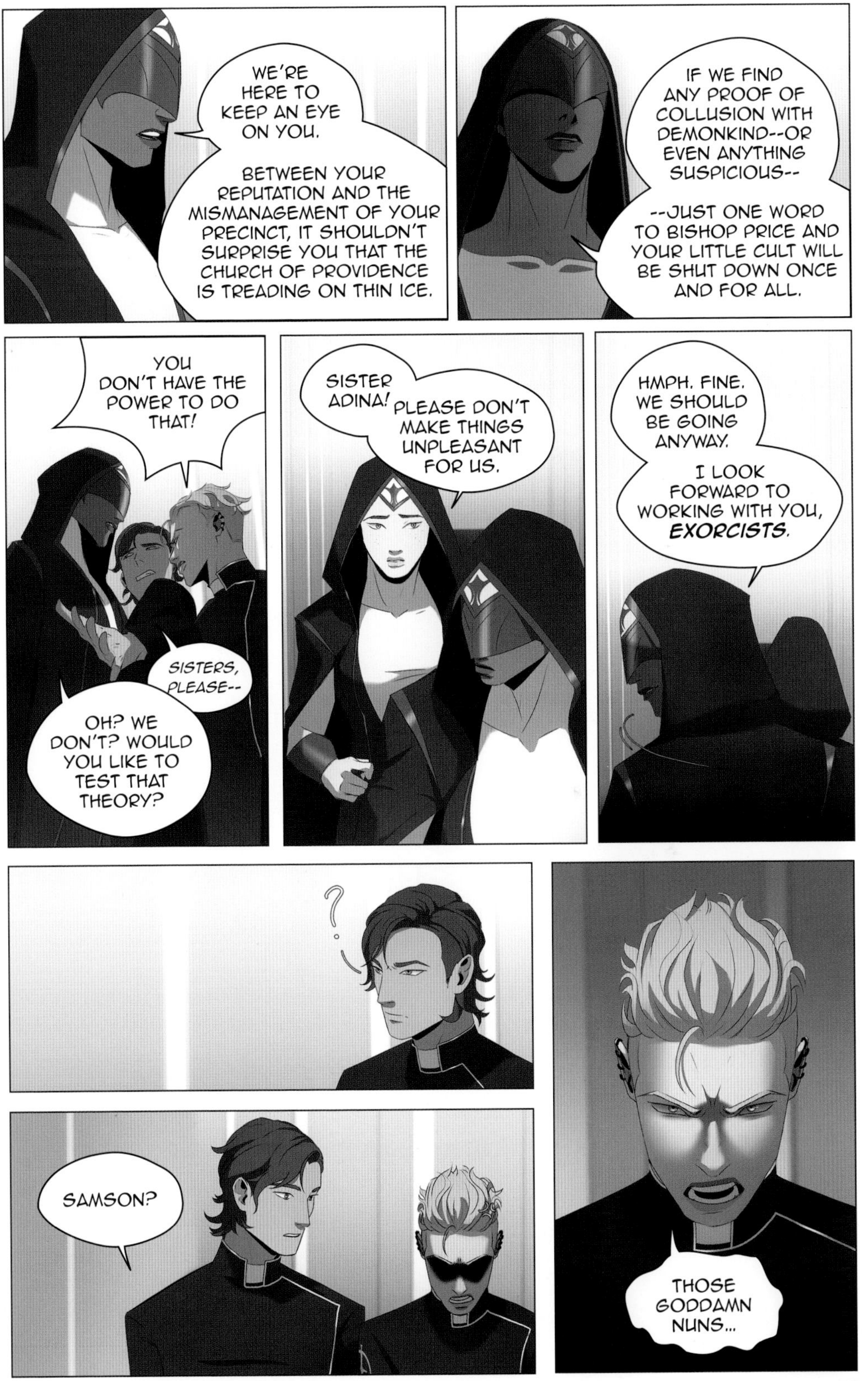
WE'RE HERE TO KEEP AN EYE ON YOU.
BETWEEN YOUR REPUTATION AND THE MISMANAGEMENT OF YOUR PRECINCT, IT SHOULDN'T SURPRISE YOU THAT THE CHURCH OF PROVIDENCE IS TREADING ON THIN ICE.
IF WE FIND ANY PROOF OF COLLUSION WITH DEMONKIND--OR EVEN ANYTHING SUSPICIOUS--
--JUST ONE WORD TO BISHOP PRICE AND YOUR LITTLE CULT WILL BE SHUT DOWN ONCE AND FOR ALL.
YOU DON'T HAVE THE POWER TO DO THAT!
SISTERS, PLEASE--
OH? WE DON'T? WOULD YOU LIKE TO TEST THAT THEORY?
SISTER ADINA!
PLEASE DON'T MAKE THINGS UNPLEASANT FOR US.
HMPH. FINE. WE SHOULD BE GOING ANYWAY.
I LOOK FORWARD TO WORKING WITH YOU, ***EXORCISTS***.
?
SAMSON?
THOSE GODDAMN NUNS...

BOOK IV

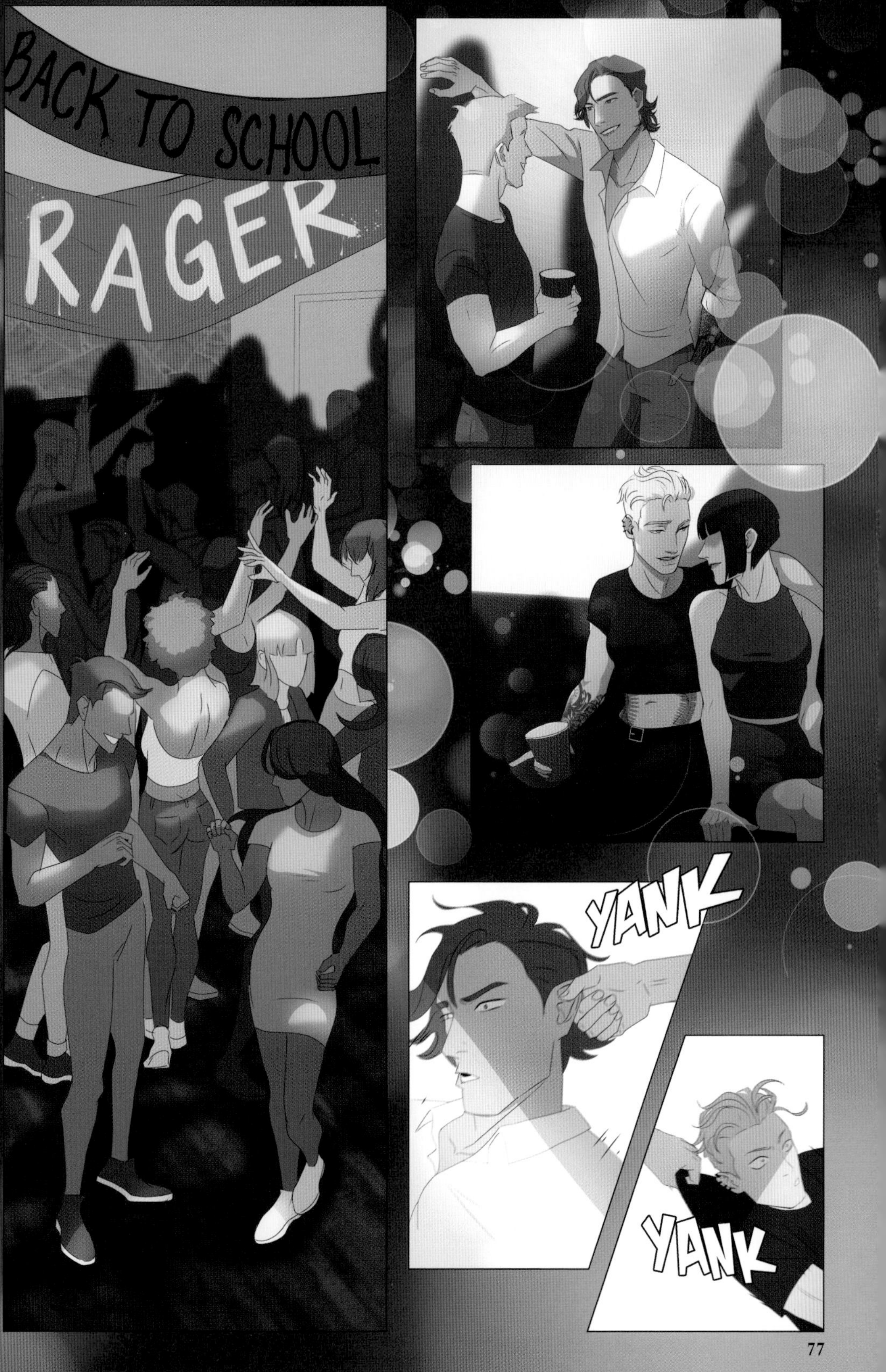
BACK TO SCHOOL
RAGER
YANK
YANK

SIGH

THEY WANT TO PLAY.

YOU MAY HAVE WON GAME #137, BUT WE'LL WIN GAME #138!

WE'RE DEFINITELY GONNA KICK YOUR BUTTS THIS TIME!

NAH, MAN.

WE'RE ON PATROL TOMORROW. WE SHOULDN'T BE GOING TOO HARD TONIGHT.

PLEASE, PLEASE, *PLEASE!!!* COME ON! THIS IS THE LAST WEEKEND BEFORE THE SEMESTER STARTS!

AND THEN BETWEEN EXTRA MISSIONS AND CLASSES,

WE'LL BE WAY TOO BUSY!

PLEASE... COME ON, SAMSON...

UGH. *FINE.*

YOU'RE ON!

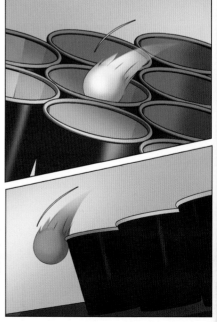

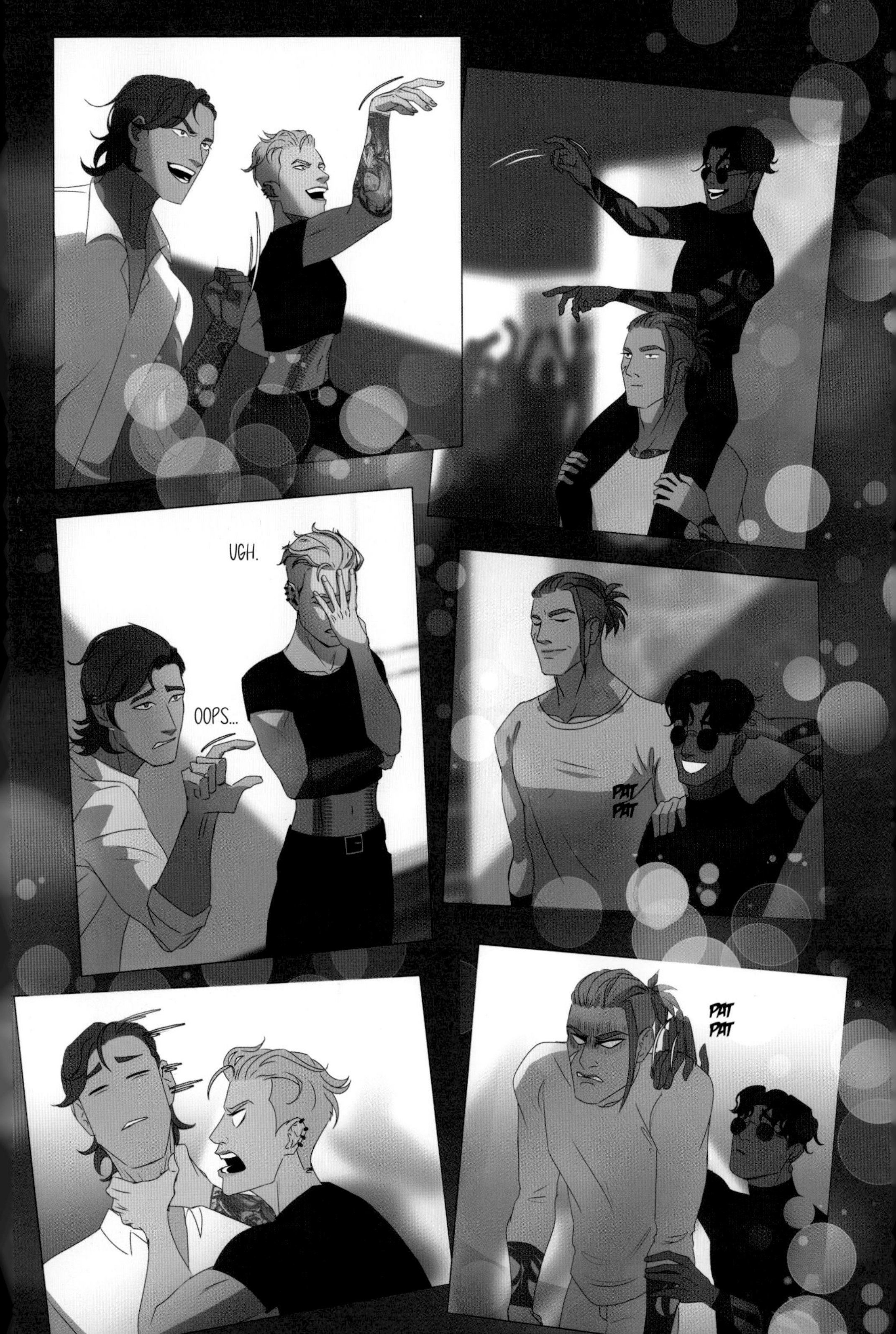
UGH.
OOPS...
PAT
PAT
PAT
PAT

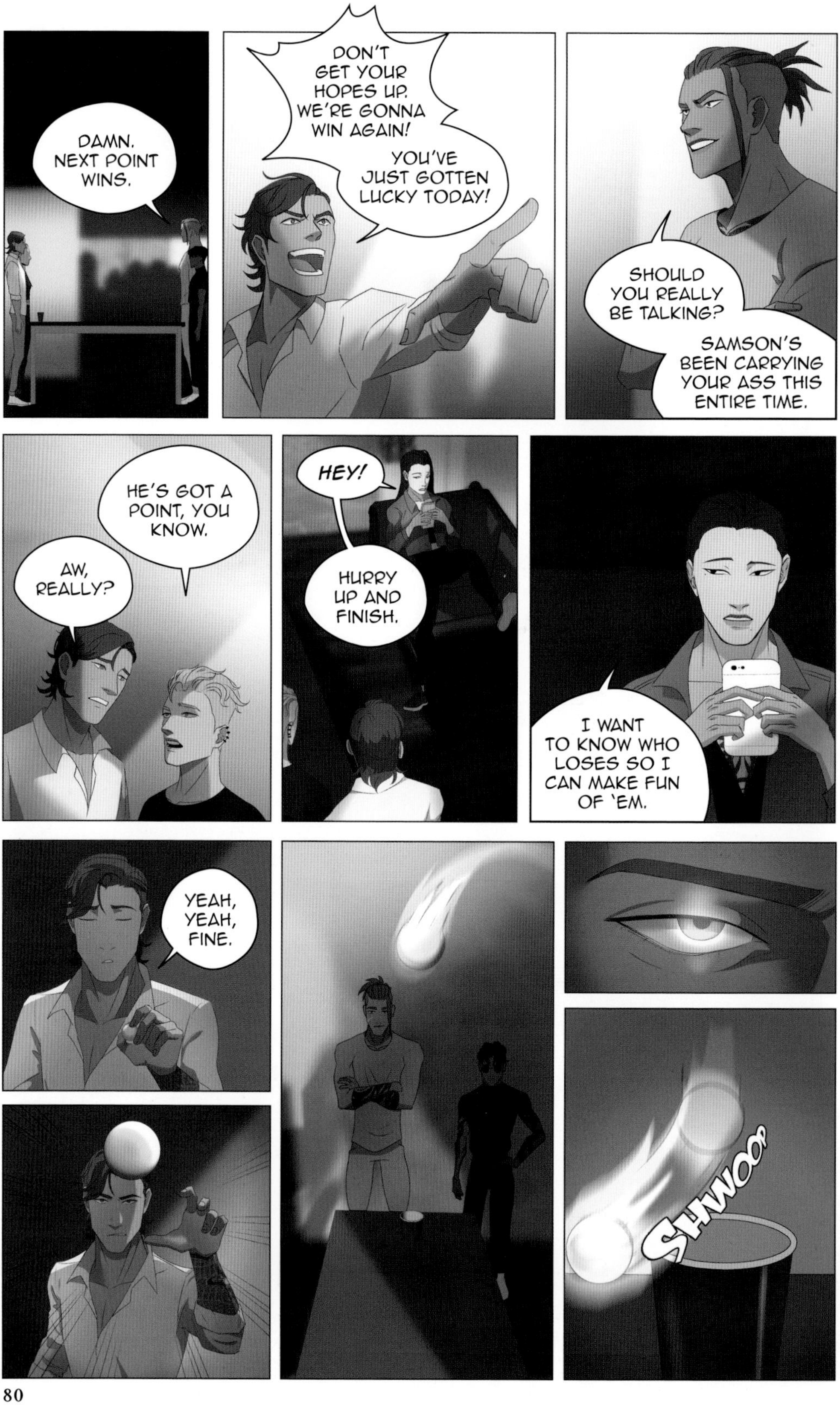

DAMN. NEXT POINT WINS.
DON'T GET YOUR HOPES UP. WE'RE GONNA WIN AGAIN!
YOU'VE JUST GOTTEN LUCKY TODAY!
SHOULD YOU REALLY BE TALKING?
SAMSON'S BEEN CARRYING YOUR ASS THIS ENTIRE TIME.
HE'S GOT A POINT, YOU KNOW.
AW, REALLY?
HEY!
HURRY UP AND FINISH.
I WANT TO KNOW WHO LOSES SO I CAN MAKE FUN OF 'EM.
YEAH, YEAH, FINE.
SHWOOP

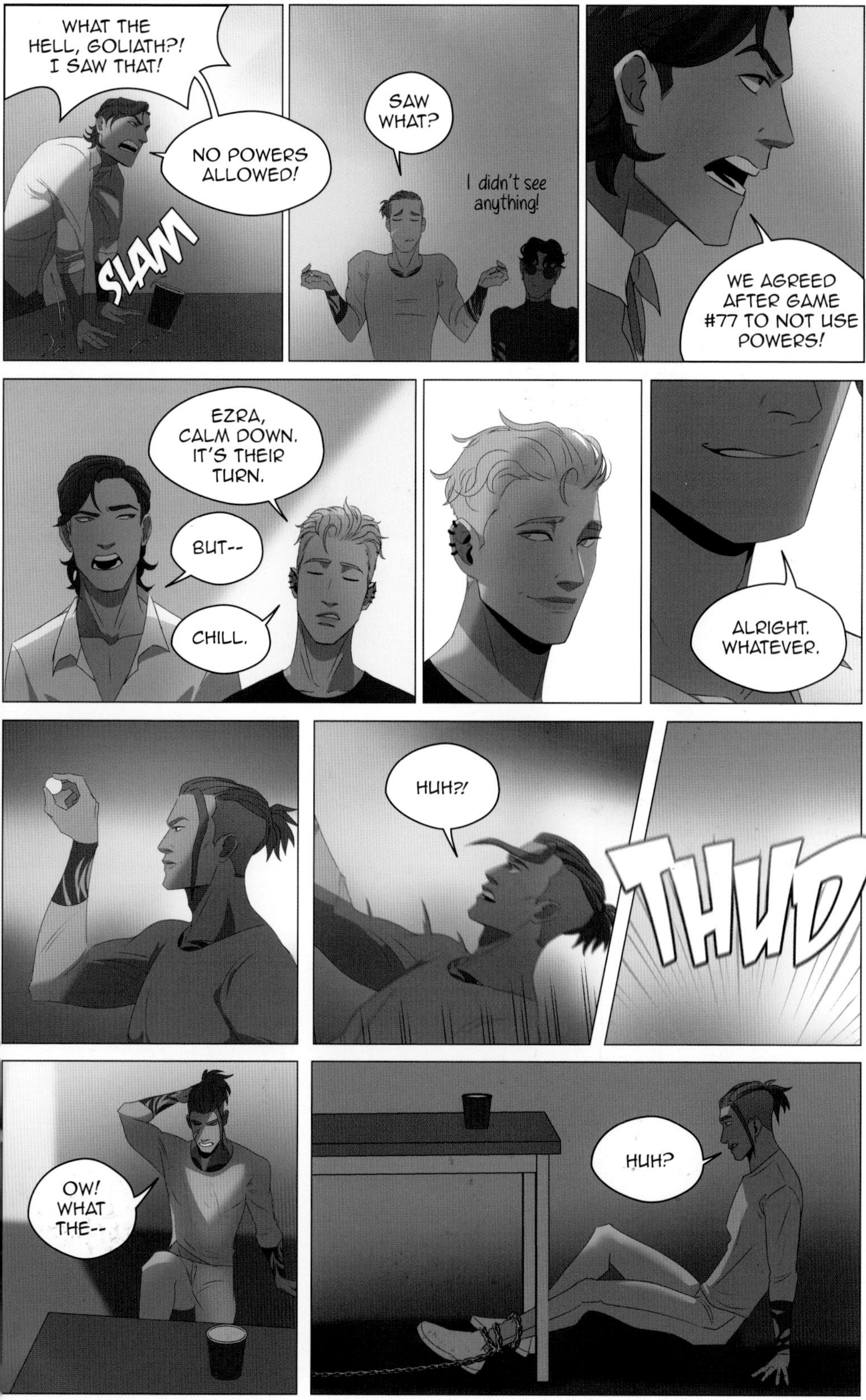

WHAT THE HELL, GOLIATH?! I SAW THAT!
NO POWERS ALLOWED!
SLAM
SAW WHAT?
I didn't see anything!
WE AGREED AFTER GAME #77 TO NOT USE POWERS!
EZRA, CALM DOWN. IT'S THEIR TURN.
BUT--
CHILL.
ALRIGHT. WHATEVER.
HUH?!
THUD
OW! WHAT THE--
HUH?

WHOA.

YOU OKAY THERE?

HA...

HA HA...

YOU'RE DEAD!

NO, *YOU'RE* DEAD, YOU CHEATER!

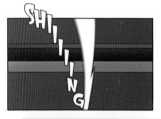

SHIIIING

SNAP

EH?

CRASH

SORRY.

I HAD TO HURT YOU MILDLY BEFORE YOU COULD HURT EACH OTHER SERIOUSLY.

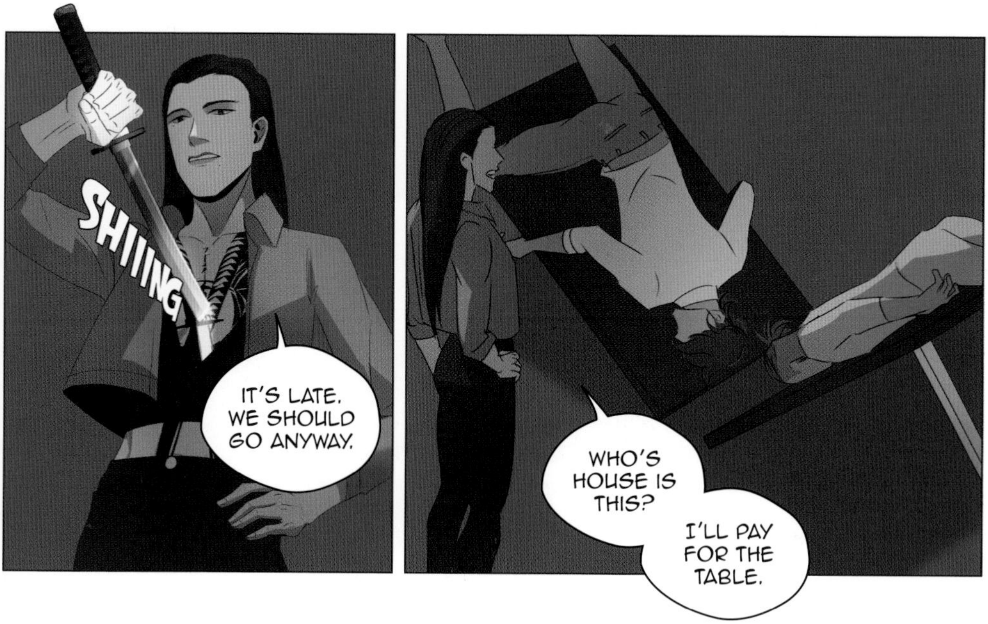
SHIIING
IT'S LATE. WE SHOULD GO ANYWAY.
WHO'S HOUSE IS THIS?
I'LL PAY FOR THE TABLE.

NEXT AFTERNOON...

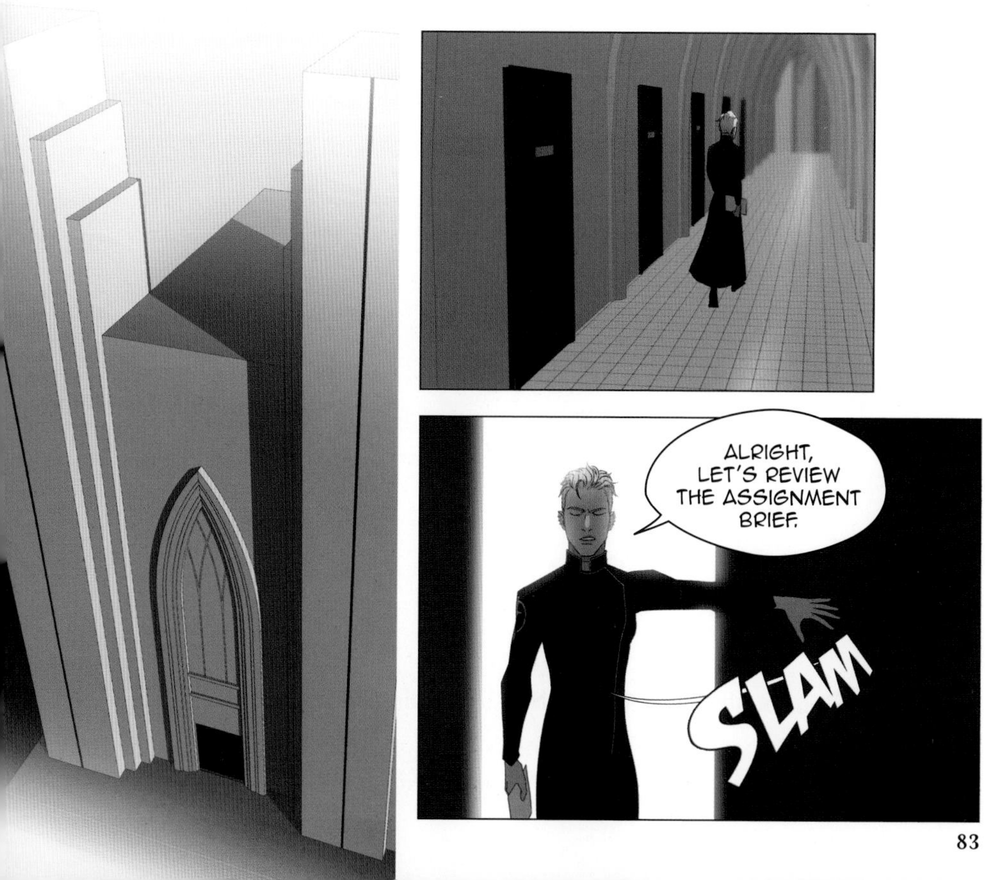
ALRIGHT, LET'S REVIEW THE ASSIGNMENT BRIEF.
SLAM

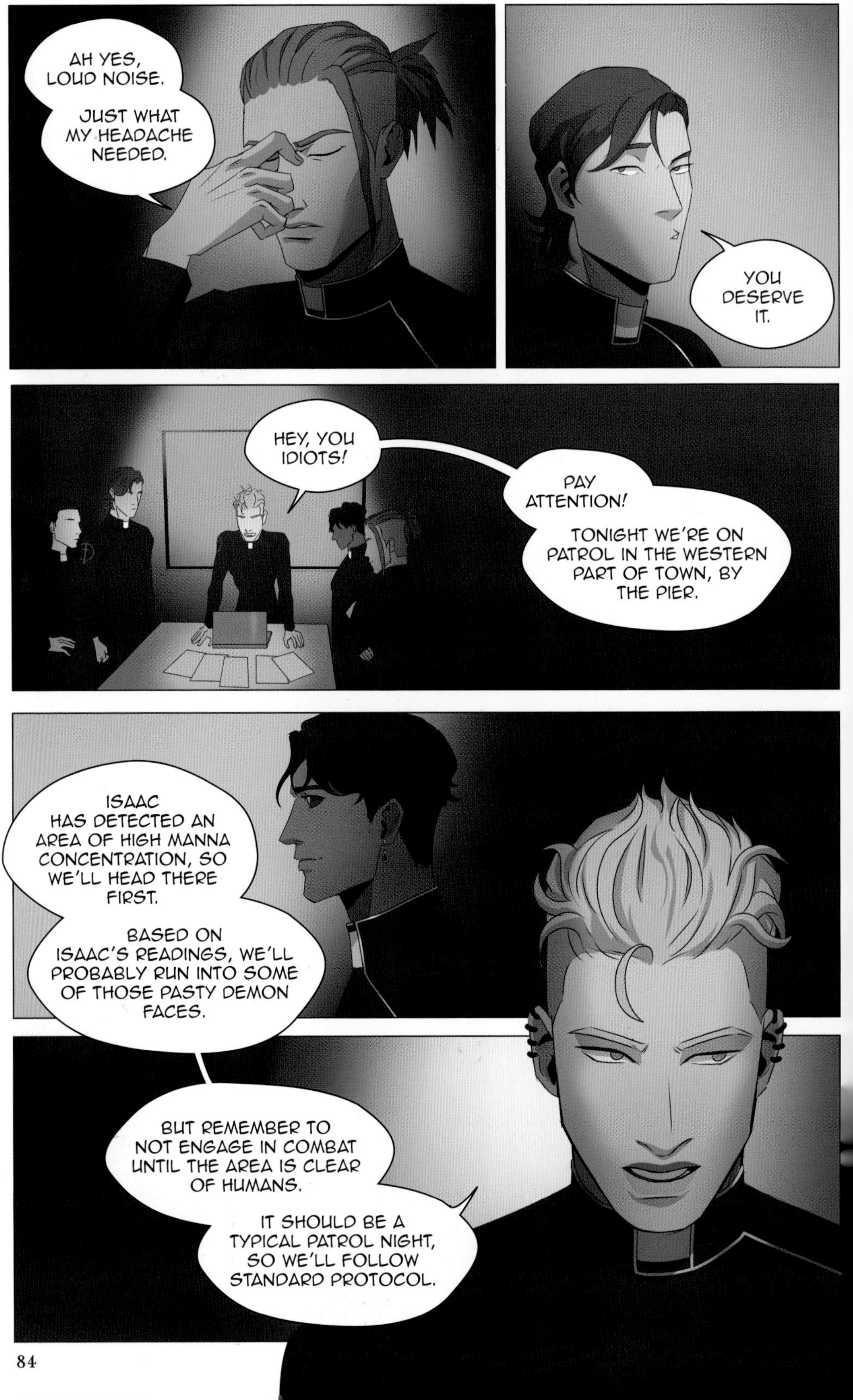
AH YES, LOUD NOISE.
JUST WHAT MY HEADACHE NEEDED.
YOU DESERVE IT.
HEY, YOU IDIOTS!
PAY ATTENTION!
TONIGHT WE'RE ON PATROL IN THE WESTERN PART OF TOWN, BY THE PIER.
ISAAC HAS DETECTED AN AREA OF HIGH MANNA CONCENTRATION, SO WE'LL HEAD THERE FIRST.
BASED ON ISAAC'S READINGS, WE'LL PROBABLY RUN INTO SOME OF THOSE PASTY DEMON FACES.
BUT REMEMBER TO NOT ENGAGE IN COMBAT UNTIL THE AREA IS CLEAR OF HUMANS.
IT SHOULD BE A TYPICAL PATROL NIGHT, SO WE'LL FOLLOW STANDARD PROTOCOL.

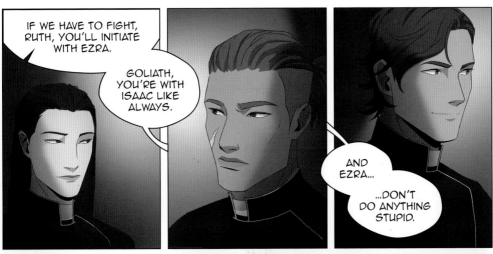

IF WE HAVE TO FIGHT, RUTH, YOU'LL INITIATE WITH EZRA.

GOLIATH, YOU'RE WITH ISAAC LIKE ALWAYS.

AND EZRA...

...DON'T DO ANYTHING STUPID.

IF THERE AREN'T ANY QUESTIONS, THEN WE SHOULD DEPART NOW.

CREAK

OH, DID NO ONE TELL YOU?

WE HAVE BEEN ASSIGNED TO YOUR PATROL SHIFT.

WE LOOK FORWARD TO WORKING TOGETHER.

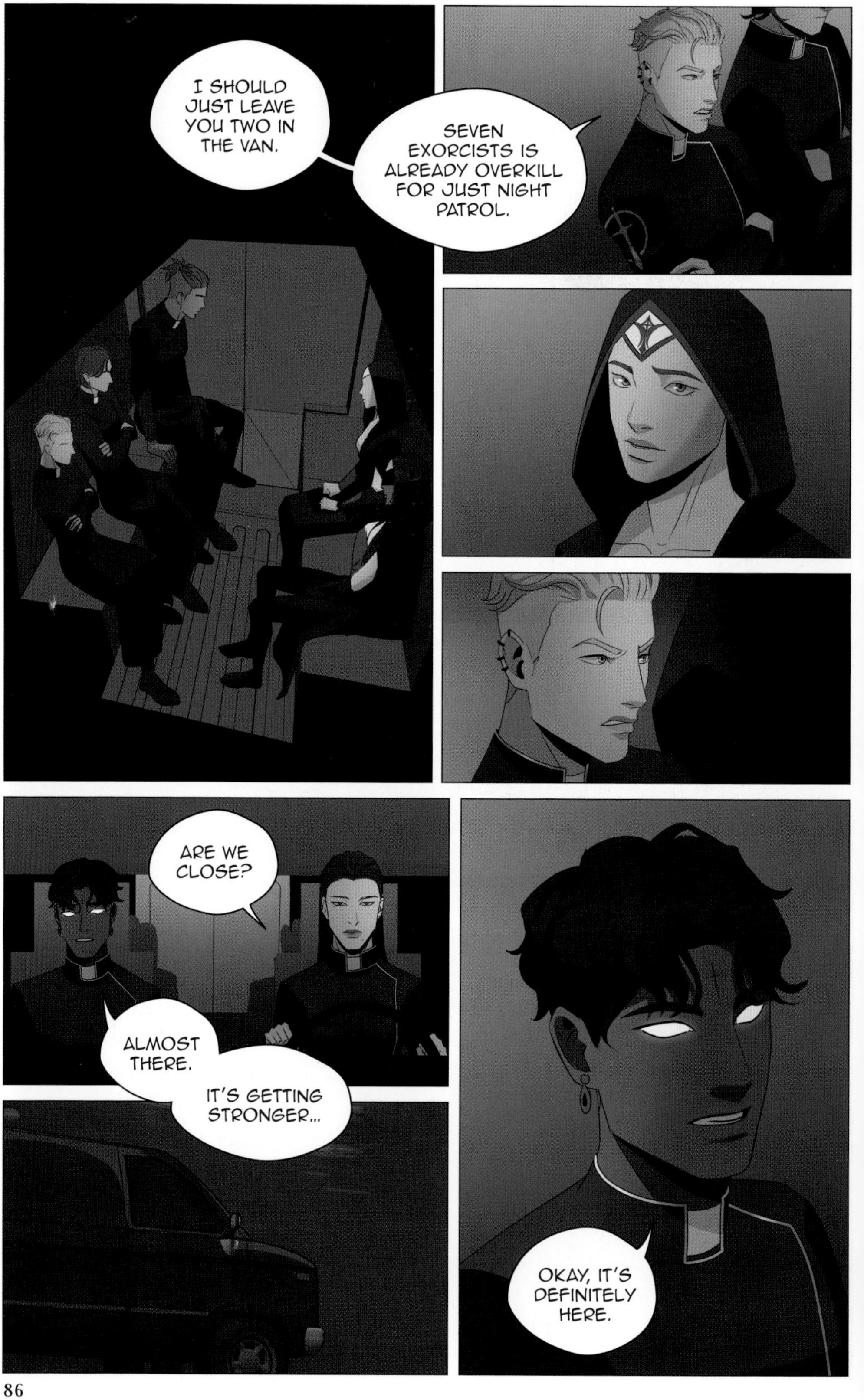
I SHOULD JUST LEAVE YOU TWO IN THE VAN.
SEVEN EXORCISTS IS ALREADY OVERKILL FOR JUST NIGHT PATROL.
ARE WE CLOSE?
ALMOST THERE.
IT'S GETTING STRONGER...
OKAY, IT'S DEFINITELY HERE.

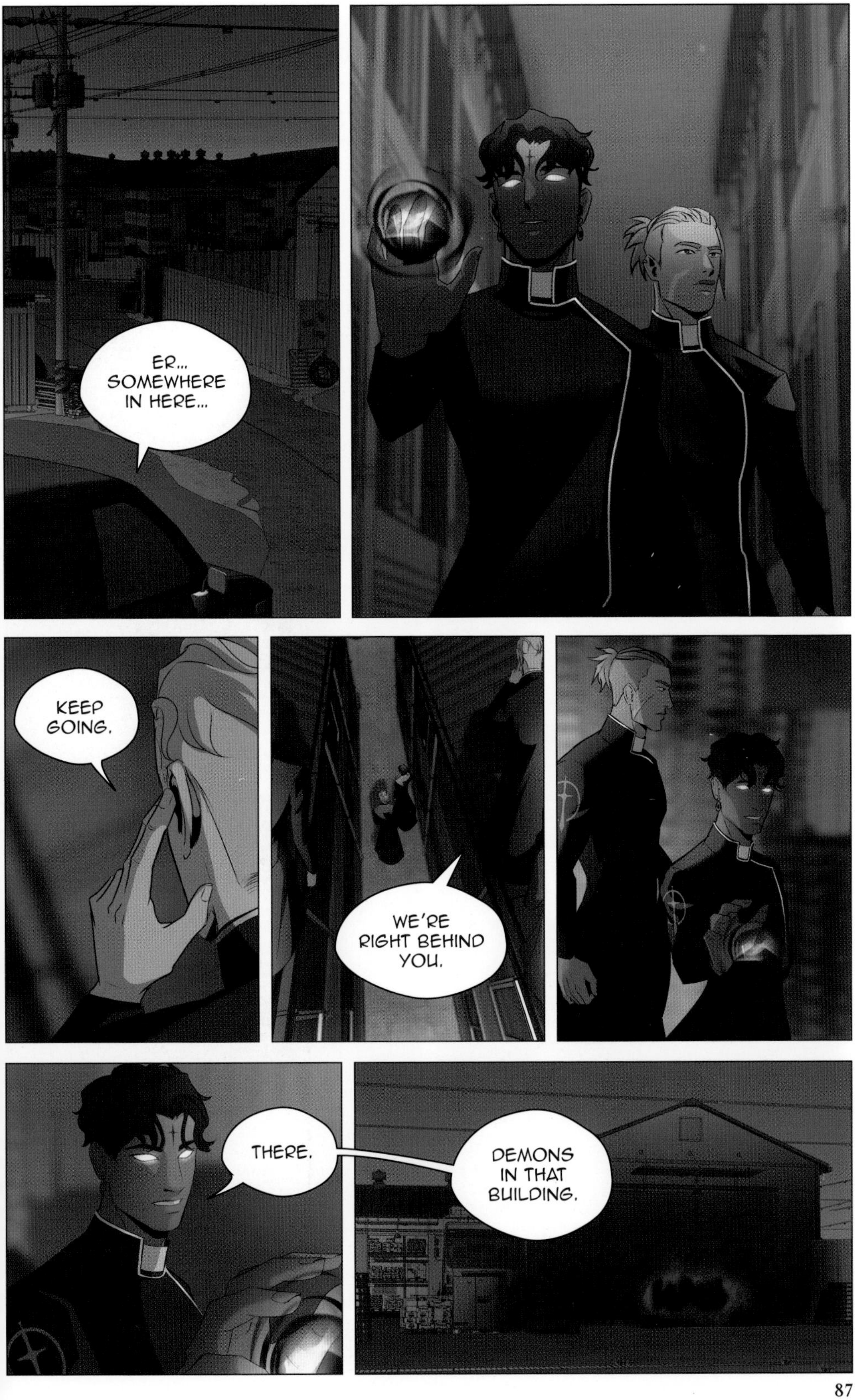
ER...
SOMEWHERE
IN HERE...
KEEP
GOING.
WE'RE
RIGHT BEHIND
YOU.
THERE.
DEMONS
IN THAT
BUILDING.

ISAAC, CAN YOU SEE ENOUGH FROM THERE?

YEAH. I'VE GOT VISUALS ON THE DEMONS.

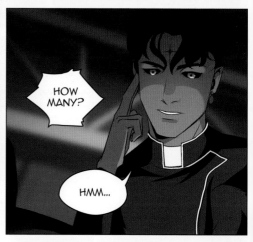

HOW MANY?

HMM...

I SEE EIGHT.

THEY MIGHT ALSO HAVE HUMANS?

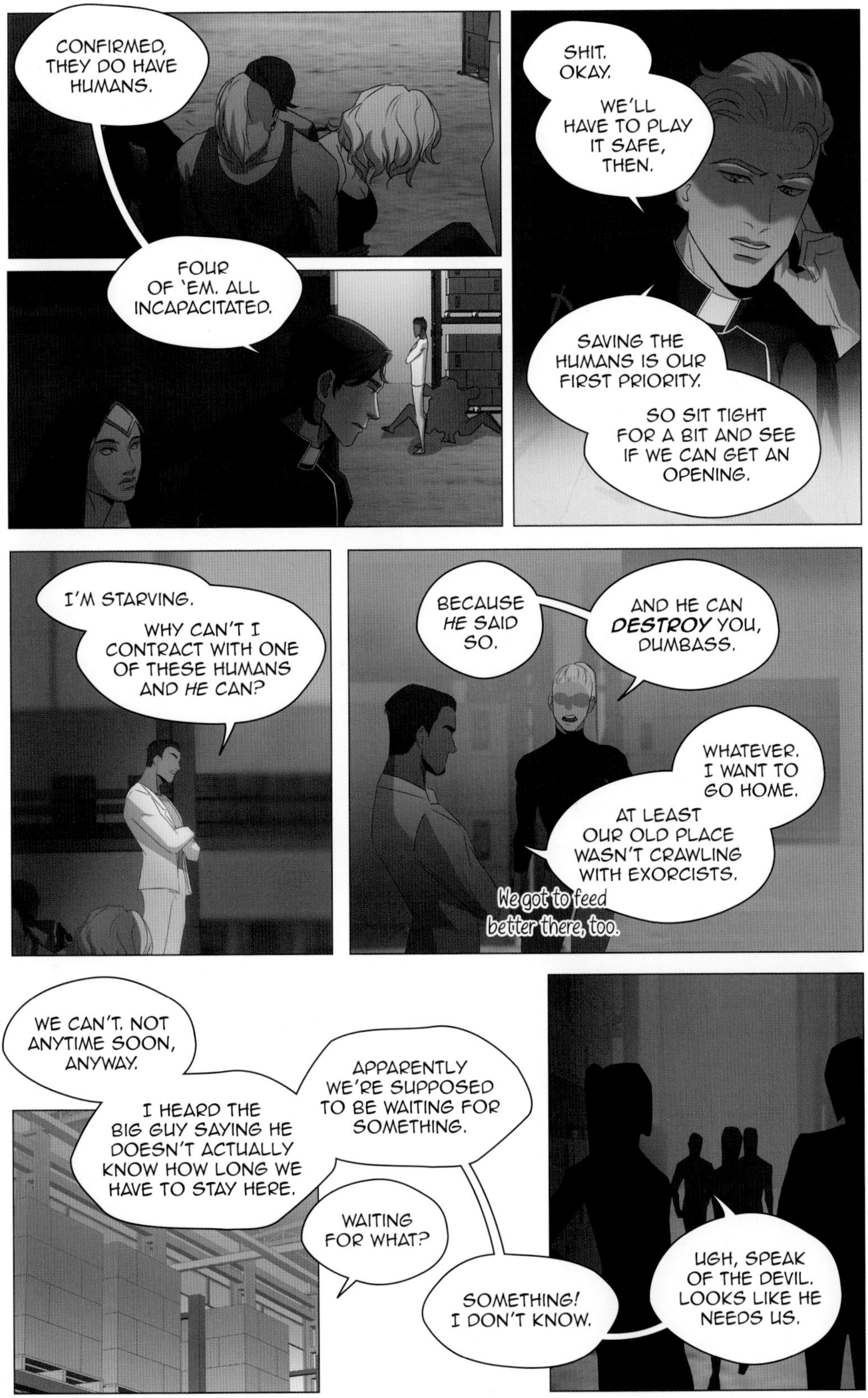
CONFIRMED, THEY DO HAVE HUMANS.
FOUR OF 'EM. ALL INCAPACITATED.
SHIT. OKAY.
WE'LL HAVE TO PLAY IT SAFE, THEN.
SAVING THE HUMANS IS OUR FIRST PRIORITY.
SO SIT TIGHT FOR A BIT AND SEE IF WE CAN GET AN OPENING.
I'M STARVING.
WHY CAN'T I CONTRACT WITH ONE OF THESE HUMANS AND HE CAN?
BECAUSE HE SAID SO.
AND HE CAN DESTROY YOU, DUMBASS.
WHATEVER. I WANT TO GO HOME.
AT LEAST OUR OLD PLACE WASN'T CRAWLING WITH EXORCISTS.
We got to feed better there, too.
WE CAN'T. NOT ANYTIME SOON, ANYWAY.
I HEARD THE BIG GUY SAYING HE DOESN'T ACTUALLY KNOW HOW LONG WE HAVE TO STAY HERE.
APPARENTLY WE'RE SUPPOSED TO BE WAITING FOR SOMETHING.
WAITING FOR WHAT?
SOMETHING! I DON'T KNOW.
UGH, SPEAK OF THE DEVIL. LOOKS LIKE HE NEEDS US.

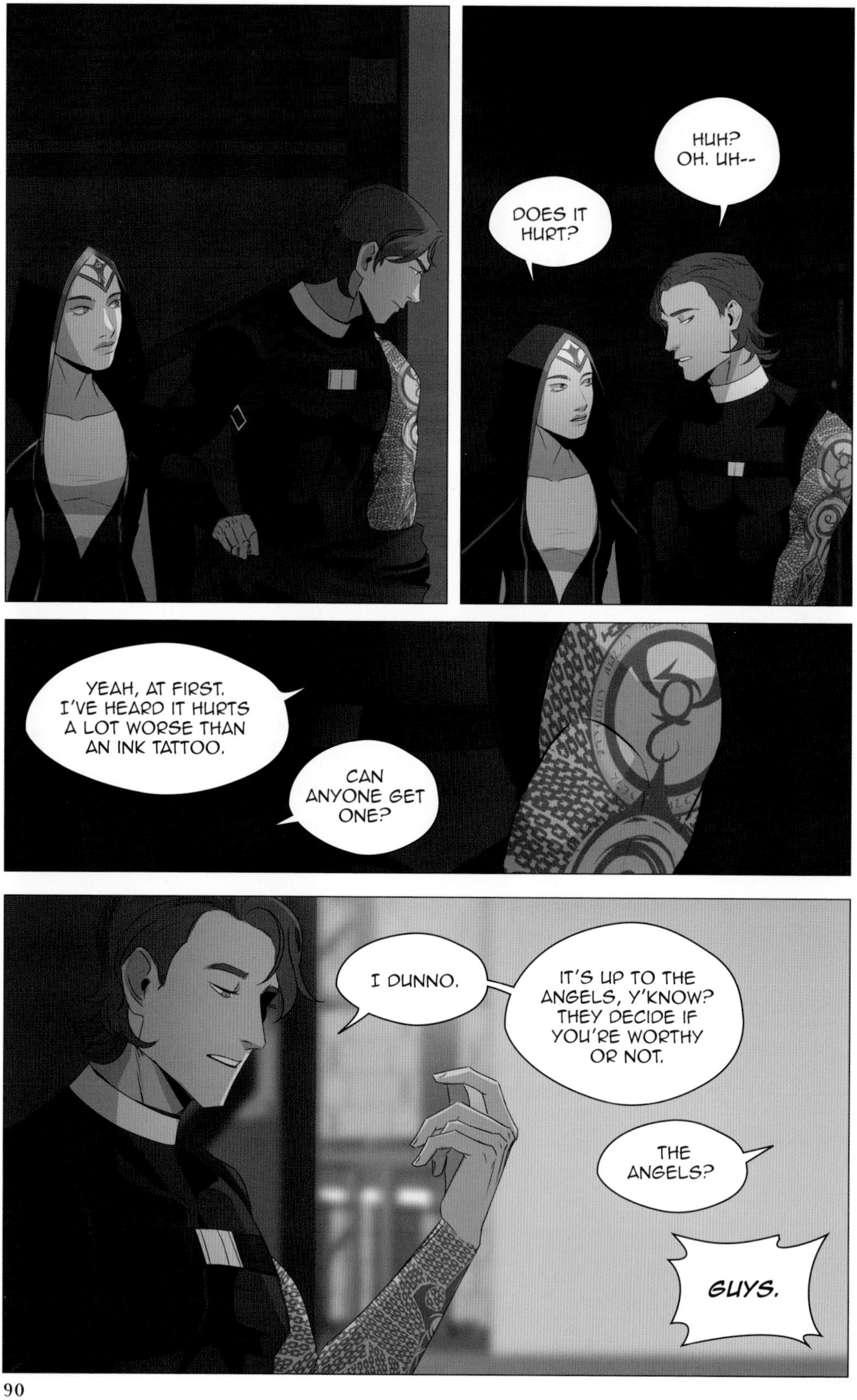
DOES IT HURT?
HUH? OH. UH--
YEAH, AT FIRST. I'VE HEARD IT HURTS A LOT WORSE THAN AN INK TATTOO.
CAN ANYONE GET ONE?
I DUNNO.
IT'S UP TO THE ANGELS, Y'KNOW? THEY DECIDE IF YOU'RE WORTHY OR NOT.
THE ANGELS?
GUYS.

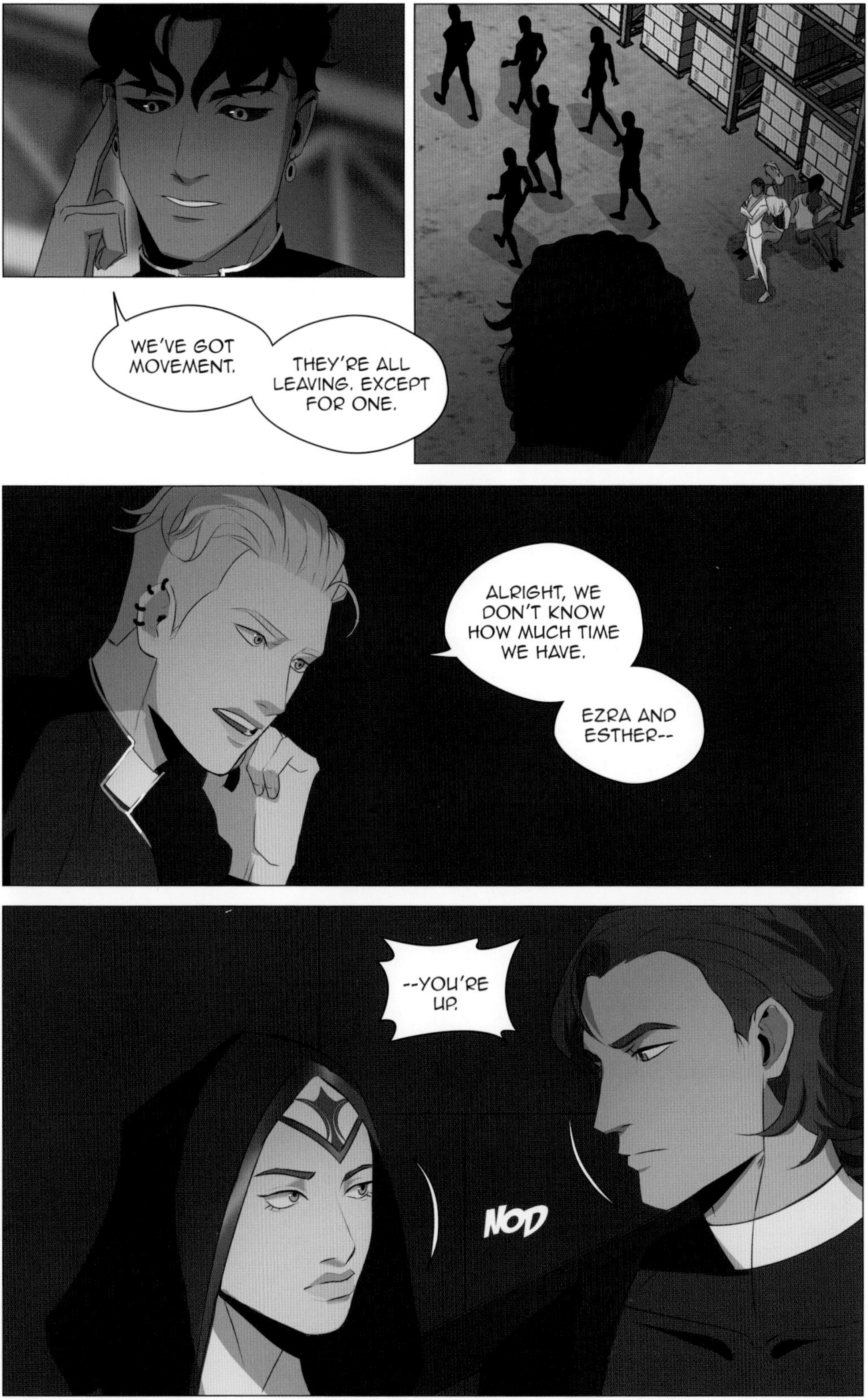
WE'VE GOT MOVEMENT.
THEY'RE ALL LEAVING. EXCEPT FOR ONE.
ALRIGHT, WE DON'T KNOW HOW MUCH TIME WE HAVE.
EZRA AND ESTHER--
--YOU'RE UP.
NOD

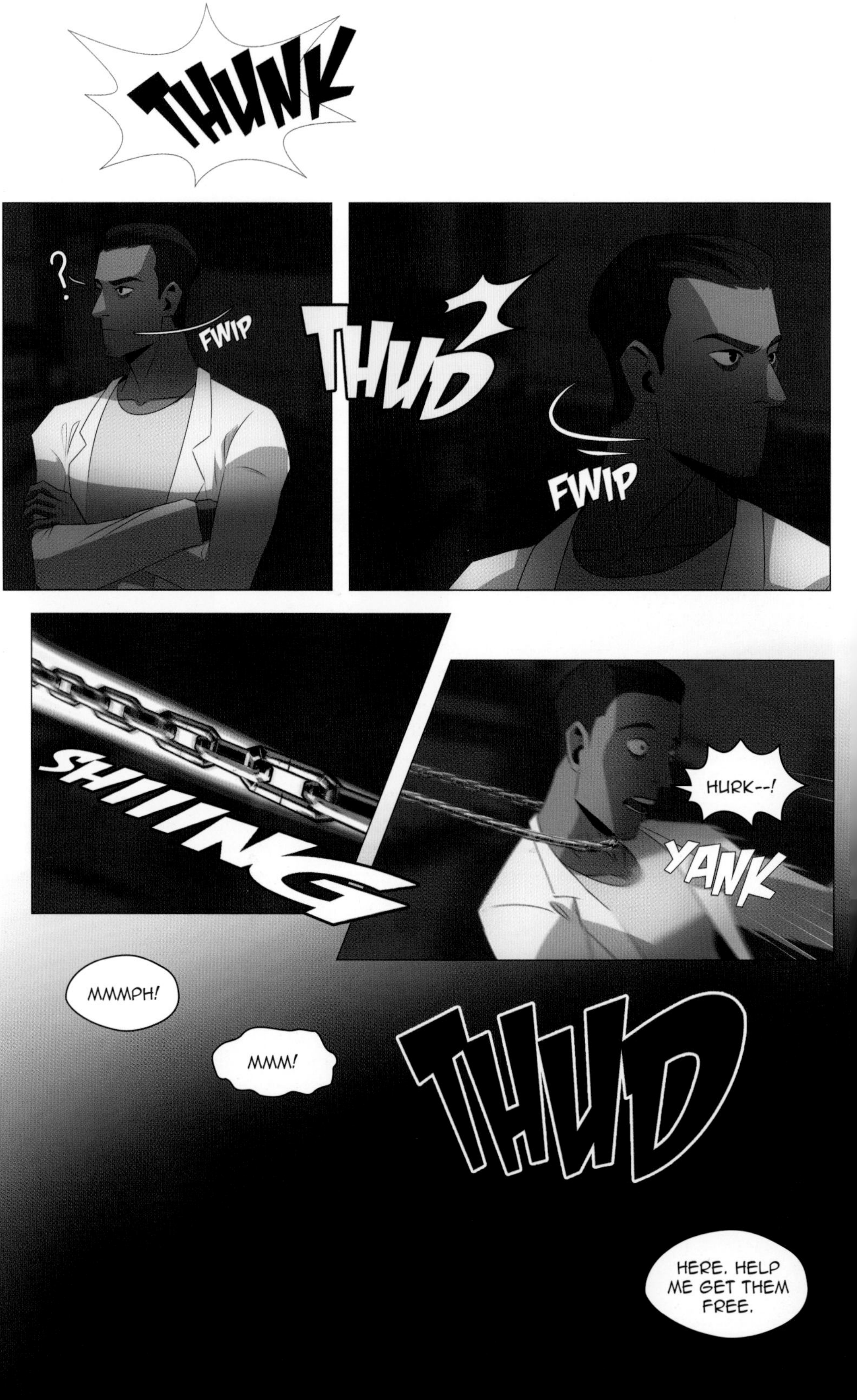
THUNK
?
FWIP
THUD
FWIP
SHIING
HURK--!
YANK
MMMPH!
MMM!
THUD
HERE. HELP ME GET THEM FREE.

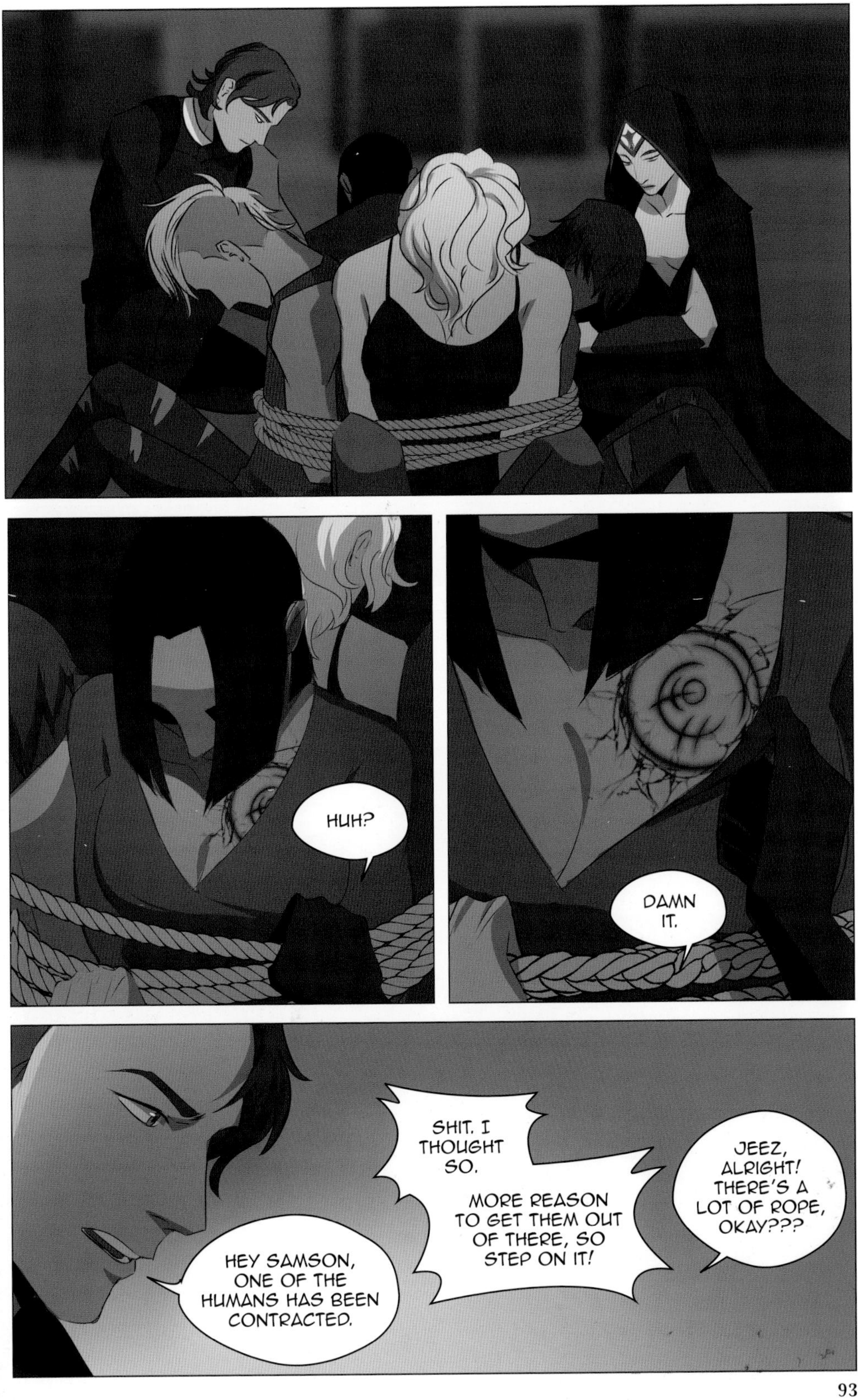
HUH?
DAMN IT.
HEY SAMSON, ONE OF THE HUMANS HAS BEEN CONTRACTED.
SHIT. I THOUGHT SO.
MORE REASON TO GET THEM OUT OF THERE, SO STEP ON IT!
JEEZ, ALRIGHT! THERE'S A LOT OF ROPE, OKAY???

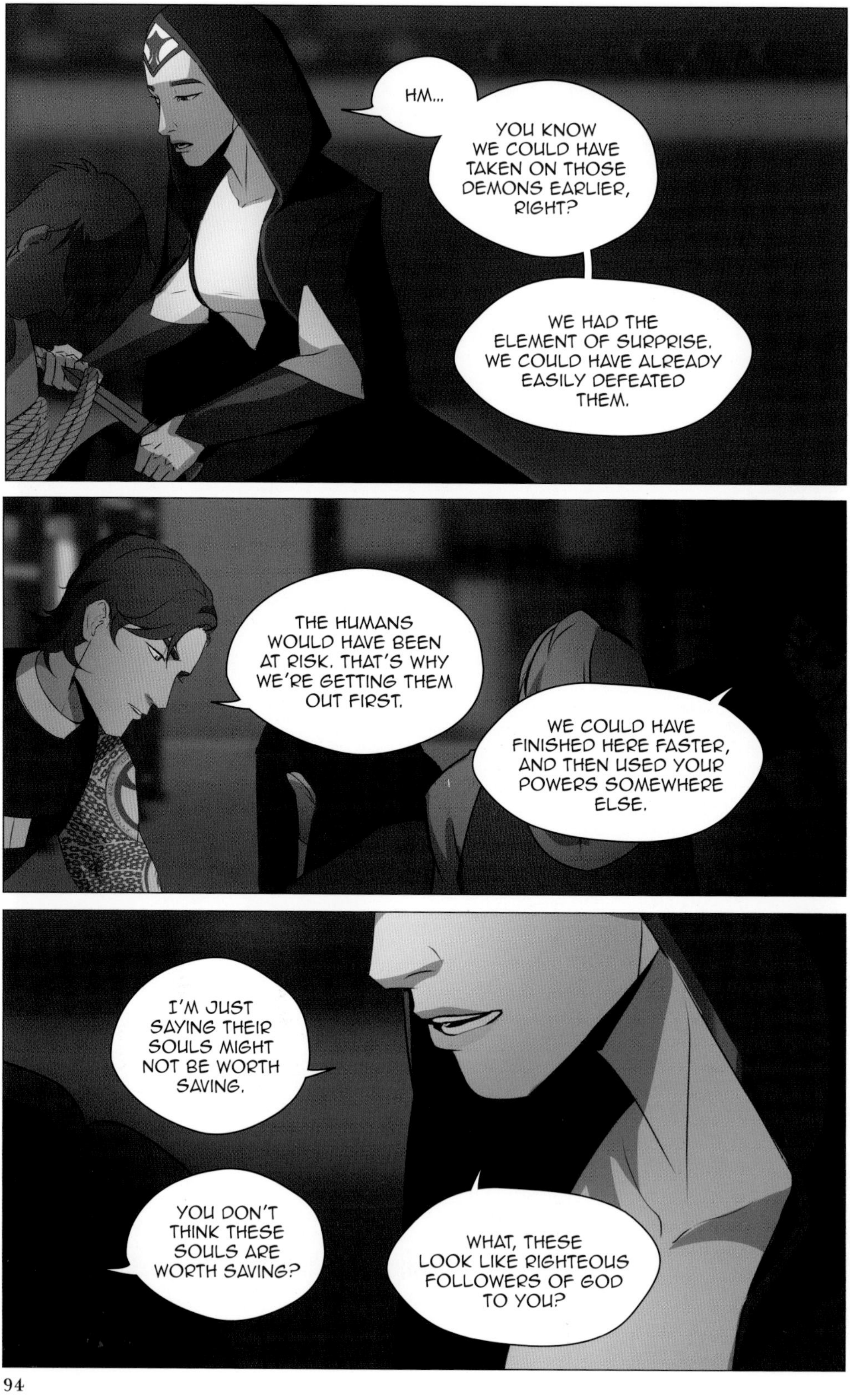
HM...
YOU KNOW WE COULD HAVE TAKEN ON THOSE DEMONS EARLIER, RIGHT?
WE HAD THE ELEMENT OF SURPRISE. WE COULD HAVE ALREADY EASILY DEFEATED THEM.
THE HUMANS WOULD HAVE BEEN AT RISK. THAT'S WHY WE'RE GETTING THEM OUT FIRST.
WE COULD HAVE FINISHED HERE FASTER, AND THEN USED YOUR POWERS SOMEWHERE ELSE.
I'M JUST SAYING THEIR SOULS MIGHT NOT BE WORTH SAVING.
YOU DON'T THINK THESE SOULS ARE WORTH SAVING?
WHAT, THESE LOOK LIKE RIGHTEOUS FOLLOWERS OF GOD TO YOU?

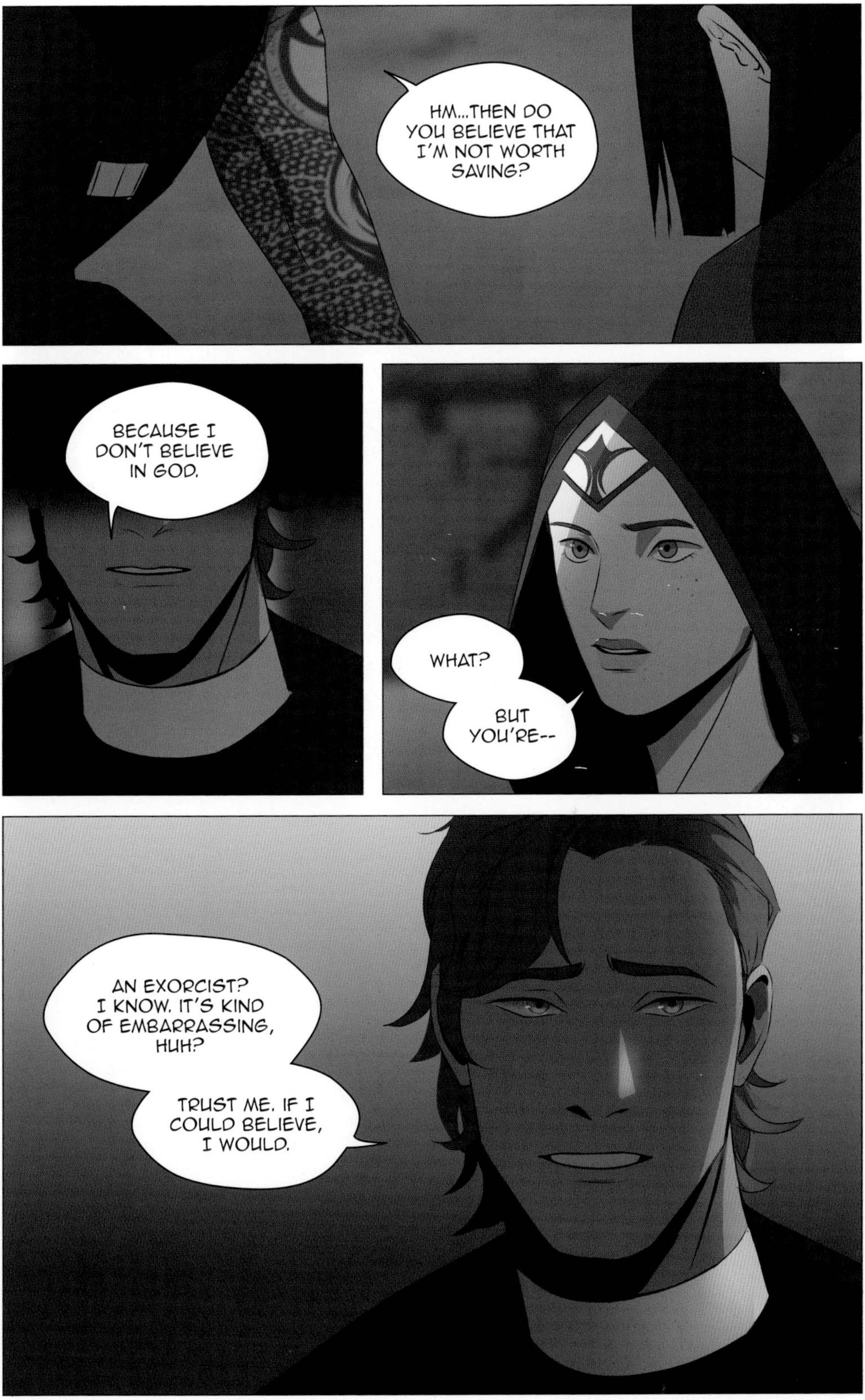
HM...THEN DO YOU BELIEVE THAT I'M NOT WORTH SAVING?
BECAUSE I DON'T BELIEVE IN GOD.
WHAT?
BUT YOU'RE--
AN EXORCIST? I KNOW. IT'S KIND OF EMBARRASSING, HUH?
TRUST ME. IF I COULD BELIEVE, I WOULD.

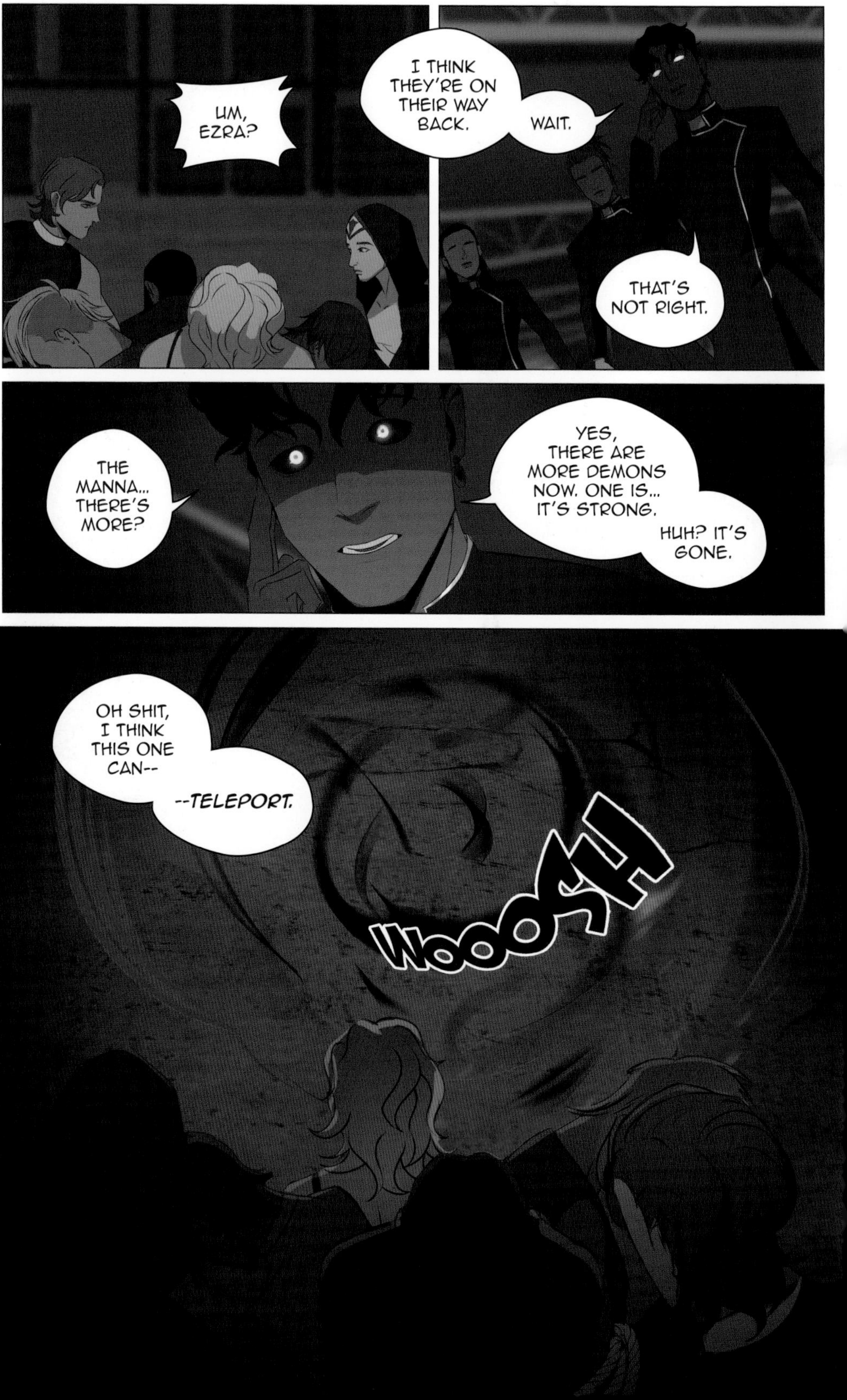
UM, EZRA?
I THINK THEY'RE ON THEIR WAY BACK.
WAIT.
THAT'S NOT RIGHT.
THE MANNA... THERE'S MORE?
YES, THERE ARE MORE DEMONS NOW. ONE IS... IT'S STRONG.
HUH? IT'S GONE.
OH SHIT, I THINK THIS ONE CAN--
--TELEPORT.
WOOOSH

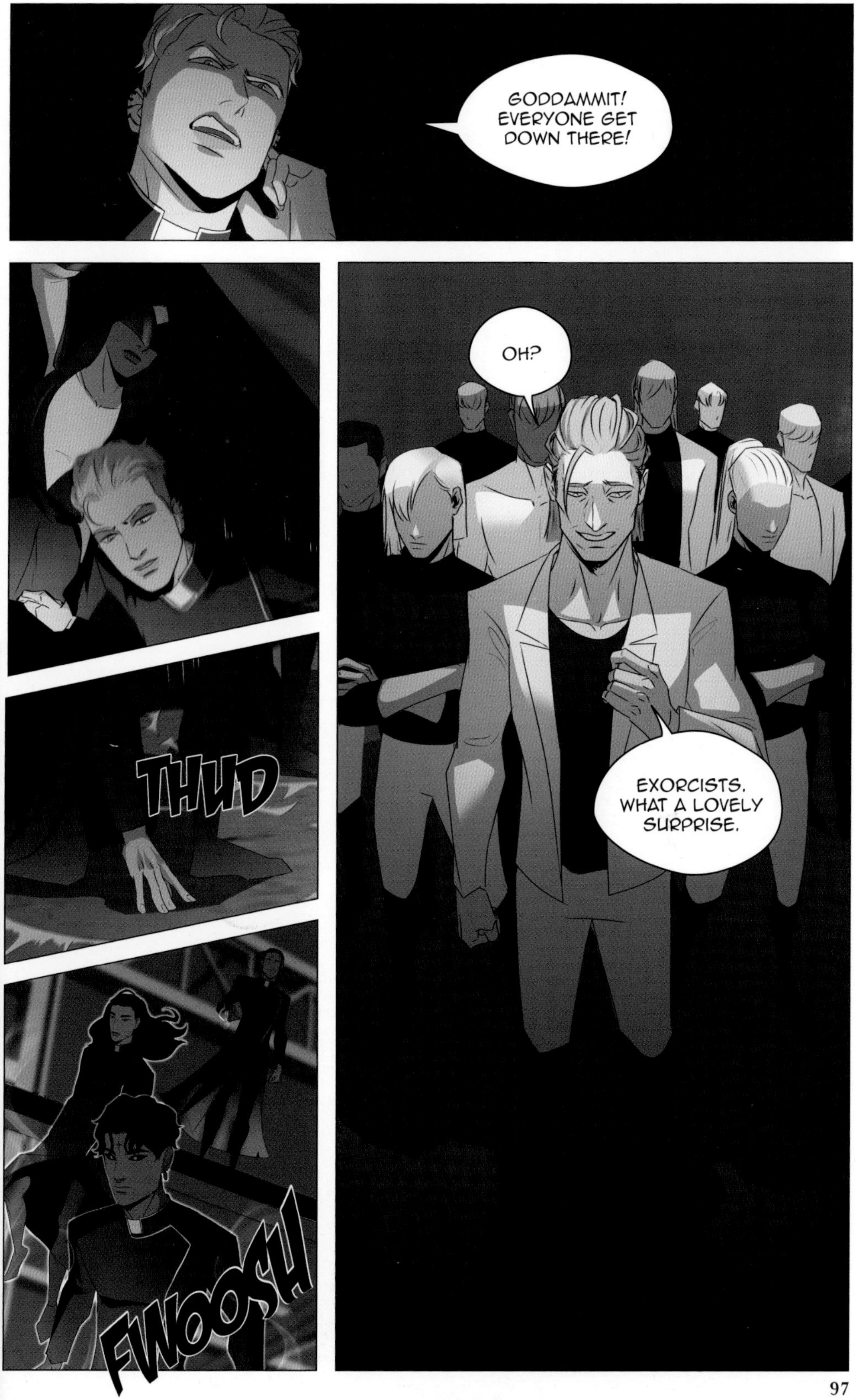
GODDAMMIT! EVERYONE GET DOWN THERE!
THUD
FWOOSH
OH?
EXORCISTS. WHAT A LOVELY SURPRISE.

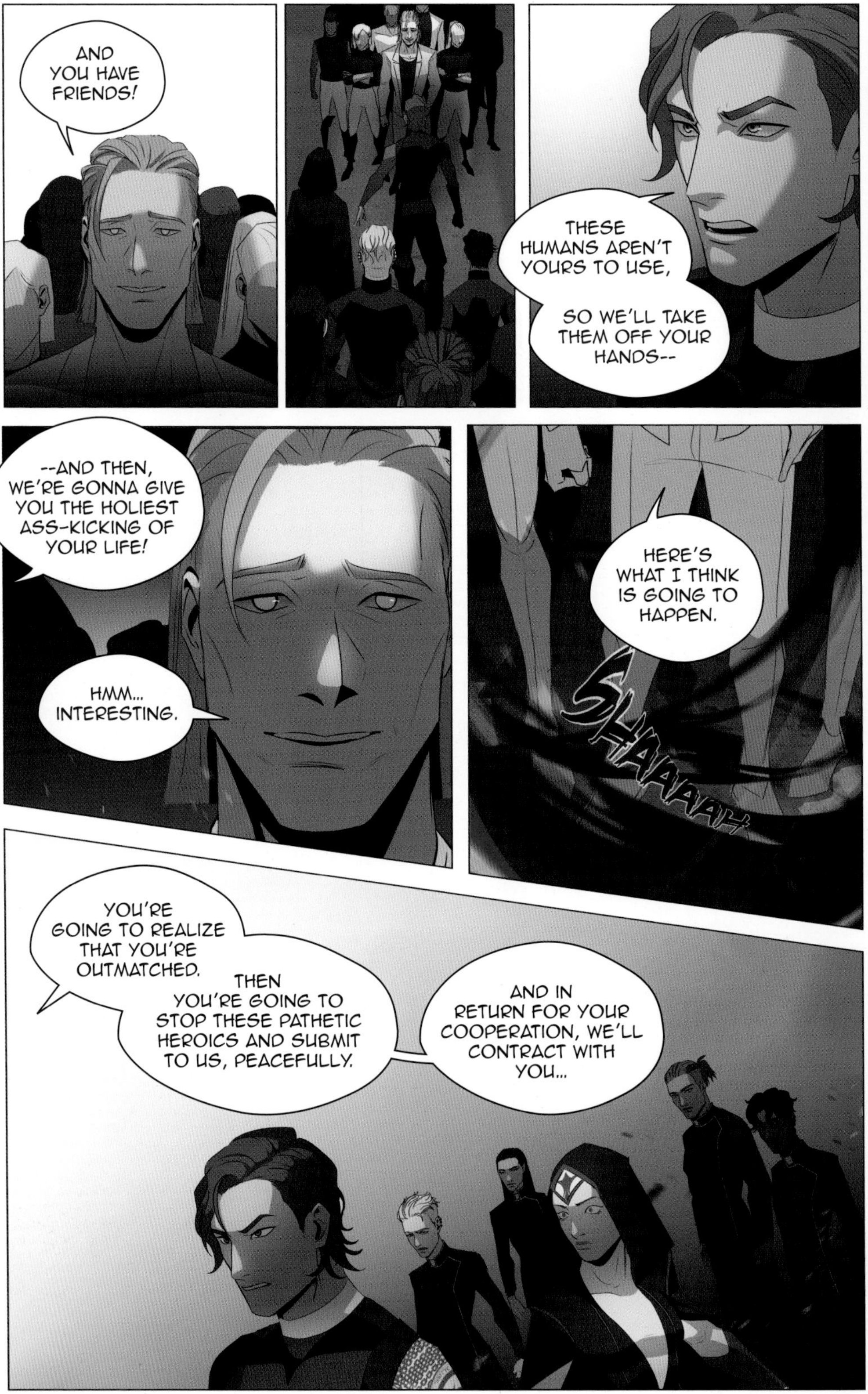

AND YOU HAVE FRIENDS!
THESE HUMANS AREN'T YOURS TO USE,
SO WE'LL TAKE THEM OFF YOUR HANDS--
--AND THEN, WE'RE GONNA GIVE YOU THE HOLIEST ASS-KICKING OF YOUR LIFE!
HMM... INTERESTING.
HERE'S WHAT I THINK IS GOING TO HAPPEN.
SHAAAAAH
YOU'RE GOING TO REALIZE THAT YOU'RE OUTMATCHED.
THEN YOU'RE GOING TO STOP THESE PATHETIC HEROICS AND SUBMIT TO US, PEACEFULLY.
AND IN RETURN FOR YOUR COOPERATION, WE'LL CONTRACT WITH YOU...

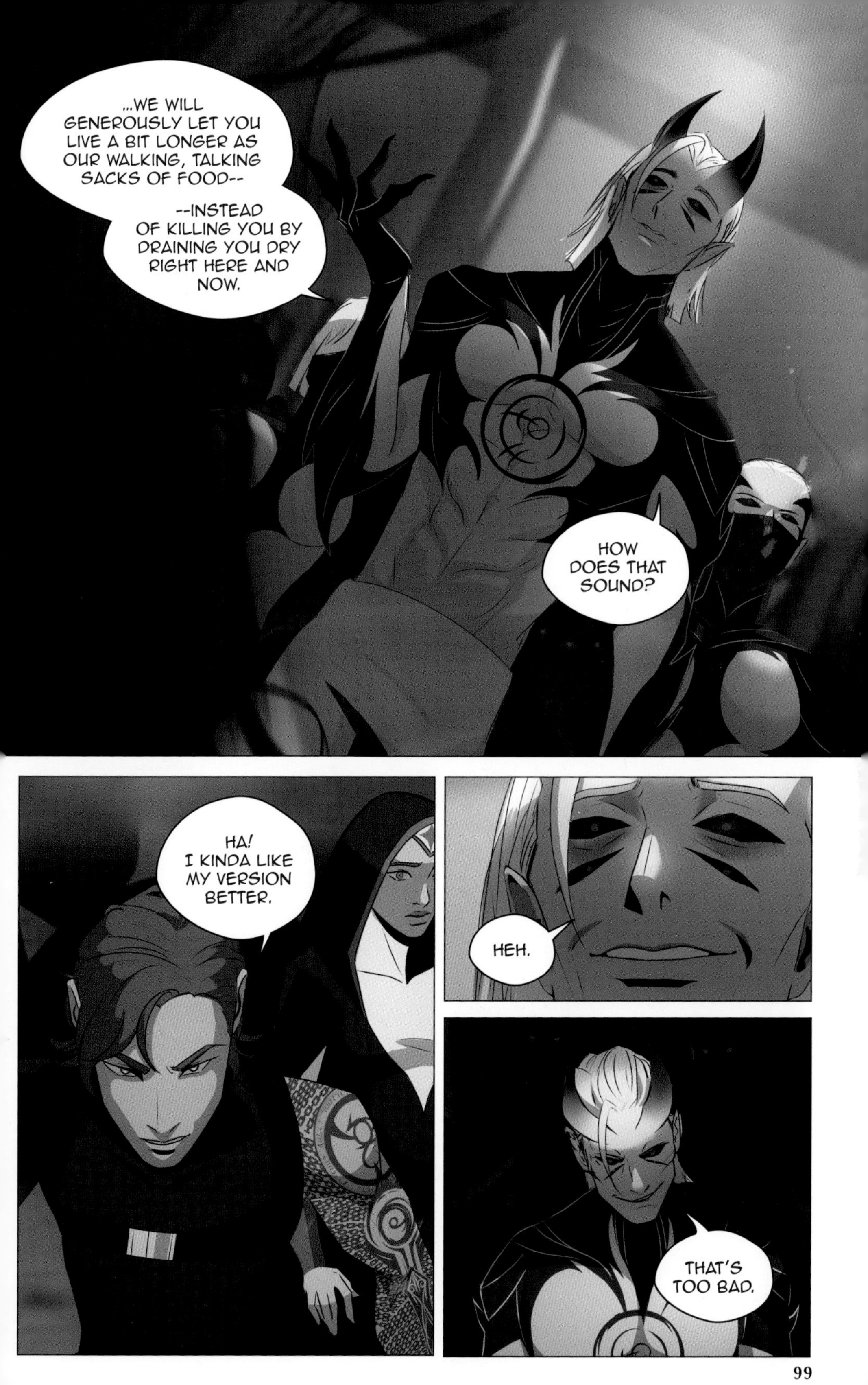
...WE WILL GENEROUSLY LET YOU LIVE A BIT LONGER AS OUR WALKING, TALKING SACKS OF FOOD--
--INSTEAD OF KILLING YOU BY DRAINING YOU DRY RIGHT HERE AND NOW.
HOW DOES THAT SOUND?
HA! I KINDA LIKE MY VERSION BETTER.
HEH.
THAT'S TOO BAD.

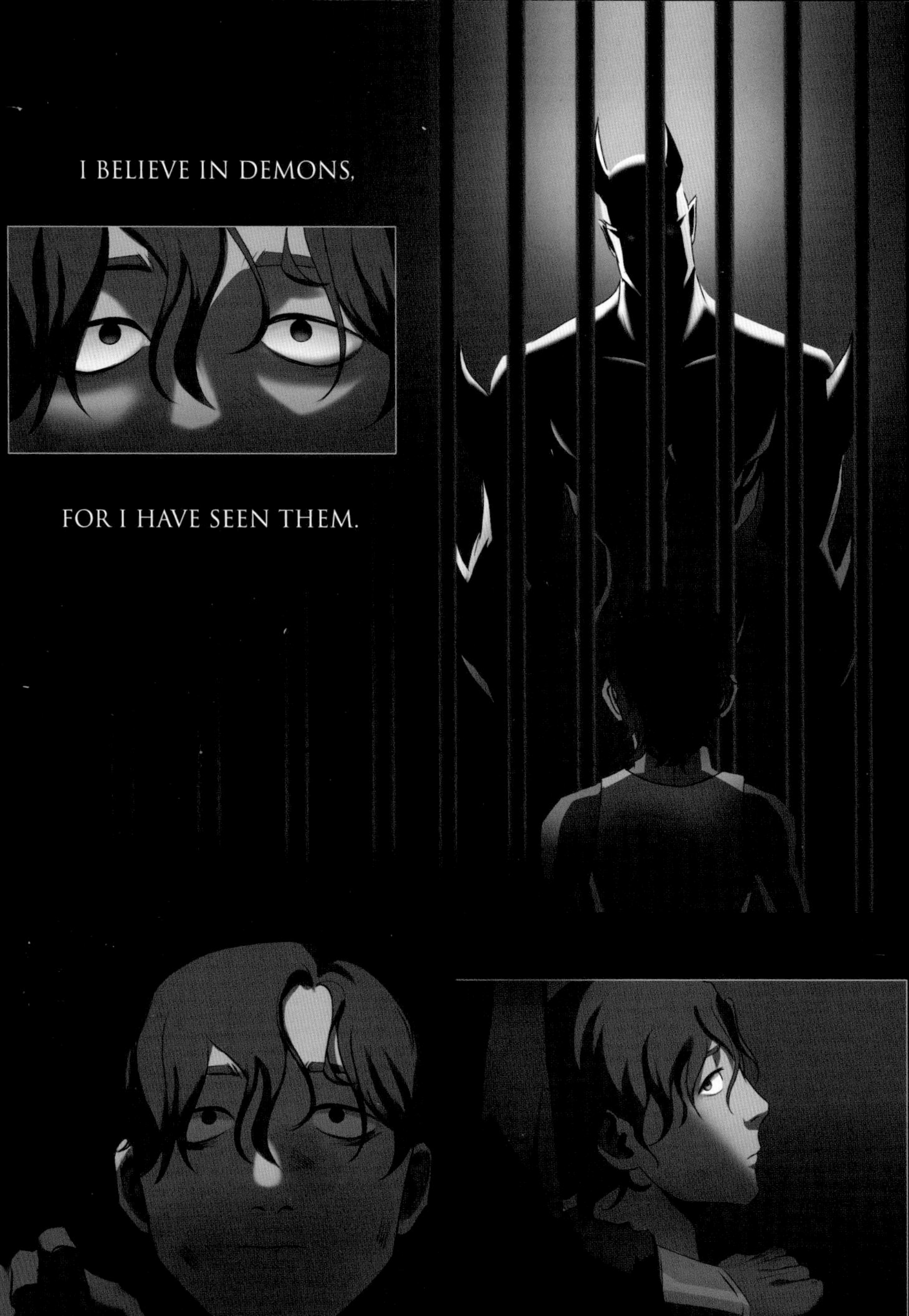
I BELIEVE IN DEMONS,
FOR I HAVE SEEN THEM.

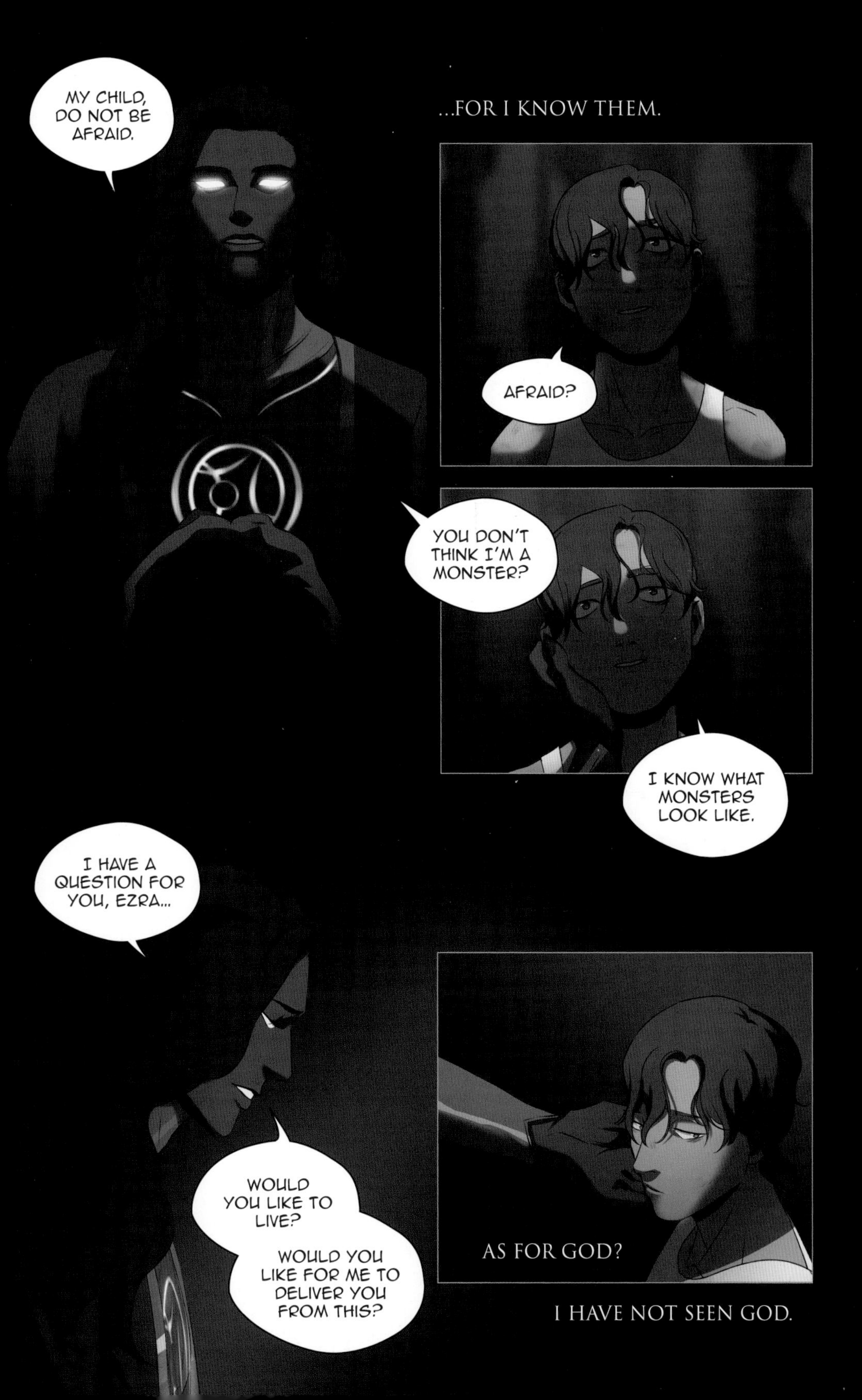
MY CHILD, DO NOT BE AFRAID.
...FOR I KNOW THEM.
AFRAID?
YOU DON'T THINK I'M A MONSTER?
I KNOW WHAT MONSTERS LOOK LIKE.
I HAVE A QUESTION FOR YOU, EZRA...
WOULD YOU LIKE TO LIVE?
WOULD YOU LIKE FOR ME TO DELIVER YOU FROM THIS?
AS FOR GOD?
I HAVE NOT SEEN GOD.

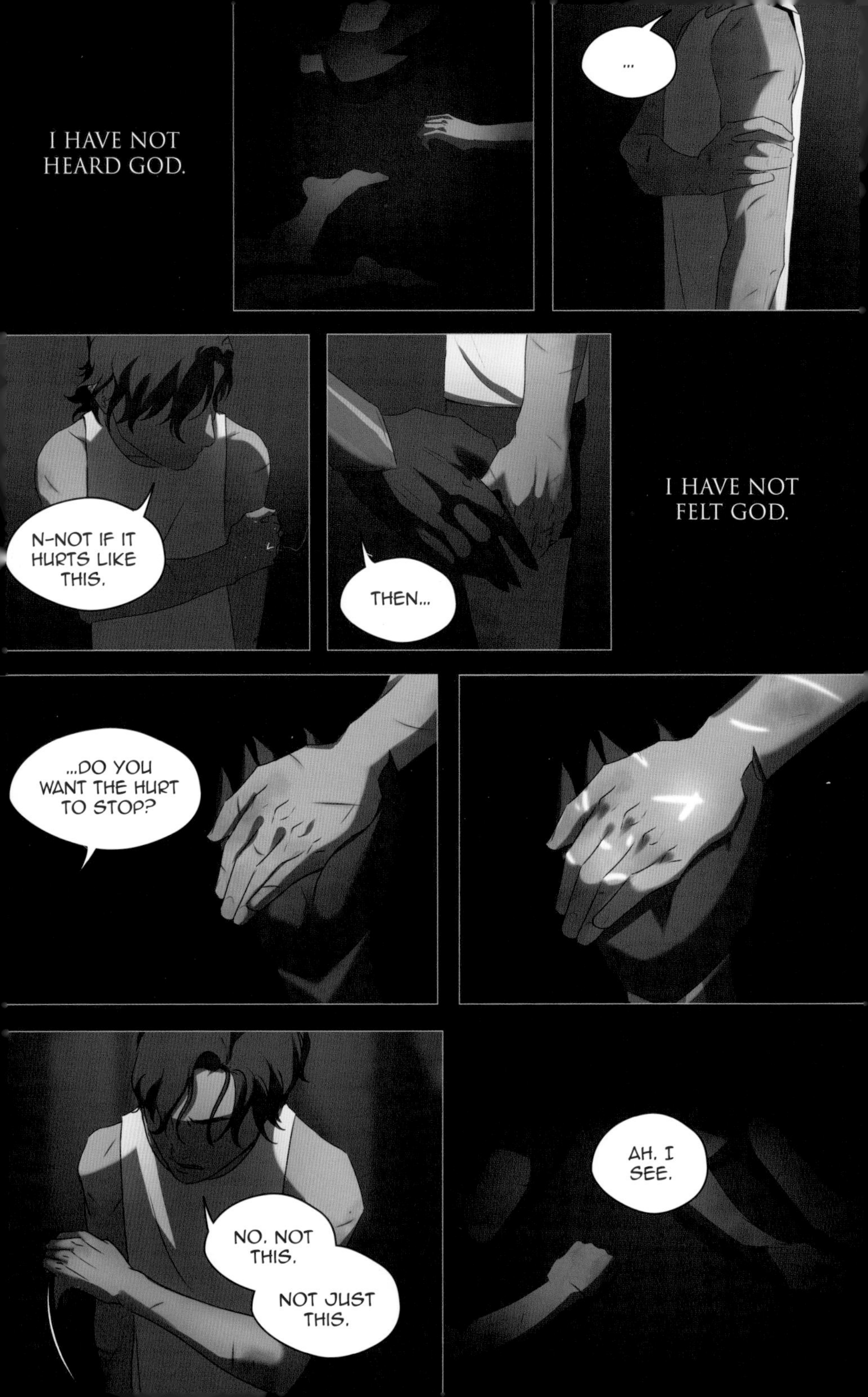
I HAVE NOT HEARD GOD.
...
N-NOT IF IT HURTS LIKE THIS.
THEN...
I HAVE NOT FELT GOD.
...DO YOU WANT THE HURT TO STOP?
NO. NOT THIS.
NOT JUST THIS.
AH. I SEE.

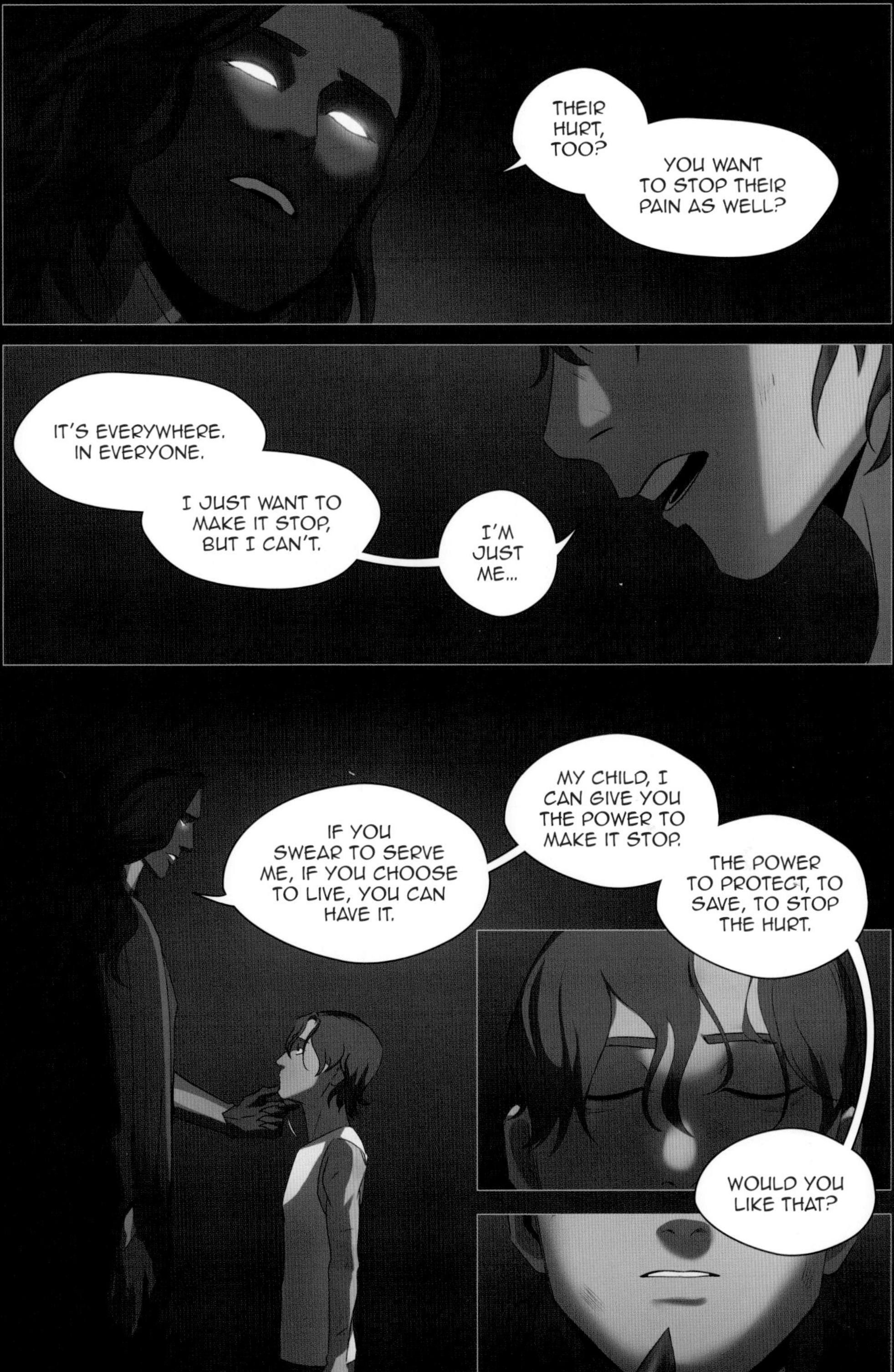
THEIR HURT, TOO?
YOU WANT TO STOP THEIR PAIN AS WELL?
IT'S EVERYWHERE. IN EVERYONE.
I JUST WANT TO MAKE IT STOP, BUT I CAN'T.
I'M JUST ME...
MY CHILD, I CAN GIVE YOU THE POWER TO MAKE IT STOP.
IF YOU SWEAR TO SERVE ME, IF YOU CHOOSE TO LIVE, YOU CAN HAVE IT.
THE POWER TO PROTECT, TO SAVE, TO STOP THE HURT.
WOULD YOU LIKE THAT?

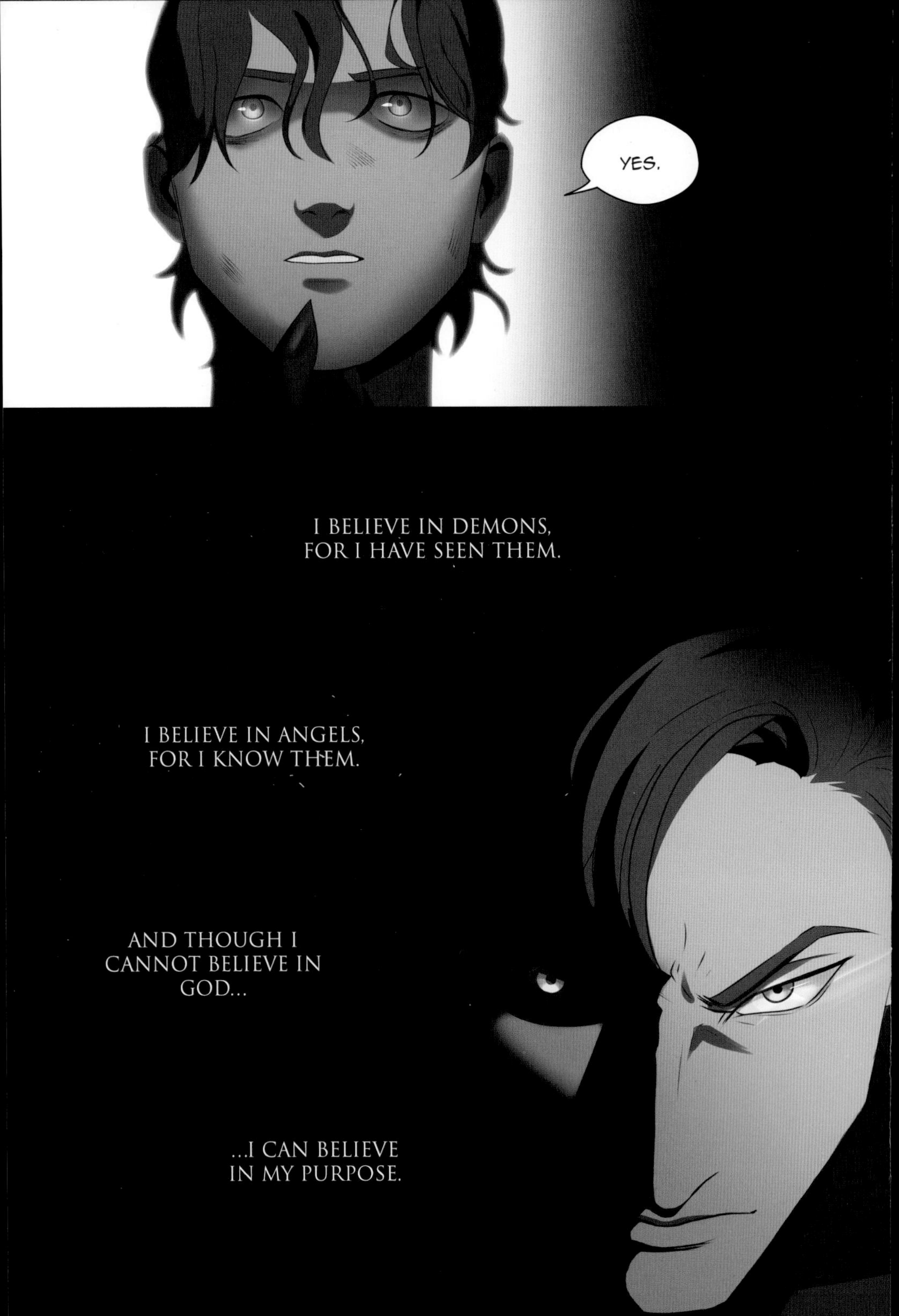
YES.
I BELIEVE IN DEMONS, FOR I HAVE SEEN THEM.
I BELIEVE IN ANGELS, FOR I KNOW THEM.
AND THOUGH I CANNOT BELIEVE IN GOD...
...I CAN BELIEVE IN MY PURPOSE.

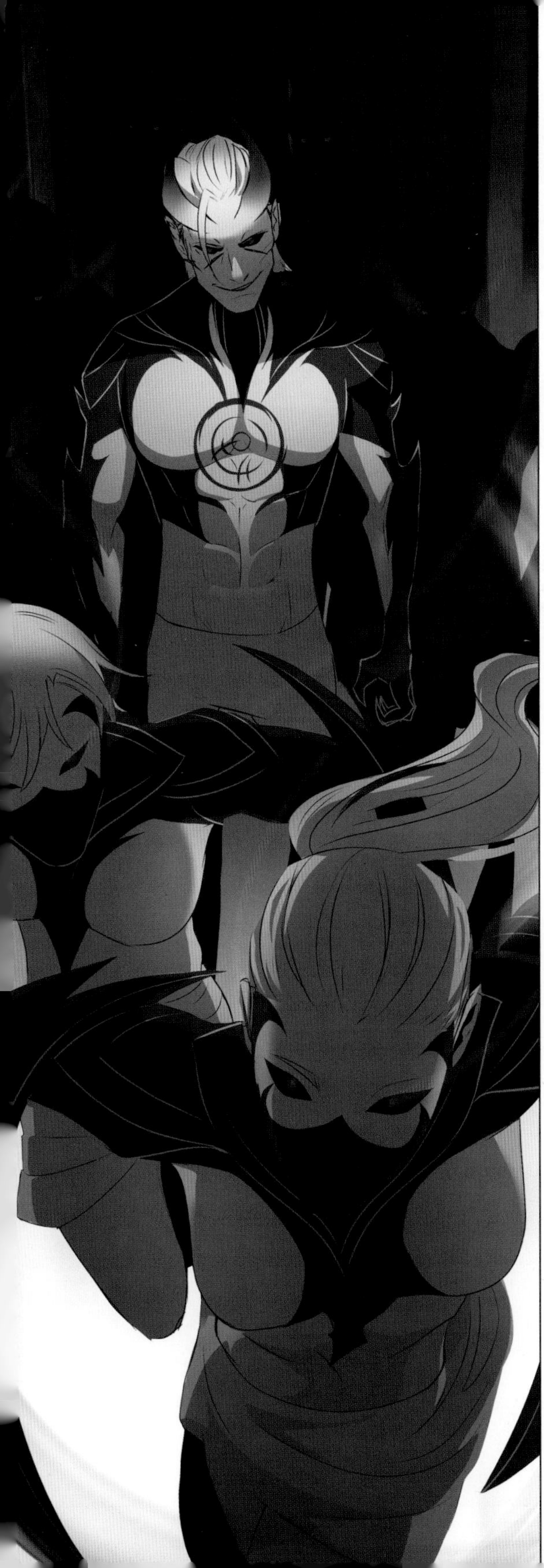

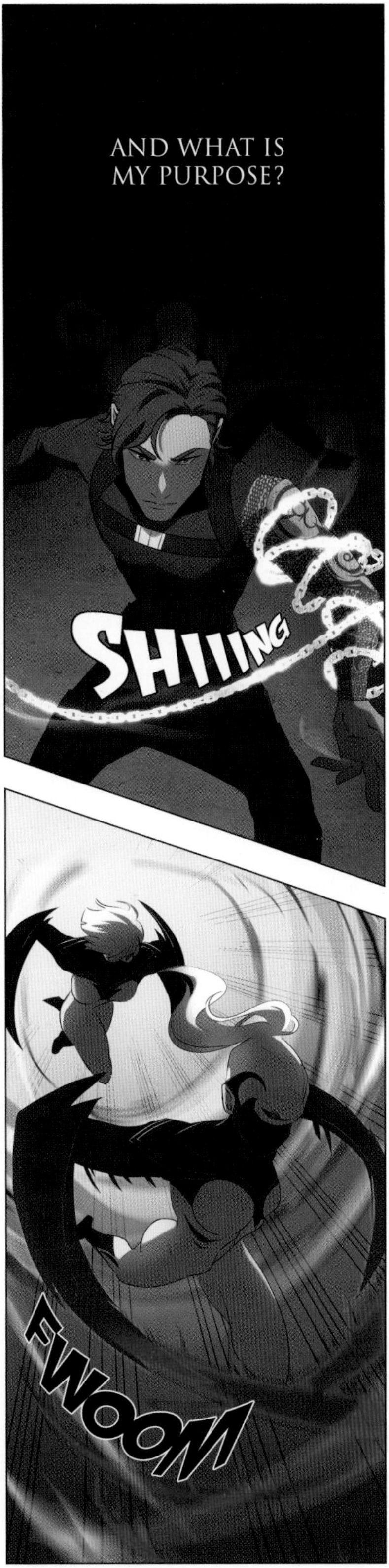
AND WHAT IS MY PURPOSE?
SHIIING
FWOOM

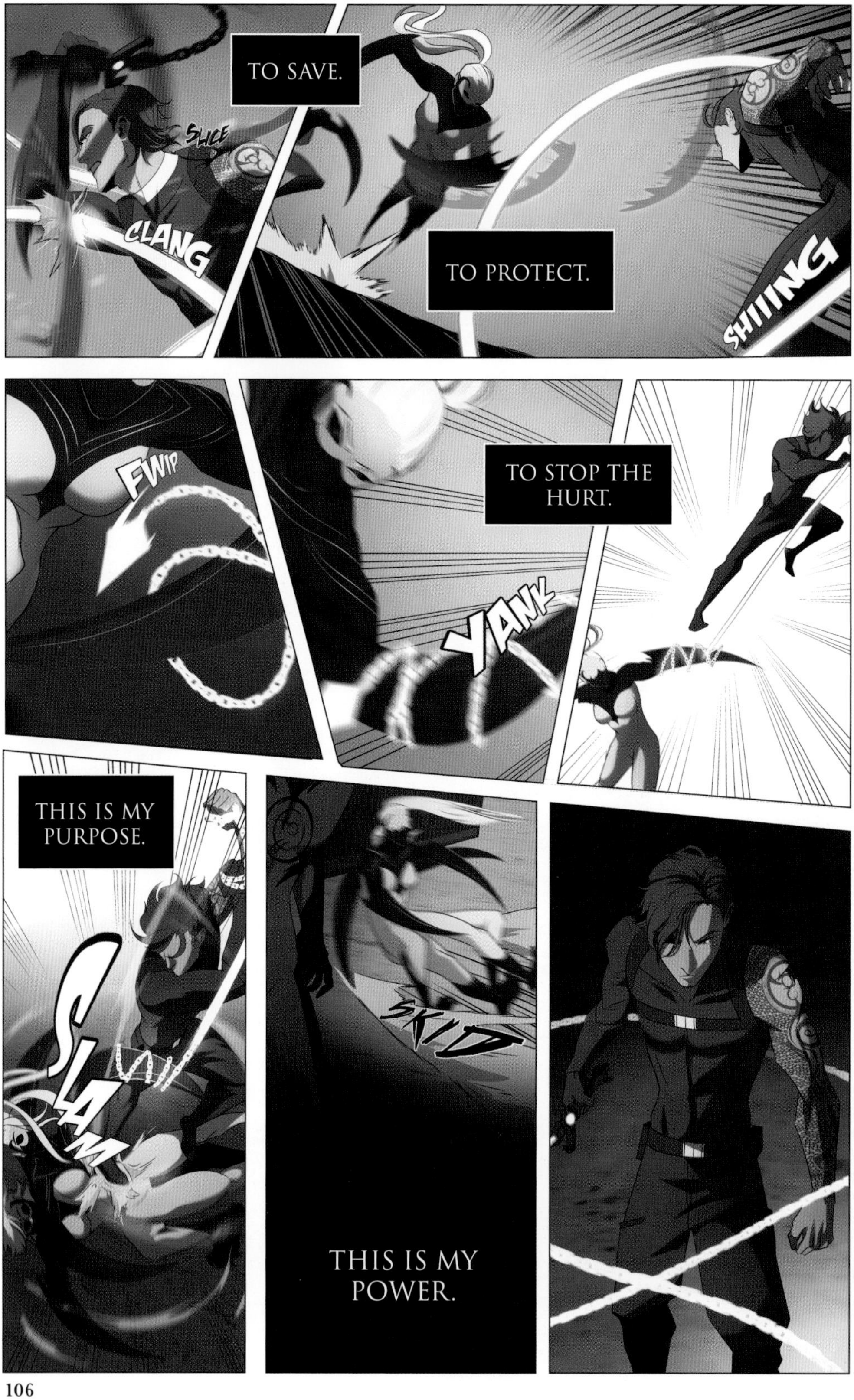
TO SAVE.
SLICE
CLANG
TO PROTECT.
SHIIING
FWIP
TO STOP THE HURT.
YANK
THIS IS MY PURPOSE.
SLAM
SKID
THIS IS MY POWER.

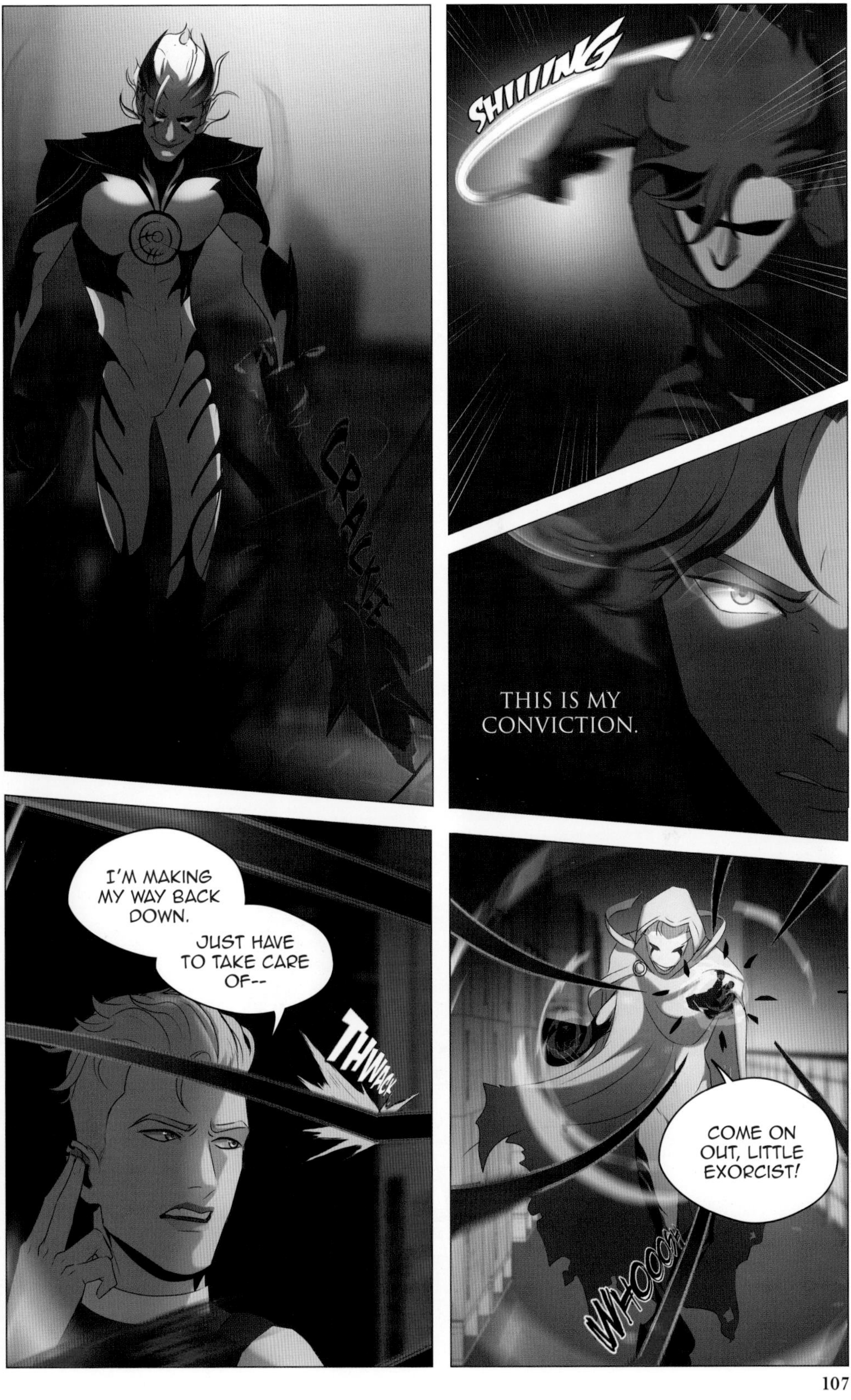
CRACKLE
SHIIIING
THIS IS MY CONVICTION.
I'M MAKING MY WAY BACK DOWN.
JUST HAVE TO TAKE CARE OF--
THWACK
COME ON OUT, LITTLE EXORCIST!

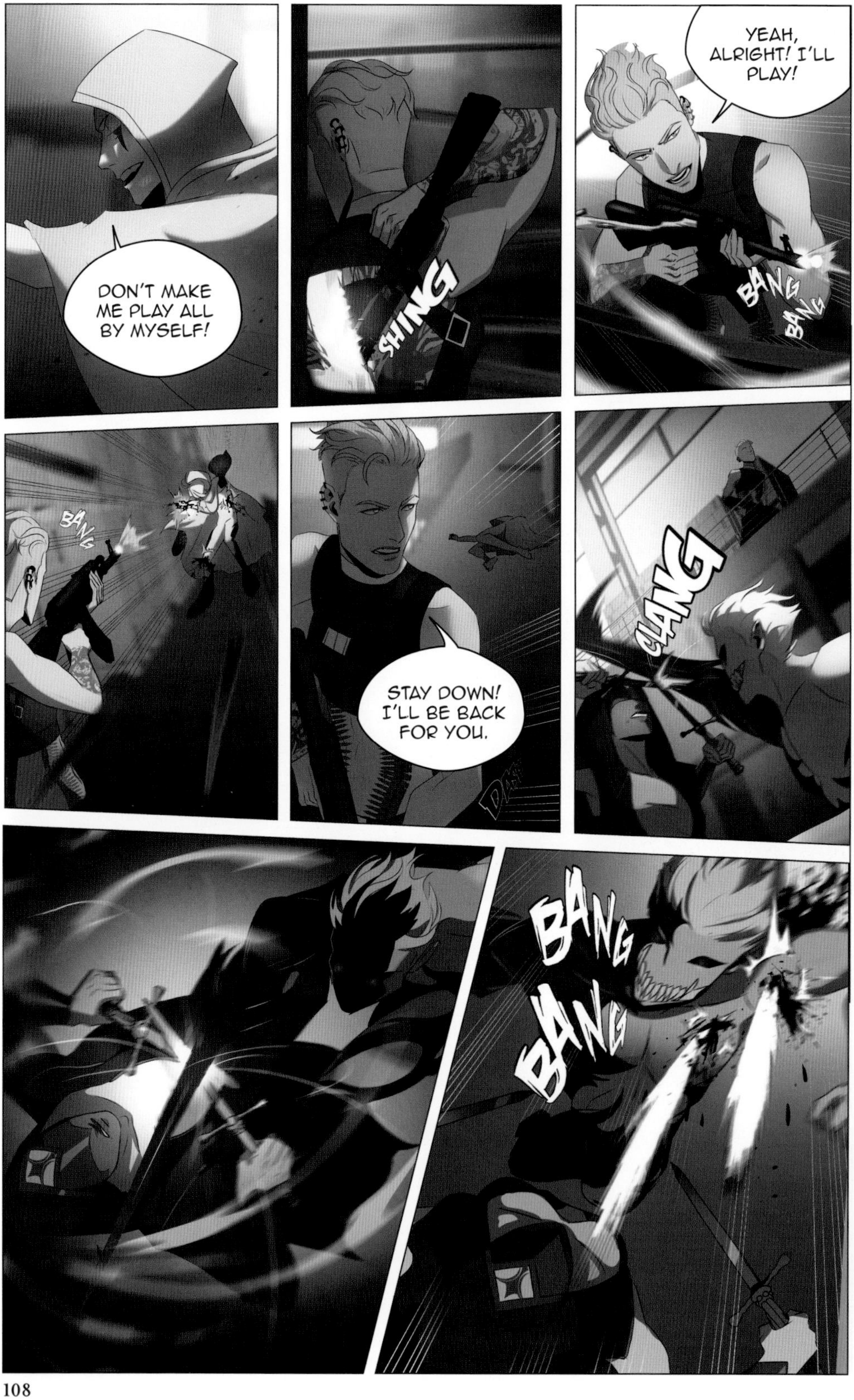
DON'T MAKE ME PLAY ALL BY MYSELF!
SHING
YEAH, ALRIGHT! I'LL PLAY!
BANG
BANG
BANG
STAY DOWN! I'LL BE BACK FOR YOU.
CLANG
BANG
BANG

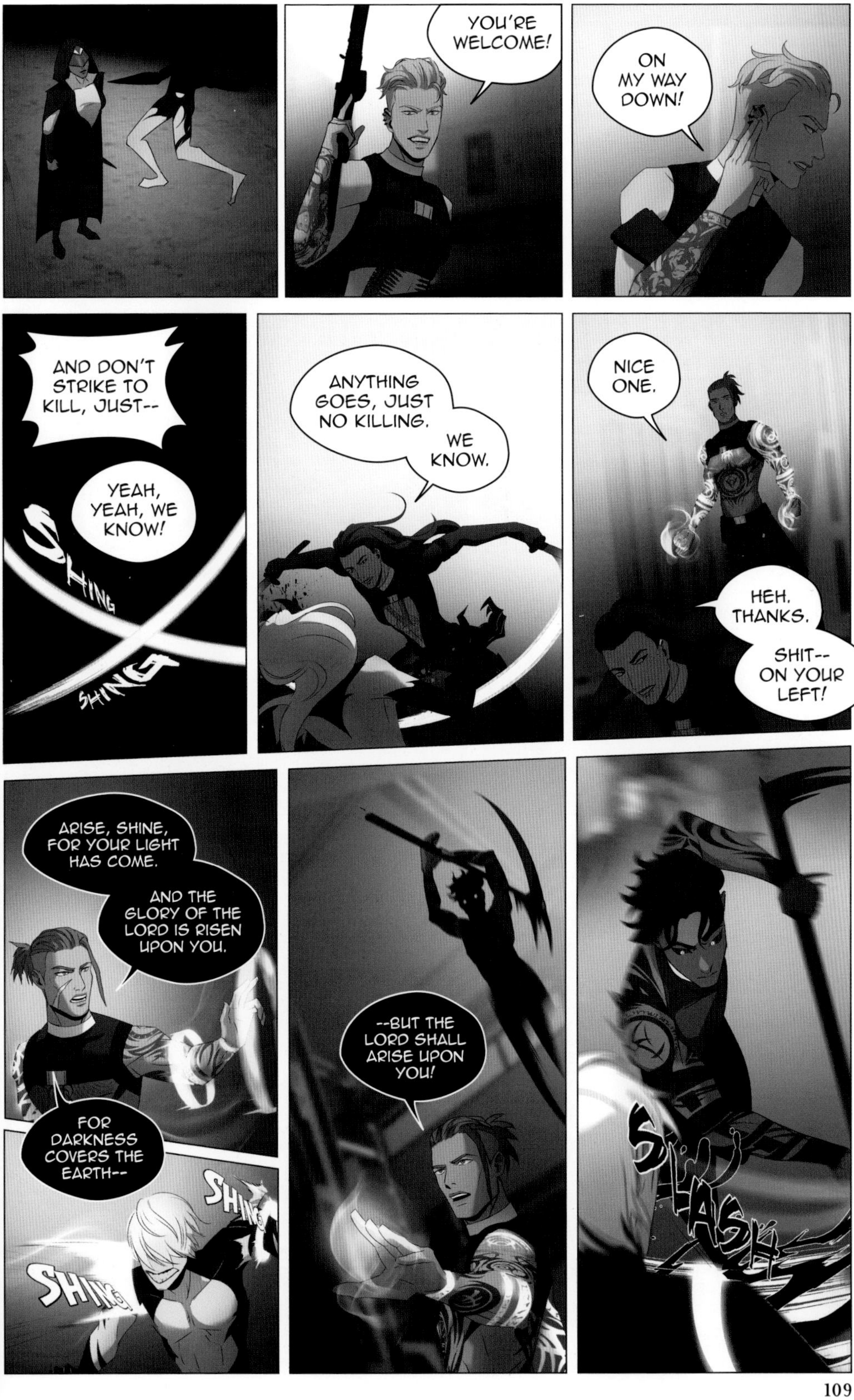
YOU'RE WELCOME!
ON MY WAY DOWN!
AND DON'T STRIKE TO KILL, JUST--
YEAH, YEAH, WE KNOW!
SHING
SHING
ANYTHING GOES, JUST NO KILLING.
WE KNOW.
NICE ONE.
HEH. THANKS.
SHIT-- ON YOUR LEFT!
ARISE, SHINE, FOR YOUR LIGHT HAS COME.
AND THE GLORY OF THE LORD IS RISEN UPON YOU.
FOR DARKNESS COVERS THE EARTH--
SHING
SHING!
--BUT THE LORD SHALL ARISE UPON YOU!
SLASH

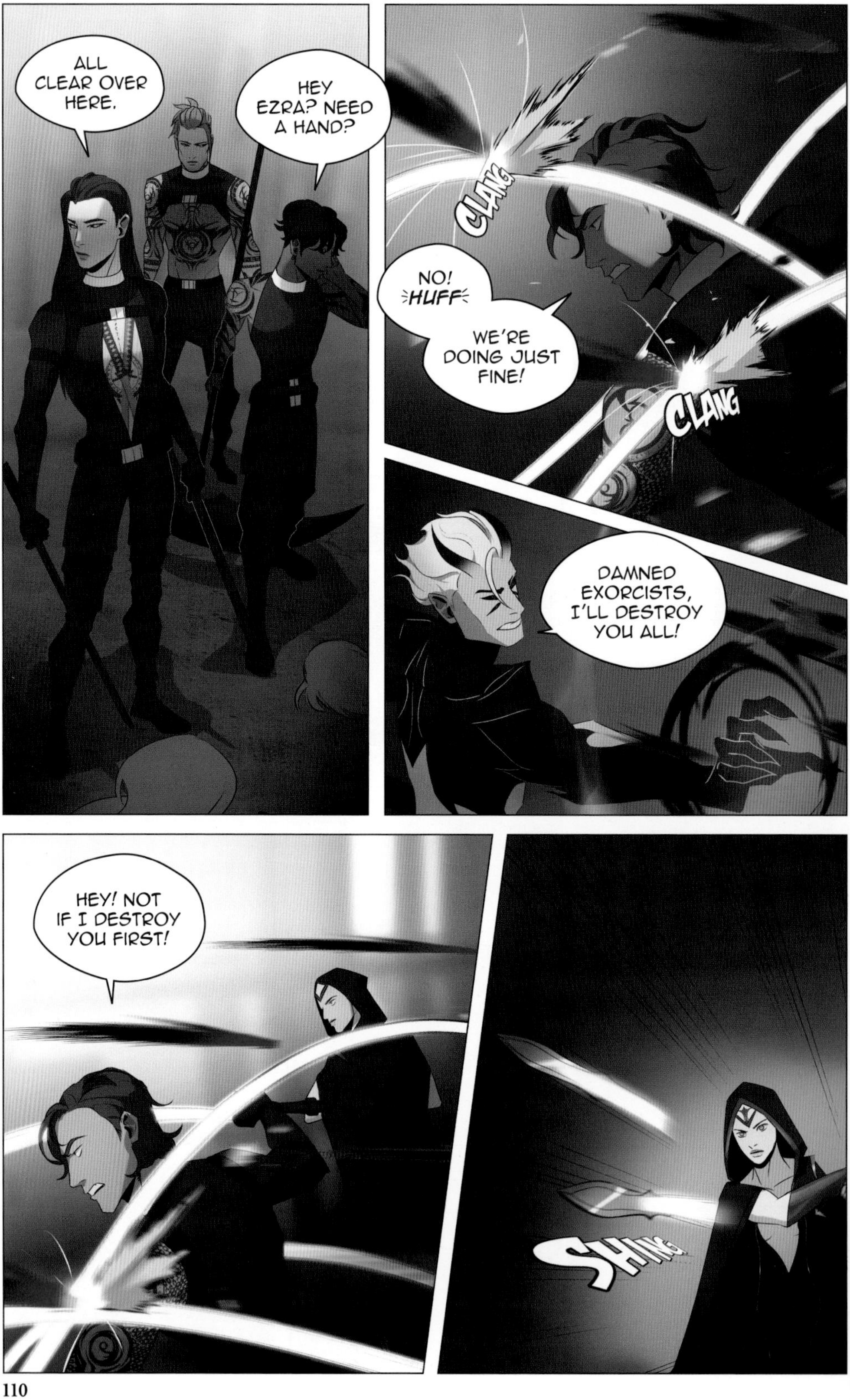

ALL CLEAR OVER HERE.
HEY EZRA? NEED A HAND?
CLANG
NO! HUFF
WE'RE DOING JUST FINE!
CLANG
DAMNED EXORCISTS, I'LL DESTROY YOU ALL!
HEY! NOT IF I DESTROY YOU FIRST!
SHING

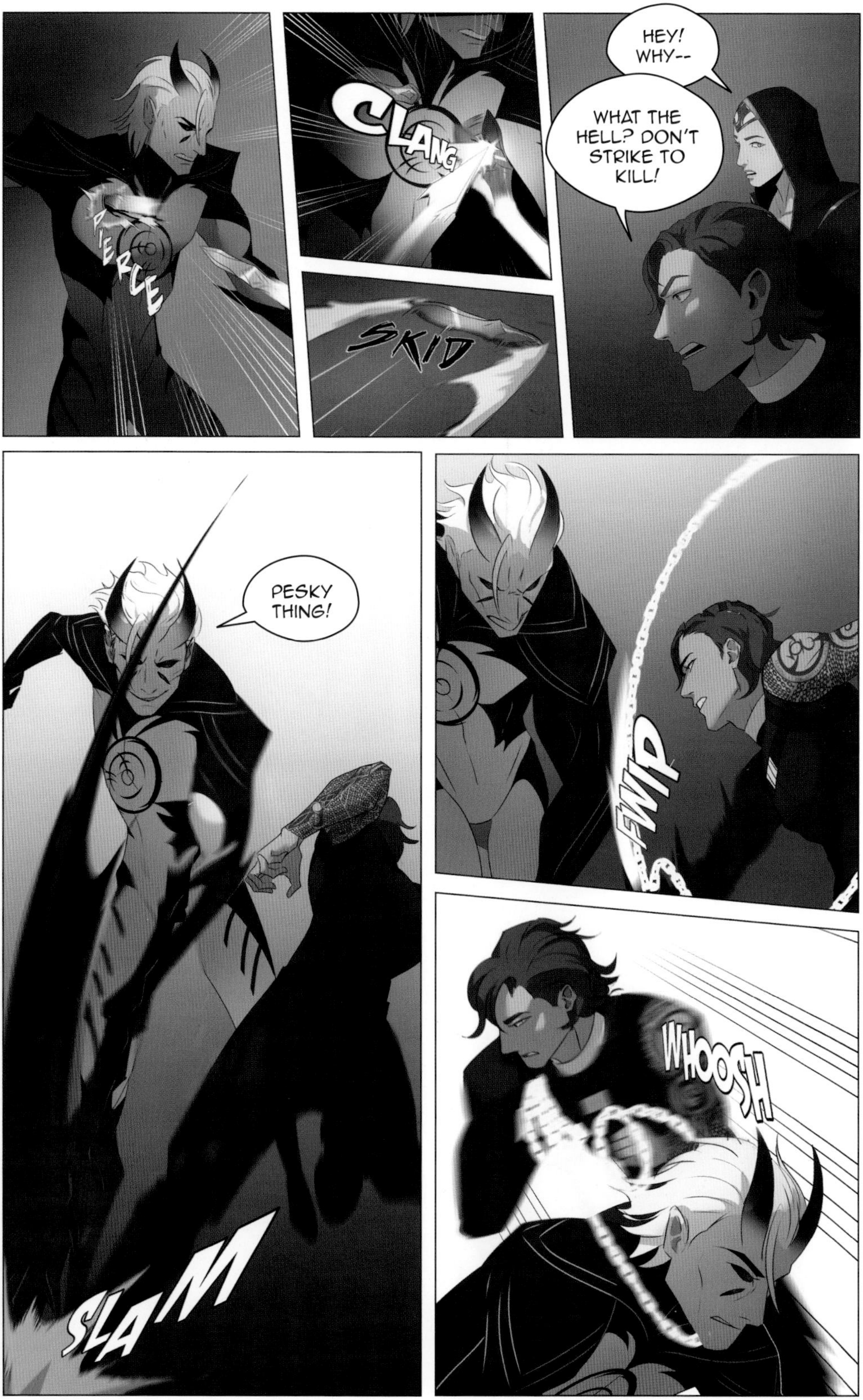
PIERCE
CLANG
SKID
HEY! WHY--
WHAT THE HELL? DON'T STRIKE TO KILL!
PESKY THING!
SLAM
FWIP
WHOOSH

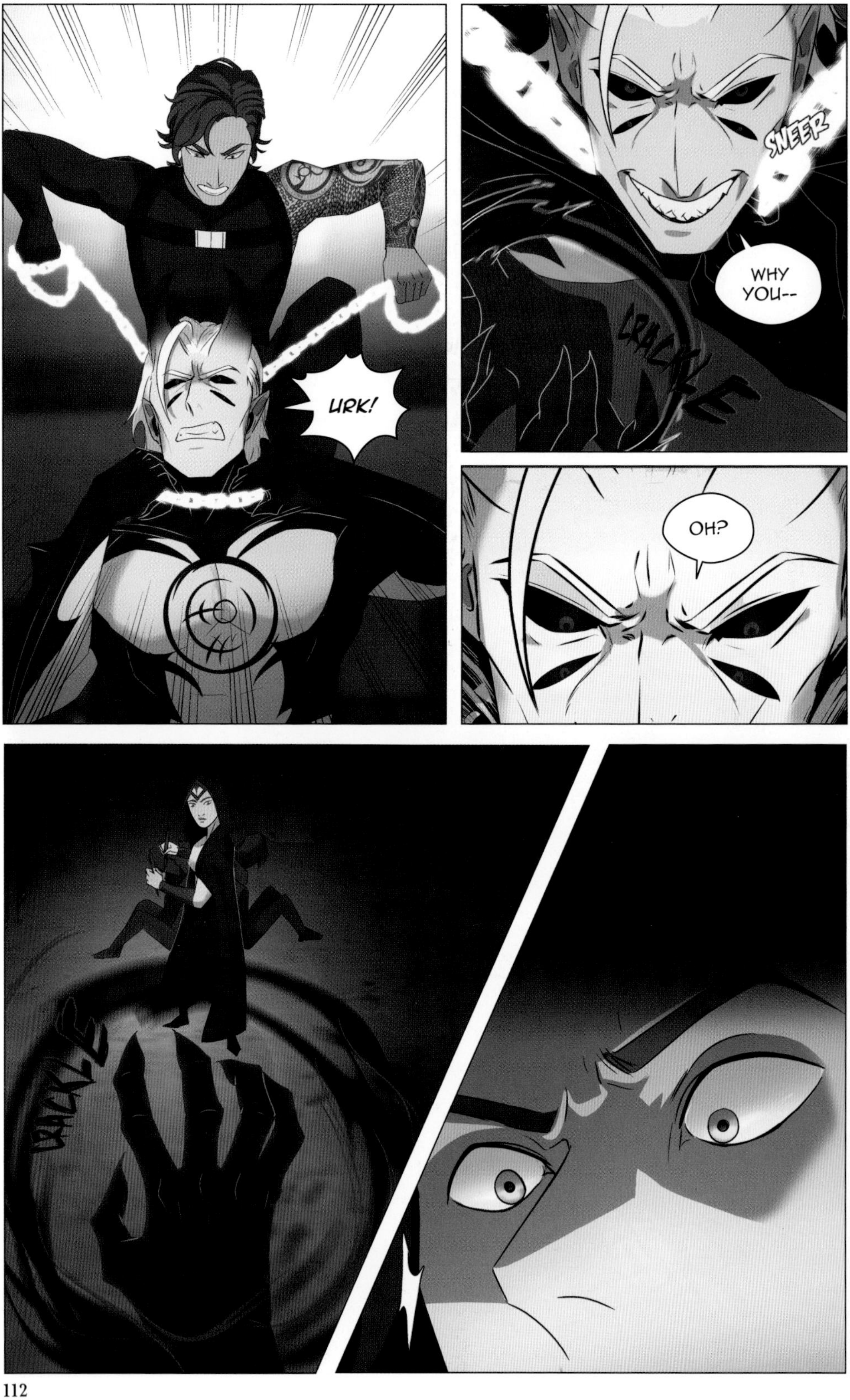
URK!
SNEER
WHY YOU--
CRACKLE
OH?
CRACKLE

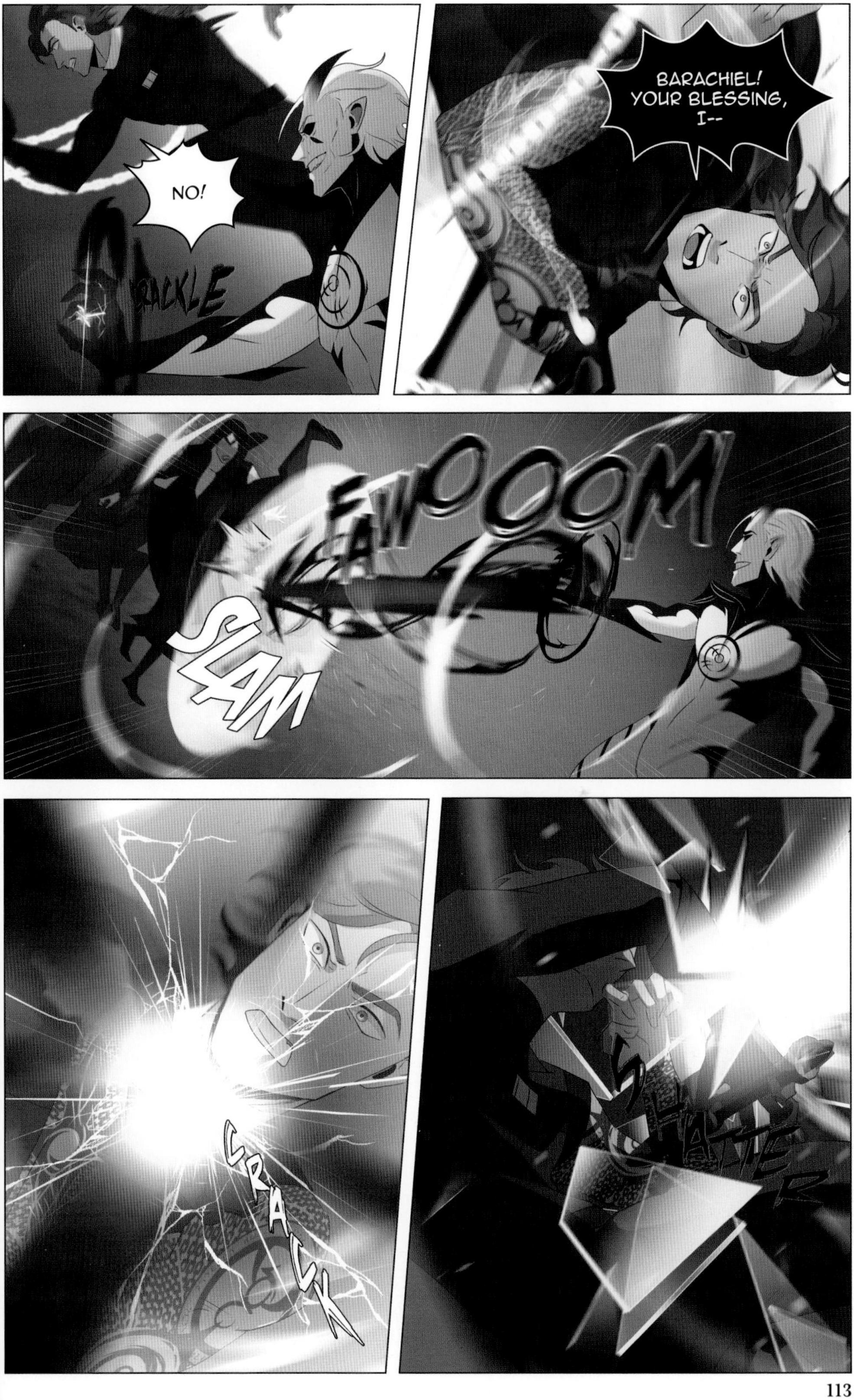
NO!
CRACKLE
BARACHIEL! YOUR BLESSING, I--
FWOOOM
SLAM
CRACK
SHATTER

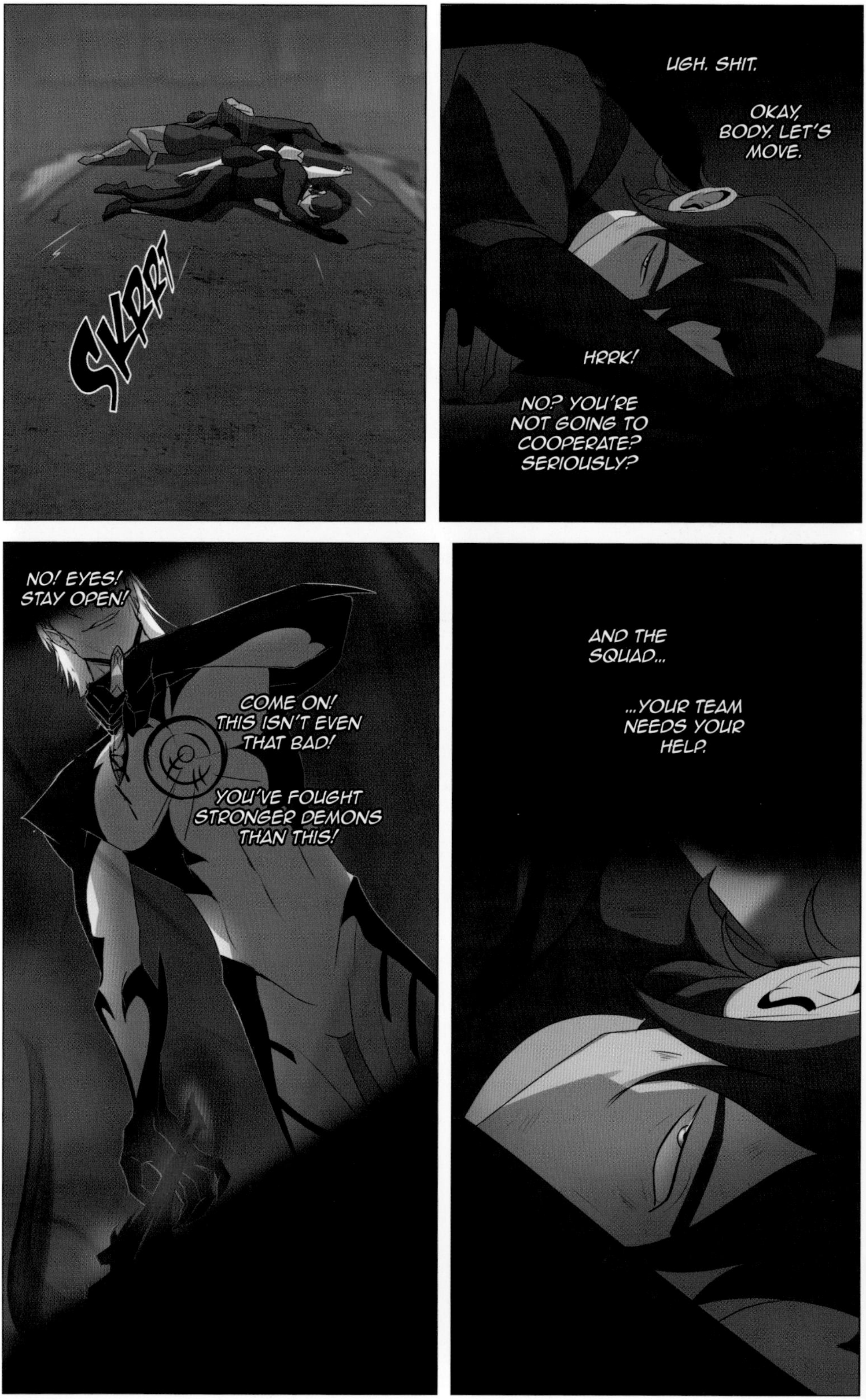
SKRRT
UGH. SHIT.
OKAY, BODY. LET'S MOVE.
HRRK!
NO? YOU'RE NOT GOING TO COOPERATE? SERIOUSLY?
NO! EYES! STAY OPEN!
COME ON! THIS ISN'T EVEN THAT BAD!
YOU'VE FOUGHT STRONGER DEMONS THAN THIS!
AND THE SQUAD...
...YOUR TEAM NEEDS YOUR HELP.

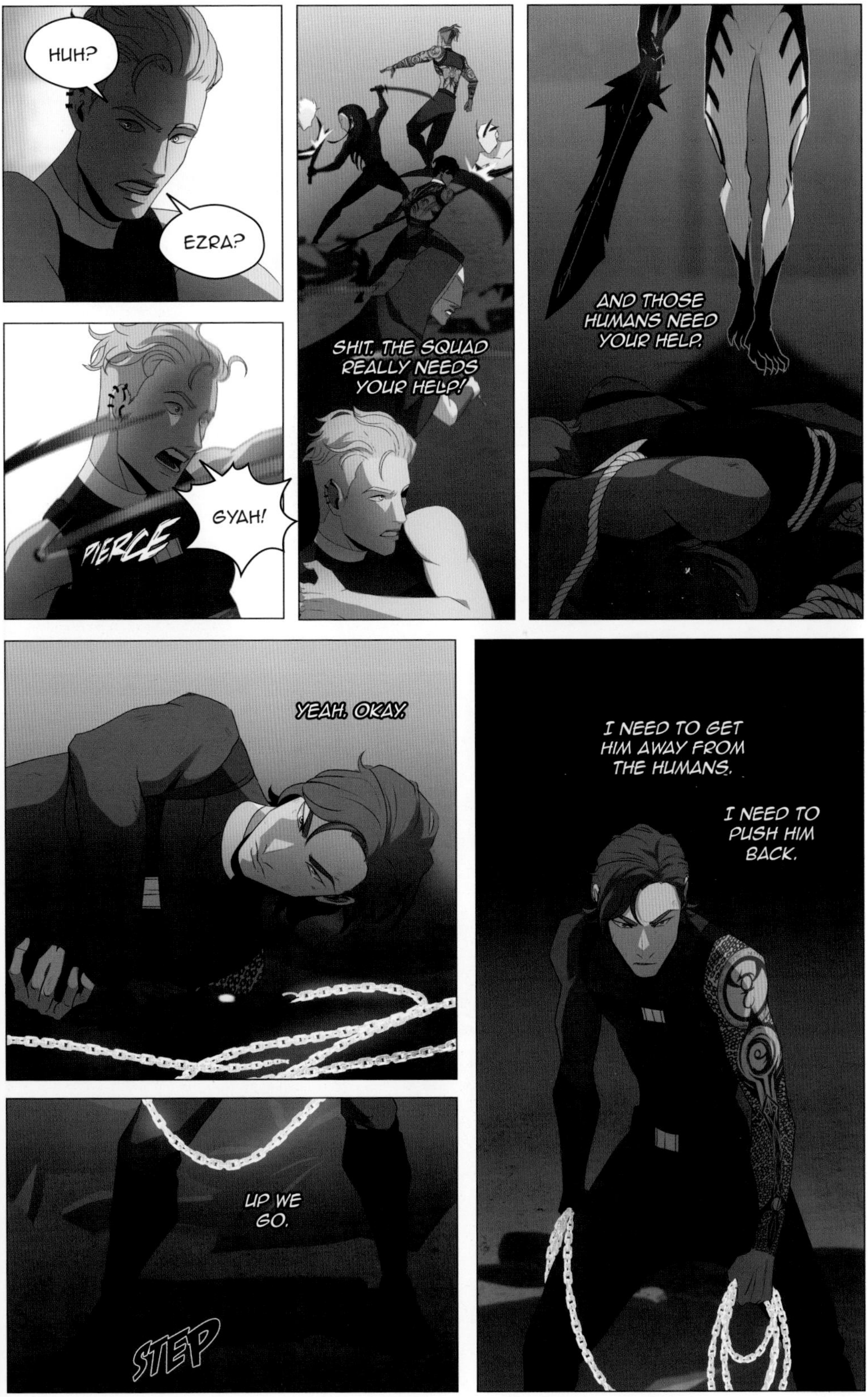
HUH?
EZRA?
SHIT. THE SQUAD REALLY NEEDS YOUR HELP!
AND THOSE HUMANS NEED YOUR HELP.
GYAH!
PIERCE
YEAH. OKAY.
I NEED TO GET HIM AWAY FROM THE HUMANS.
I NEED TO PUSH HIM BACK.
UP WE GO.
STEP

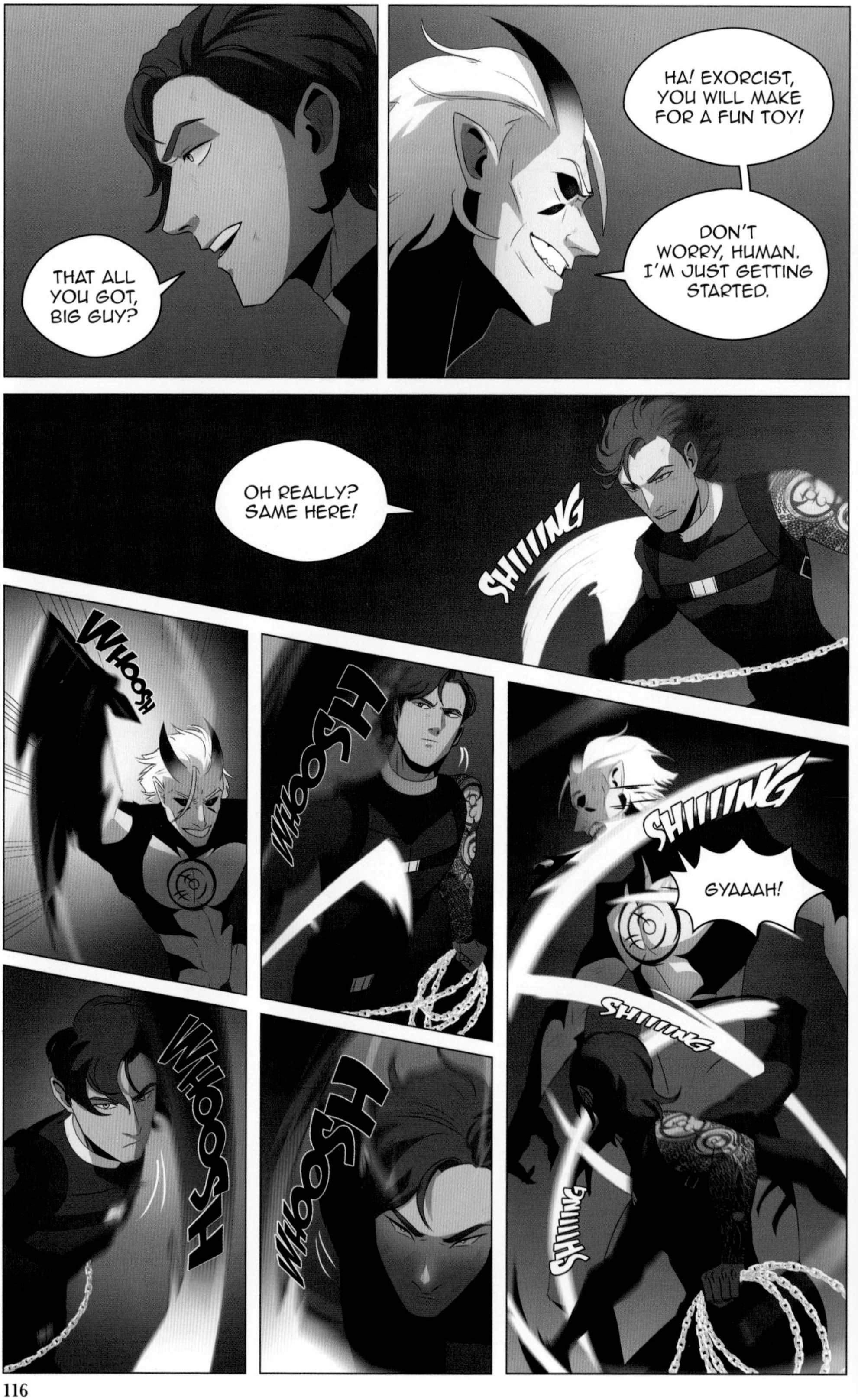
THAT ALL YOU GOT, BIG GUY?
HA! EXORCIST, YOU WILL MAKE FOR A FUN TOY!
DON'T WORRY, HUMAN. I'M JUST GETTING STARTED.
OH REALLY? SAME HERE!
SHIIIING
WHOOSH
WHOOSH
SHIIIING
GYAAAH!
SHIIIING
WHOOSH
WHOOSH
SHIIIING

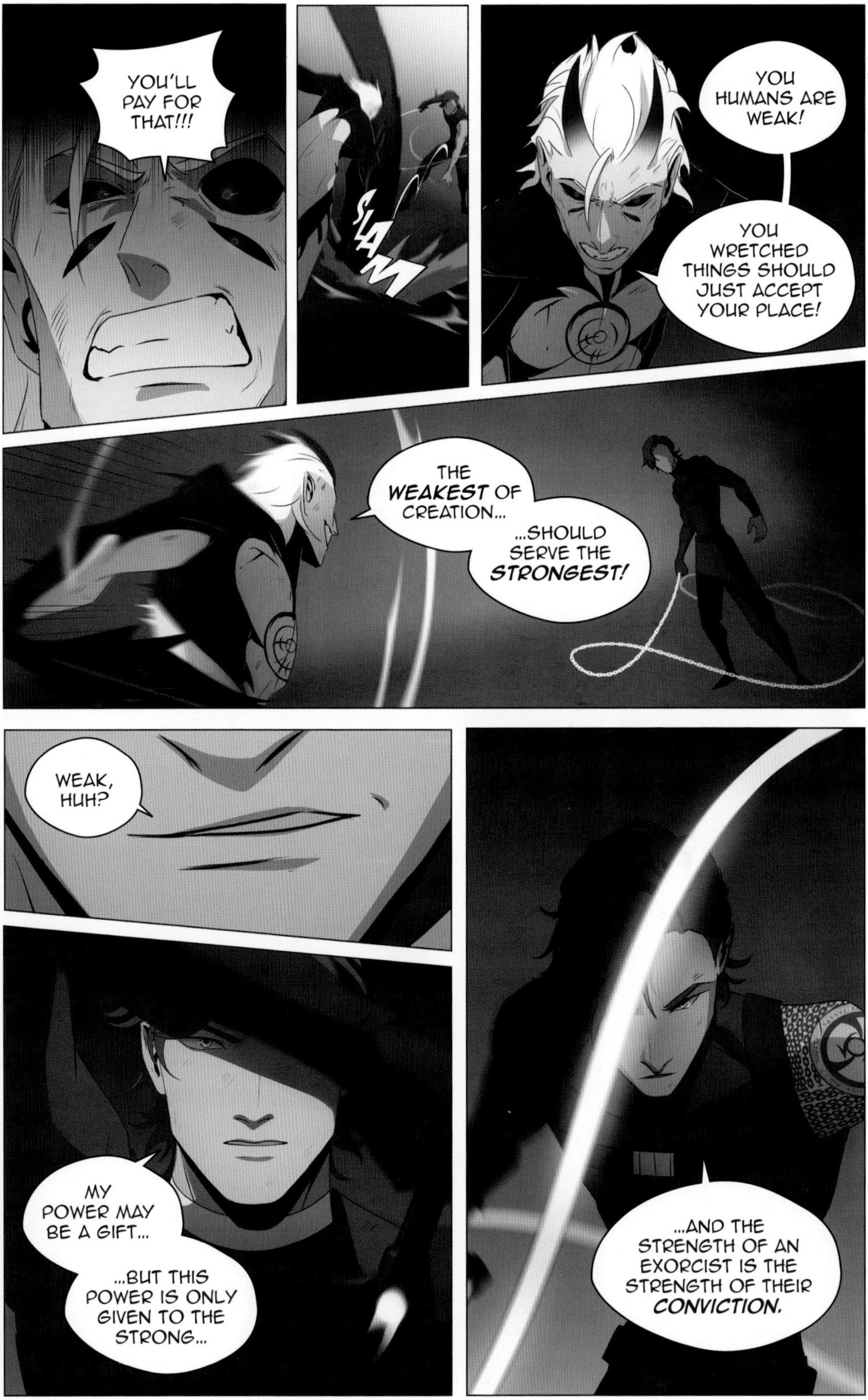
YOU'LL PAY FOR THAT!!!
SLAM
YOU HUMANS ARE WEAK!
YOU WRETCHED THINGS SHOULD JUST ACCEPT YOUR PLACE!
THE WEAKEST OF CREATION...
...SHOULD SERVE THE STRONGEST!
WEAK, HUH?
MY POWER MAY BE A GIFT...
...BUT THIS POWER IS ONLY GIVEN TO THE STRONG...
...AND THE STRENGTH OF AN EXORCIST IS THE STRENGTH OF THEIR CONVICTION.

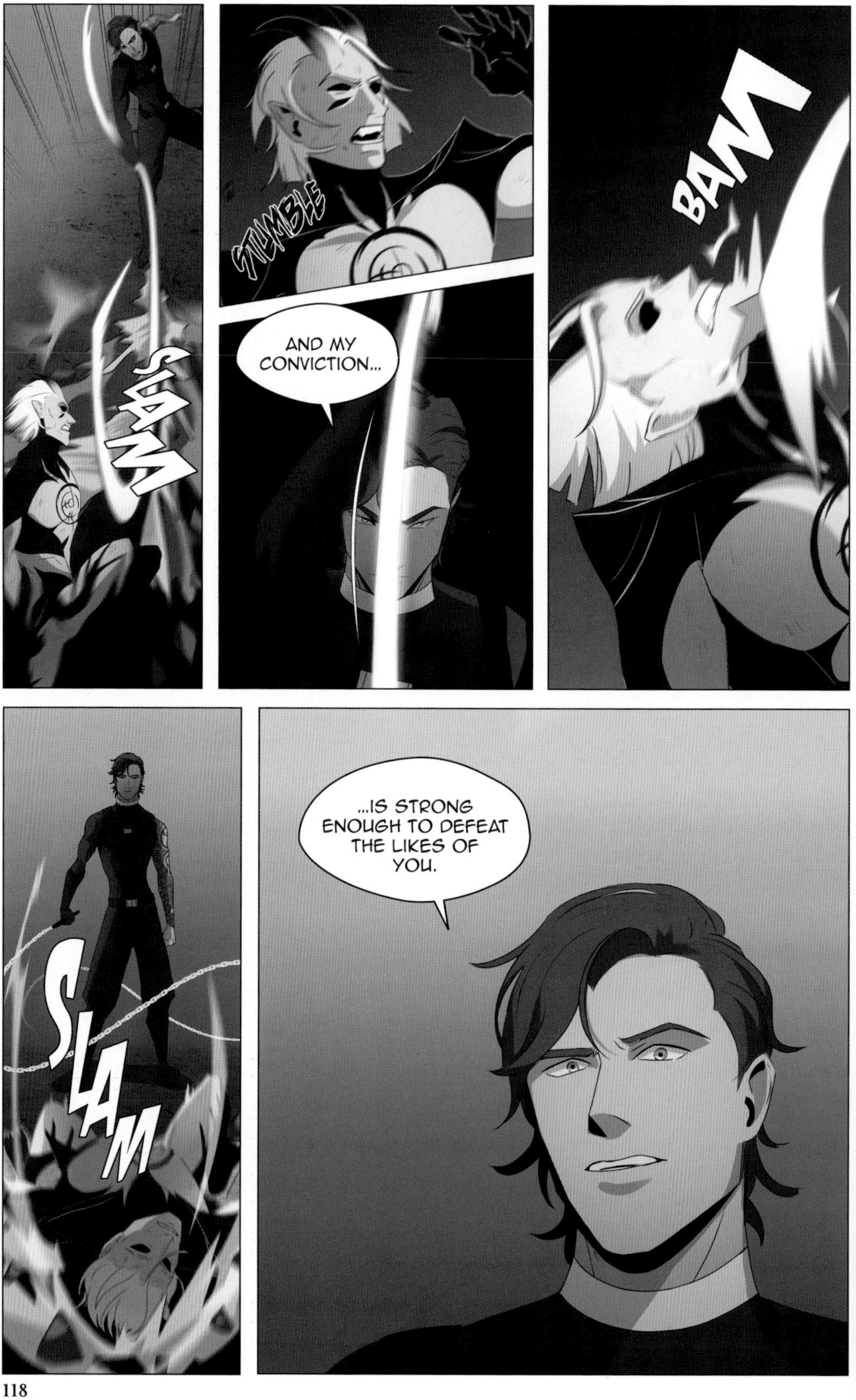
SLAM
STUMBLE
AND MY CONVICTION...
BAM
...IS STRONG ENOUGH TO DEFEAT THE LIKES OF YOU.
SLAM

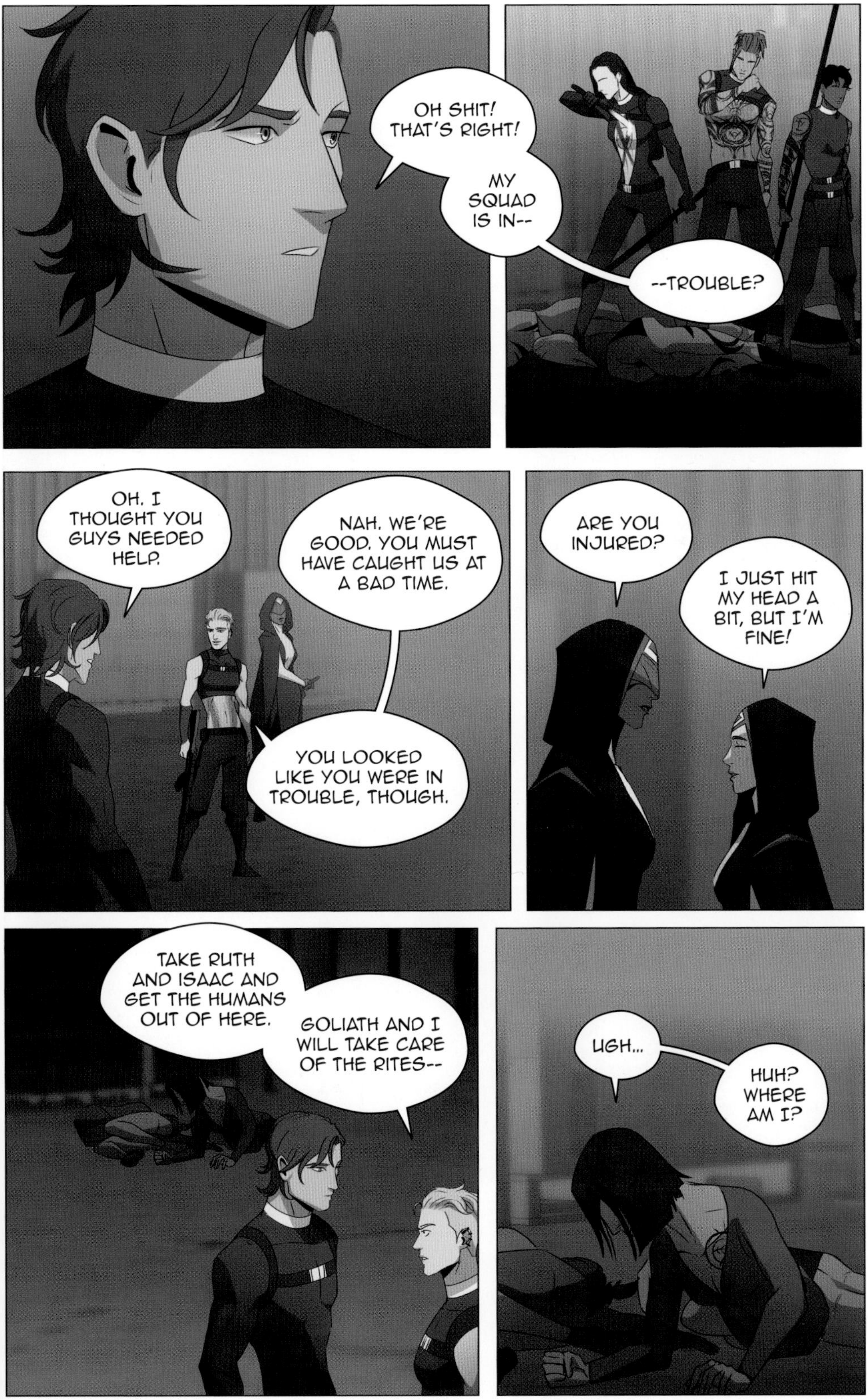
OH SHIT! THAT'S RIGHT!
MY SQUAD IS IN--
--TROUBLE?
OH. I THOUGHT YOU GUYS NEEDED HELP.
NAH. WE'RE GOOD. YOU MUST HAVE CAUGHT US AT A BAD TIME.
YOU LOOKED LIKE YOU WERE IN TROUBLE, THOUGH.
ARE YOU INJURED?
I JUST HIT MY HEAD A BIT, BUT I'M FINE!
TAKE RUTH AND ISAAC AND GET THE HUMANS OUT OF HERE.
GOLIATH AND I WILL TAKE CARE OF THE RITES--
UGH...
HUH? WHERE AM I?

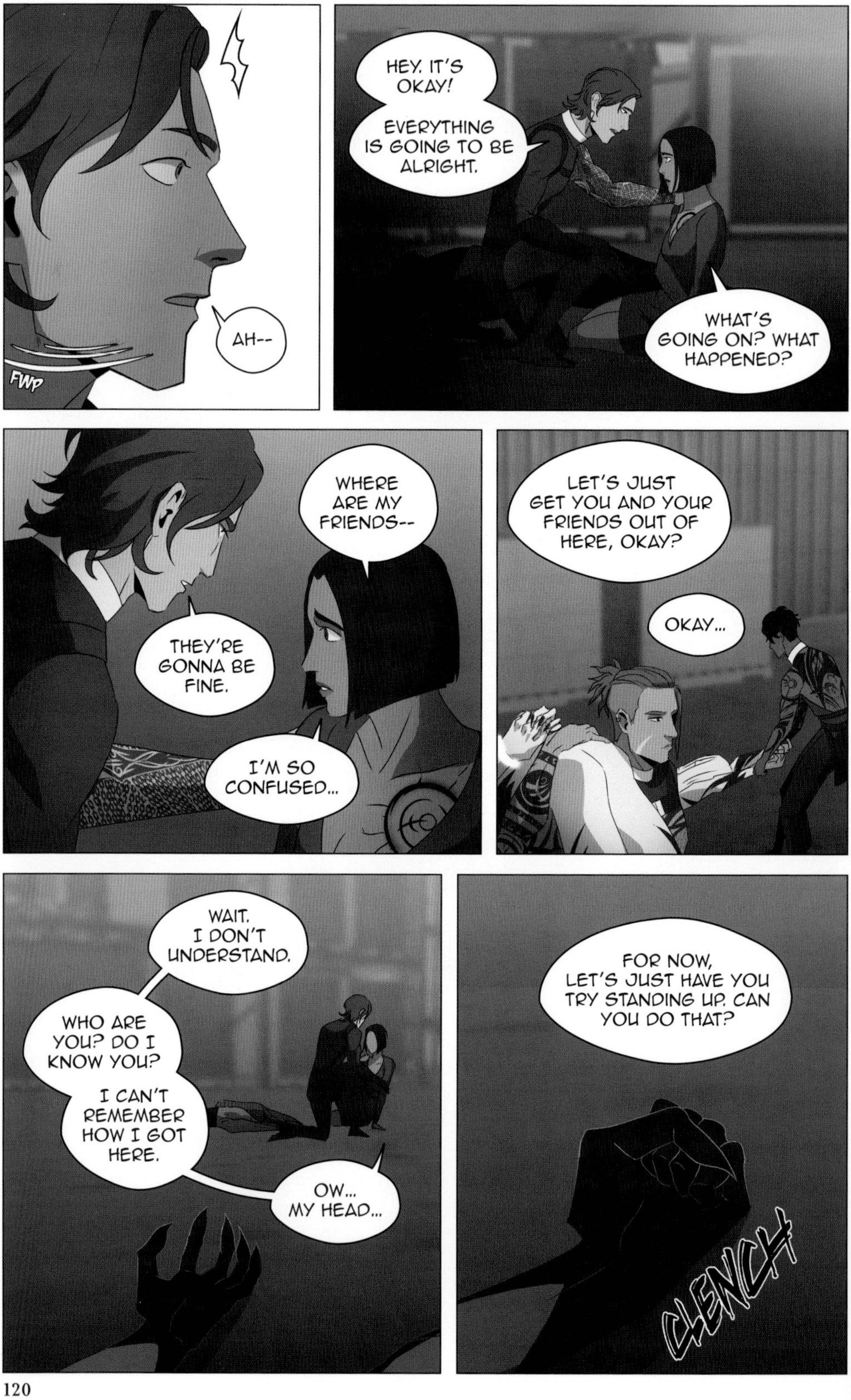
AH--
FWP
HEY. IT'S OKAY!
EVERYTHING IS GOING TO BE ALRIGHT.
WHAT'S GOING ON? WHAT HAPPENED?
WHERE ARE MY FRIENDS--
THEY'RE GONNA BE FINE.
I'M SO CONFUSED...
LET'S JUST GET YOU AND YOUR FRIENDS OUT OF HERE, OKAY?
OKAY...
WAIT. I DON'T UNDERSTAND.
WHO ARE YOU? DO I KNOW YOU?
I CAN'T REMEMBER HOW I GOT HERE.
OW... MY HEAD...
FOR NOW, LET'S JUST HAVE YOU TRY STANDING UP. CAN YOU DO THAT?
CLENCH

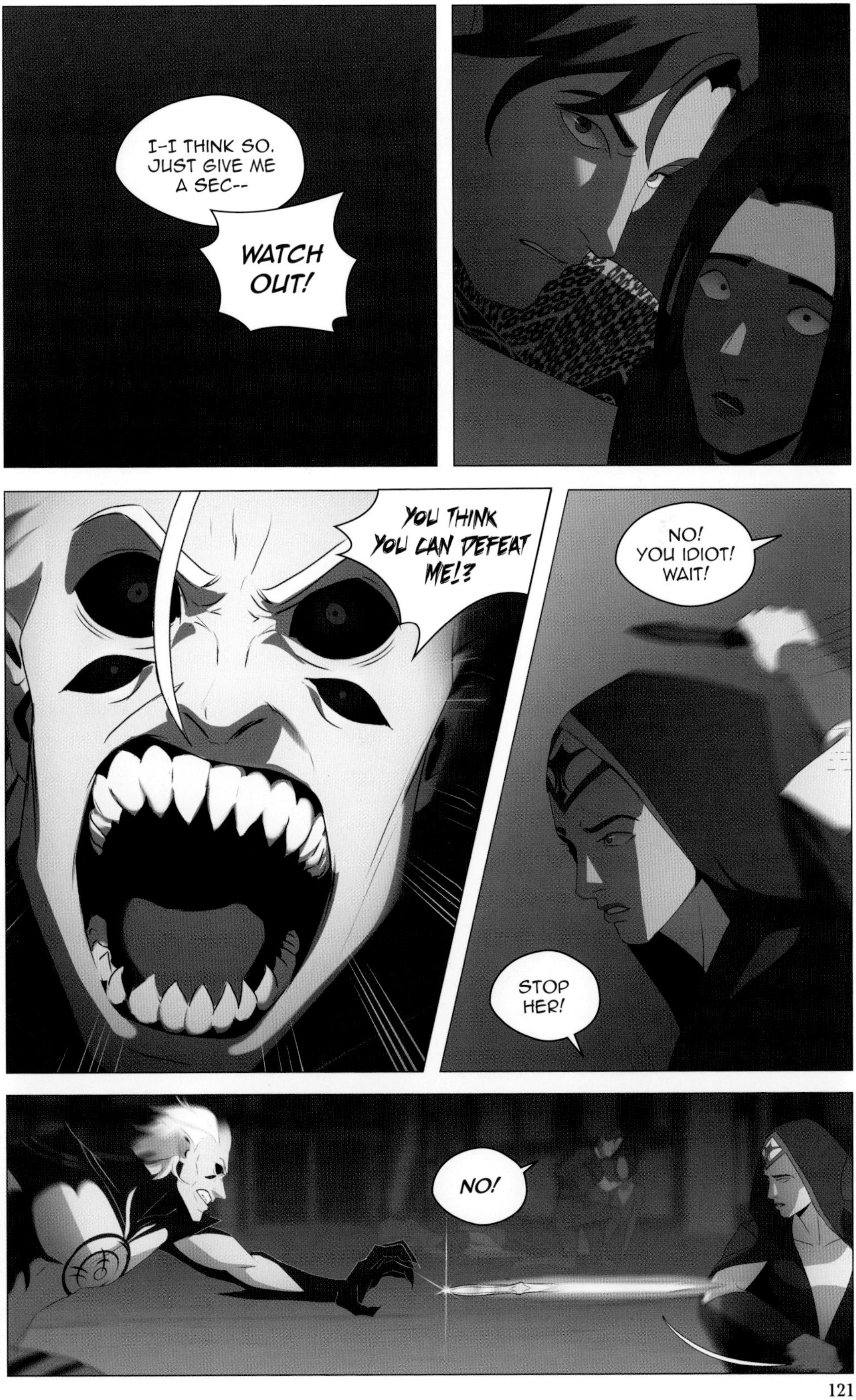
I-I THINK SO. JUST GIVE ME A SEC--
WATCH OUT!
YOU THINK YOU CAN DEFEAT ME!?
NO! YOU IDIOT! WAIT!
STOP HER!
NO!

NO.
NO. NO. NO.

I HAVE TO STOP IT.

IF ONLY I COULD JUST--

GABRIEL, PLEASE!

JUST THIS ONCE--

--YOUR BLESSING, LET ME USE IT--

--I BEG OF YOU!

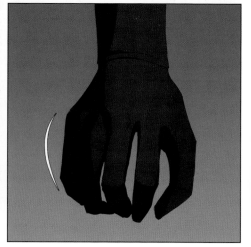

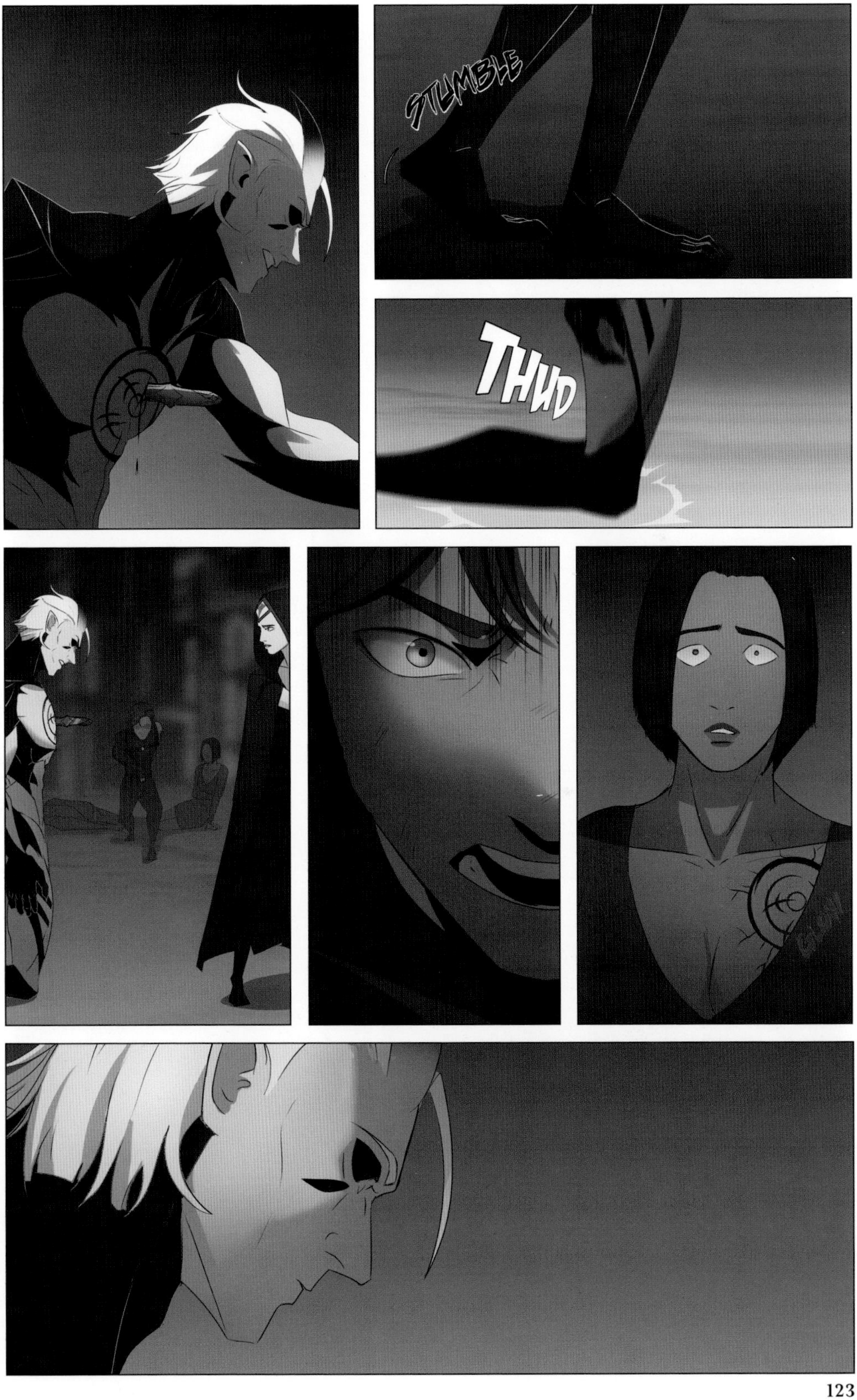
STUMBLE
THUD

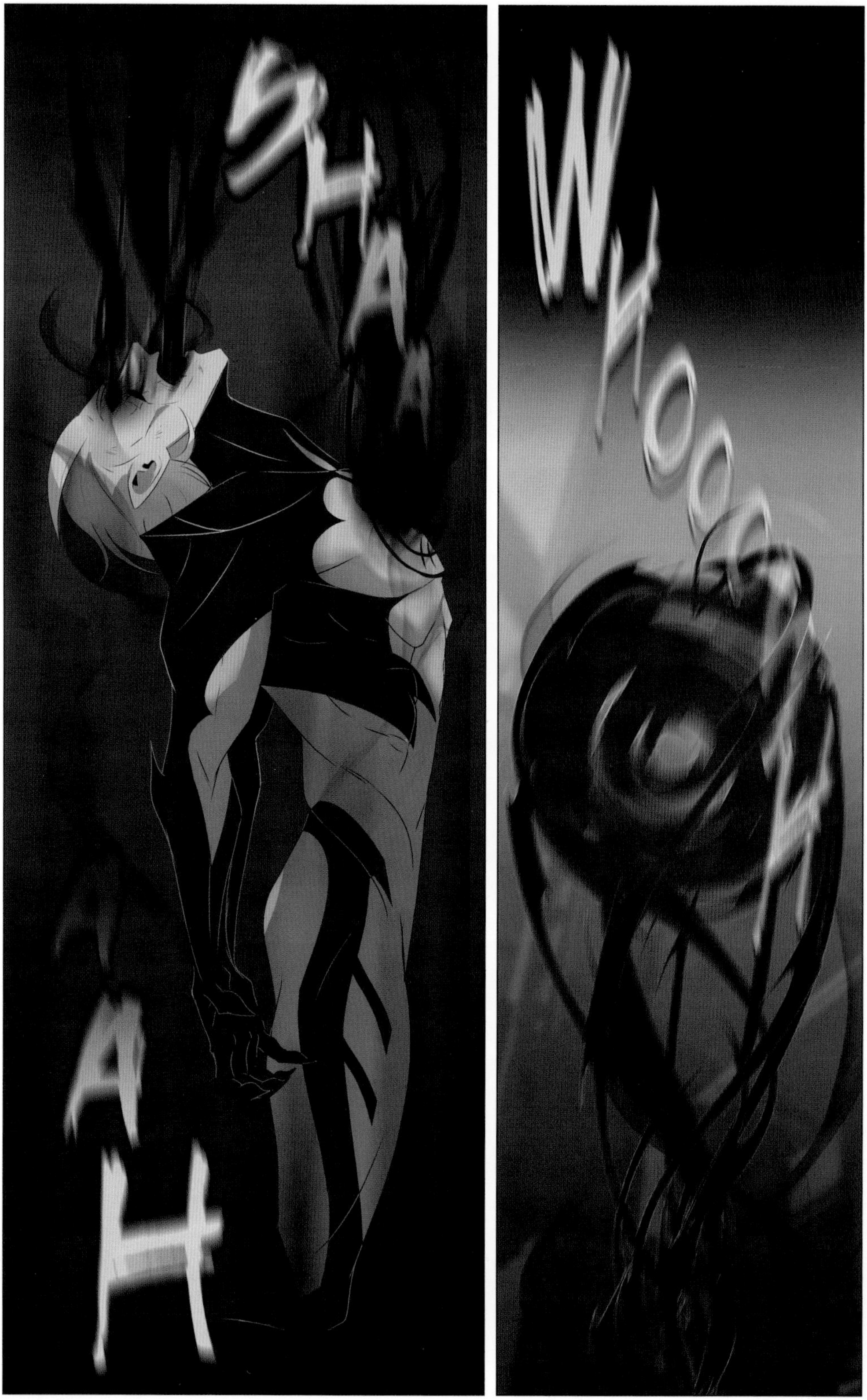
SHAAAH
WHOOOSH

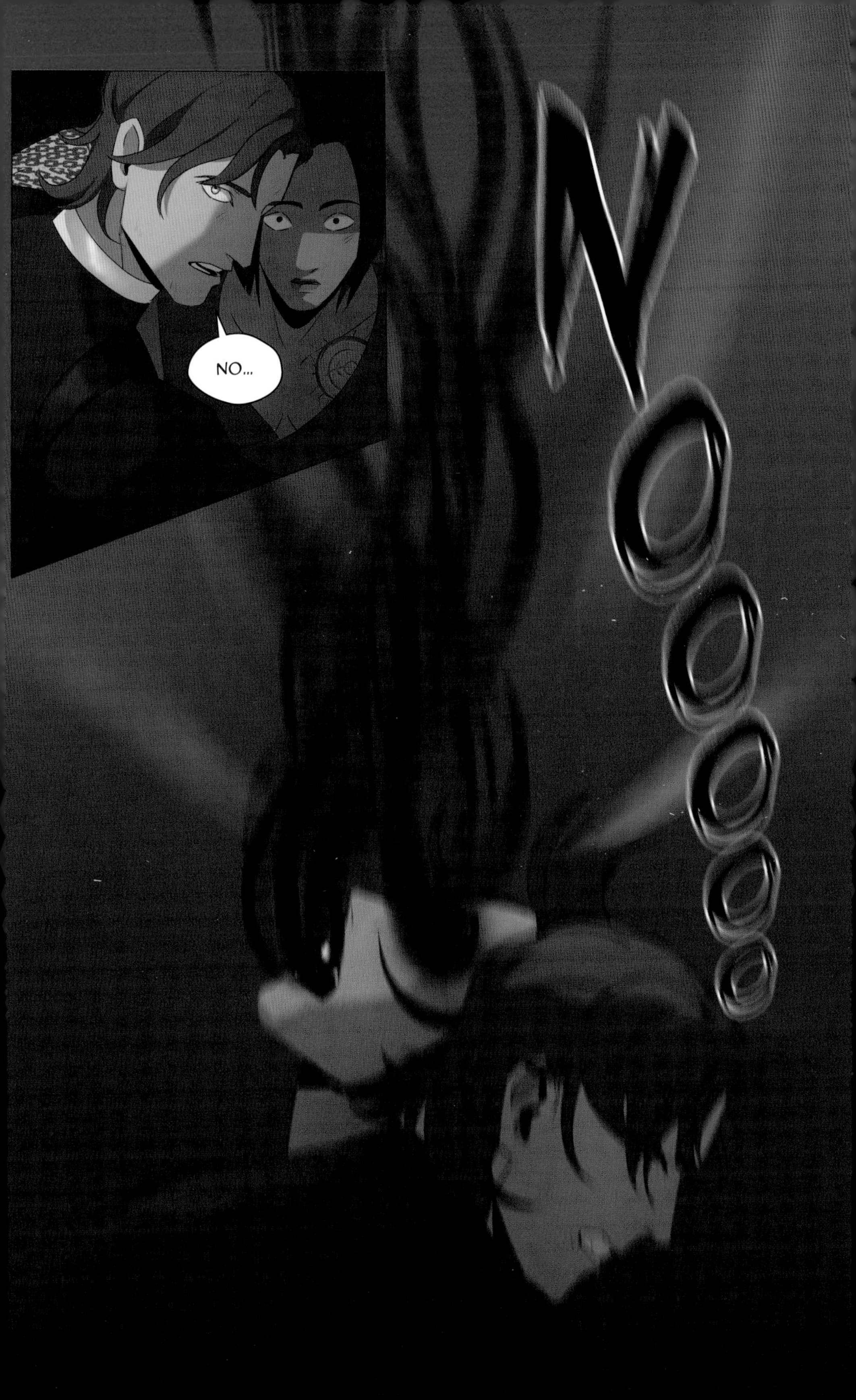
NO...
NOOOOOO

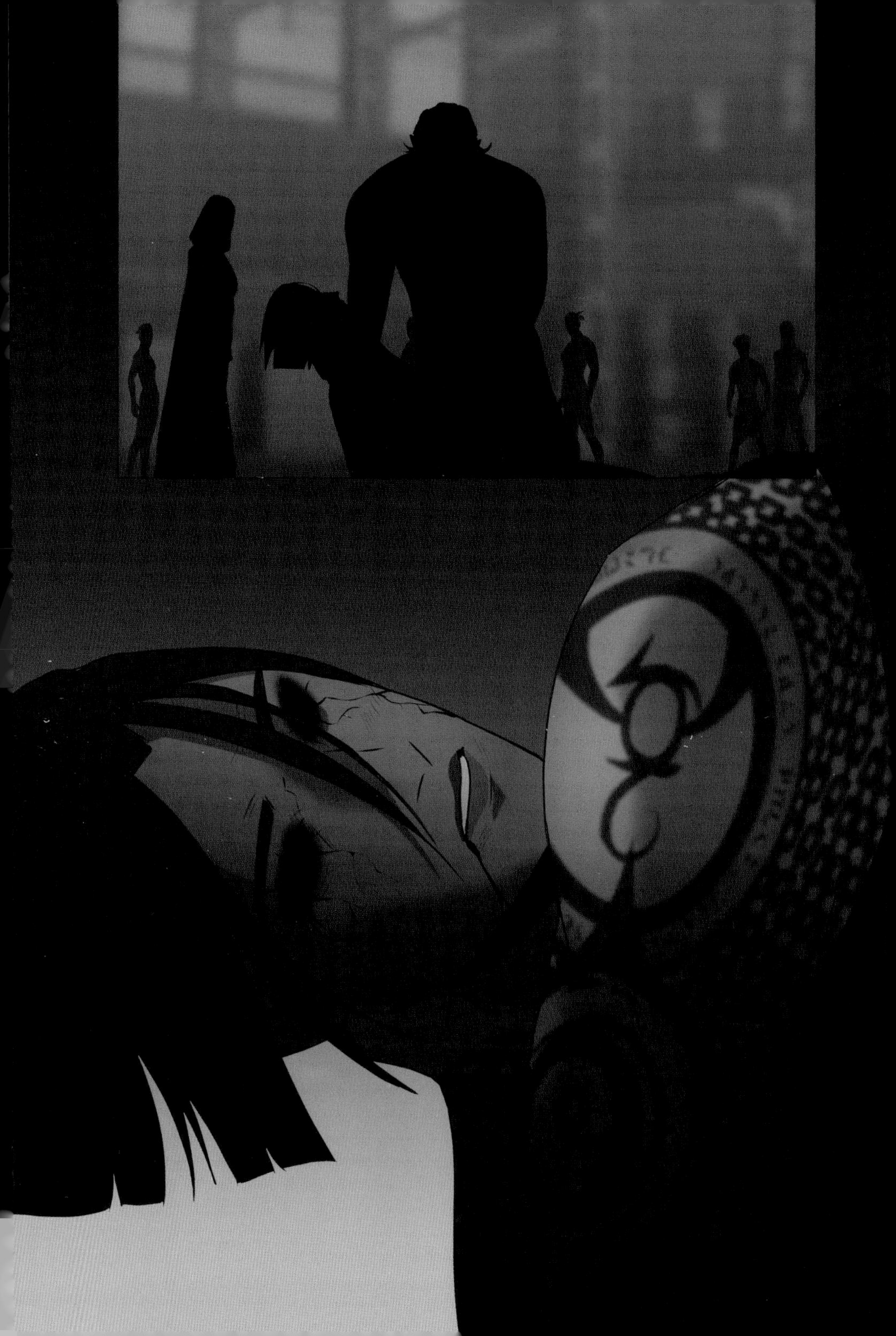

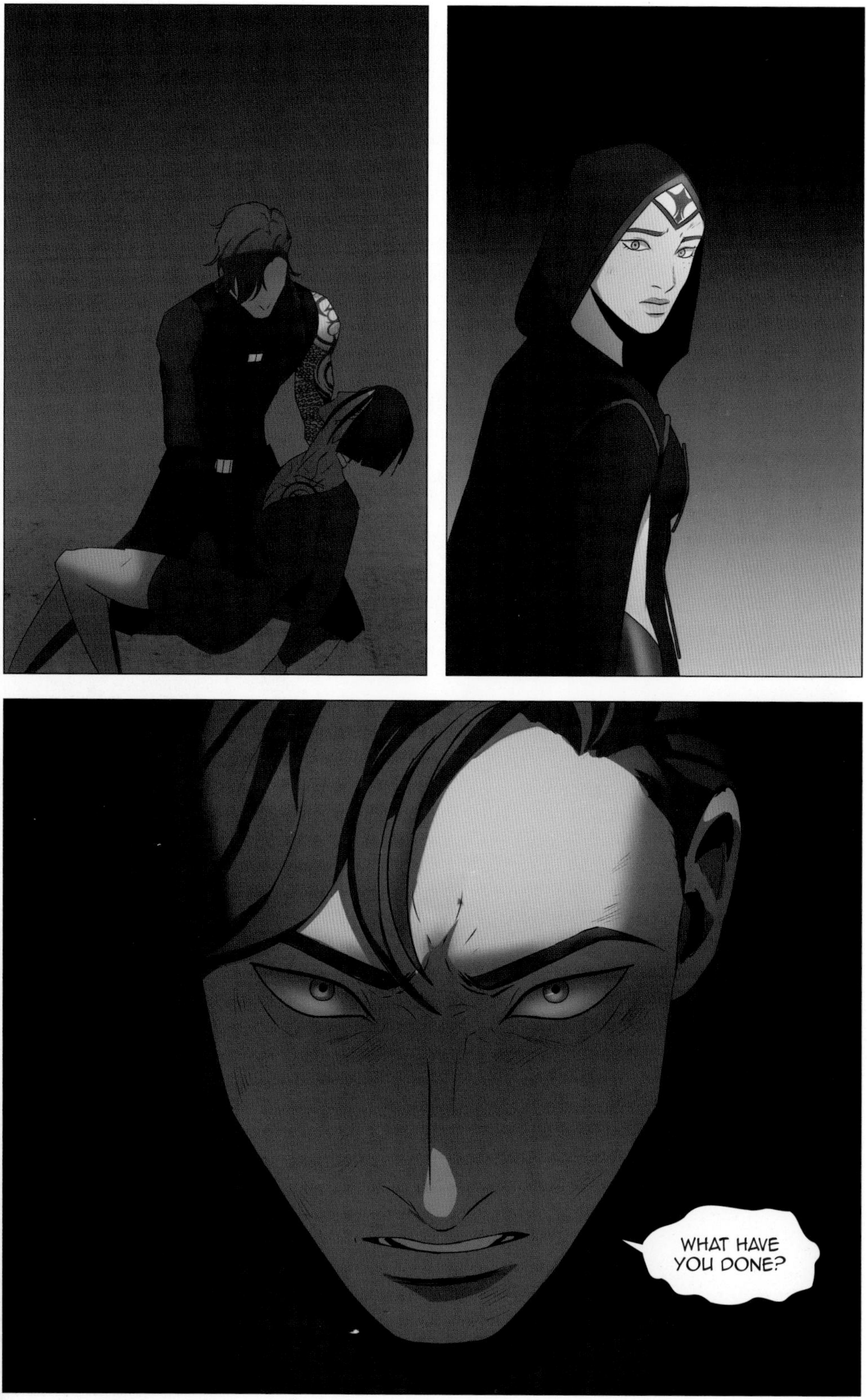
WHAT HAVE YOU DONE?

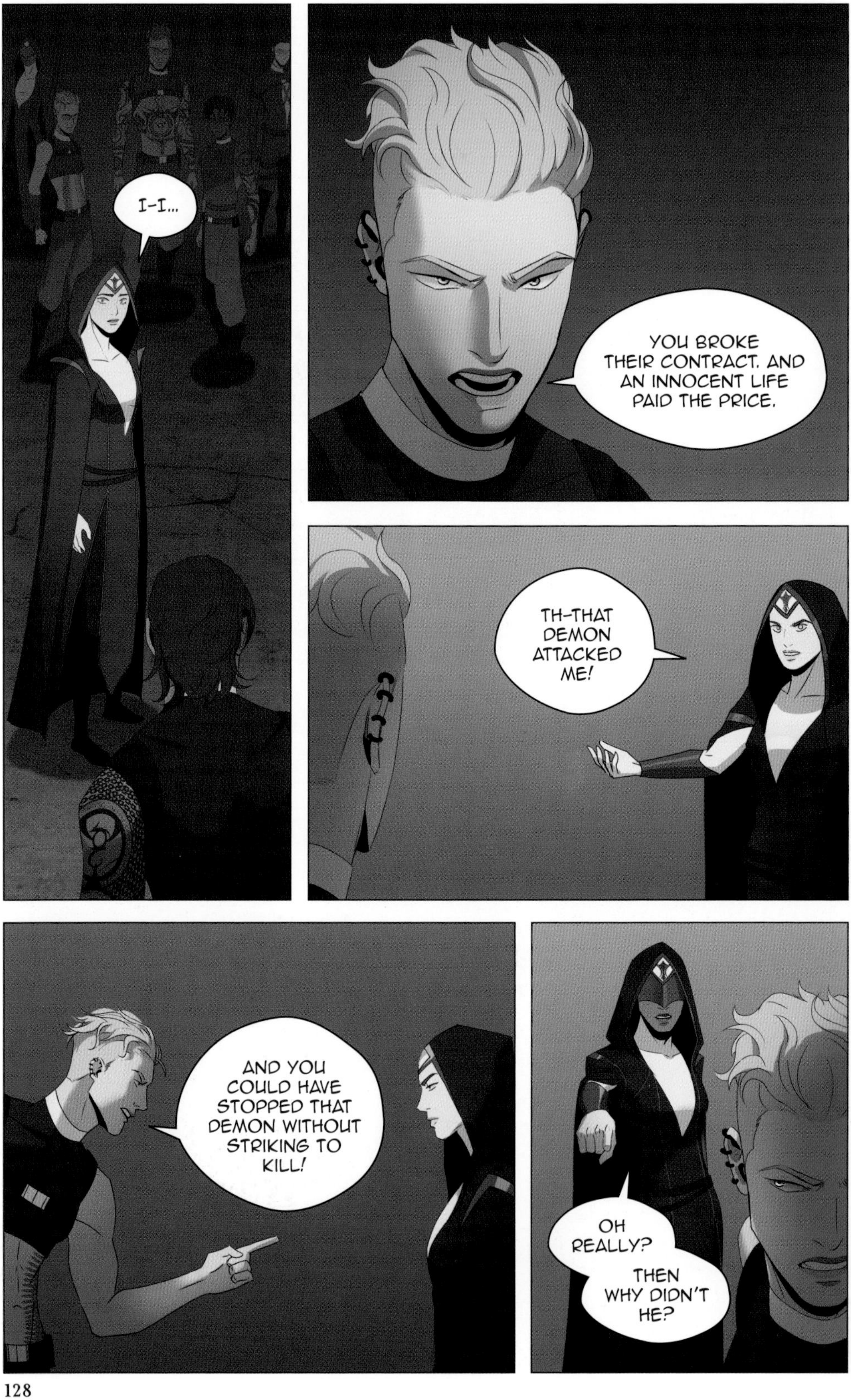
I-I...
YOU BROKE THEIR CONTRACT. AND AN INNOCENT LIFE PAID THE PRICE.
TH-THAT DEMON ATTACKED ME!
AND YOU COULD HAVE STOPPED THAT DEMON WITHOUT STRIKING TO KILL!
OH REALLY?
THEN WHY DIDN'T HE?

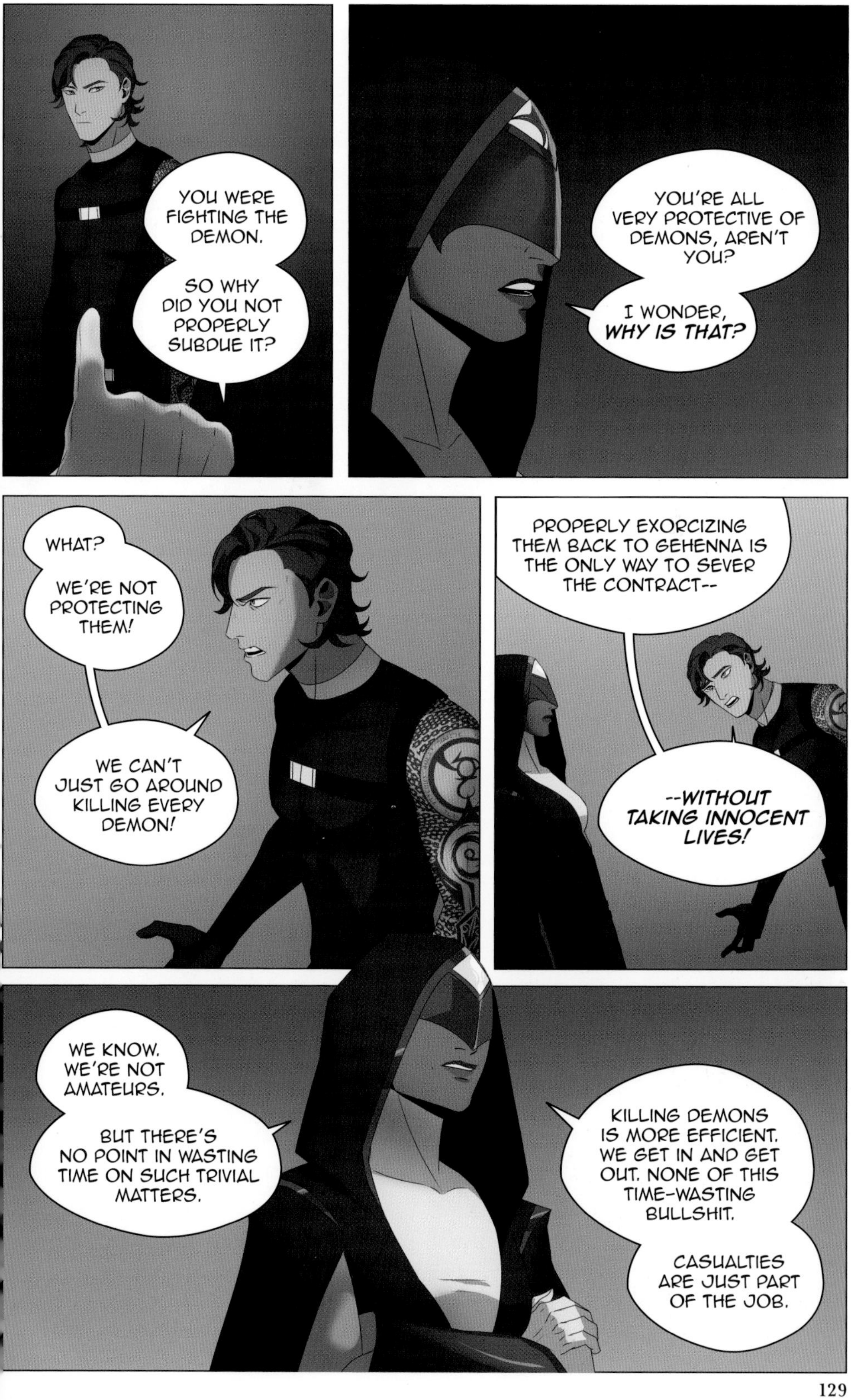
YOU WERE FIGHTING THE DEMON.
SO WHY DID YOU NOT PROPERLY SUBDUE IT?
YOU'RE ALL VERY PROTECTIVE OF DEMONS, AREN'T YOU?
I WONDER, *WHY IS THAT?*
WHAT?
WE'RE NOT PROTECTING THEM!
WE CAN'T JUST GO AROUND KILLING EVERY DEMON!
PROPERLY EXORCIZING THEM BACK TO GEHENNA IS THE ONLY WAY TO SEVER THE CONTRACT--
--WITHOUT TAKING INNOCENT LIVES!
WE KNOW. WE'RE NOT AMATEURS.
BUT THERE'S NO POINT IN WASTING TIME ON SUCH TRIVIAL MATTERS.
KILLING DEMONS IS MORE EFFICIENT. WE GET IN AND GET OUT. NONE OF THIS TIME-WASTING BULLSHIT.
CASUALTIES ARE JUST PART OF THE JOB.

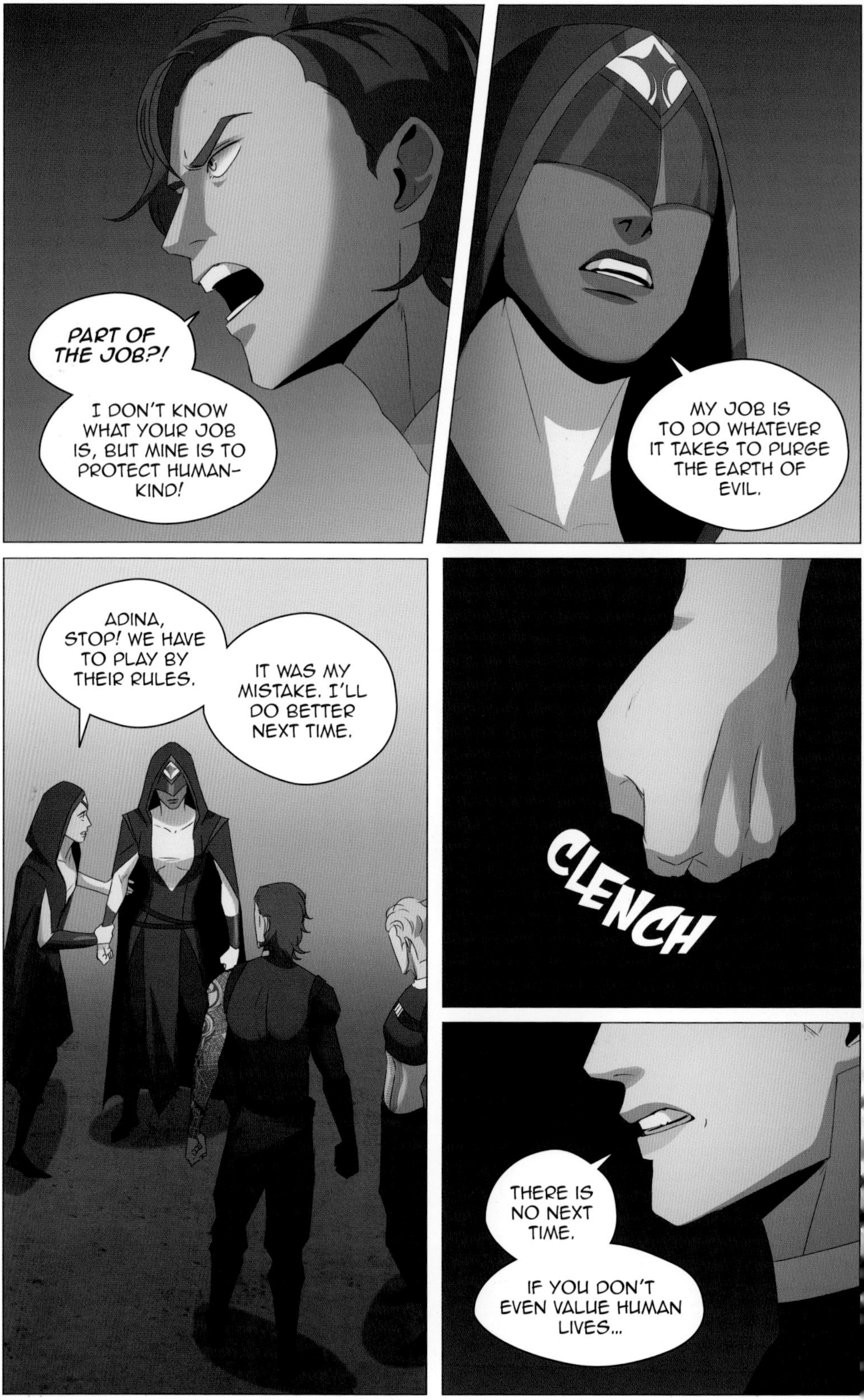
PART OF THE JOB?!
I DON'T KNOW WHAT YOUR JOB IS, BUT MINE IS TO PROTECT HUMAN-KIND!
MY JOB IS TO DO WHATEVER IT TAKES TO PURGE THE EARTH OF EVIL.
ADINA, STOP! WE HAVE TO PLAY BY THEIR RULES.
IT WAS MY MISTAKE. I'LL DO BETTER NEXT TIME.
CLENCH
THERE IS NO NEXT TIME.
IF YOU DON'T EVEN VALUE HUMAN LIVES...

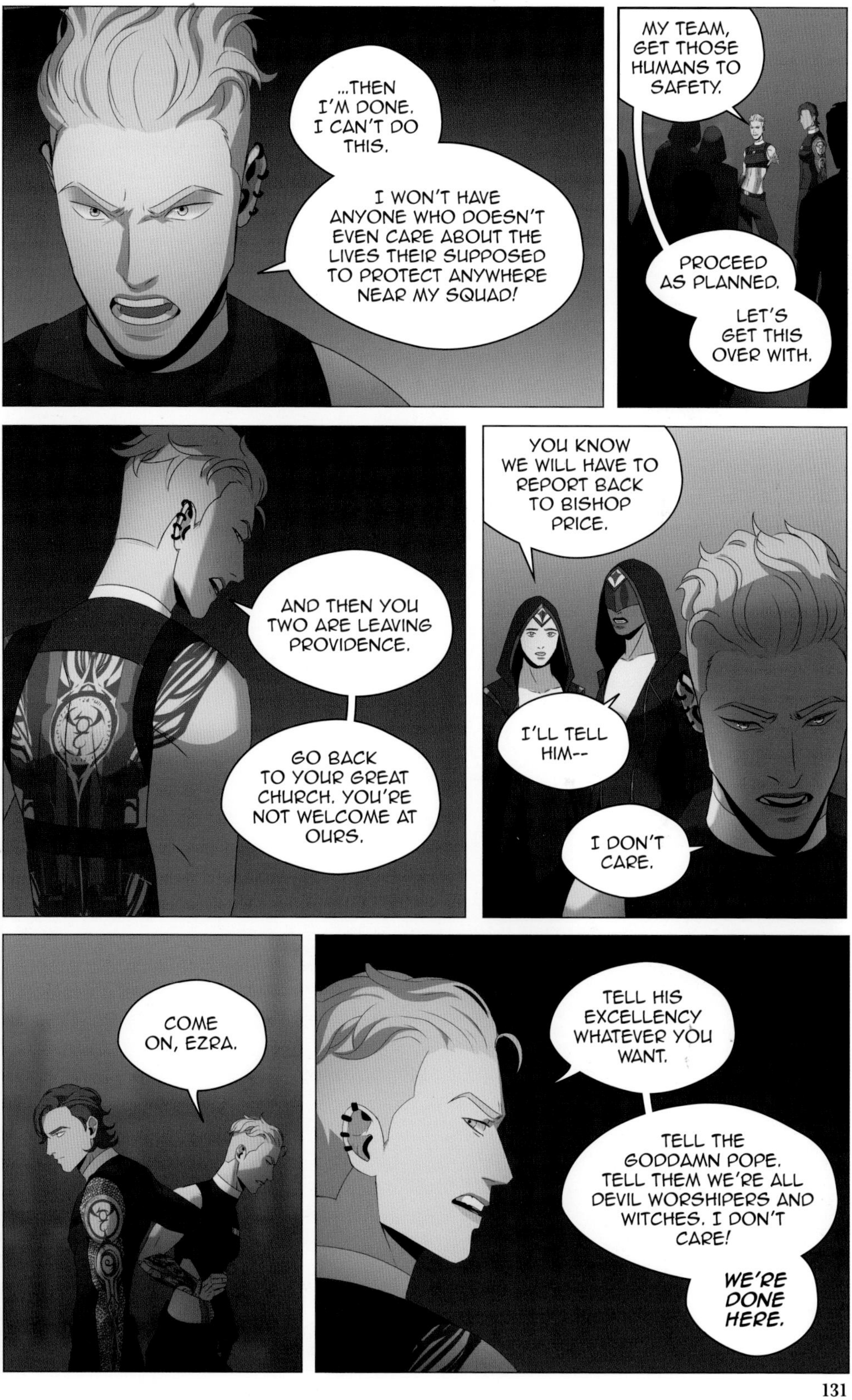

...THEN I'M DONE. I CAN'T DO THIS.
I WON'T HAVE ANYONE WHO DOESN'T EVEN CARE ABOUT THE LIVES THEIR SUPPOSED TO PROTECT ANYWHERE NEAR MY SQUAD!
MY TEAM, GET THOSE HUMANS TO SAFETY.
PROCEED AS PLANNED.
LET'S GET THIS OVER WITH.
AND THEN YOU TWO ARE LEAVING PROVIDENCE.
GO BACK TO YOUR GREAT CHURCH. YOU'RE NOT WELCOME AT OURS.
YOU KNOW WE WILL HAVE TO REPORT BACK TO BISHOP PRICE.
I'LL TELL HIM--
I DON'T CARE.
COME ON, EZRA.
TELL HIS EXCELLENCY WHATEVER YOU WANT.
TELL THE GODDAMN POPE. TELL THEM WE'RE ALL DEVIL WORSHIPERS AND WITCHES. I DON'T CARE!
WE'RE DONE HERE.

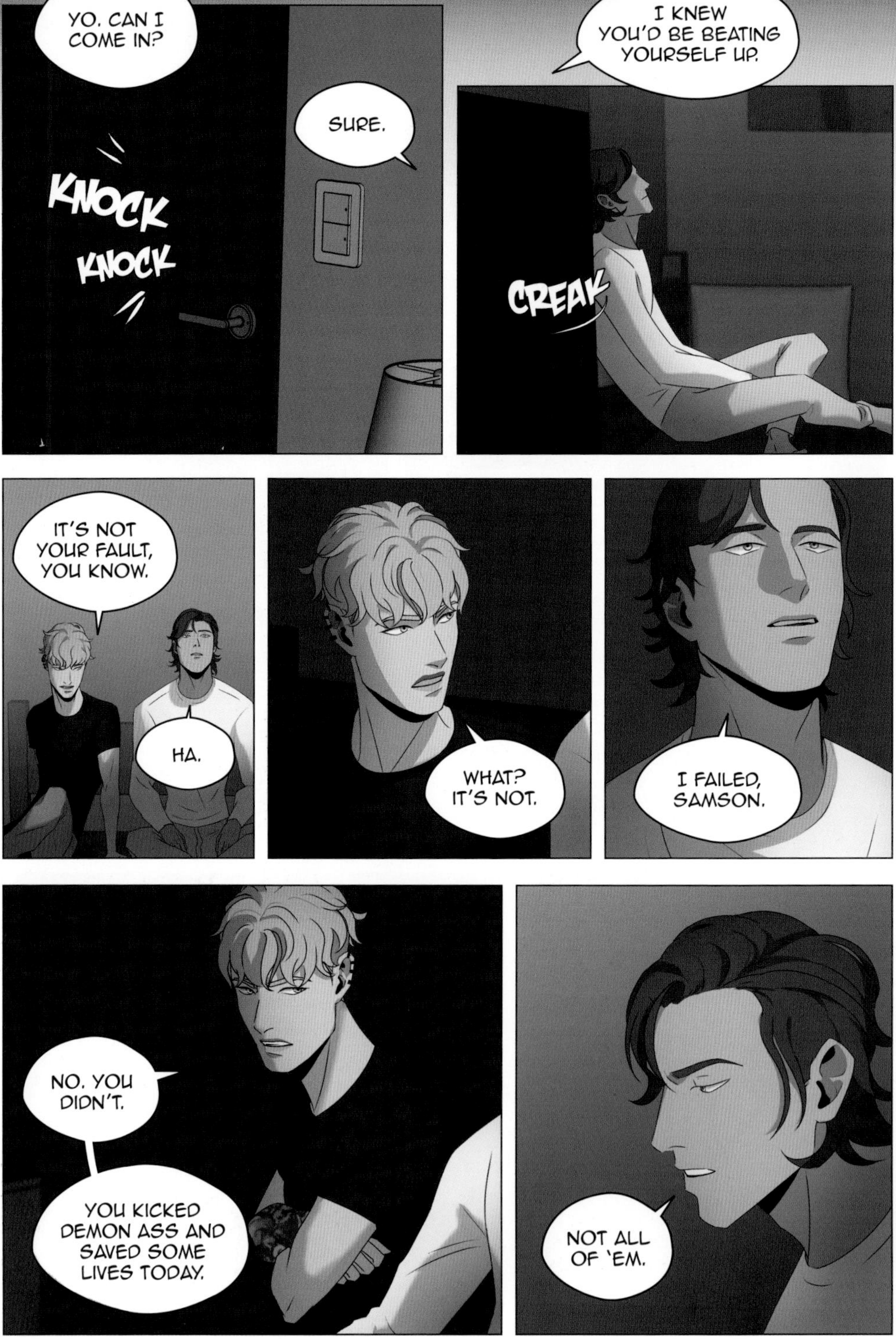
YO. CAN I COME IN?
KNOCK
KNOCK
SURE.
I KNEW YOU'D BE BEATING YOURSELF UP.
CREAK
IT'S NOT YOUR FAULT, YOU KNOW.
HA.
WHAT? IT'S NOT.
I FAILED, SAMSON.
NO. YOU DIDN'T.
YOU KICKED DEMON ASS AND SAVED SOME LIVES TODAY.
NOT ALL OF 'EM.

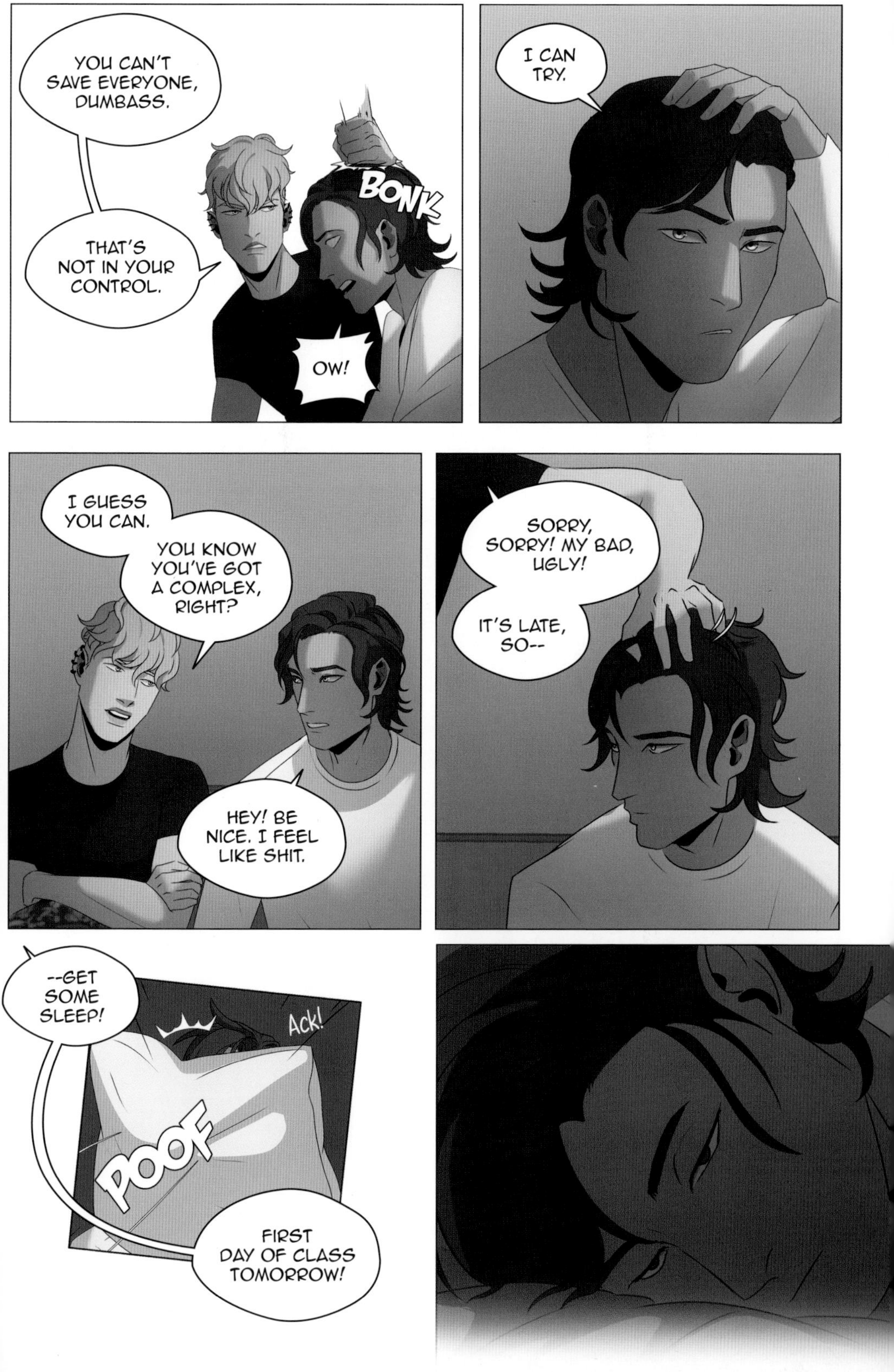
YOU CAN'T SAVE EVERYONE, DUMBASS.
THAT'S NOT IN YOUR CONTROL.
BONK
OW!
I CAN TRY.
I GUESS YOU CAN.
YOU KNOW YOU'VE GOT A COMPLEX, RIGHT?
HEY! BE NICE. I FEEL LIKE SHIT.
SORRY, SORRY! MY BAD, UGLY!
IT'S LATE, SO--
--GET SOME SLEEP!
Ack!
POOF
FIRST DAY OF CLASS TOMORROW!

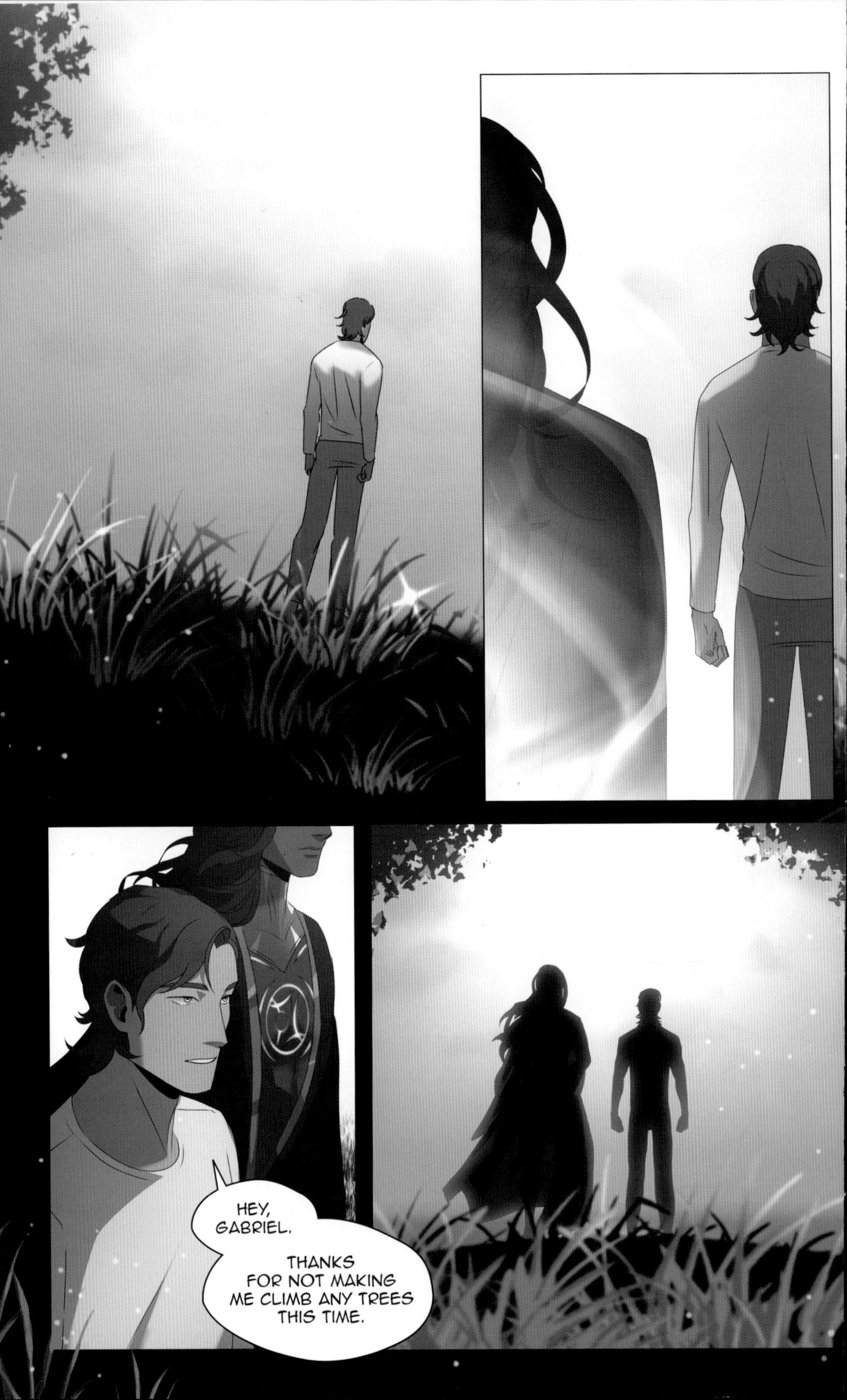
HEY, GABRIEL.
THANKS FOR NOT MAKING ME CLIMB ANY TREES THIS TIME.

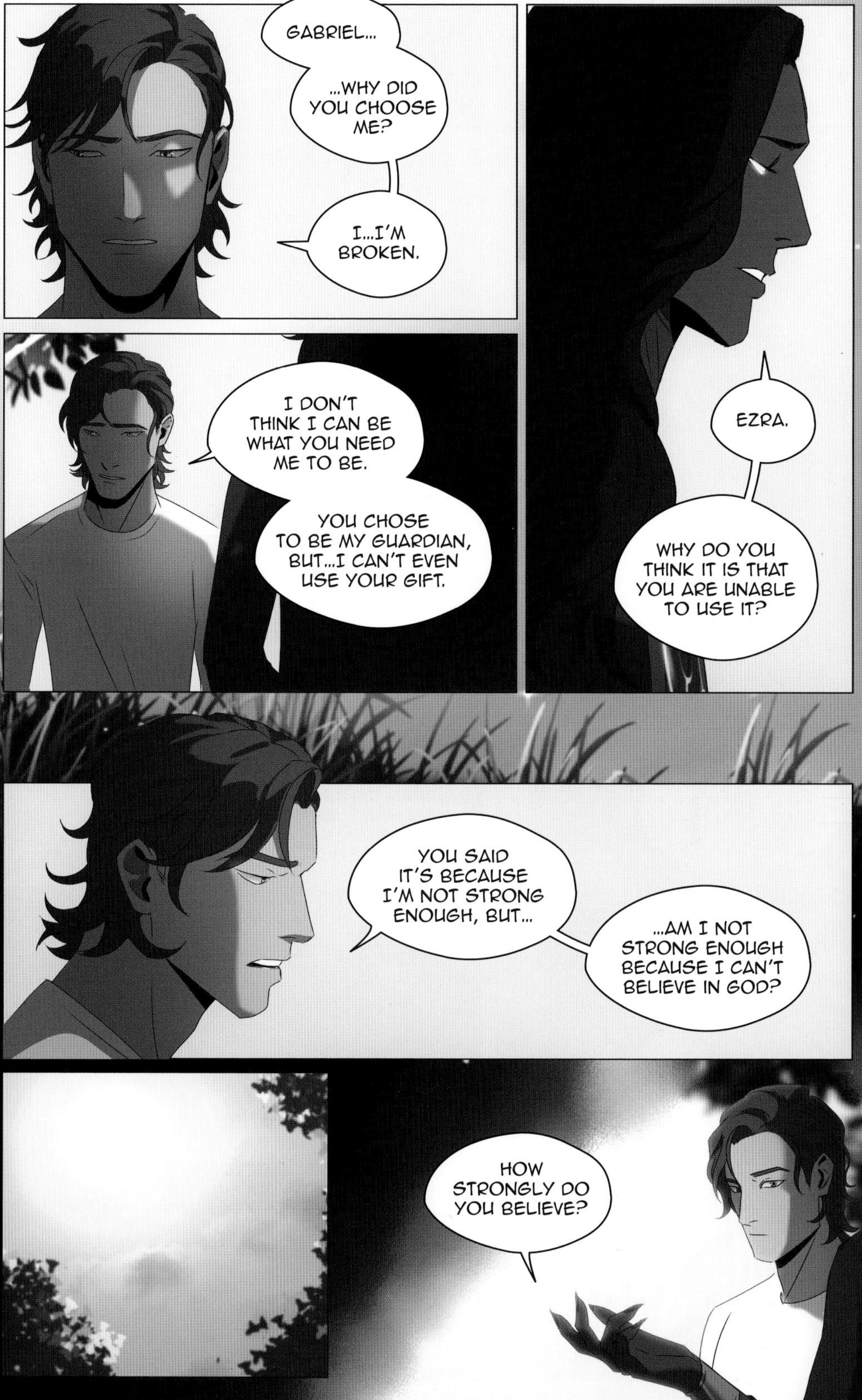
GABRIEL...
...WHY DID YOU CHOOSE ME?
I...I'M BROKEN.
EZRA.
I DON'T THINK I CAN BE WHAT YOU NEED ME TO BE.
YOU CHOSE TO BE MY GUARDIAN, BUT...I CAN'T EVEN USE YOUR GIFT.
WHY DO YOU THINK IT IS THAT YOU ARE UNABLE TO USE IT?
YOU SAID IT'S BECAUSE I'M NOT STRONG ENOUGH, BUT...
...AM I NOT STRONG ENOUGH BECAUSE I CAN'T BELIEVE IN GOD?
HOW STRONGLY DO YOU BELIEVE?

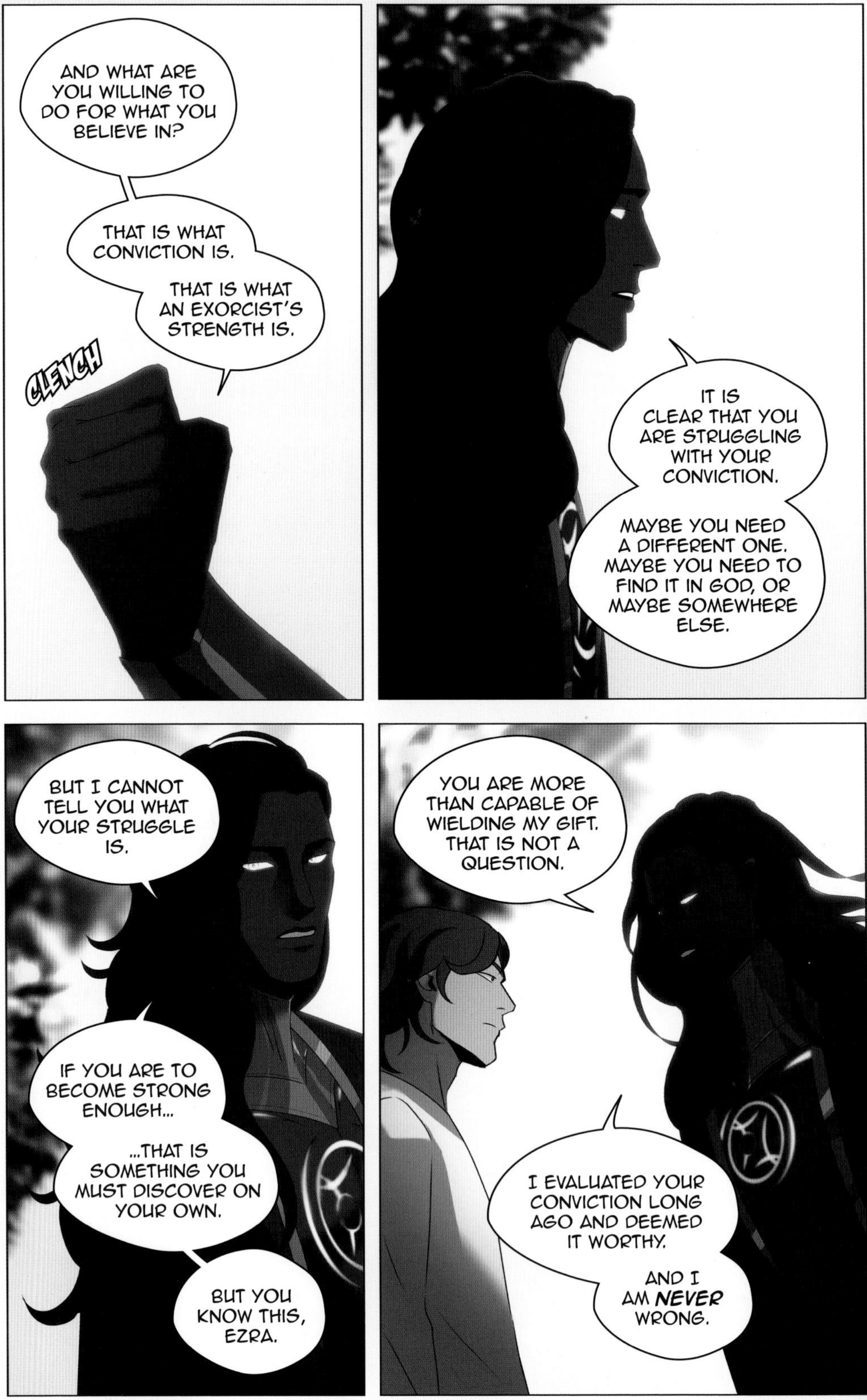
AND WHAT ARE YOU WILLING TO DO FOR WHAT YOU BELIEVE IN?
THAT IS WHAT CONVICTION IS.
THAT IS WHAT AN EXORCIST'S STRENGTH IS.
CLENCH
IT IS CLEAR THAT YOU ARE STRUGGLING WITH YOUR CONVICTION.
MAYBE YOU NEED A DIFFERENT ONE. MAYBE YOU NEED TO FIND IT IN GOD, OR MAYBE SOMEWHERE ELSE.
BUT I CANNOT TELL YOU WHAT YOUR STRUGGLE IS.
IF YOU ARE TO BECOME STRONG ENOUGH...
...THAT IS SOMETHING YOU MUST DISCOVER ON YOUR OWN.
BUT YOU KNOW THIS, EZRA.
YOU ARE MORE THAN CAPABLE OF WIELDING MY GIFT. THAT IS NOT A QUESTION.
I EVALUATED YOUR CONVICTION LONG AGO AND DEEMED IT WORTHY.
AND I AM ***NEVER*** WRONG.

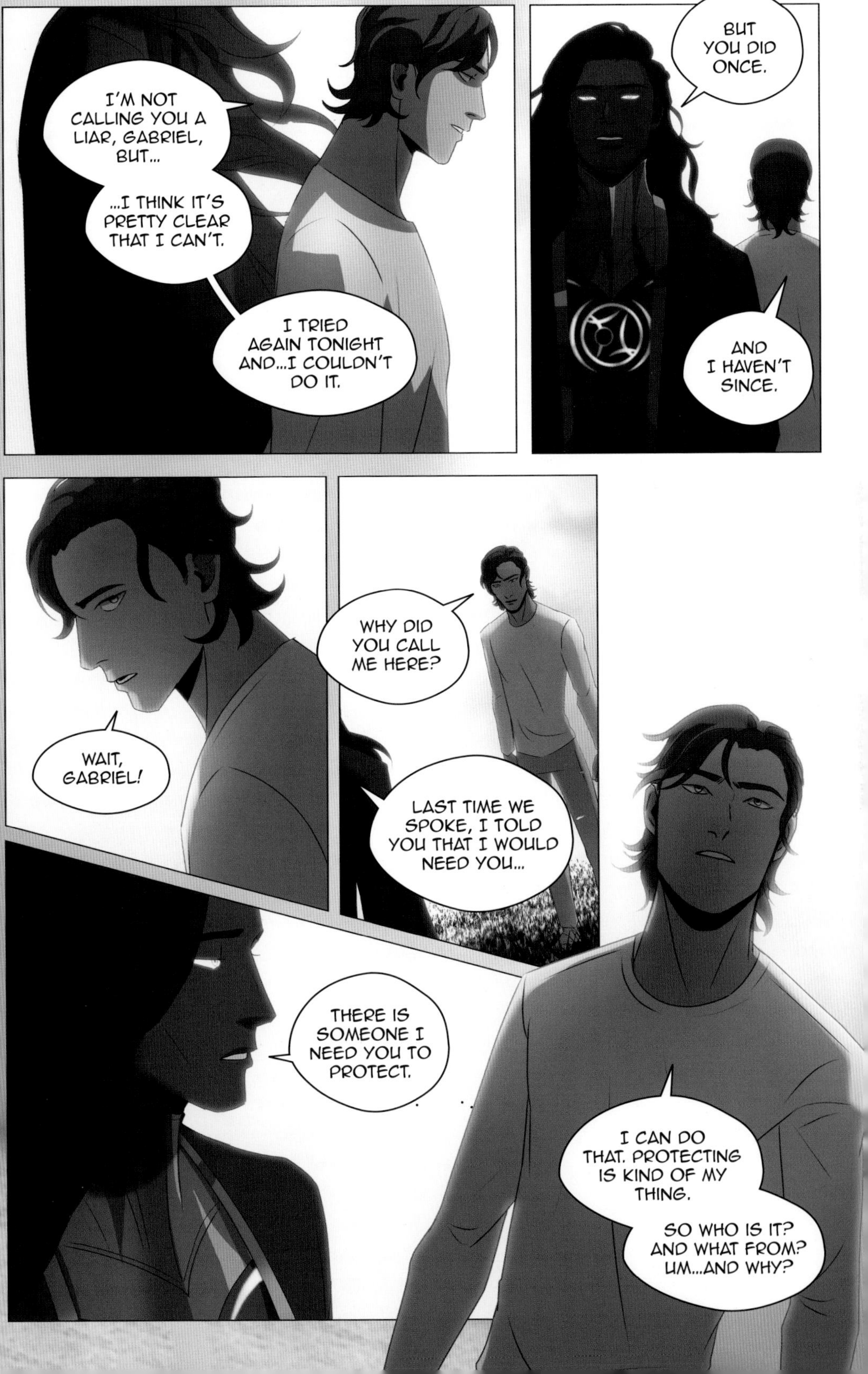
I'M NOT CALLING YOU A LIAR, GABRIEL, BUT...
...I THINK IT'S PRETTY CLEAR THAT I CAN'T.
I TRIED AGAIN TONIGHT AND...I COULDN'T DO IT.
BUT YOU DID ONCE.
AND I HAVEN'T SINCE.
WAIT, GABRIEL!
WHY DID YOU CALL ME HERE?
LAST TIME WE SPOKE, I TOLD YOU THAT I WOULD NEED YOU...
THERE IS SOMEONE I NEED YOU TO PROTECT.
I CAN DO THAT. PROTECTING IS KIND OF MY THING.
SO WHO IS IT? AND WHAT FROM? UM...AND WHY?

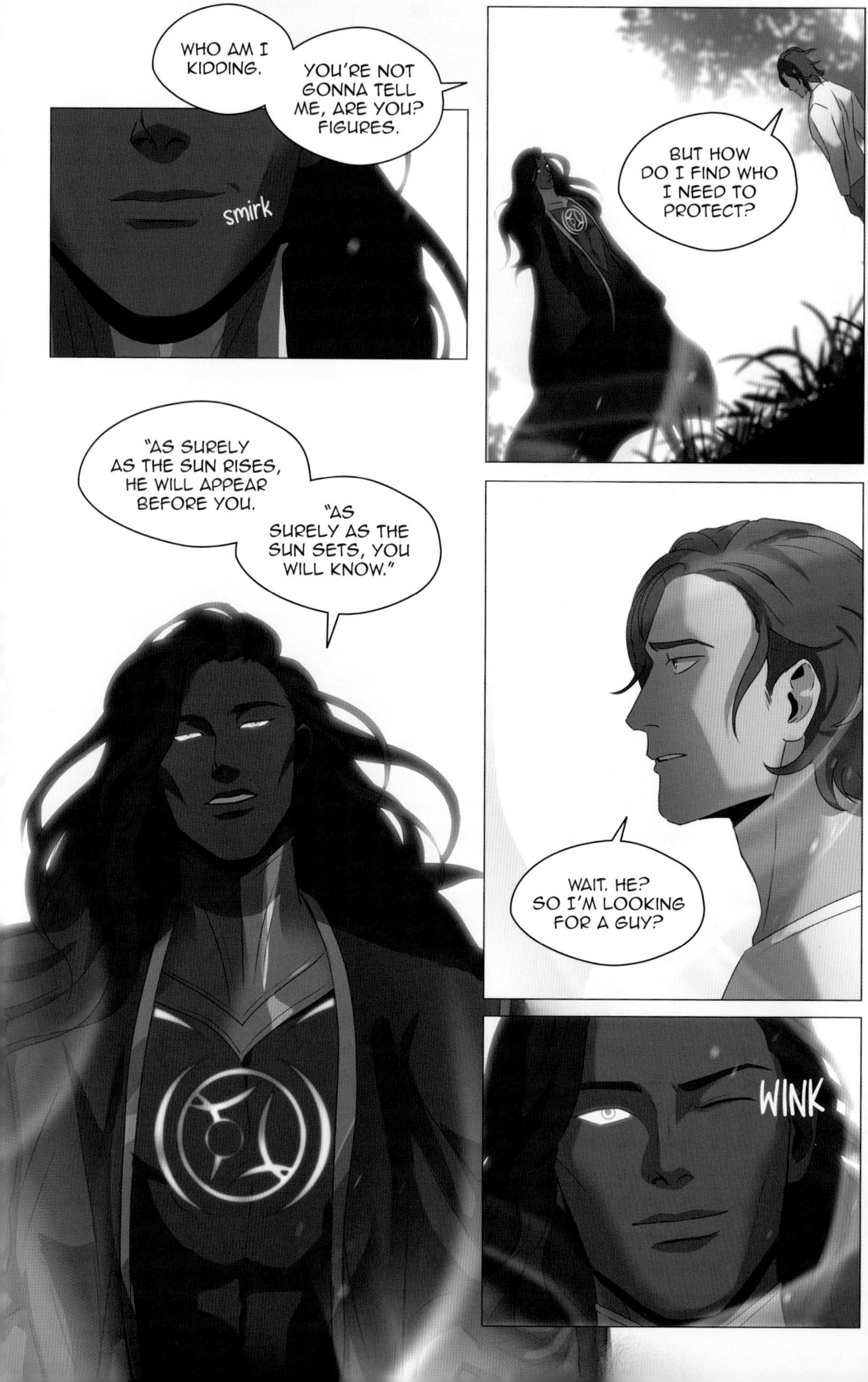
WHO AM I KIDDING.
YOU'RE NOT GONNA TELL ME, ARE YOU? FIGURES.
smirk
BUT HOW DO I FIND WHO I NEED TO PROTECT?
"AS SURELY AS THE SUN RISES, HE WILL APPEAR BEFORE YOU.
"AS SURELY AS THE SUN SETS, YOU WILL KNOW."
WAIT. HE? SO I'M LOOKING FOR A GUY?
WINK

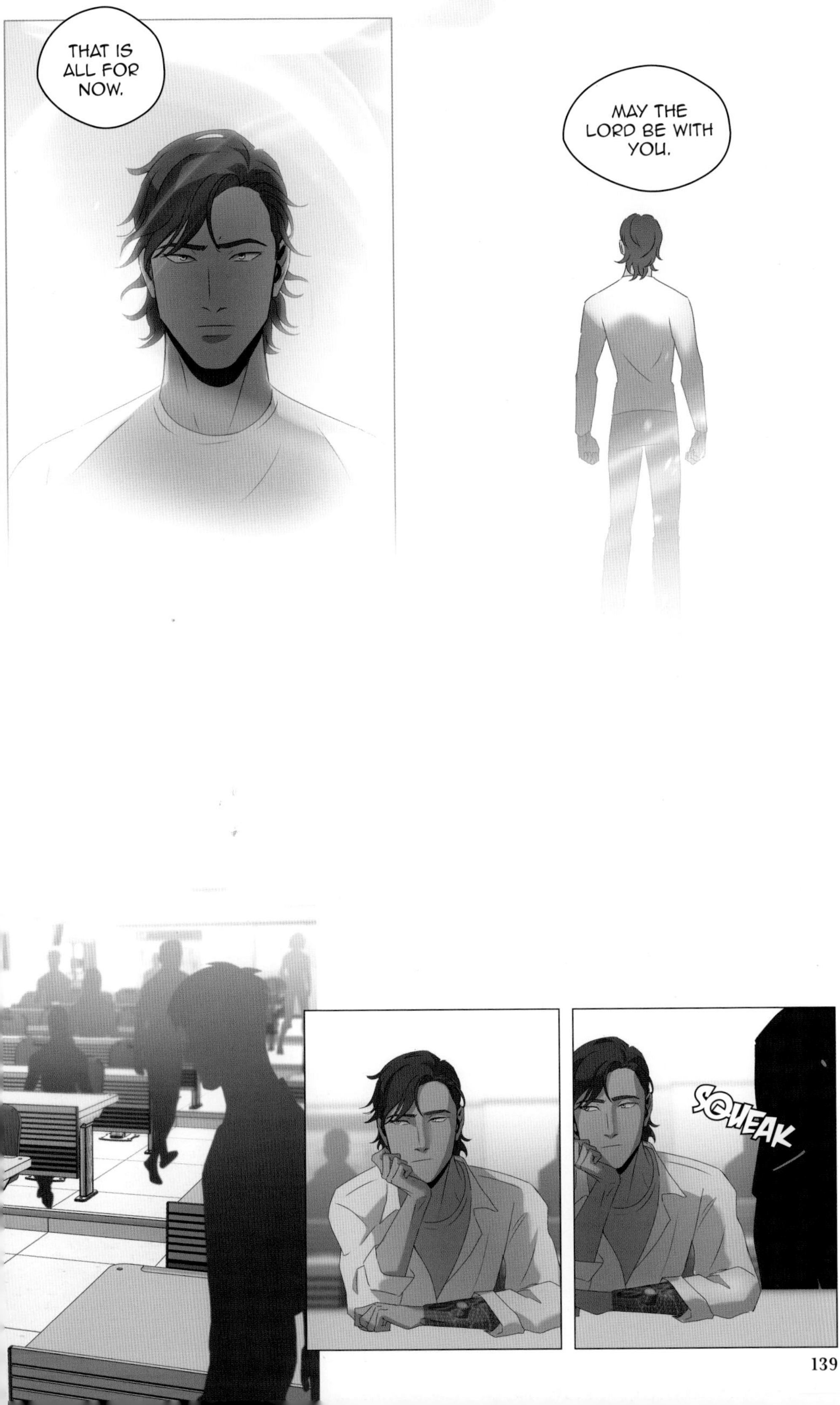
THAT IS ALL FOR NOW.
MAY THE LORD BE WITH YOU.
SQUEAK

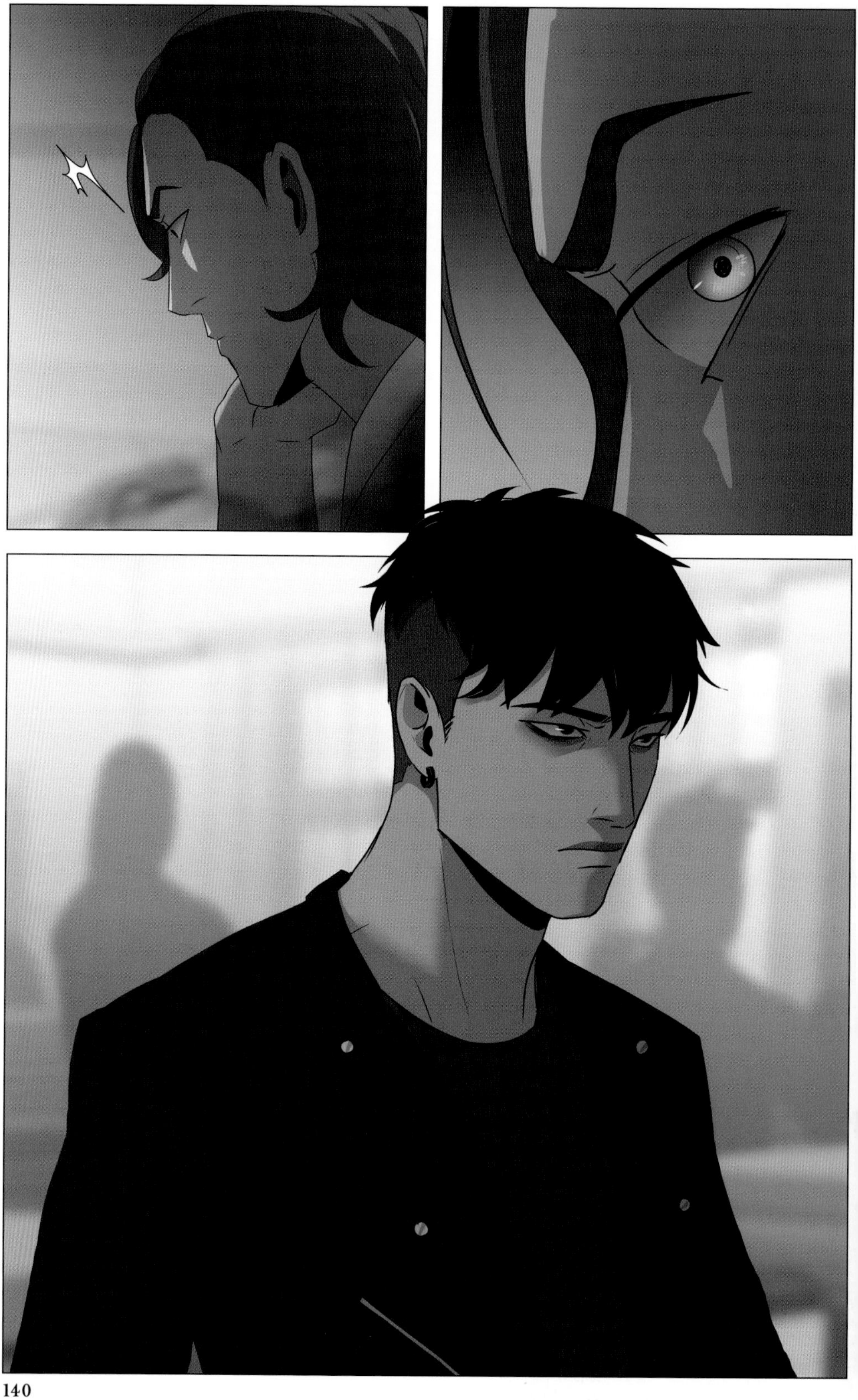

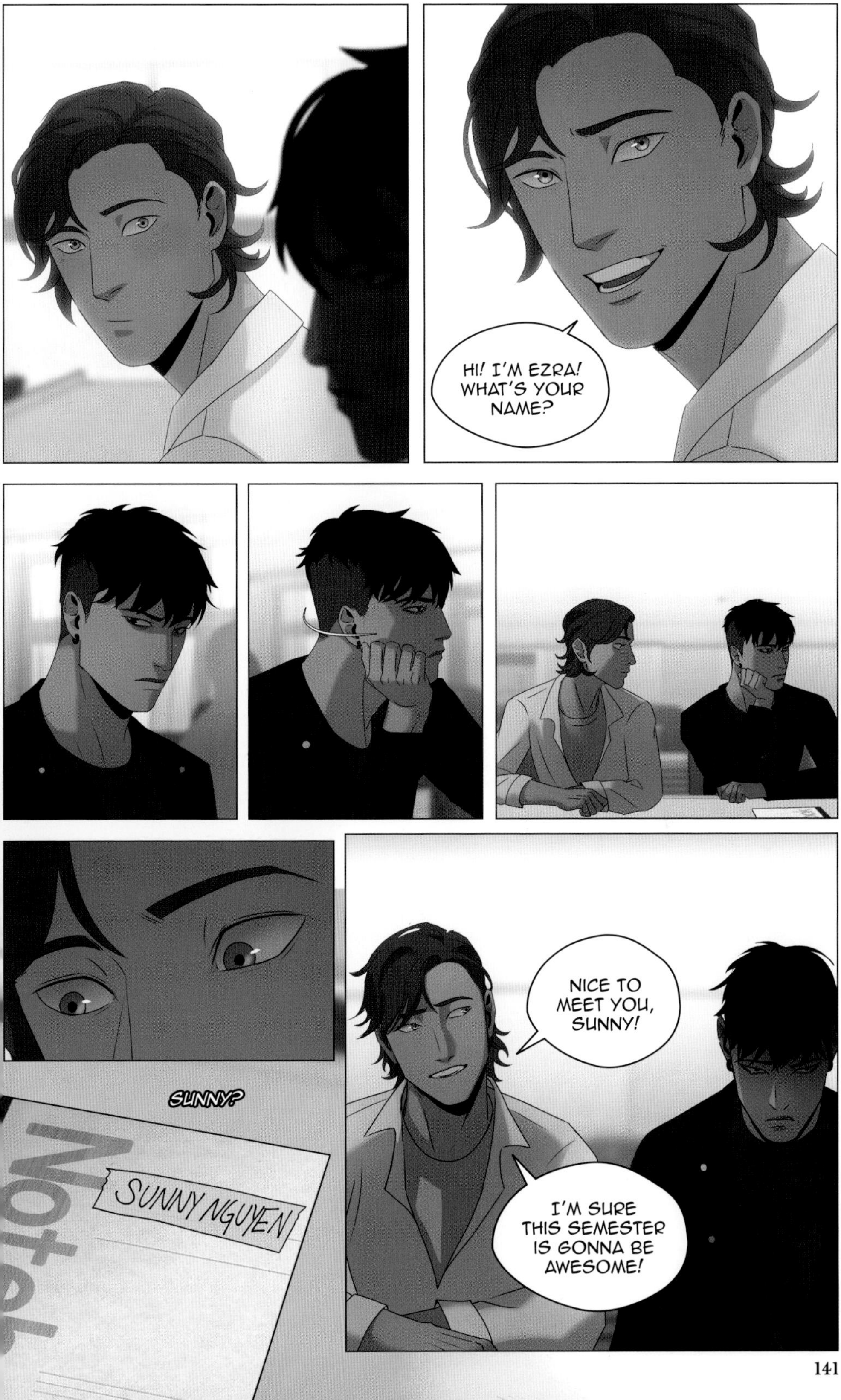
HI! I'M EZRA! WHAT'S YOUR NAME?
SUNNY?
SUNNY NGUYEN
NICE TO MEET YOU, SUNNY!
I'M SURE THIS SEMESTER IS GONNA BE AWESOME!

BOOK V

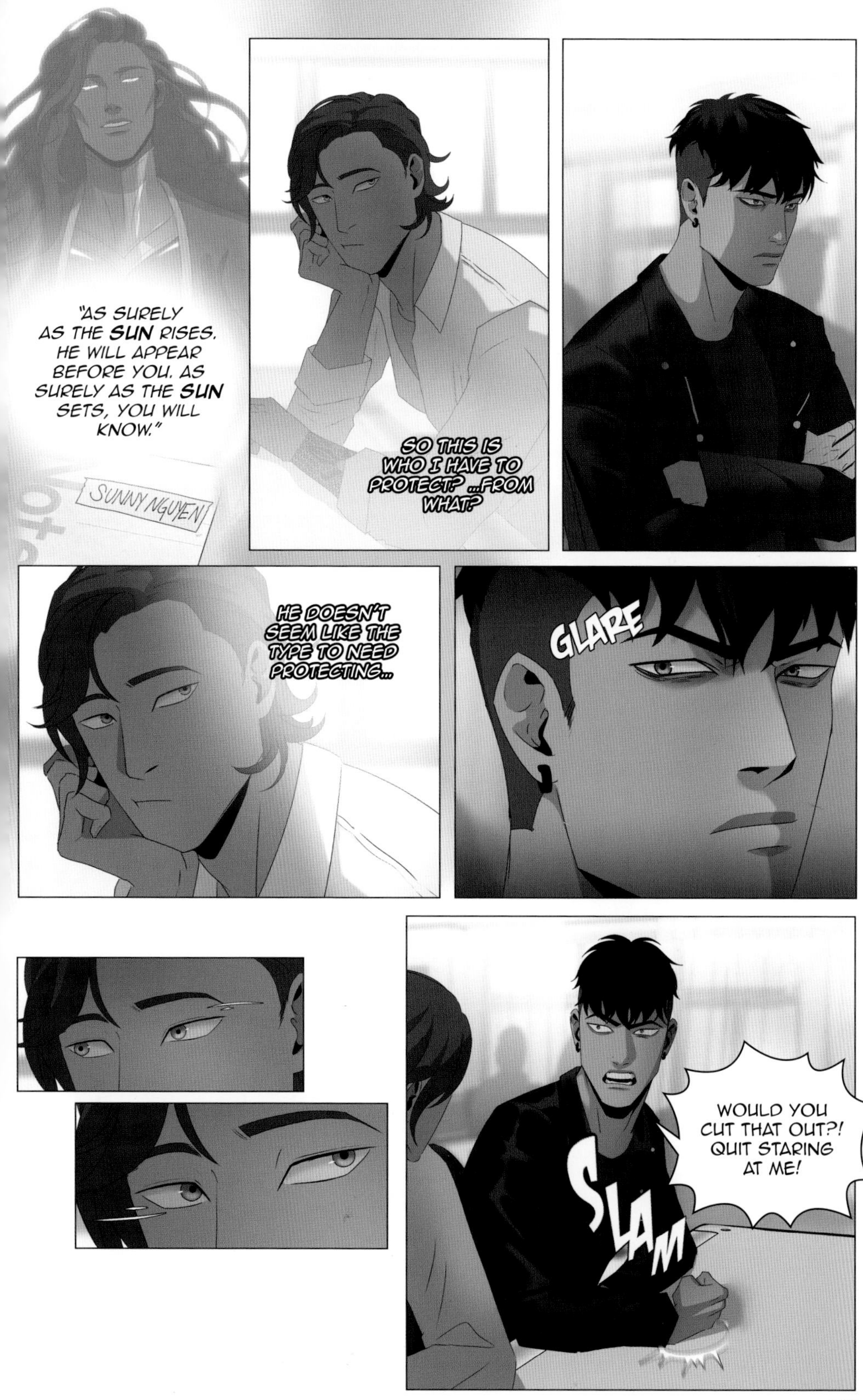
"AS SURELY AS THE SUN RISES, HE WILL APPEAR BEFORE YOU. AS SURELY AS THE SUN SETS, YOU WILL KNOW."
SUNNY NGUYEN
SO THIS IS WHO I HAVE TO PROTECT? ...FROM WHAT?
HE DOESN'T SEEM LIKE THE TYPE TO NEED PROTECTING...
GLARE
WOULD YOU CUT THAT OUT?! QUIT STARING AT ME!
SLAM

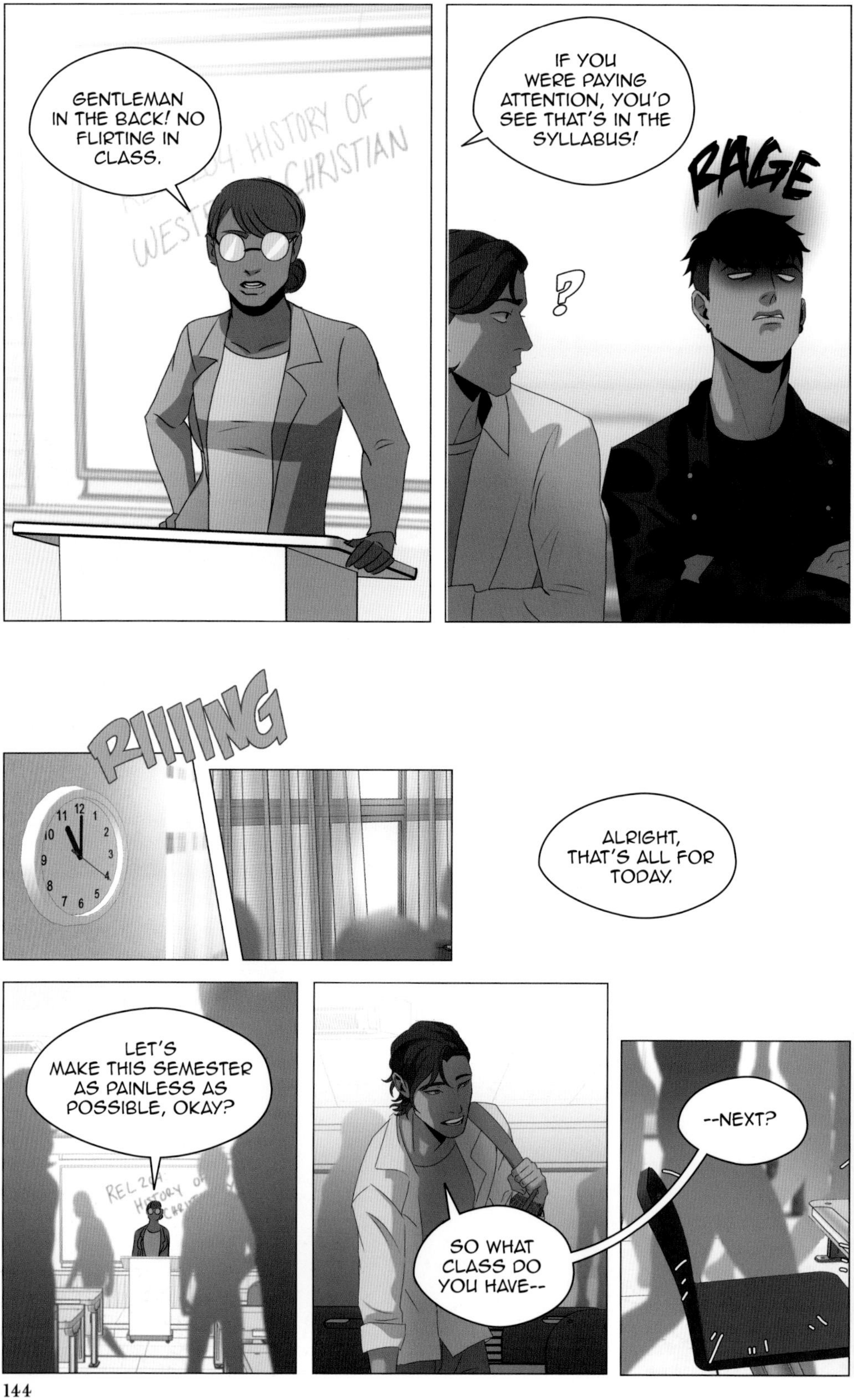
GENTLEMAN IN THE BACK! NO FLIRTING IN CLASS.
IF YOU WERE PAYING ATTENTION, YOU'D SEE THAT'S IN THE SYLLABUS!
RAGE
?
RIIING
ALRIGHT, THAT'S ALL FOR TODAY.
LET'S MAKE THIS SEMESTER AS PAINLESS AS POSSIBLE, OKAY?
SO WHAT CLASS DO YOU HAVE--
--NEXT?

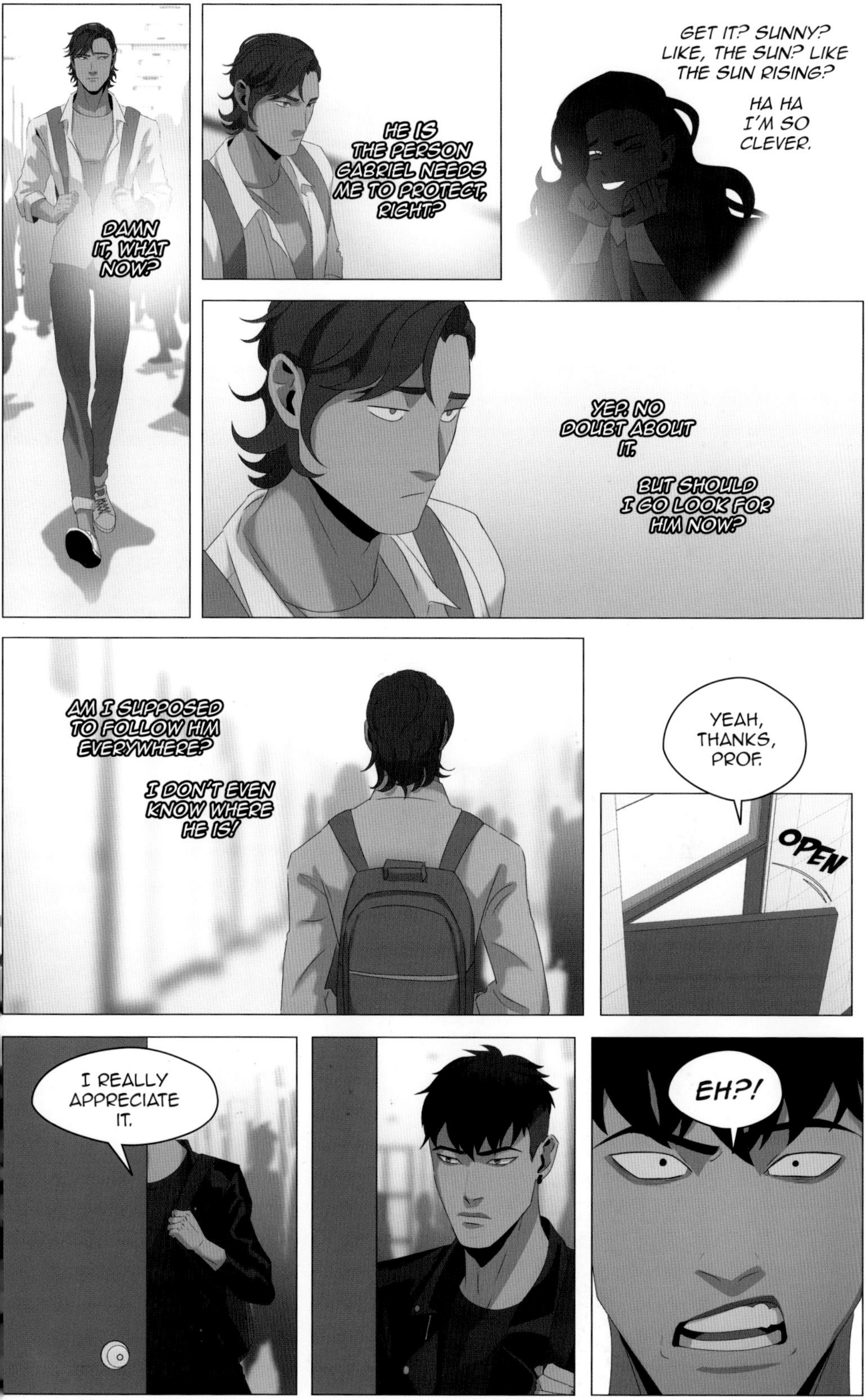
DAMN IT, WHAT NOW?
HE IS THE PERSON GABRIEL NEEDS ME TO PROTECT, RIGHT?
GET IT? SUNNY? LIKE, THE SUN? LIKE THE SUN RISING?
HA HA I'M SO CLEVER.
YEP. NO DOUBT ABOUT IT.
BUT SHOULD I GO LOOK FOR HIM NOW?
AM I SUPPOSED TO FOLLOW HIM EVERYWHERE?
I DON'T EVEN KNOW WHERE HE IS!
YEAH, THANKS, PROF.
OPEN
I REALLY APPRECIATE IT.
EH?!

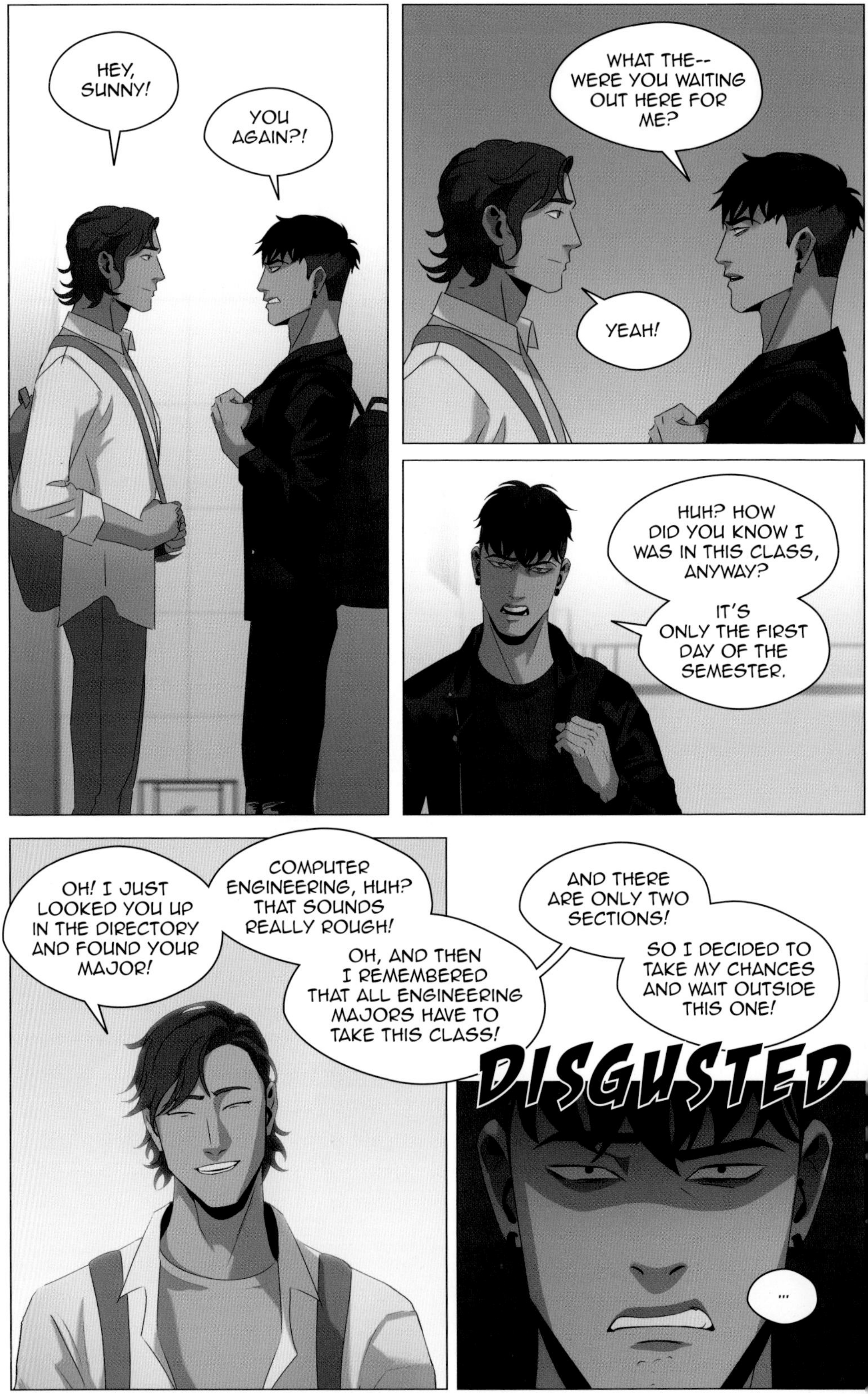
HEY, SUNNY!
YOU AGAIN?!
WHAT THE-- WERE YOU WAITING OUT HERE FOR ME?
YEAH!
HUH? HOW DID YOU KNOW I WAS IN THIS CLASS, ANYWAY?
IT'S ONLY THE FIRST DAY OF THE SEMESTER.
OH! I JUST LOOKED YOU UP IN THE DIRECTORY AND FOUND YOUR MAJOR!
COMPUTER ENGINEERING, HUH? THAT SOUNDS REALLY ROUGH!
OH, AND THEN I REMEMBERED THAT ALL ENGINEERING MAJORS HAVE TO TAKE THIS CLASS!
AND THERE ARE ONLY TWO SECTIONS!
SO I DECIDED TO TAKE MY CHANCES AND WAIT OUTSIDE THIS ONE!
DISGUSTED
...

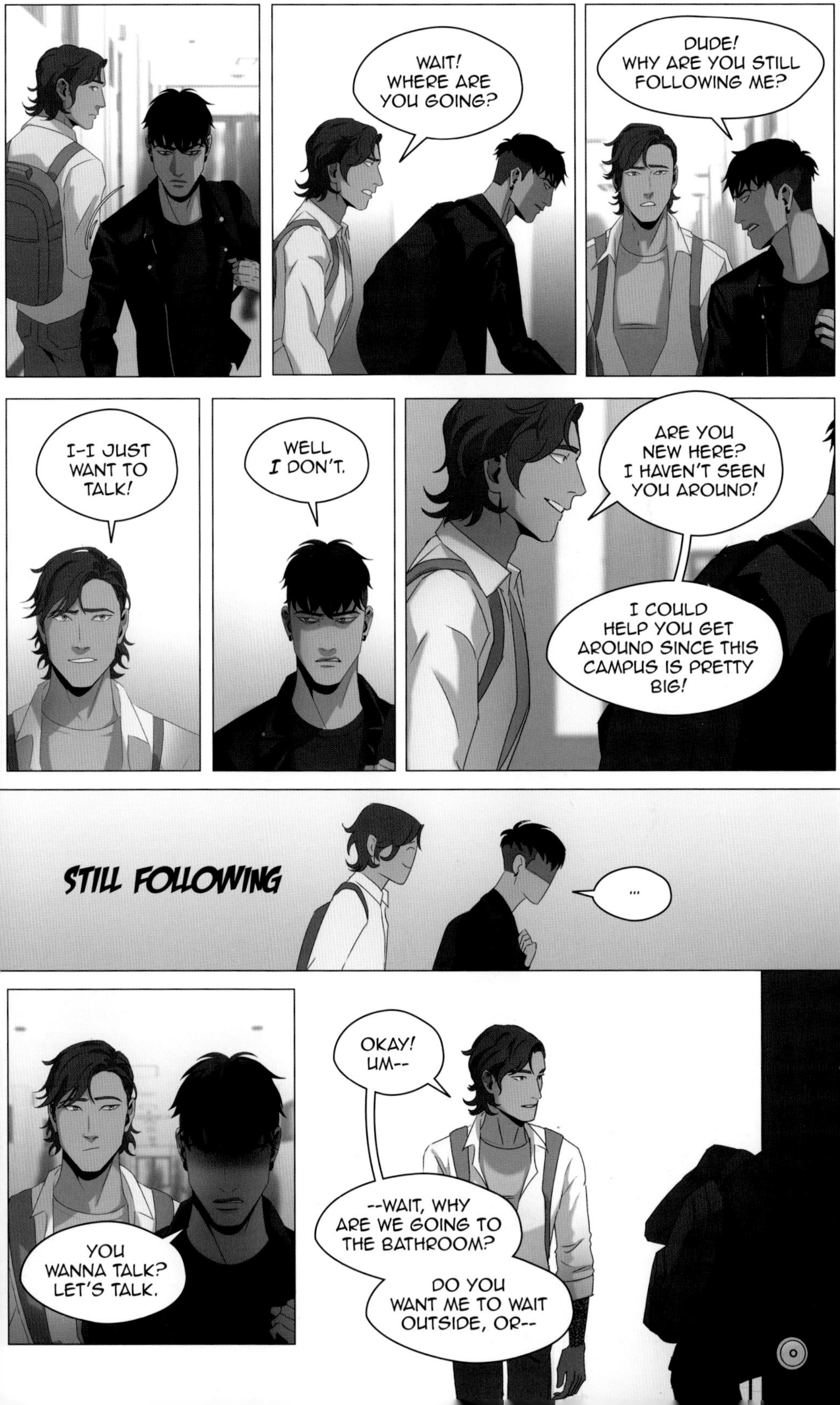
WAIT!
WHERE ARE
YOU GOING?
DUDE!
WHY ARE YOU STILL
FOLLOWING ME?
I-I JUST
WANT TO
TALK!
WELL
I DON'T.
ARE YOU
NEW HERE?
I HAVEN'T SEEN
YOU AROUND!
I COULD
HELP YOU GET
AROUND SINCE THIS
CAMPUS IS PRETTY
BIG!
STILL FOLLOWING
...
YOU
WANNA TALK?
LET'S TALK.
OKAY!
UM--
--WAIT, WHY
ARE WE GOING TO
THE BATHROOM?
DO YOU
WANT ME TO WAIT
OUTSIDE, OR--

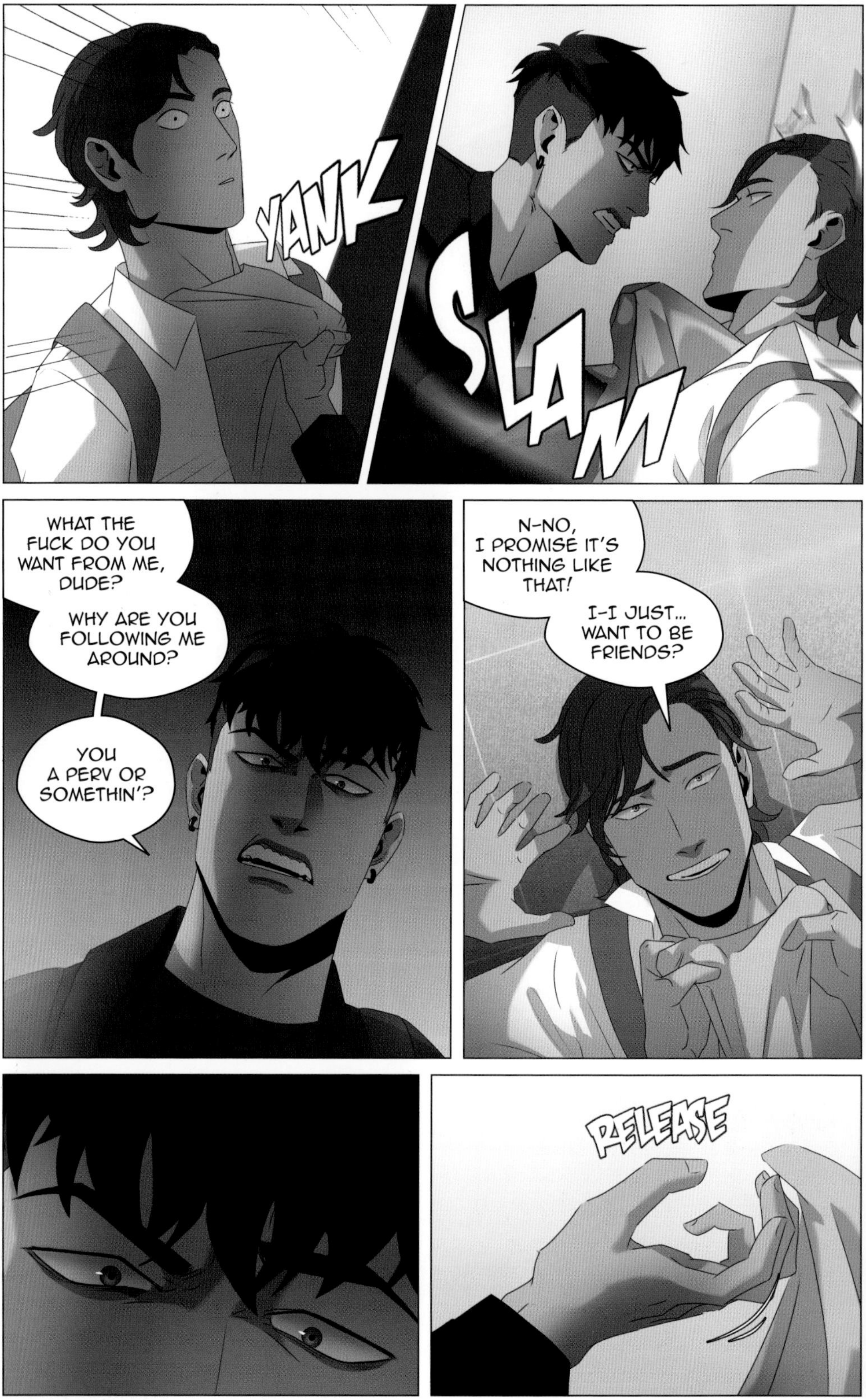
YANK
SLAM
WHAT THE FUCK DO YOU WANT FROM ME, DUDE?
WHY ARE YOU FOLLOWING ME AROUND?
YOU A PERV OR SOMETHIN'?
N-NO, I PROMISE IT'S NOTHING LIKE THAT!
I-I JUST... WANT TO BE FRIENDS?
RELEASE

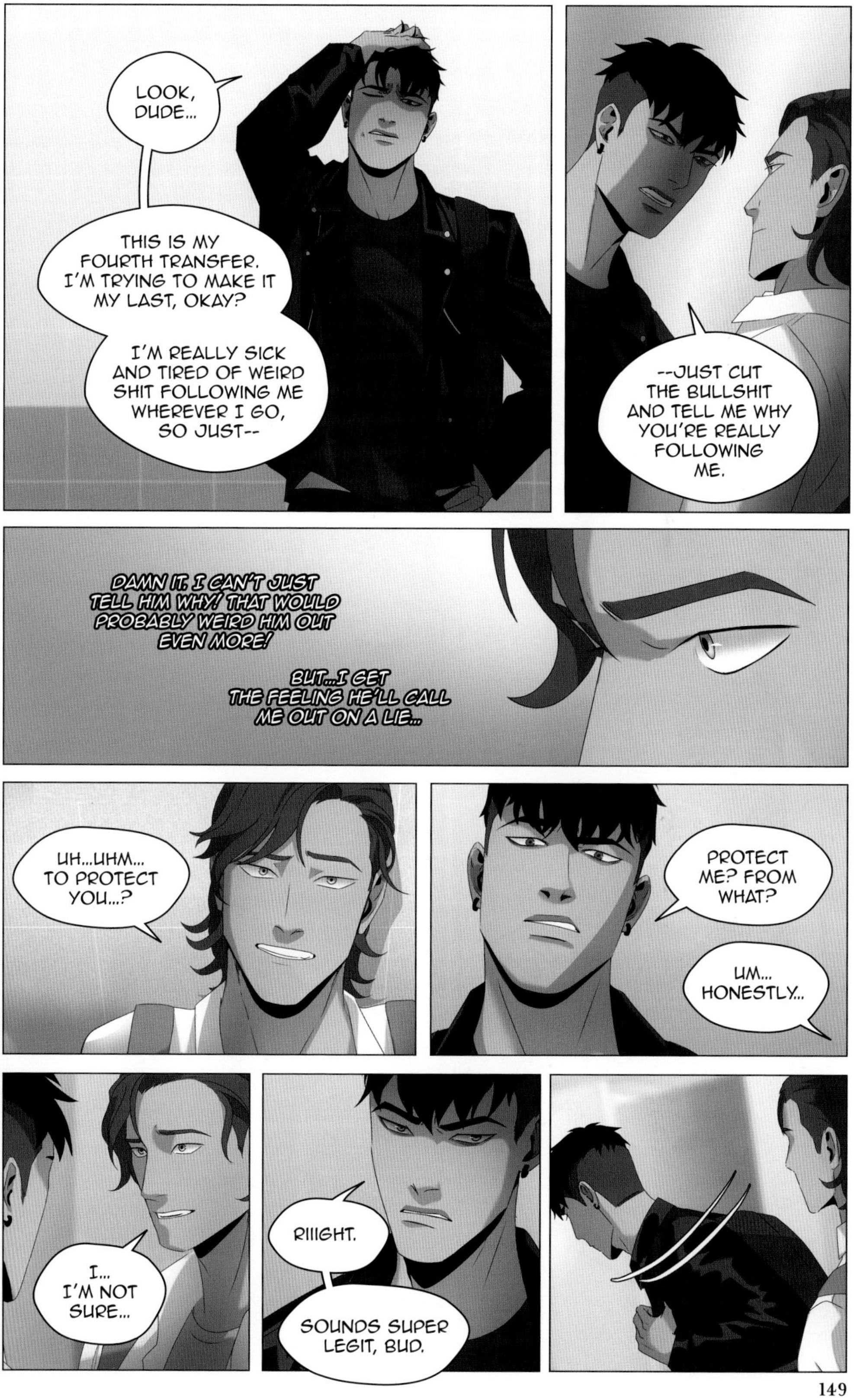
LOOK, DUDE...
THIS IS MY FOURTH TRANSFER. I'M TRYING TO MAKE IT MY LAST, OKAY?
I'M REALLY SICK AND TIRED OF WEIRD SHIT FOLLOWING ME WHEREVER I GO, SO JUST--
--JUST CUT THE BULLSHIT AND TELL ME WHY YOU'RE REALLY FOLLOWING ME.
DAMN IT. I CAN'T JUST TELL HIM WHY! THAT WOULD PROBABLY WEIRD HIM OUT EVEN MORE!
BUT...I GET THE FEELING HE'LL CALL ME OUT ON A LIE...
UH...UHM... TO PROTECT YOU...?
PROTECT ME? FROM WHAT?
UM... HONESTLY...
I... I'M NOT SURE...
RIIIGHT.
SOUNDS SUPER LEGIT, BUD.

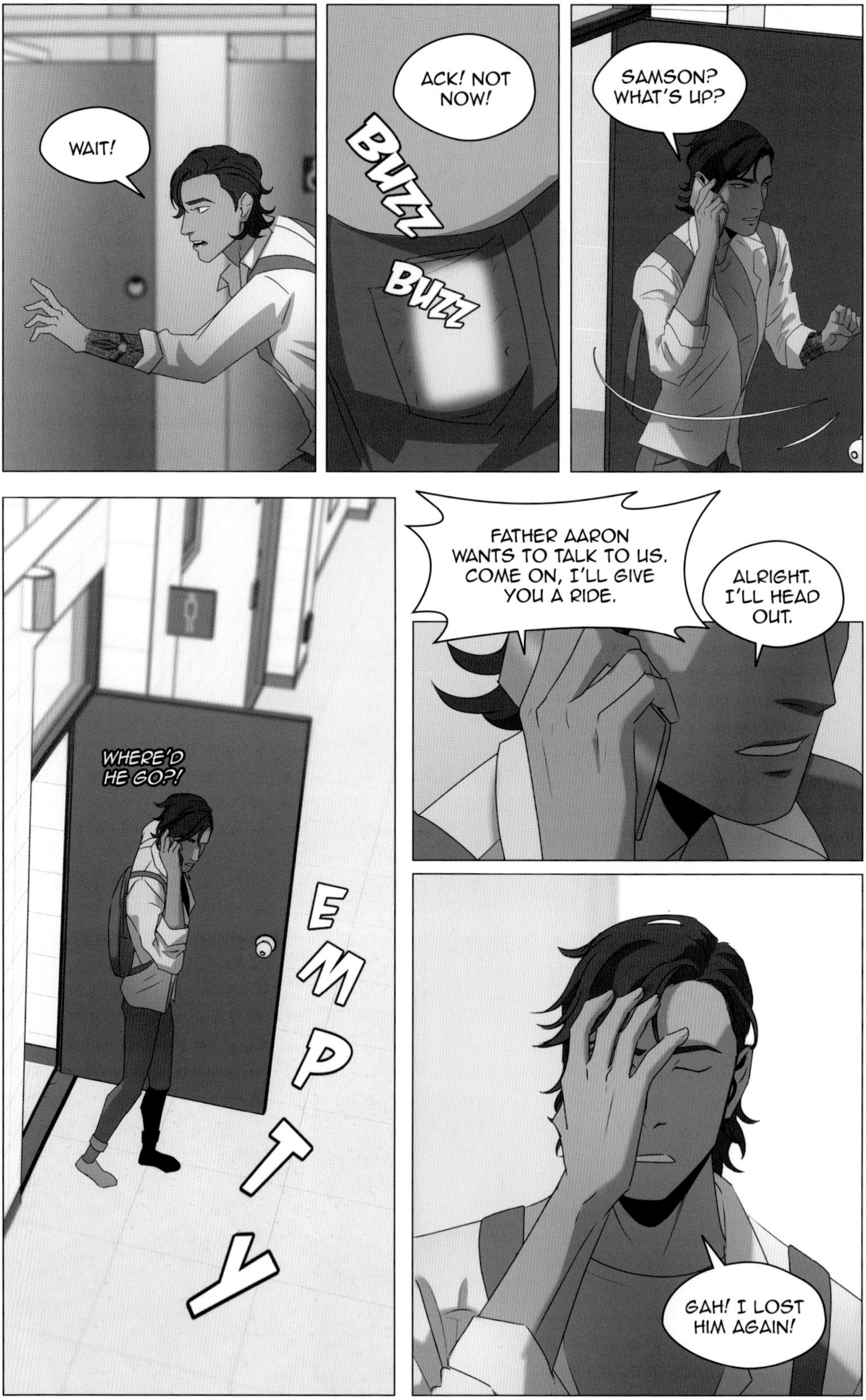
WAIT!
ACK! NOT NOW!
BUZZ
BUZZ
SAMSON? WHAT'S UP?
WHERE'D HE GO?!
EMPTY
FATHER AARON WANTS TO TALK TO US. COME ON, I'LL GIVE YOU A RIDE.
ALRIGHT. I'LL HEAD OUT.
GAH! I LOST HIM AGAIN!

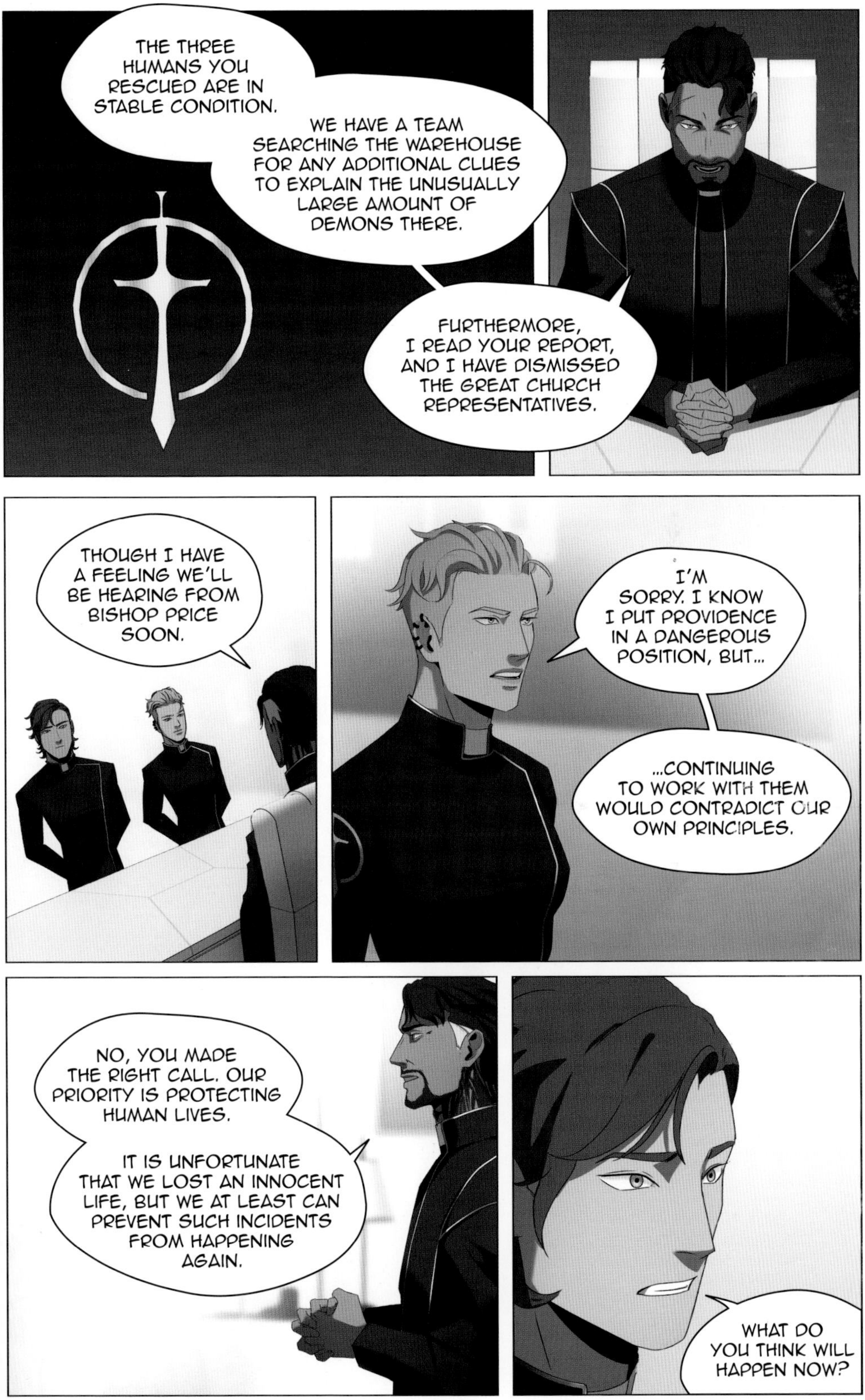
THE THREE HUMANS YOU RESCUED ARE IN STABLE CONDITION.
WE HAVE A TEAM SEARCHING THE WAREHOUSE FOR ANY ADDITIONAL CLUES TO EXPLAIN THE UNUSUALLY LARGE AMOUNT OF DEMONS THERE.
FURTHERMORE, I READ YOUR REPORT, AND I HAVE DISMISSED THE GREAT CHURCH REPRESENTATIVES.
THOUGH I HAVE A FEELING WE'LL BE HEARING FROM BISHOP PRICE SOON.
I'M SORRY. I KNOW I PUT PROVIDENCE IN A DANGEROUS POSITION, BUT...
...CONTINUING TO WORK WITH THEM WOULD CONTRADICT OUR OWN PRINCIPLES.
NO, YOU MADE THE RIGHT CALL. OUR PRIORITY IS PROTECTING HUMAN LIVES.
IT IS UNFORTUNATE THAT WE LOST AN INNOCENT LIFE, BUT WE AT LEAST CAN PREVENT SUCH INCIDENTS FROM HAPPENING AGAIN.
WHAT DO YOU THINK WILL HAPPEN NOW?

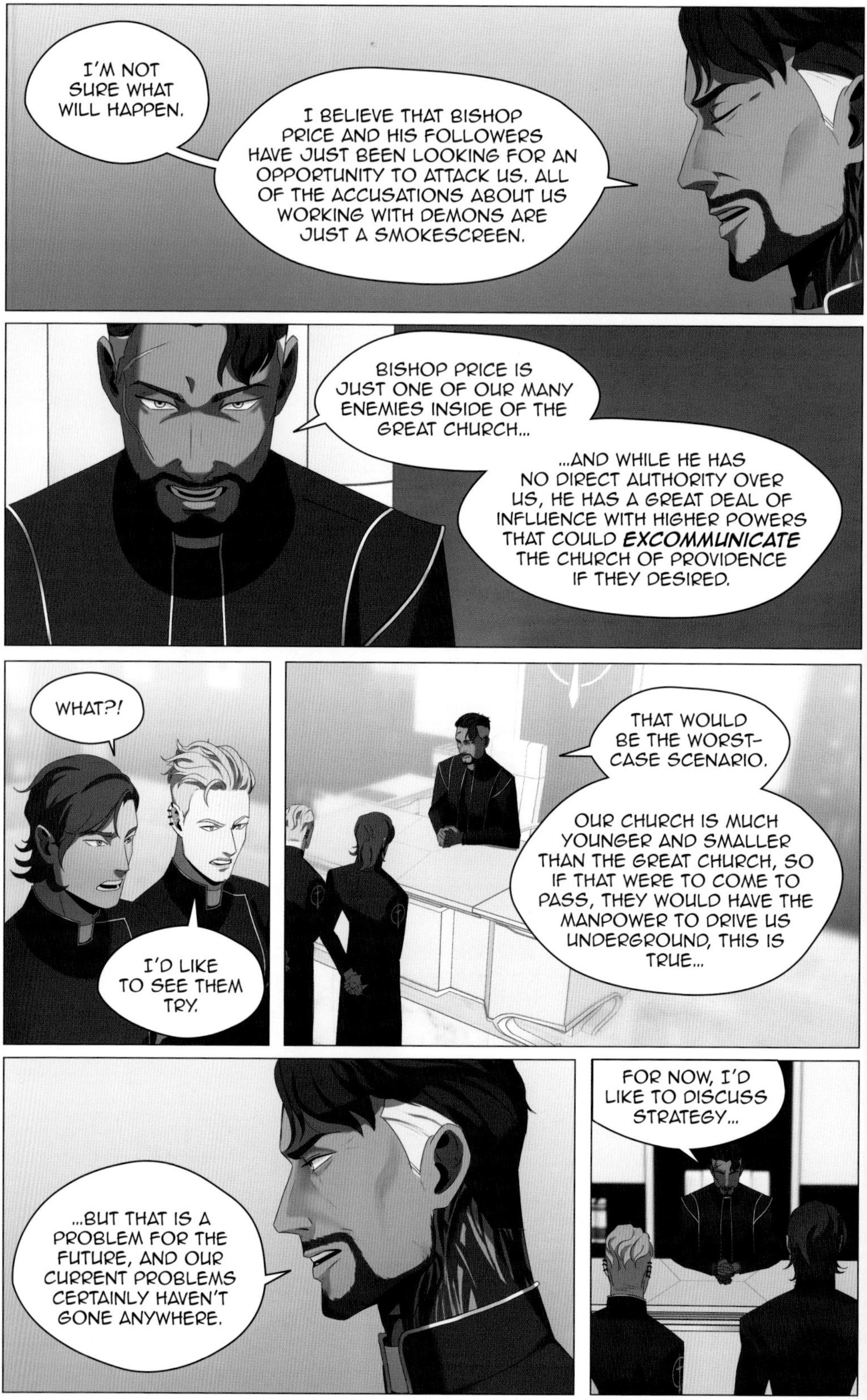
I'M NOT SURE WHAT WILL HAPPEN.
I BELIEVE THAT BISHOP PRICE AND HIS FOLLOWERS HAVE JUST BEEN LOOKING FOR AN OPPORTUNITY TO ATTACK US. ALL OF THE ACCUSATIONS ABOUT US WORKING WITH DEMONS ARE JUST A SMOKESCREEN.
BISHOP PRICE IS JUST ONE OF OUR MANY ENEMIES INSIDE OF THE GREAT CHURCH...
...AND WHILE HE HAS NO DIRECT AUTHORITY OVER US, HE HAS A GREAT DEAL OF INFLUENCE WITH HIGHER POWERS THAT COULD ***EXCOMMUNICATE*** THE CHURCH OF PROVIDENCE IF THEY DESIRED.
WHAT?!
I'D LIKE TO SEE THEM TRY.
THAT WOULD BE THE WORST-CASE SCENARIO.
OUR CHURCH IS MUCH YOUNGER AND SMALLER THAN THE GREAT CHURCH, SO IF THAT WERE TO COME TO PASS, THEY WOULD HAVE THE MANPOWER TO DRIVE US UNDERGROUND, THIS IS TRUE...
...BUT THAT IS A PROBLEM FOR THE FUTURE, AND OUR CURRENT PROBLEMS CERTAINLY HAVEN'T GONE ANYWHERE.
FOR NOW, I'D LIKE TO DISCUSS STRATEGY...

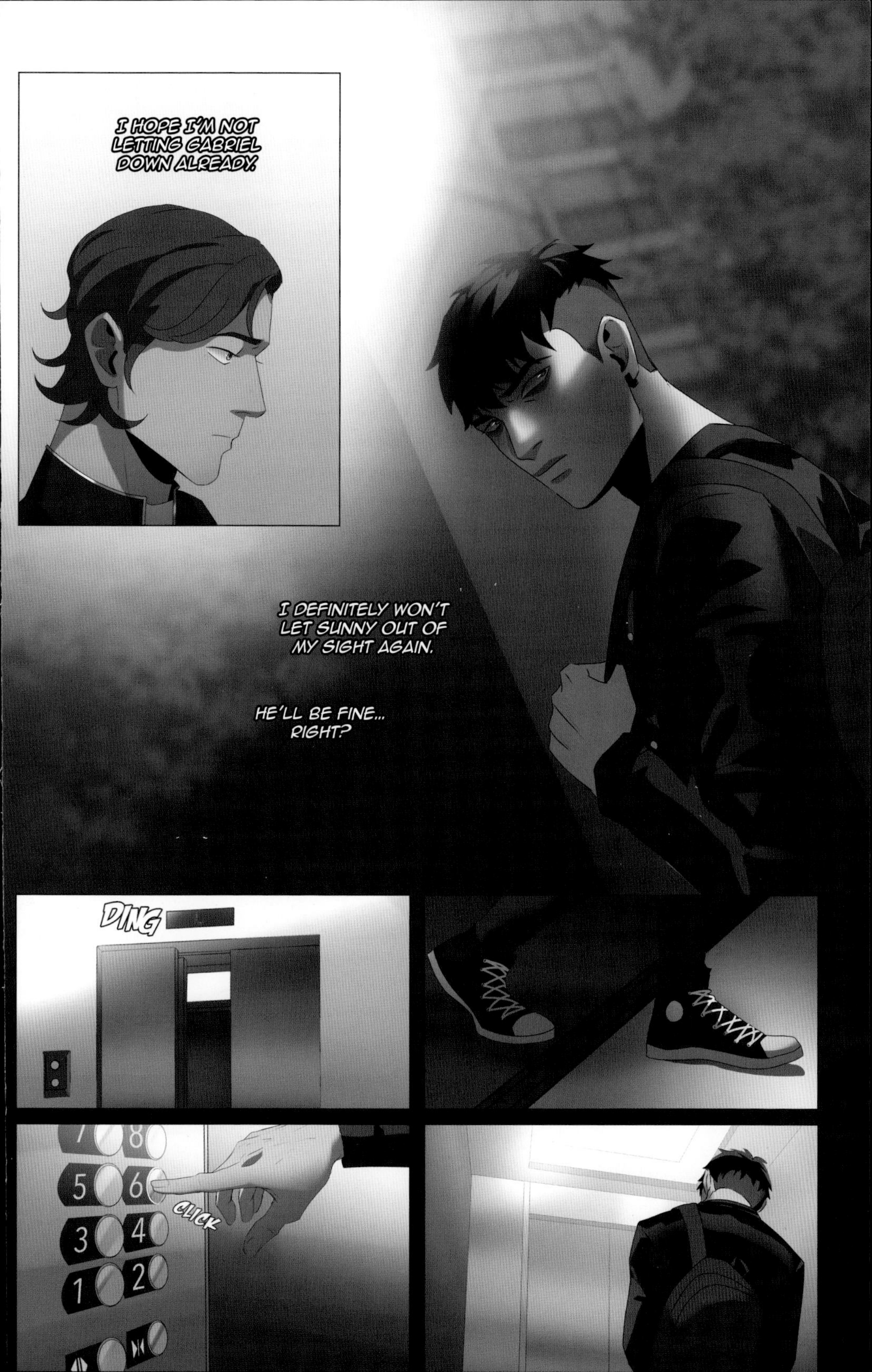
I HOPE I'M NOT LETTING GABRIEL DOWN ALREADY.
I DEFINITELY WON'T LET SUNNY OUT OF MY SIGHT AGAIN.
HE'LL BE FINE... RIGHT?
DING
CLICK

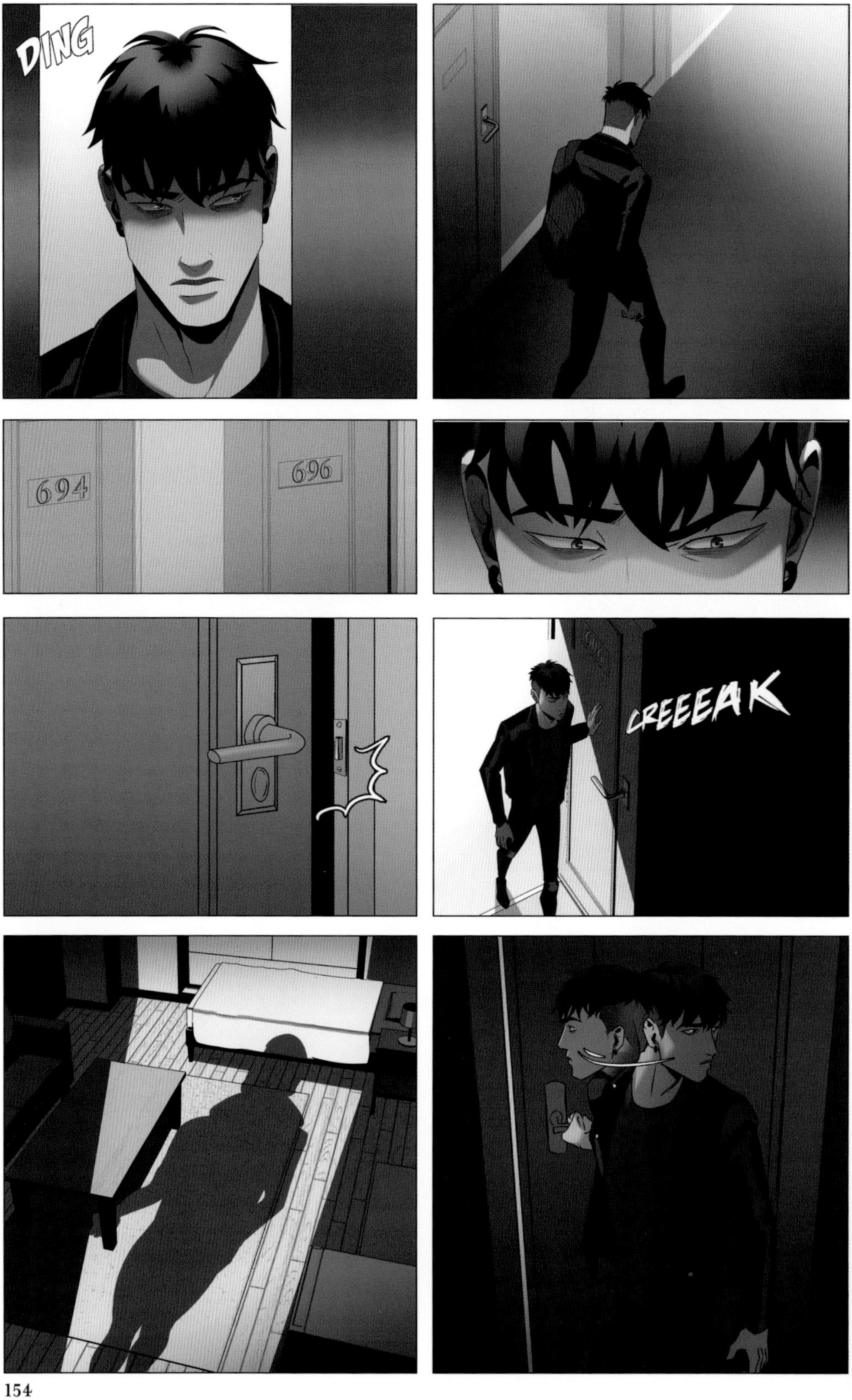
DING
694
696
CREEEAK

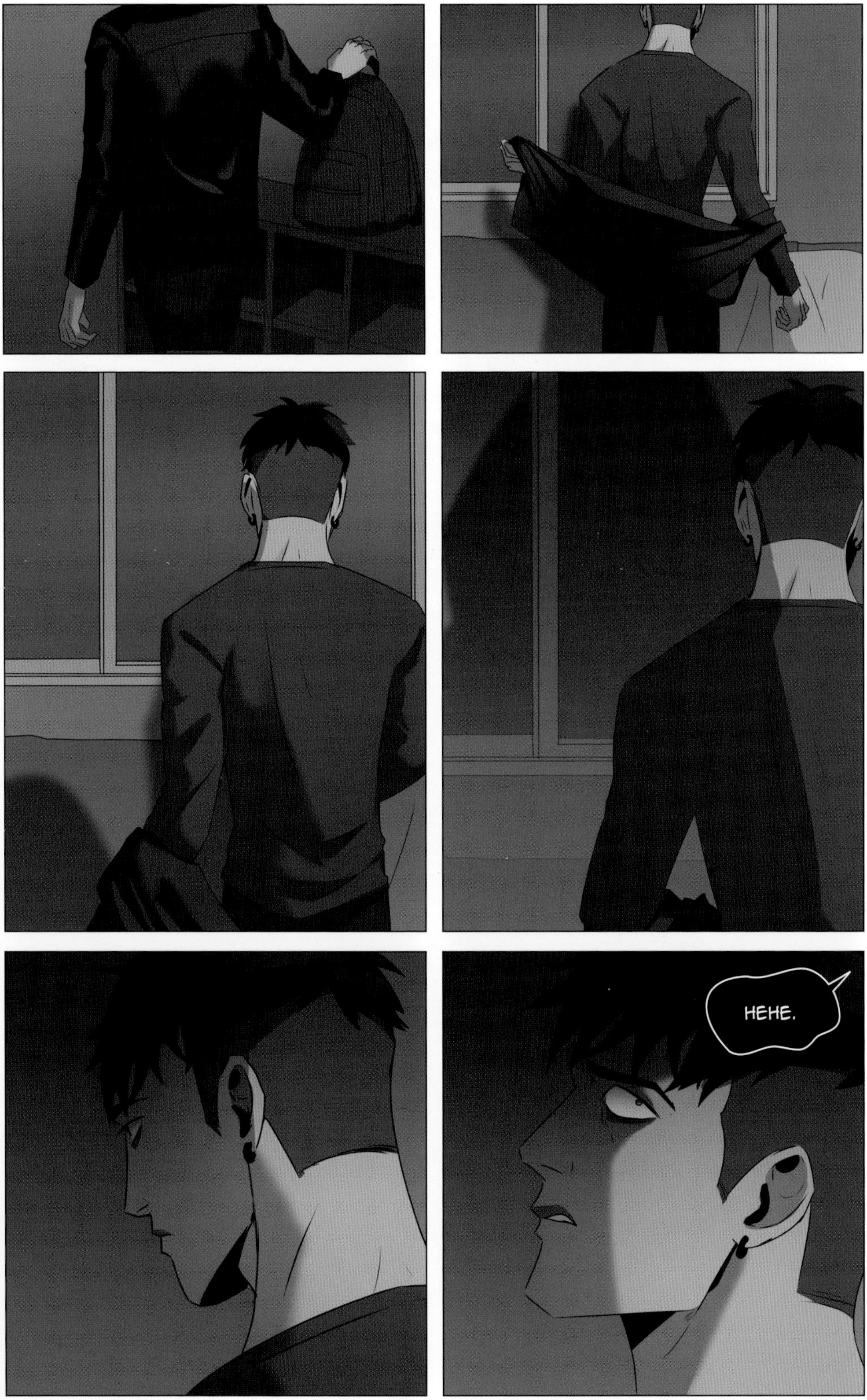
HEHE.

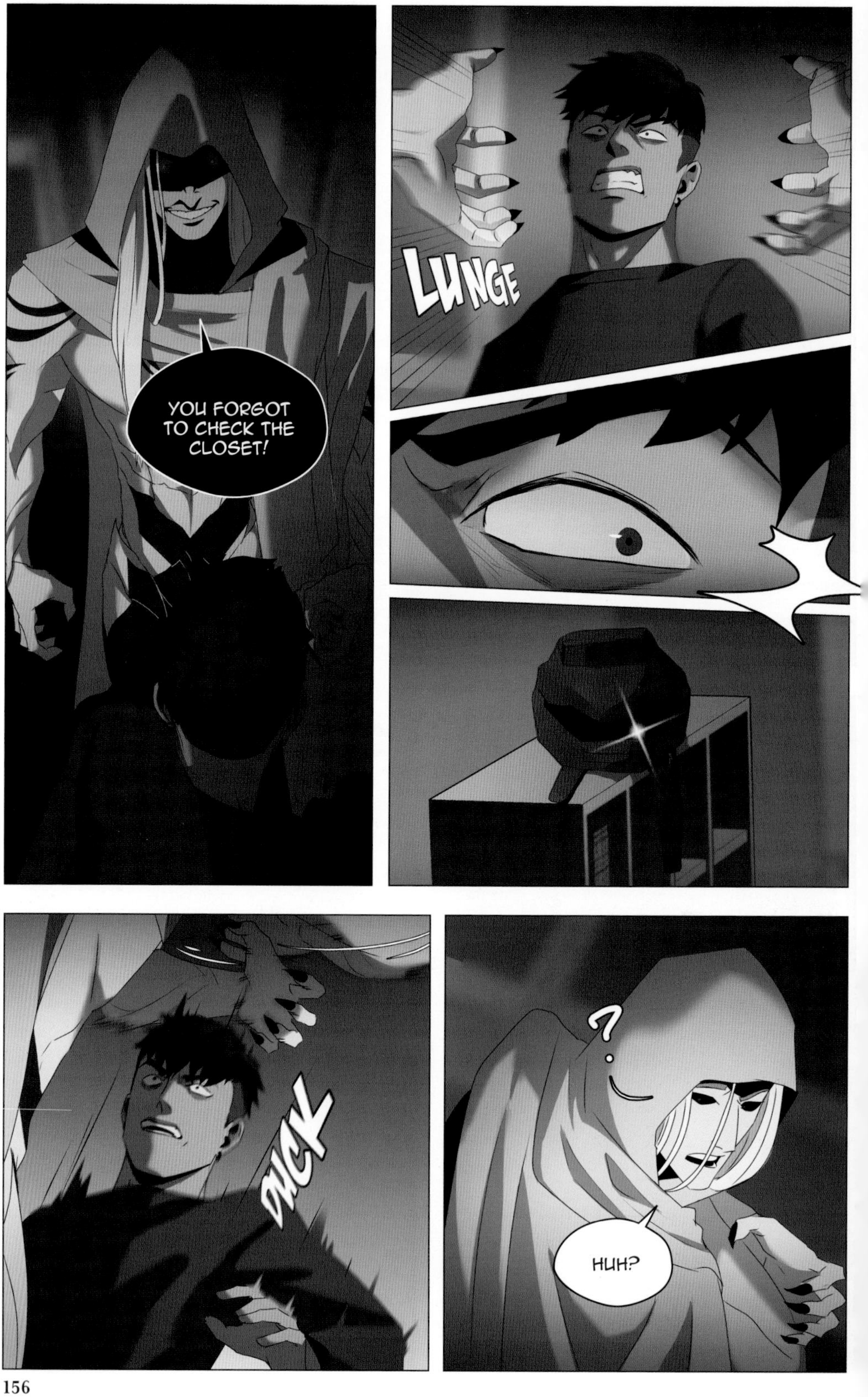
YOU FORGOT TO CHECK THE CLOSET!
LUNGE
DUCK
?
HUH?

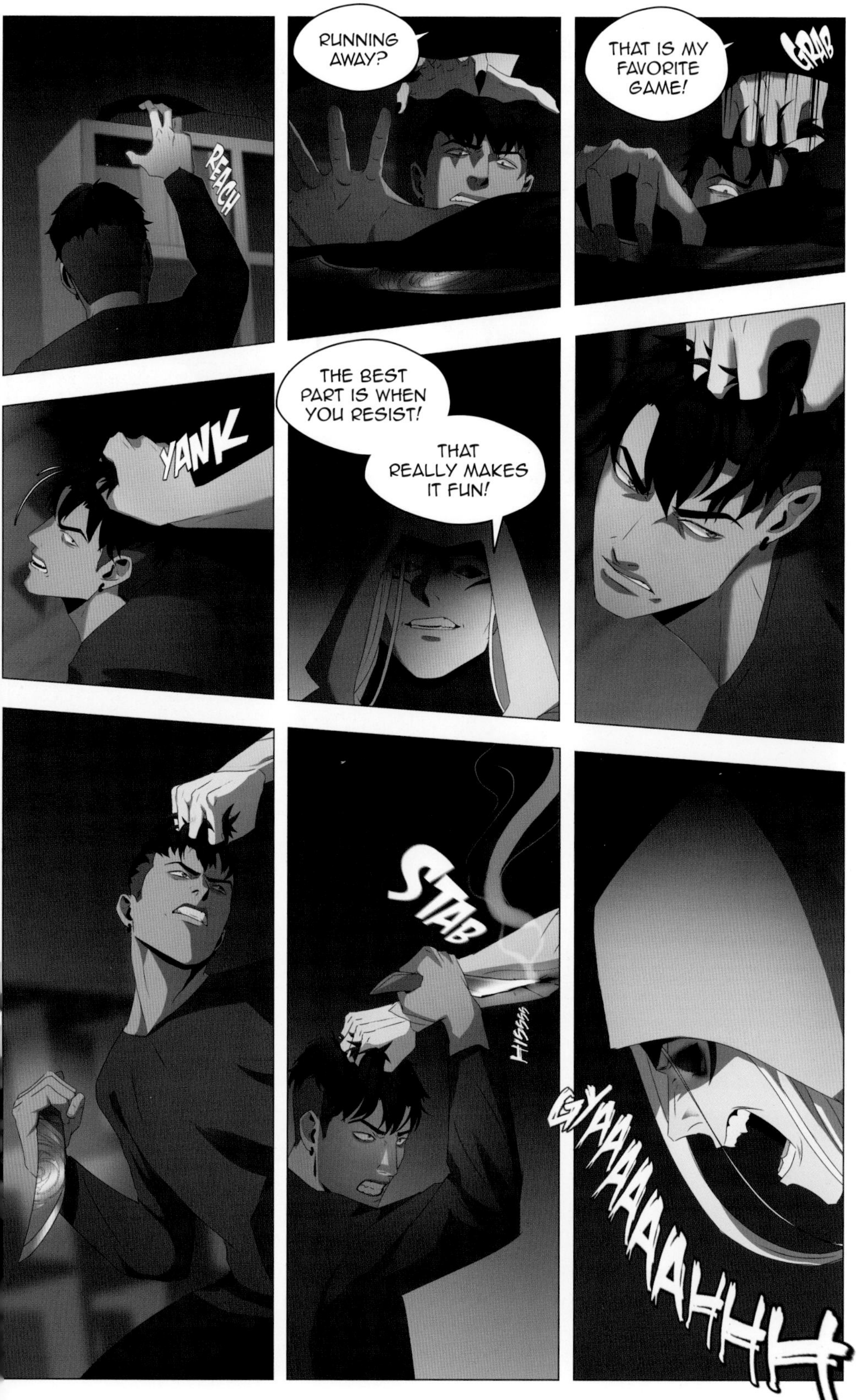
REACH
RUNNING AWAY?
THAT IS MY FAVORITE GAME!
GRAB
YANK
THE BEST PART IS WHEN YOU RESIST!
THAT REALLY MAKES IT FUN!
STAB
HISSSS
GYAAAAAAHHH

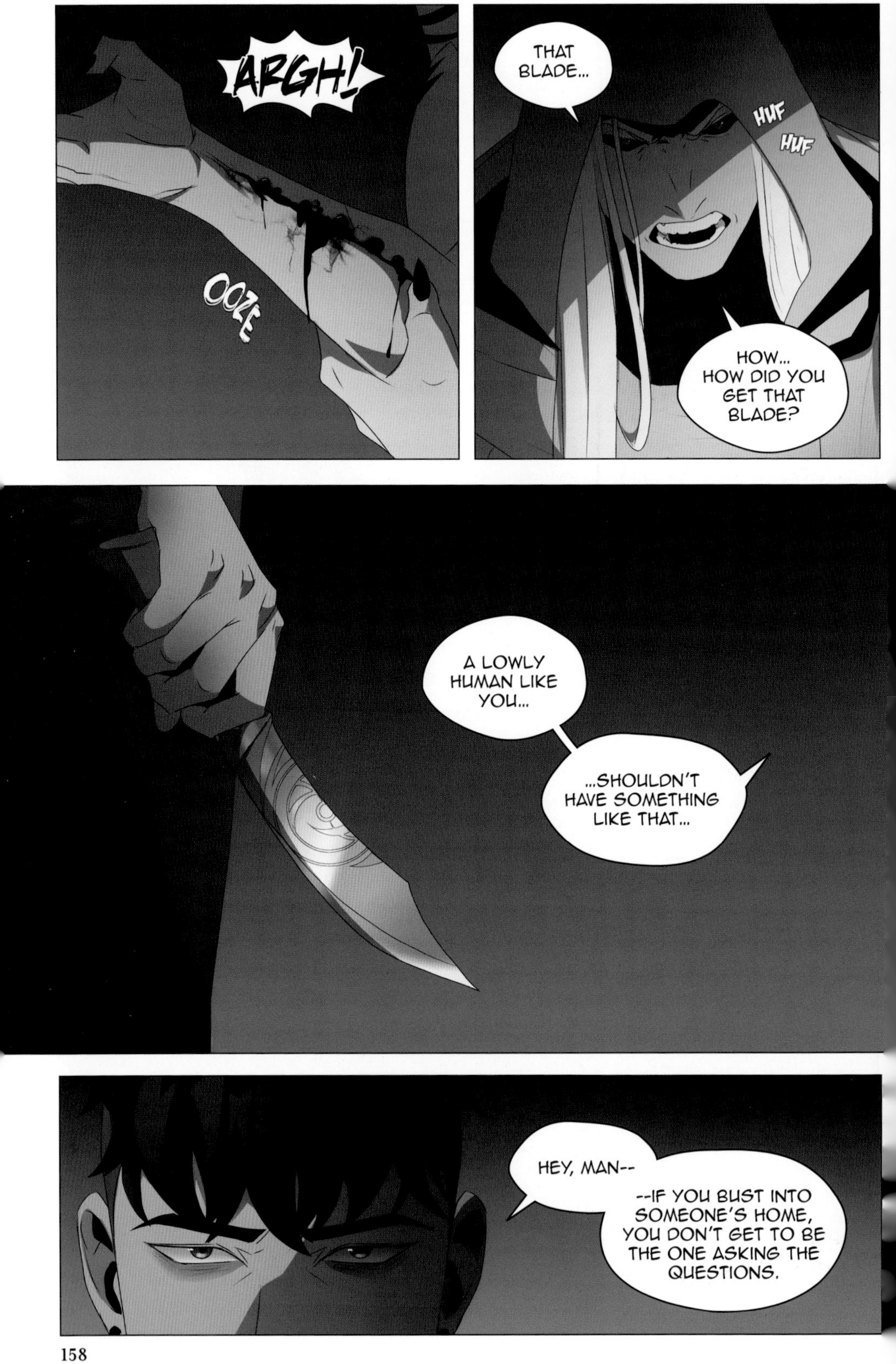
ARGH!
OOZE
THAT BLADE...
HUF
HUF
HOW... HOW DID YOU GET THAT BLADE?
A LOWLY HUMAN LIKE YOU...
...SHOULDN'T HAVE SOMETHING LIKE THAT...
HEY, MAN--
--IF YOU BUST INTO SOMEONE'S HOME, YOU DON'T GET TO BE THE ONE ASKING THE QUESTIONS.

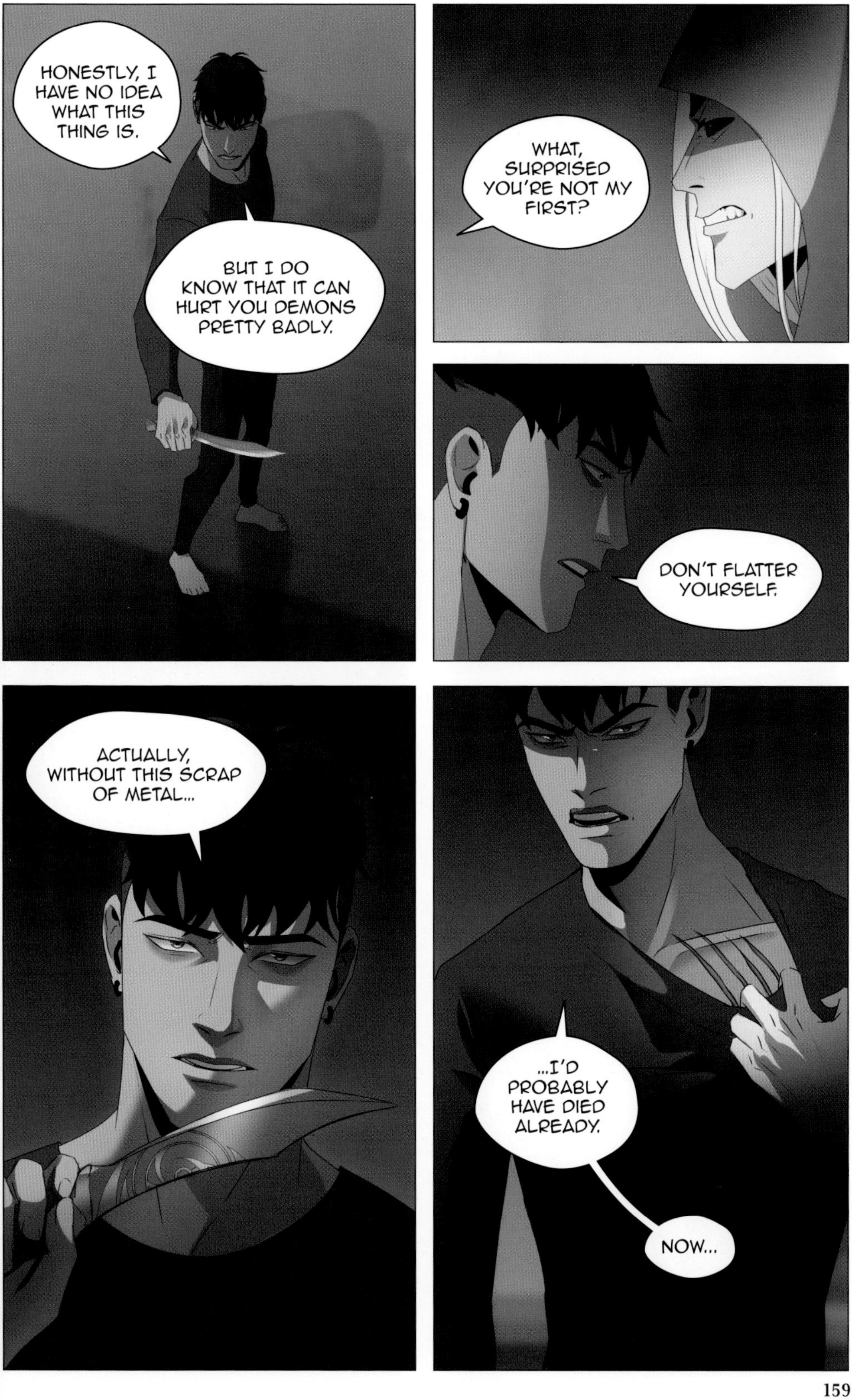
HONESTLY, I HAVE NO IDEA WHAT THIS THING IS.
BUT I DO KNOW THAT IT CAN HURT YOU DEMONS PRETTY BADLY.
WHAT, SURPRISED YOU'RE NOT MY FIRST?
DON'T FLATTER YOURSELF.
ACTUALLY, WITHOUT THIS SCRAP OF METAL...
...I'D PROBABLY HAVE DIED ALREADY.
NOW...

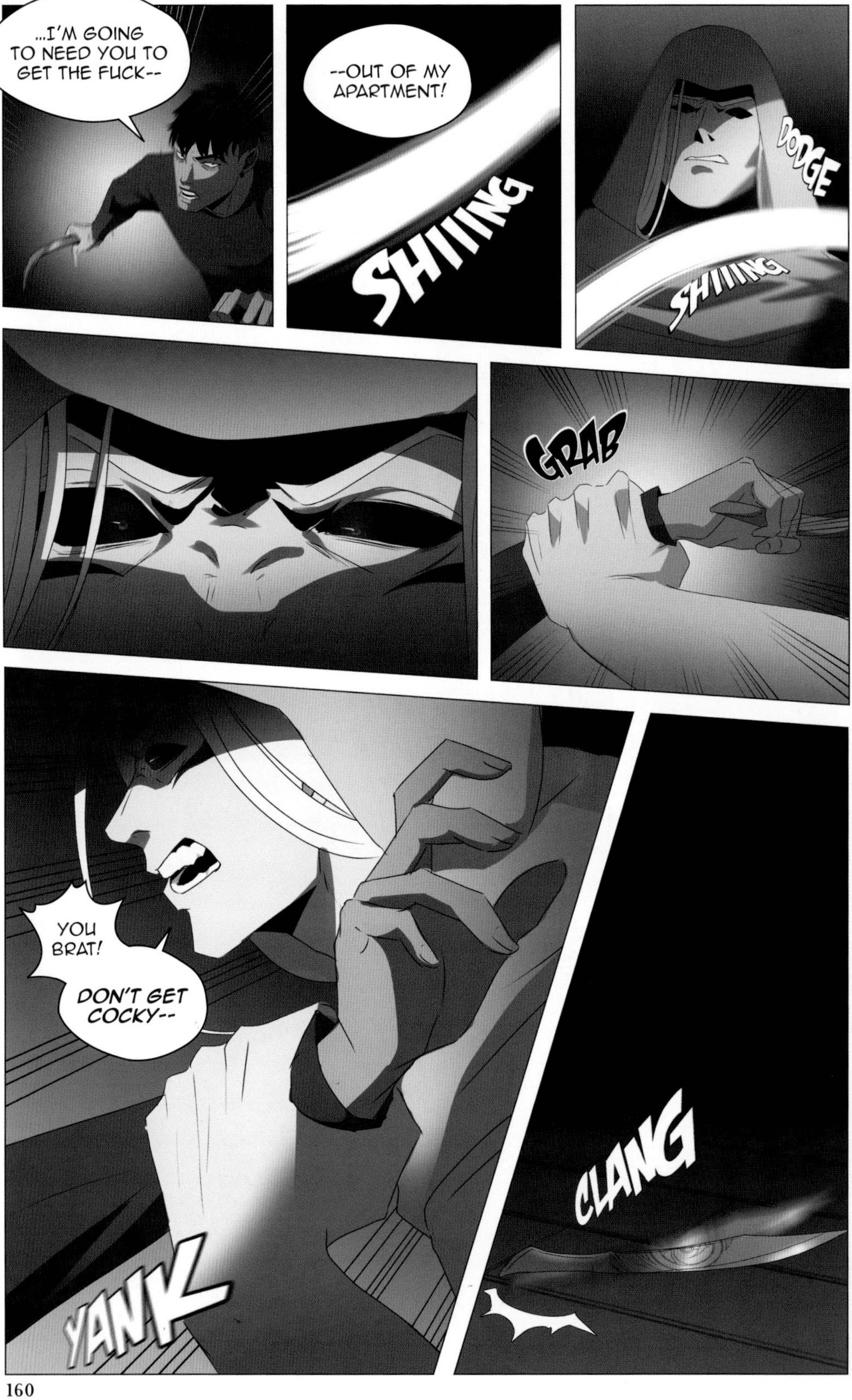
...I'M GOING TO NEED YOU TO GET THE FUCK--
--OUT OF MY APARTMENT!
SHIIING
DODGE
SHIIING
GRAB
YOU BRAT!
DON'T GET COCKY--
YANK
CLANG

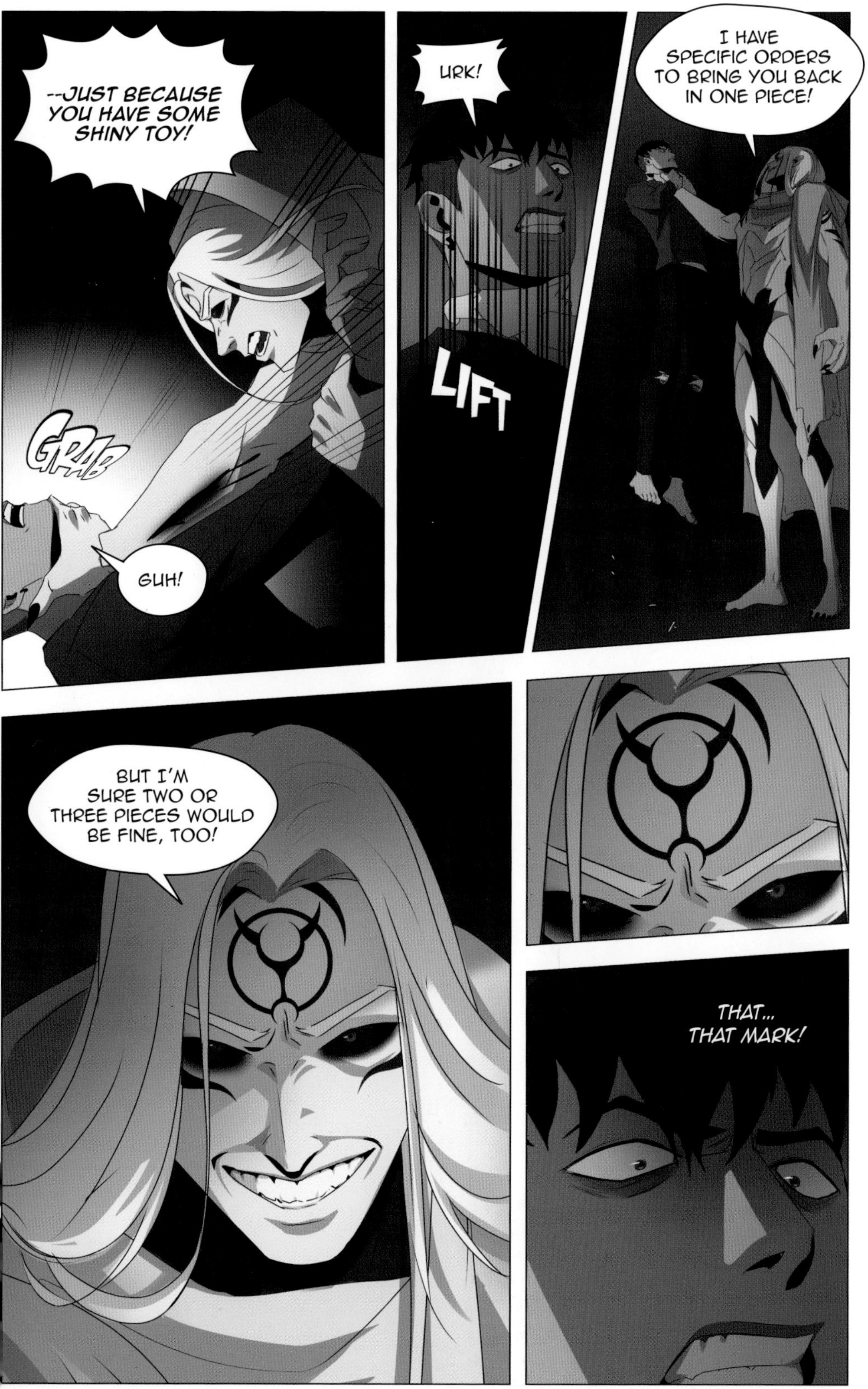
--JUST BECAUSE YOU HAVE SOME SHINY TOY!
GRAB
GUH!
URK!
LIFT
I HAVE SPECIFIC ORDERS TO BRING YOU BACK IN ONE PIECE!
BUT I'M SURE TWO OR THREE PIECES WOULD BE FINE, TOO!
THAT... THAT MARK!

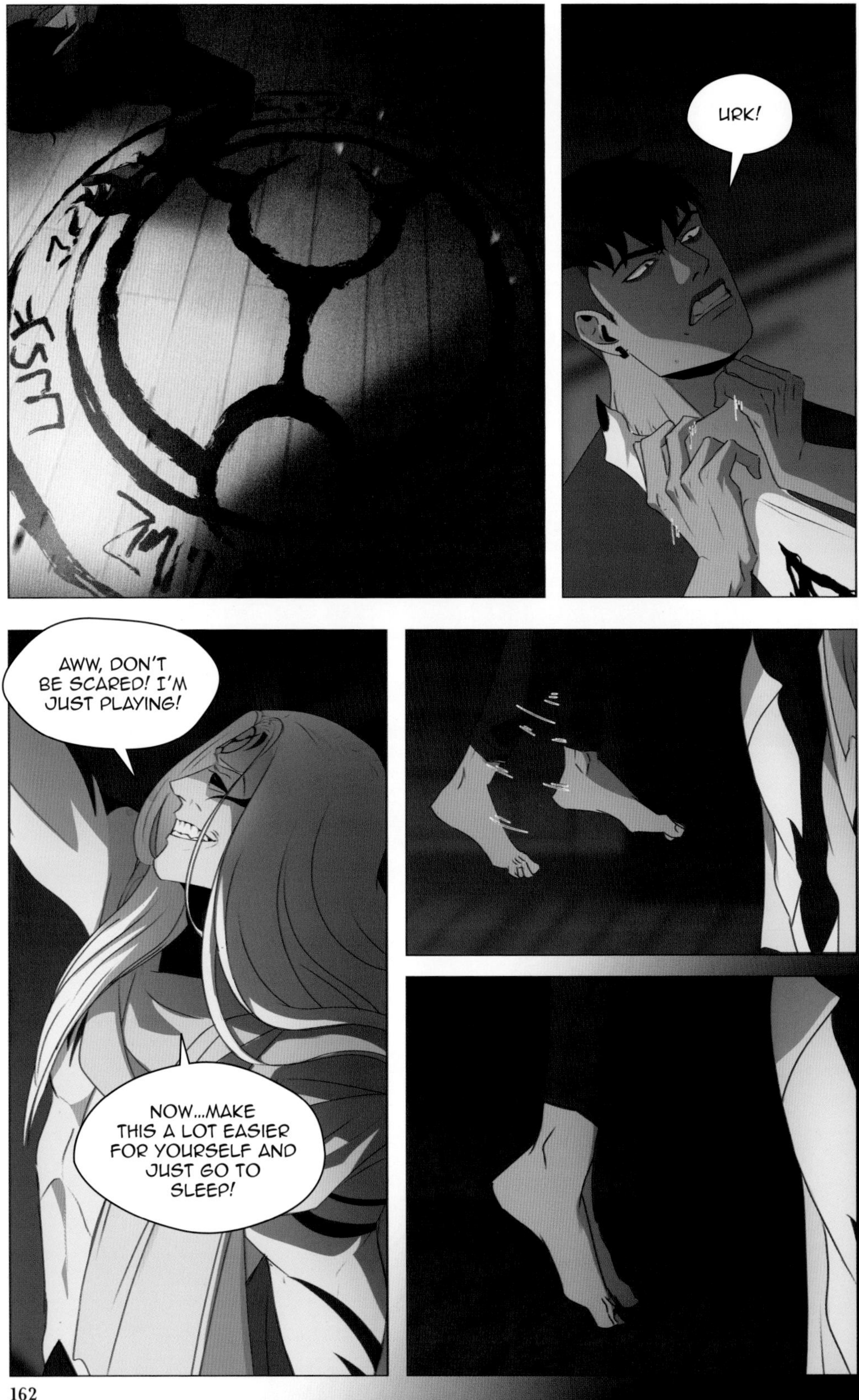
URK!
AWW, DON'T BE SCARED! I'M JUST PLAYING!
NOW...MAKE THIS A LOT EASIER FOR YOURSELF AND JUST GO TO SLEEP!

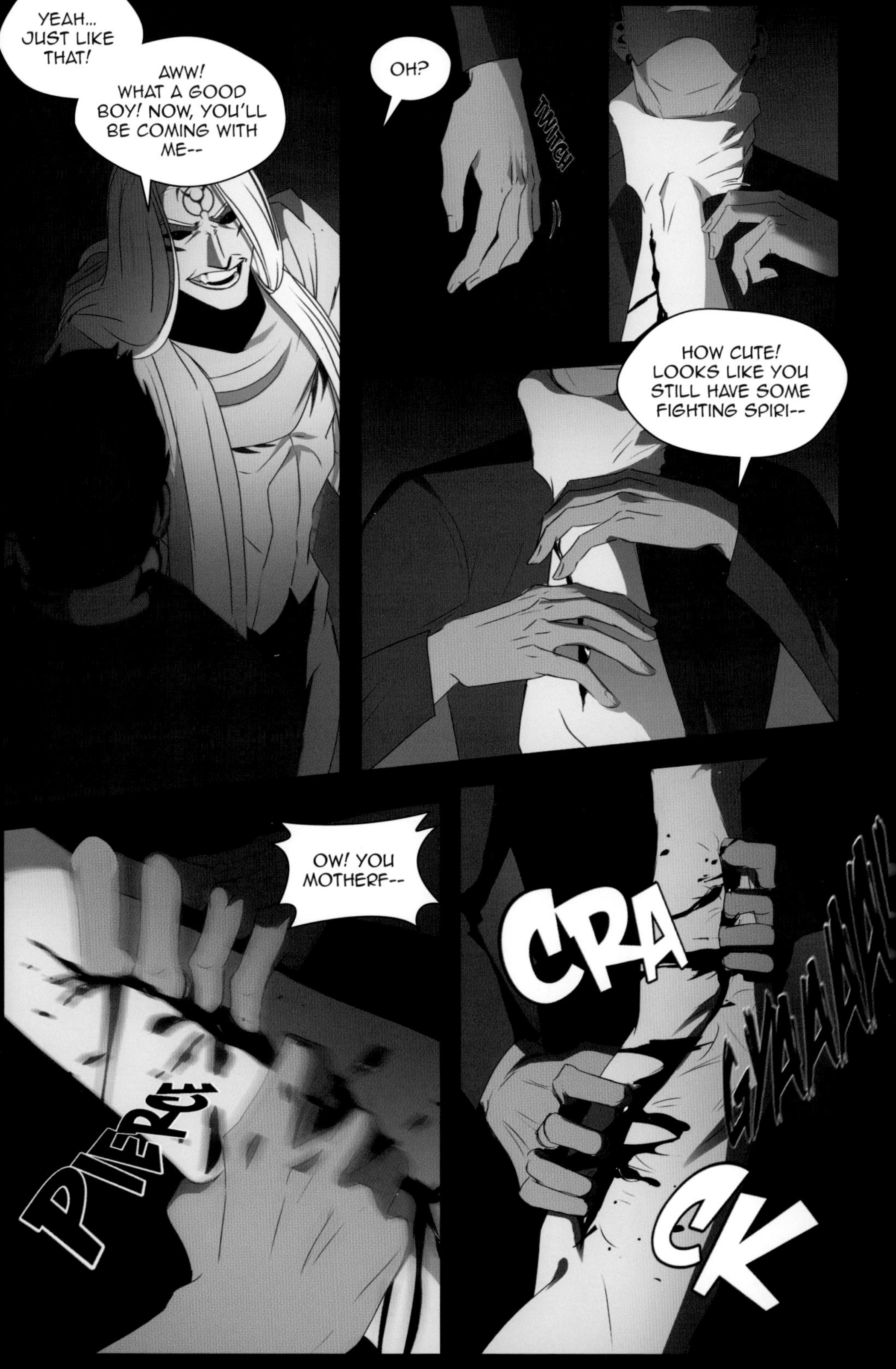
YEAH... JUST LIKE THAT!
AWW! WHAT A GOOD BOY! NOW, YOU'LL BE COMING WITH ME--
OH?
TWITCH
HOW CUTE! LOOKS LIKE YOU STILL HAVE SOME FIGHTING SPIRI--
OW! YOU MOTHERF--
PIERCE
CRACK
GYAAAH!

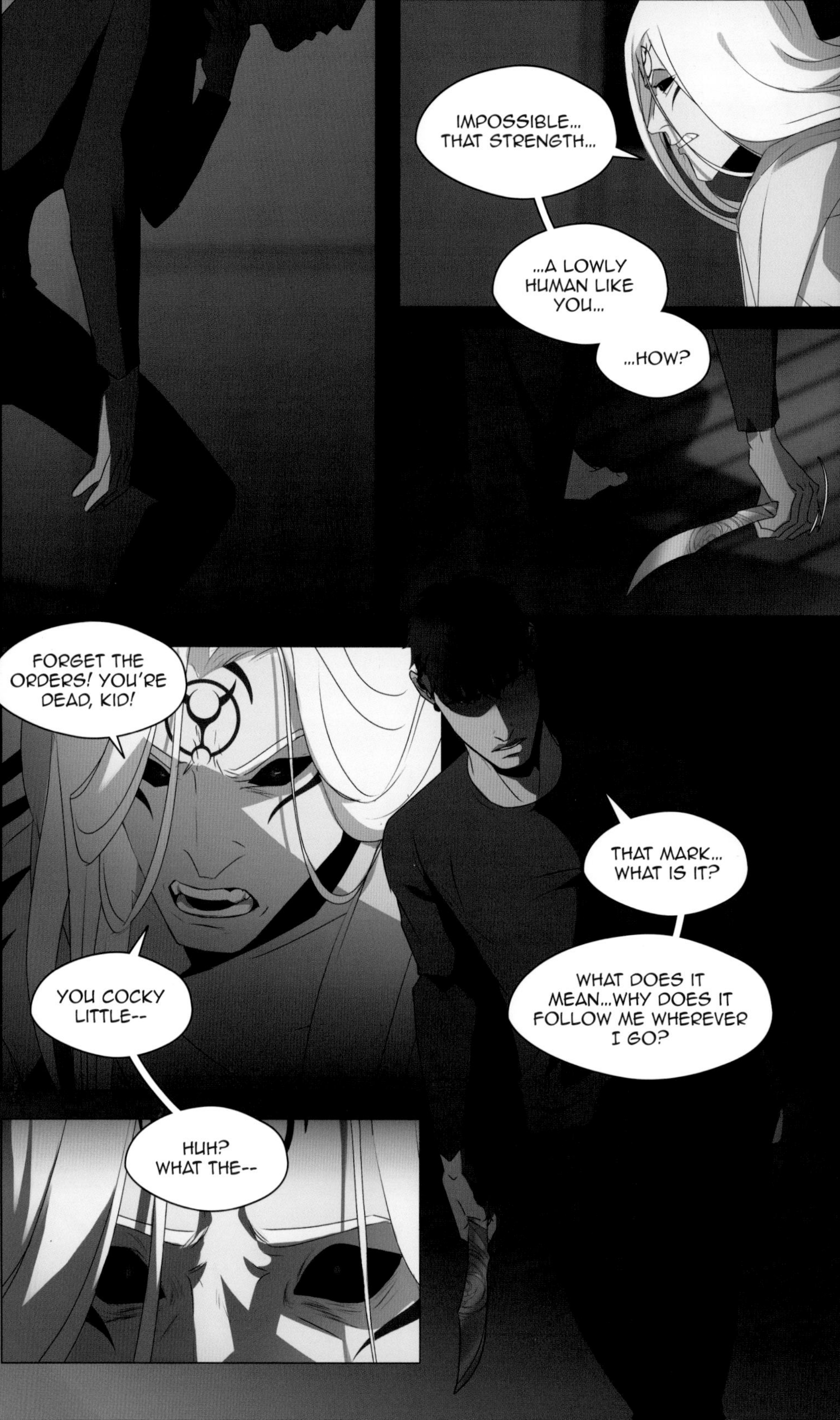
IMPOSSIBLE... THAT STRENGTH...
...A LOWLY HUMAN LIKE YOU...
...HOW?
FORGET THE ORDERS! YOU'RE DEAD, KID!
THAT MARK... WHAT IS IT?
WHAT DOES IT MEAN...WHY DOES IT FOLLOW ME WHEREVER I GO?
YOU COCKY LITTLE--
HUH? WHAT THE--

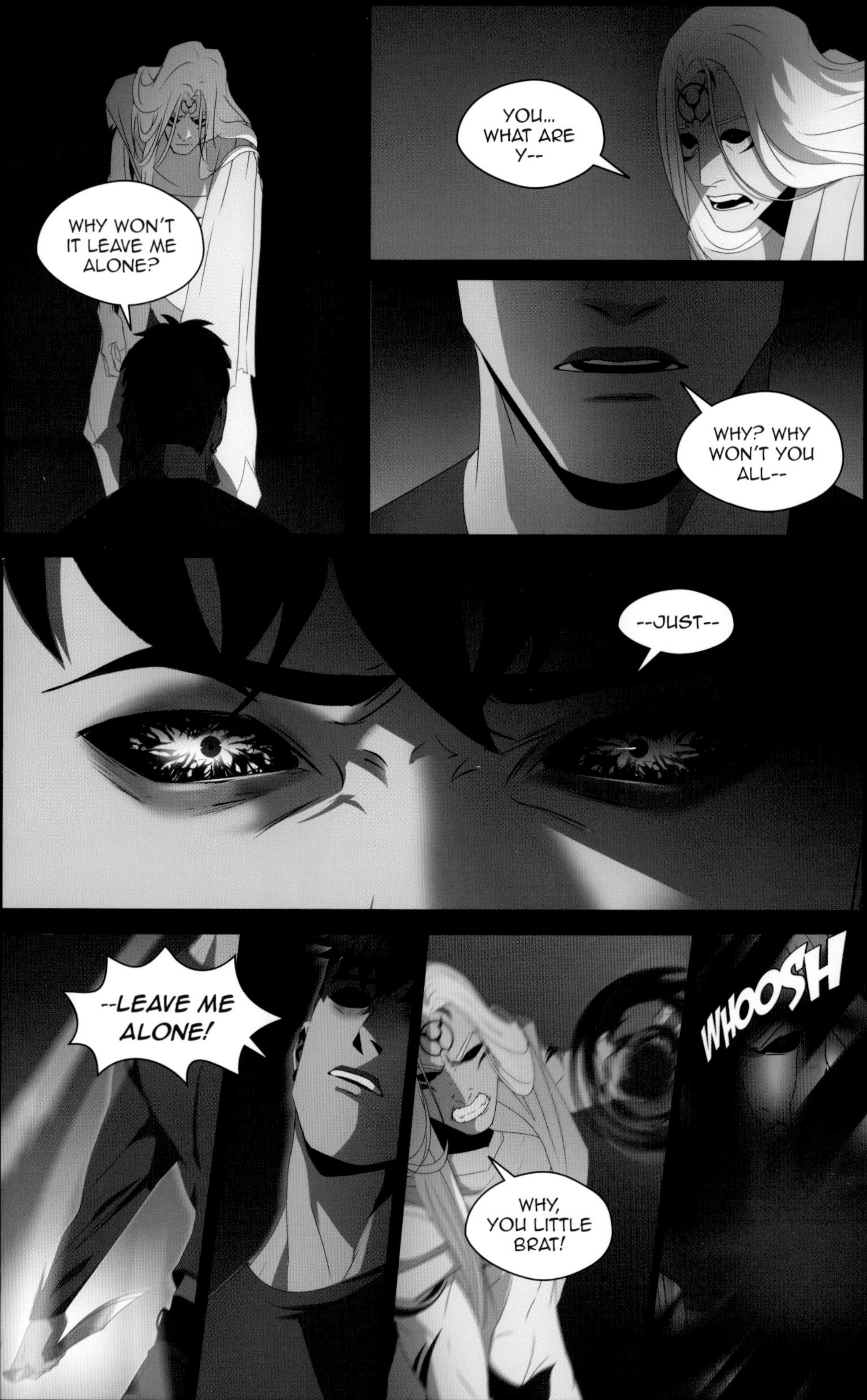
YOU... WHAT ARE Y--
WHY WON'T IT LEAVE ME ALONE?
WHY? WHY WON'T YOU ALL--
--JUST--
--LEAVE ME ALONE!
WHOOSH
WHY, YOU LITTLE BRAT!

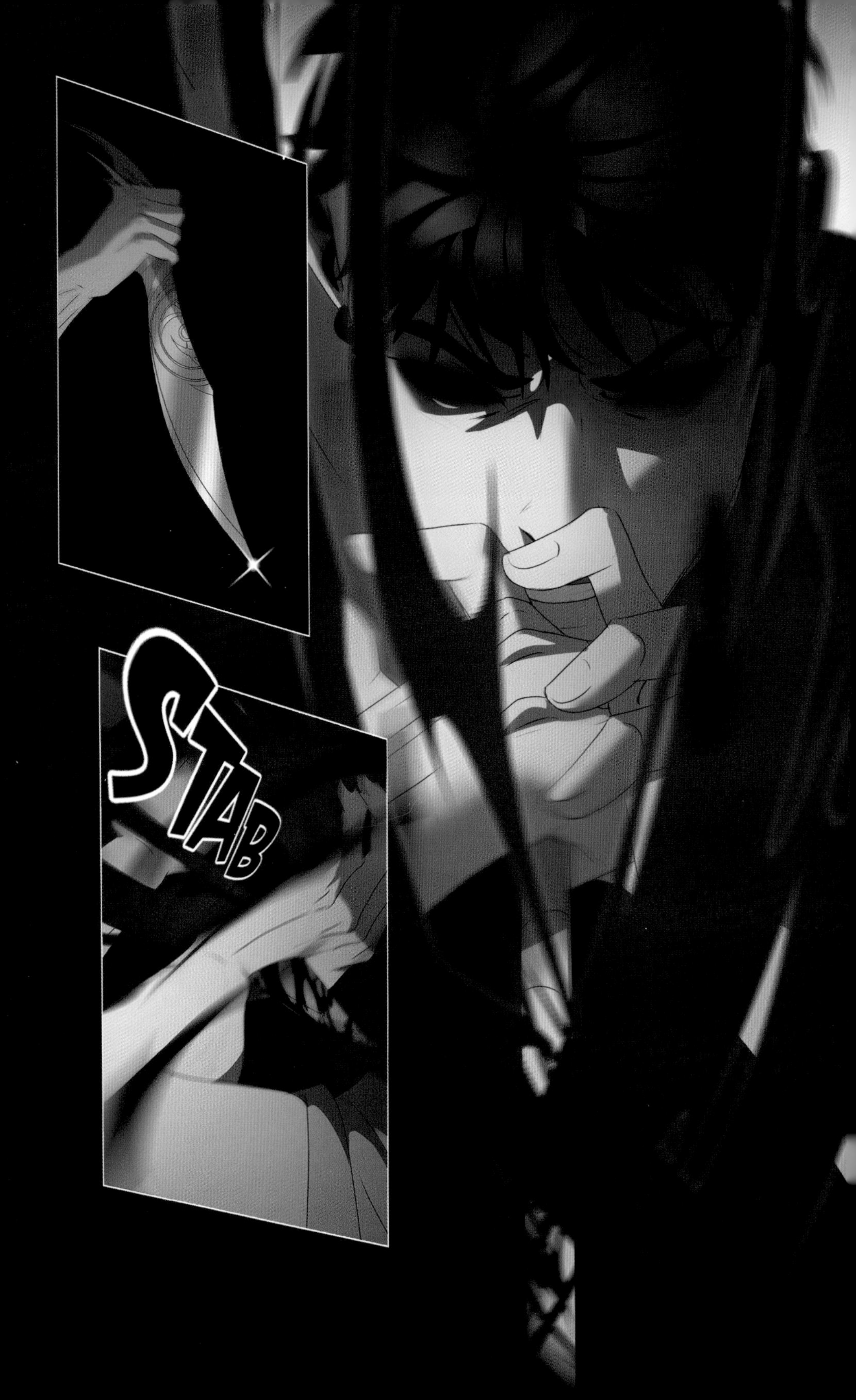
STAB

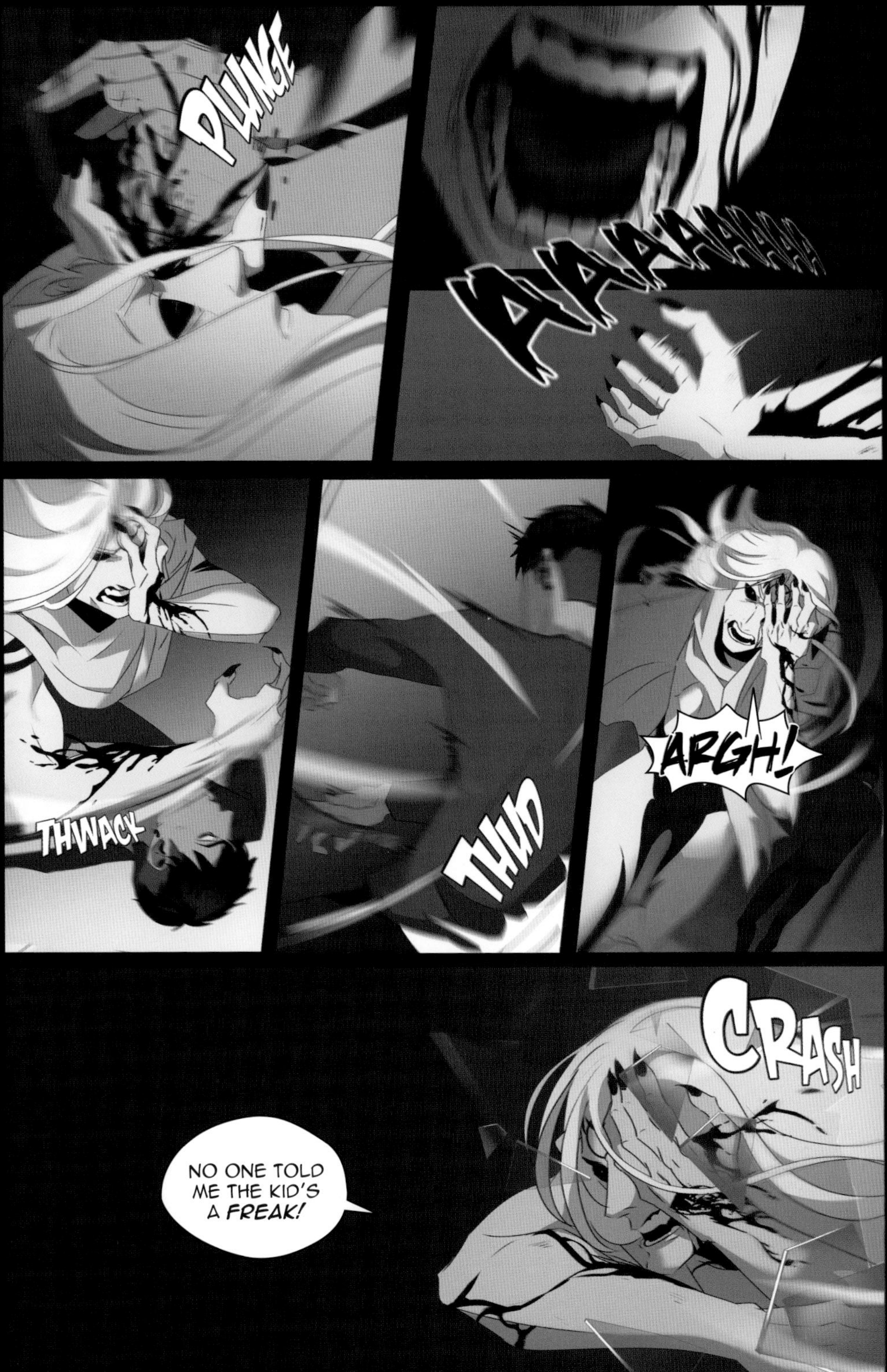
PLUNGE
AAAAAAAAA
THWACK
THUD
ARGH!
CRASH
NO ONE TOLD ME THE KID'S A *FREAK!*

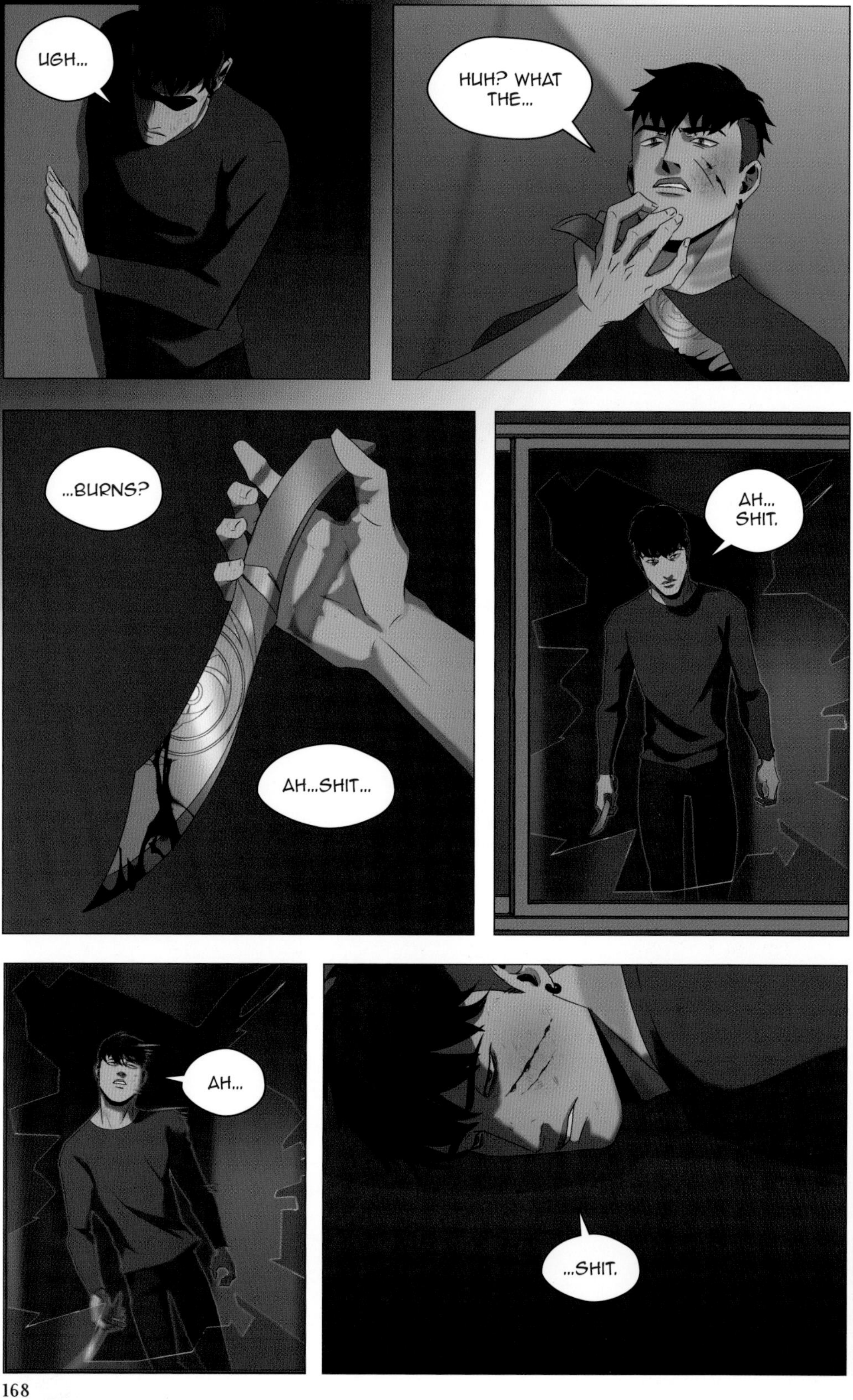
UGH...
HUH? WHAT THE...
...BURNS?
AH...SHIT...
AH... SHIT.
AH...
...SHIT.

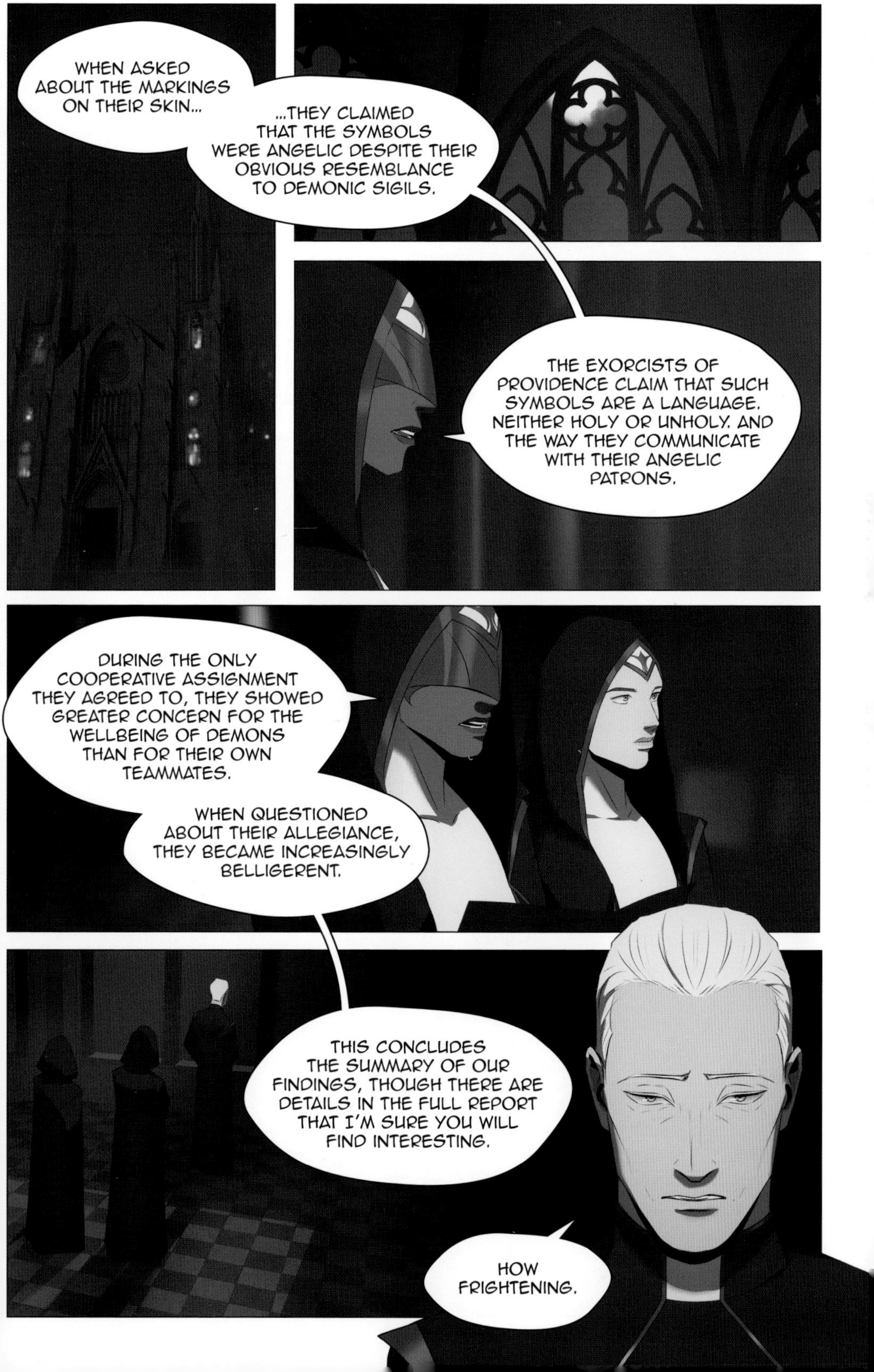

WHEN ASKED ABOUT THE MARKINGS ON THEIR SKIN...
...THEY CLAIMED THAT THE SYMBOLS WERE ANGELIC DESPITE THEIR OBVIOUS RESEMBLANCE TO DEMONIC SIGILS.
THE EXORCISTS OF PROVIDENCE CLAIM THAT SUCH SYMBOLS ARE A LANGUAGE. NEITHER HOLY OR UNHOLY. AND THE WAY THEY COMMUNICATE WITH THEIR ANGELIC PATRONS.
DURING THE ONLY COOPERATIVE ASSIGNMENT THEY AGREED TO, THEY SHOWED GREATER CONCERN FOR THE WELLBEING OF DEMONS THAN FOR THEIR OWN TEAMMATES.
WHEN QUESTIONED ABOUT THEIR ALLEGIANCE, THEY BECAME INCREASINGLY BELLIGERENT.
THIS CONCLUDES THE SUMMARY OF OUR FINDINGS, THOUGH THERE ARE DETAILS IN THE FULL REPORT THAT I'M SURE YOU WILL FIND INTERESTING.
HOW FRIGHTENING.

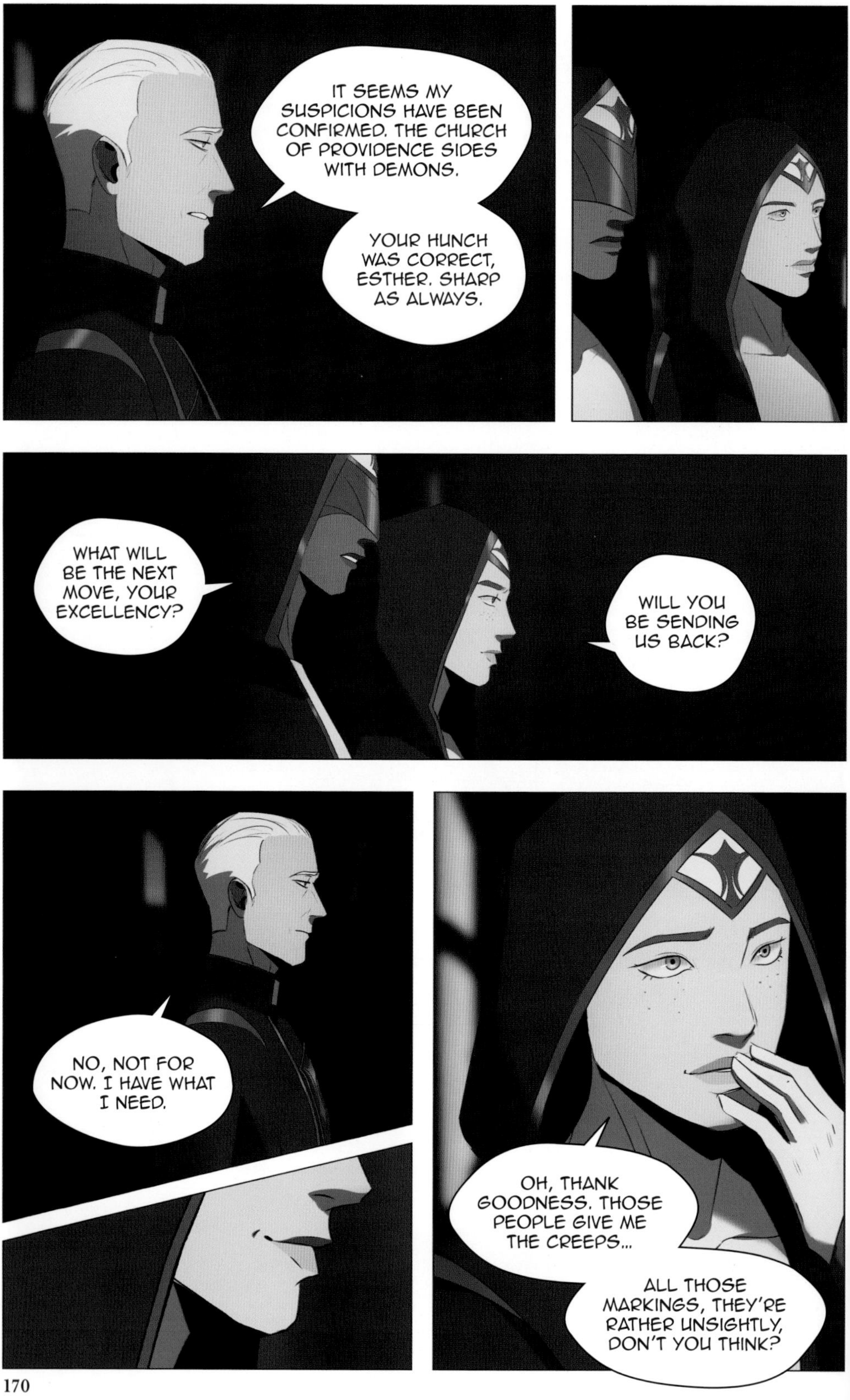
IT SEEMS MY SUSPICIONS HAVE BEEN CONFIRMED. THE CHURCH OF PROVIDENCE SIDES WITH DEMONS.
YOUR HUNCH WAS CORRECT, ESTHER. SHARP AS ALWAYS.
WHAT WILL BE THE NEXT MOVE, YOUR EXCELLENCY?
WILL YOU BE SENDING US BACK?
NO, NOT FOR NOW. I HAVE WHAT I NEED.
OH, THANK GOODNESS. THOSE PEOPLE GIVE ME THE CREEPS...
ALL THOSE MARKINGS, THEY'RE RATHER UNSIGHTLY, DON'T YOU THINK?

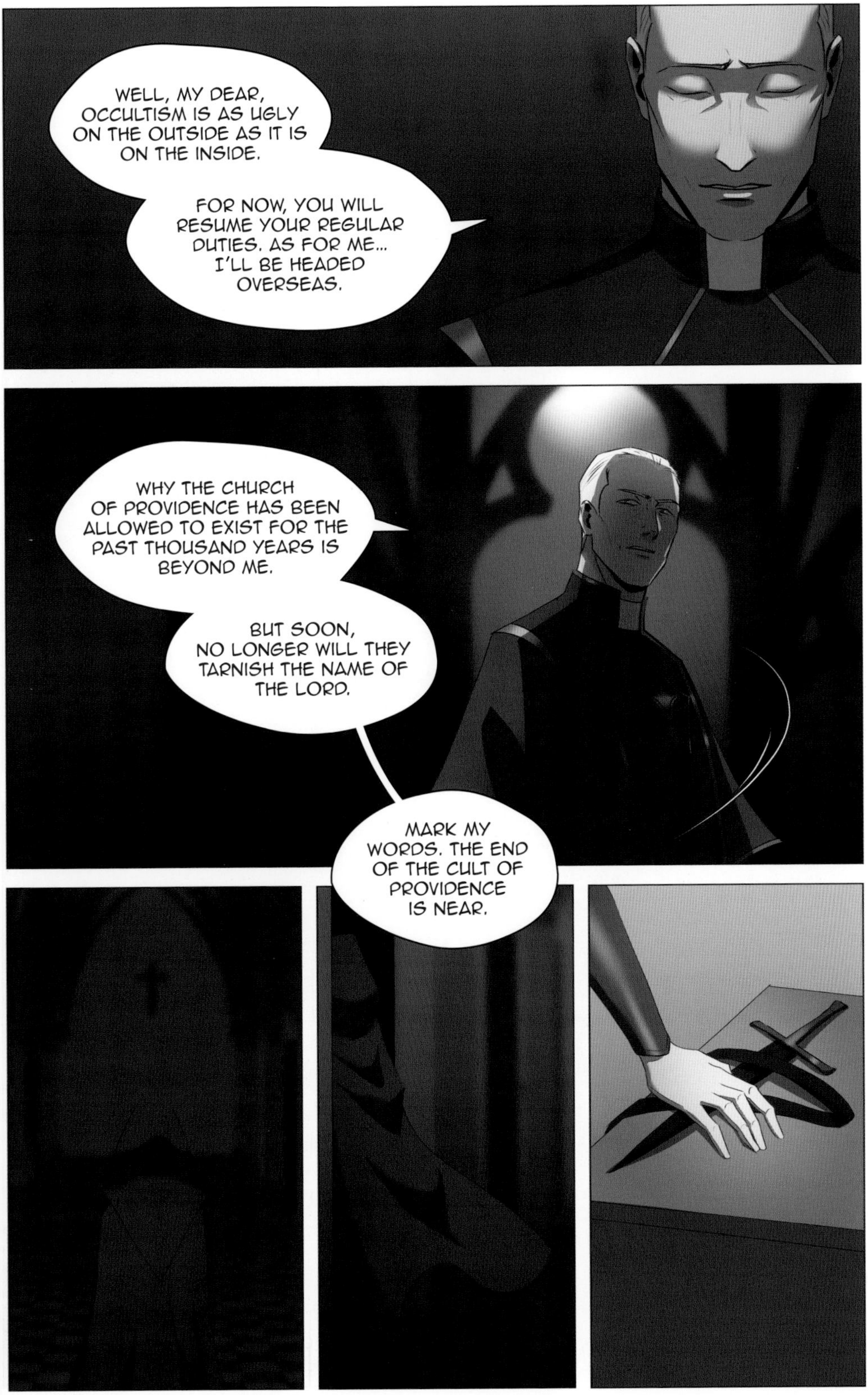
WELL, MY DEAR, OCCULTISM IS AS UGLY ON THE OUTSIDE AS IT IS ON THE INSIDE.
FOR NOW, YOU WILL RESUME YOUR REGULAR DUTIES. AS FOR ME... I'LL BE HEADED OVERSEAS.
WHY THE CHURCH OF PROVIDENCE HAS BEEN ALLOWED TO EXIST FOR THE PAST THOUSAND YEARS IS BEYOND ME.
BUT SOON, NO LONGER WILL THEY TARNISH THE NAME OF THE LORD.
MARK MY WORDS. THE END OF THE CULT OF PROVIDENCE IS NEAR.

HOW
UNSIGHTLY
INDEED.

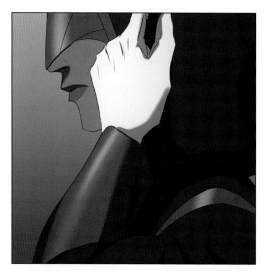

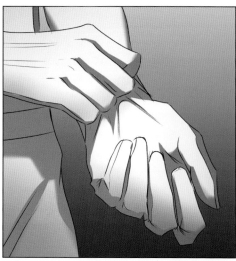

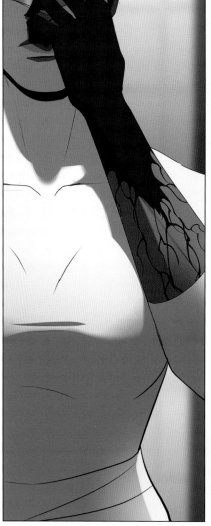

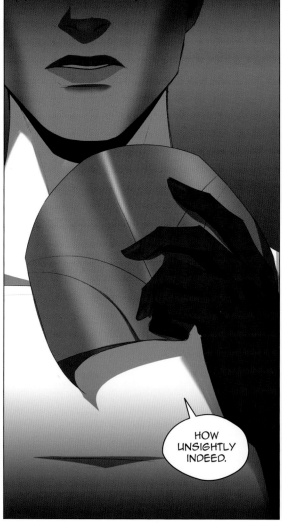

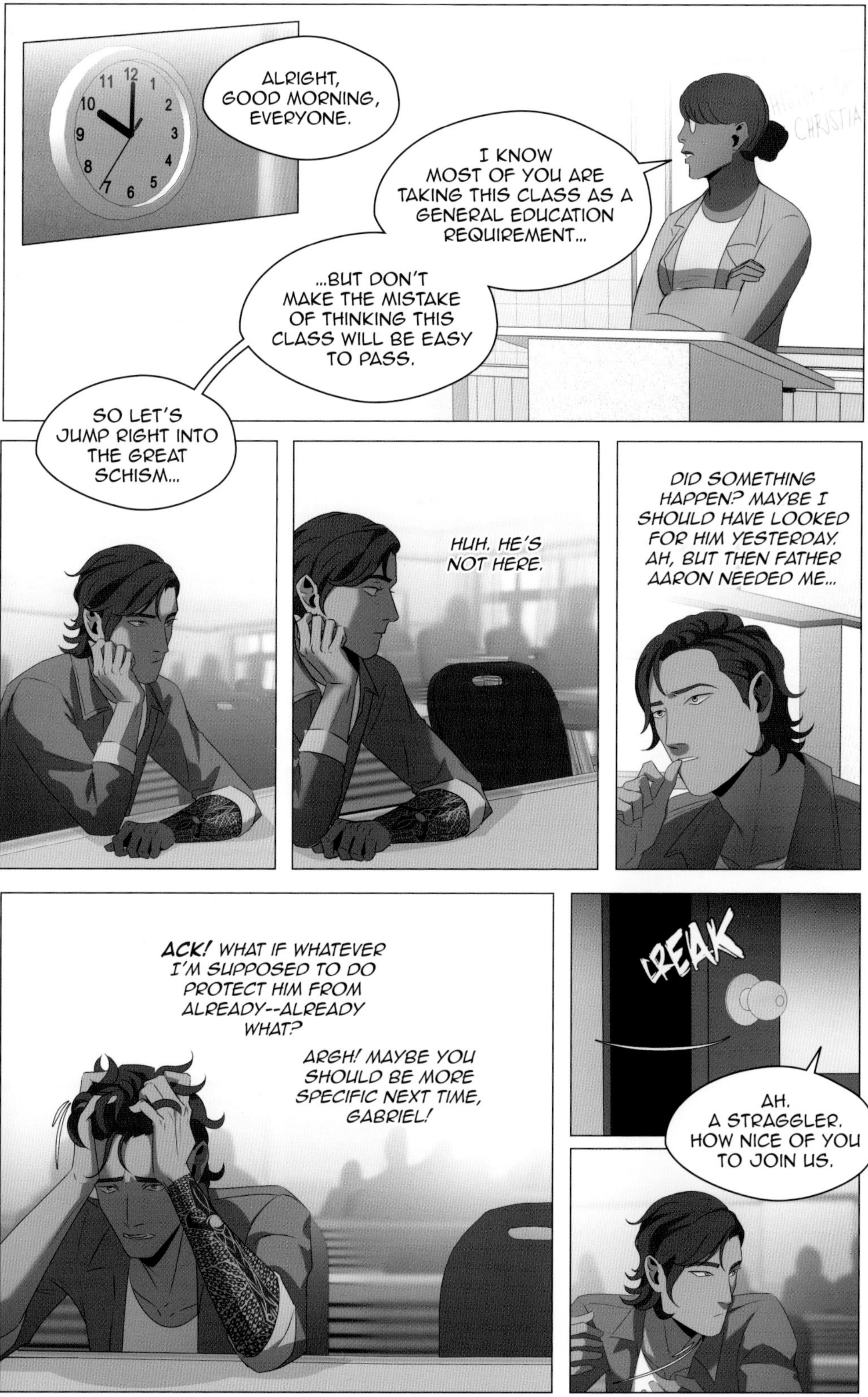
ALRIGHT, GOOD MORNING, EVERYONE.
I KNOW MOST OF YOU ARE TAKING THIS CLASS AS A GENERAL EDUCATION REQUIREMENT...
...BUT DON'T MAKE THE MISTAKE OF THINKING THIS CLASS WILL BE EASY TO PASS.
SO LET'S JUMP RIGHT INTO THE GREAT SCHISM...
HUH. HE'S NOT HERE.
DID SOMETHING HAPPEN? MAYBE I SHOULD HAVE LOOKED FOR HIM YESTERDAY. AH, BUT THEN FATHER AARON NEEDED ME...
ACK! WHAT IF WHATEVER I'M SUPPOSED TO DO PROTECT HIM FROM ALREADY--ALREADY WHAT?
ARGH! MAYBE YOU SHOULD BE MORE SPECIFIC NEXT TIME, GABRIEL!
CREAK
AH. A STRAGGLER. HOW NICE OF YOU TO JOIN US.

QUICKLY TAKE YOUR SEAT.

NOW, AS I WAS SAYING...

HUH?

WHAT...

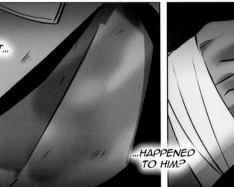

...HAPPENED TO HIM?

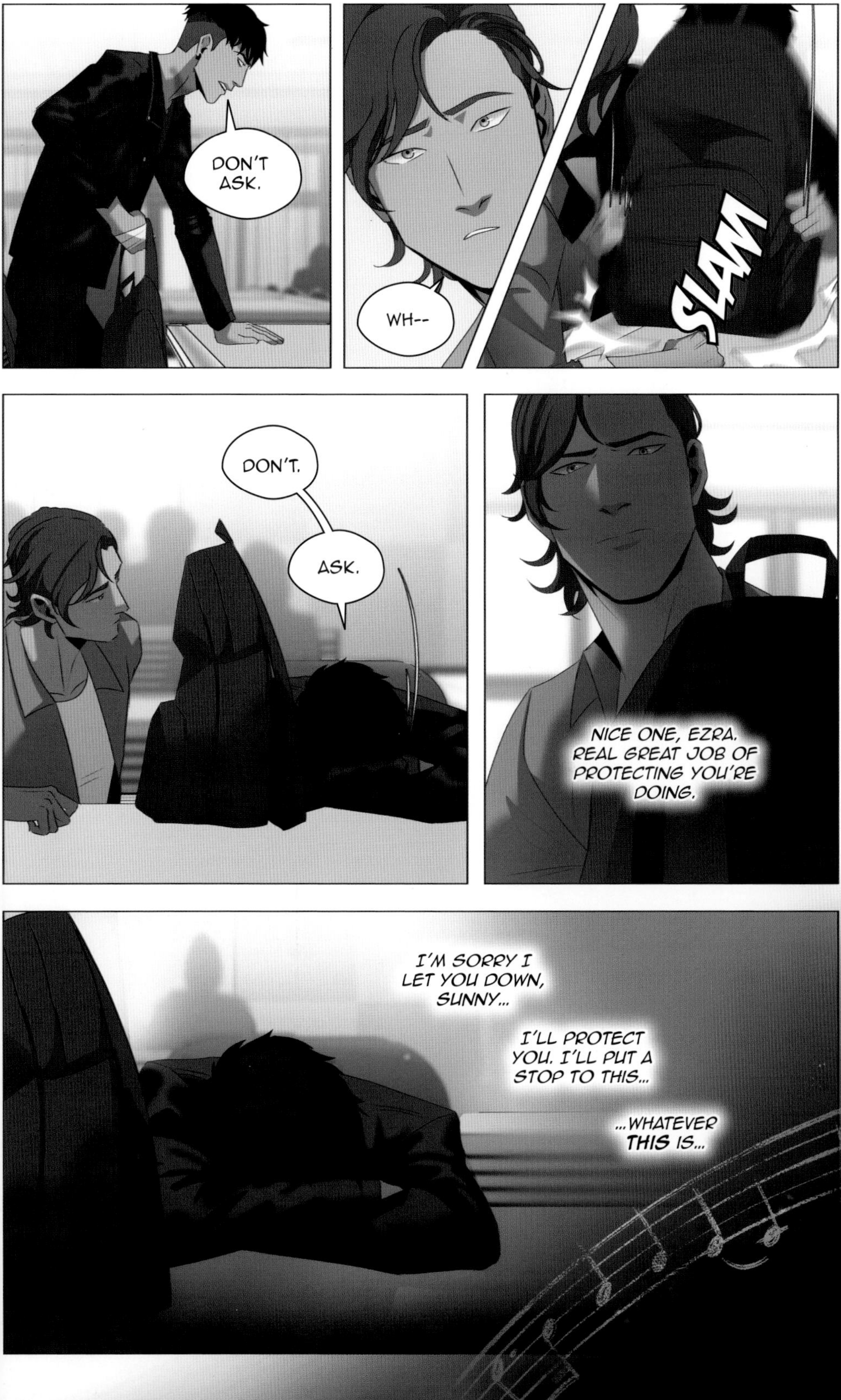
DON'T ASK.
WH--
SLAM
DON'T.
ASK.
NICE ONE, EZRA. REAL GREAT JOB OF PROTECTING YOU'RE DOING.
I'M SORRY I LET YOU DOWN, SUNNY...
I'LL PROTECT YOU. I'LL PUT A STOP TO THIS...
...WHATEVER THIS IS...

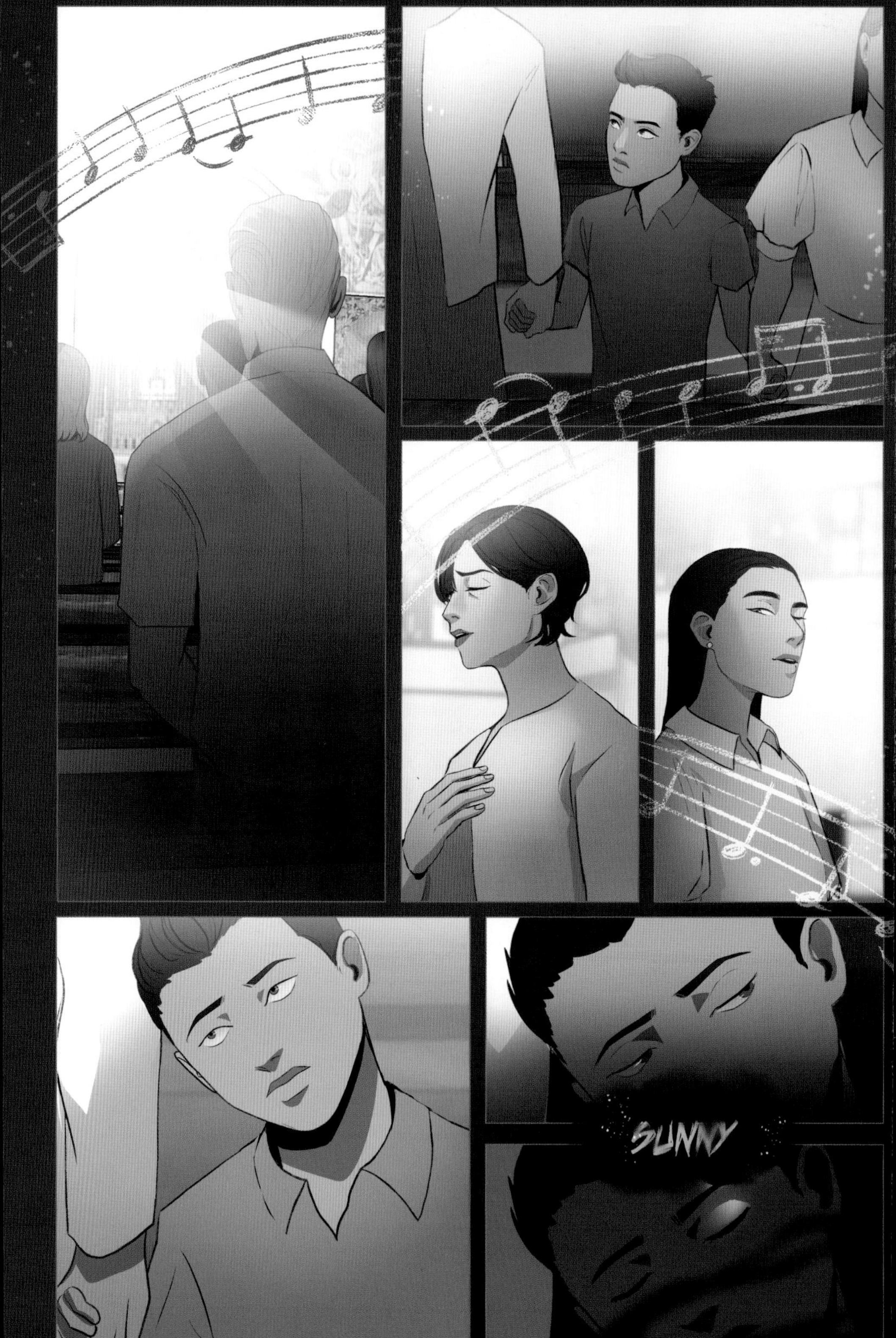
SUNNY

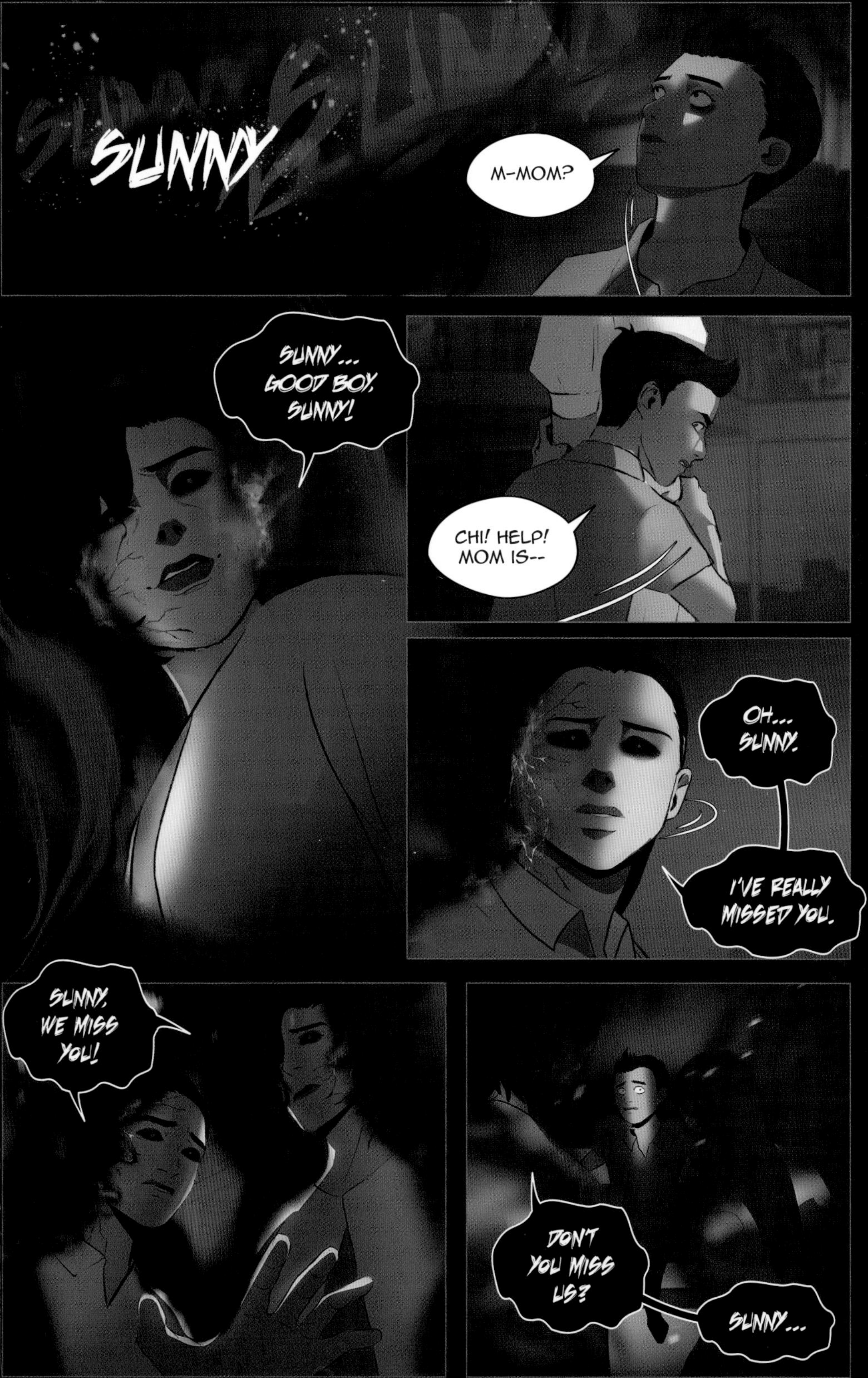
SUNNY
M-MOM?
SUNNY... GOOD BOY, SUNNY!
CHI! HELP! MOM IS--
OH... SUNNY.
I'VE REALLY MISSED YOU.
SUNNY, WE MISS YOU!
DON'T YOU MISS US?
SUNNY...

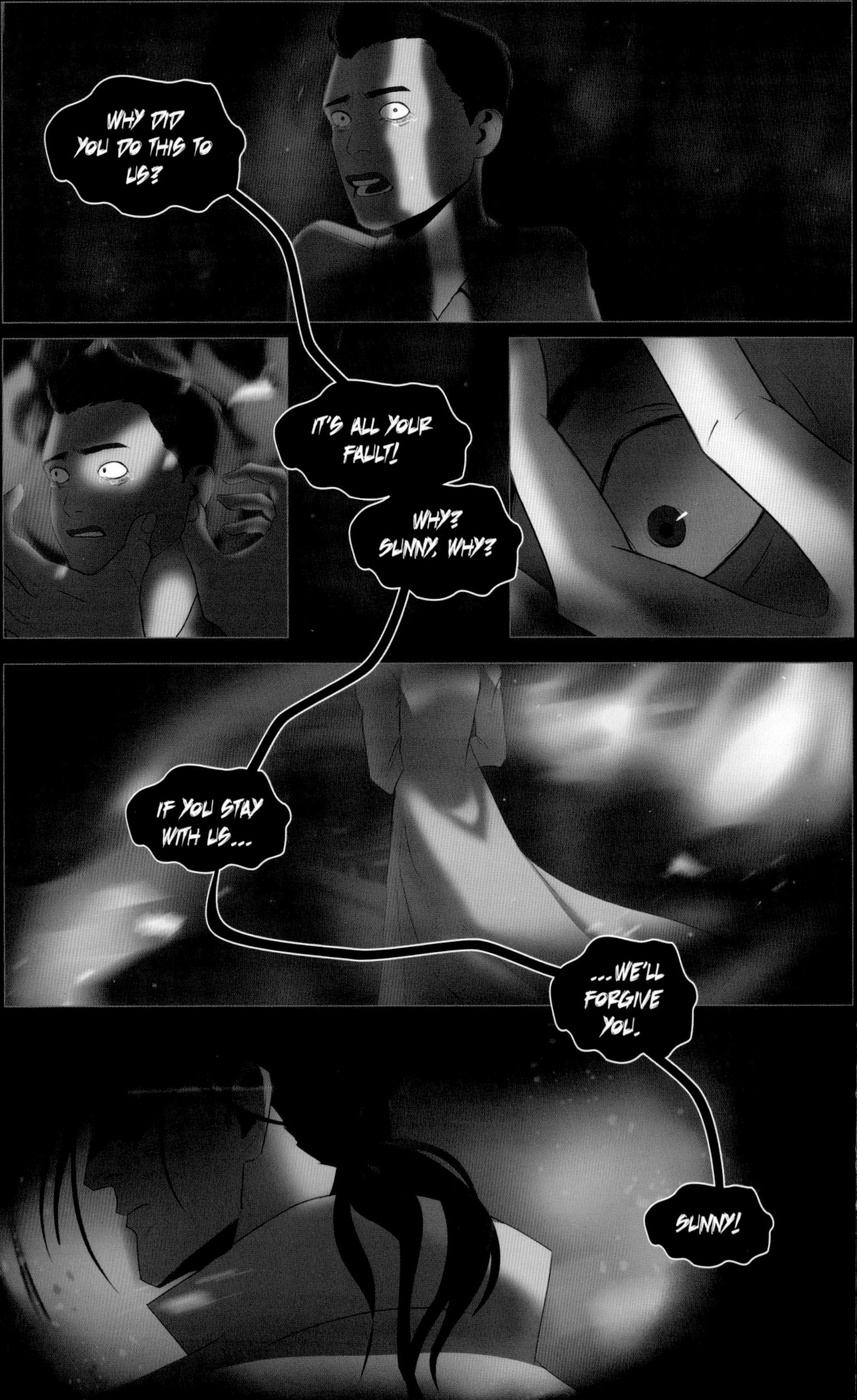
WHY DID YOU DO THIS TO US?
IT'S ALL YOUR FAULT!
WHY? SUNNY, WHY?
IF YOU STAY WITH US...
...WE'LL FORGIVE YOU.
SUNNY!

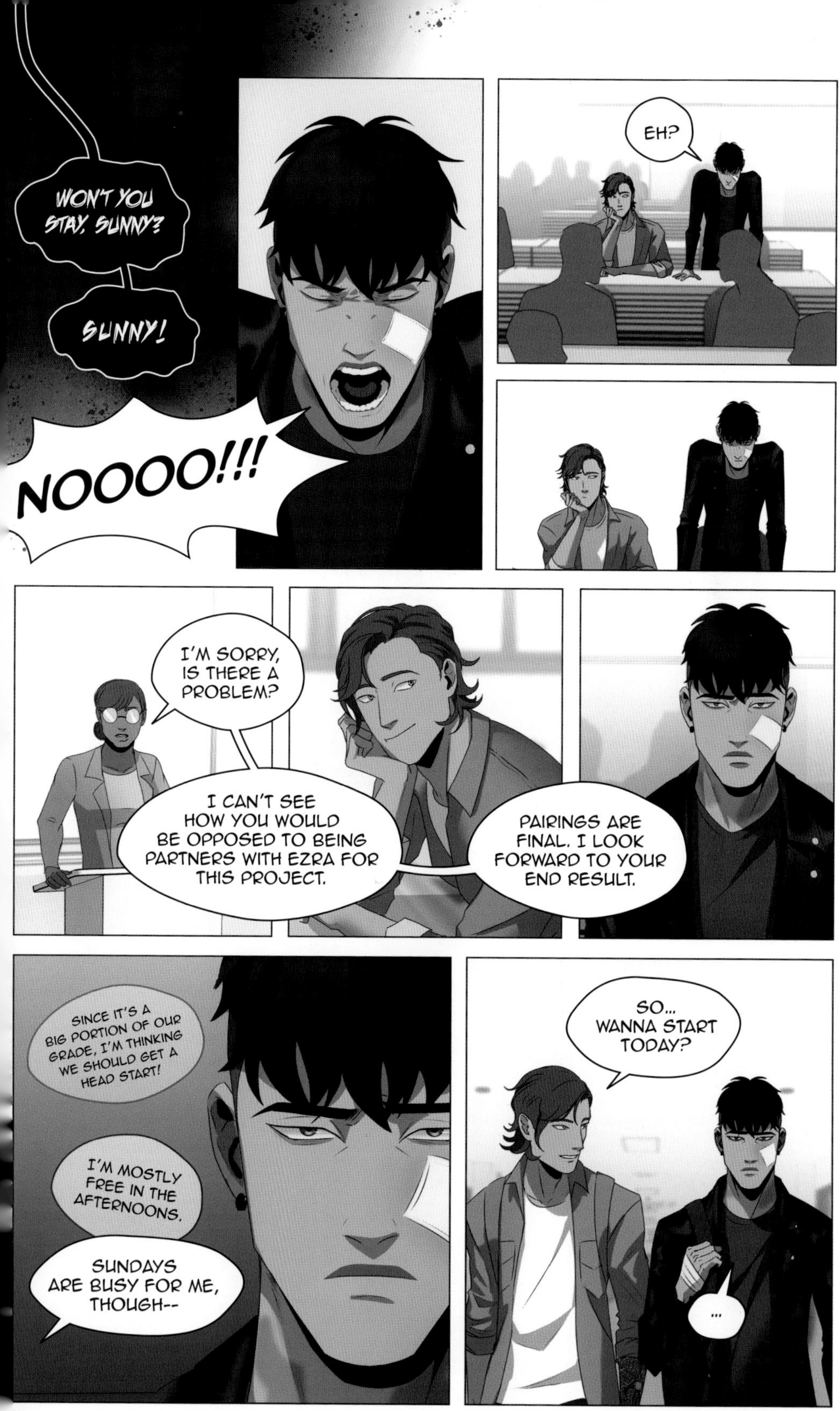
WON'T YOU STAY, SUNNY?
SUNNY!
NOOOO!!!
EH?
I'M SORRY, IS THERE A PROBLEM?
I CAN'T SEE HOW YOU WOULD BE OPPOSED TO BEING PARTNERS WITH EZRA FOR THIS PROJECT.
PAIRINGS ARE FINAL. I LOOK FORWARD TO YOUR END RESULT.
SINCE IT'S A BIG PORTION OF OUR GRADE, I'M THINKING WE SHOULD GET A HEAD START!
I'M MOSTLY FREE IN THE AFTERNOONS.
SUNDAYS ARE BUSY FOR ME, THOUGH--
SO... WANNA START TODAY?
...

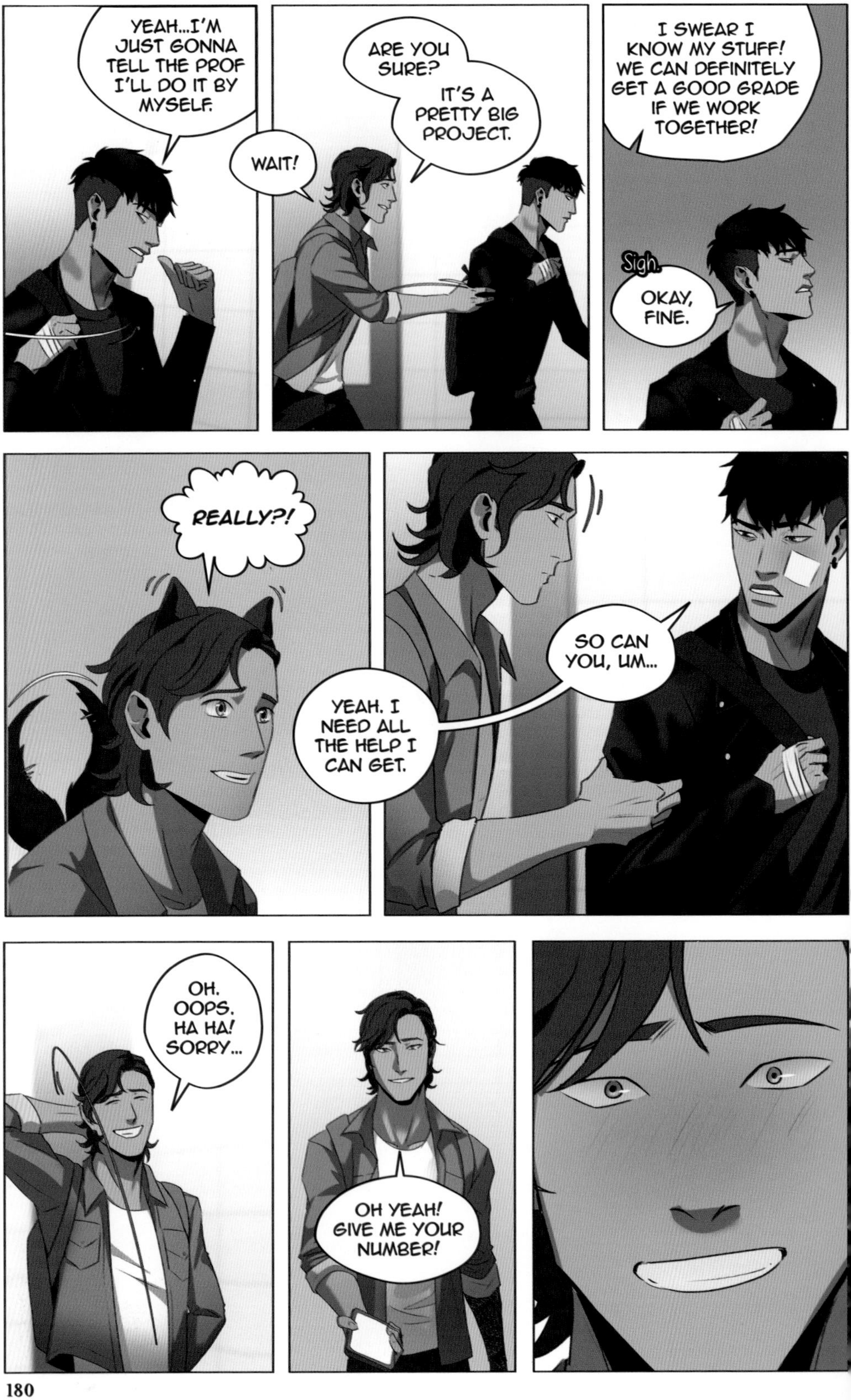
YEAH...I'M JUST GONNA TELL THE PROF I'LL DO IT BY MYSELF.
WAIT!
ARE YOU SURE?
IT'S A PRETTY BIG PROJECT.
I SWEAR I KNOW MY STUFF! WE CAN DEFINITELY GET A GOOD GRADE IF WE WORK TOGETHER!
Sigh.
OKAY, FINE.
REALLY?!
SO CAN YOU, UM...
YEAH. I NEED ALL THE HELP I CAN GET.
OH. OOPS. HA HA! SORRY...
OH YEAH! GIVE ME YOUR NUMBER!

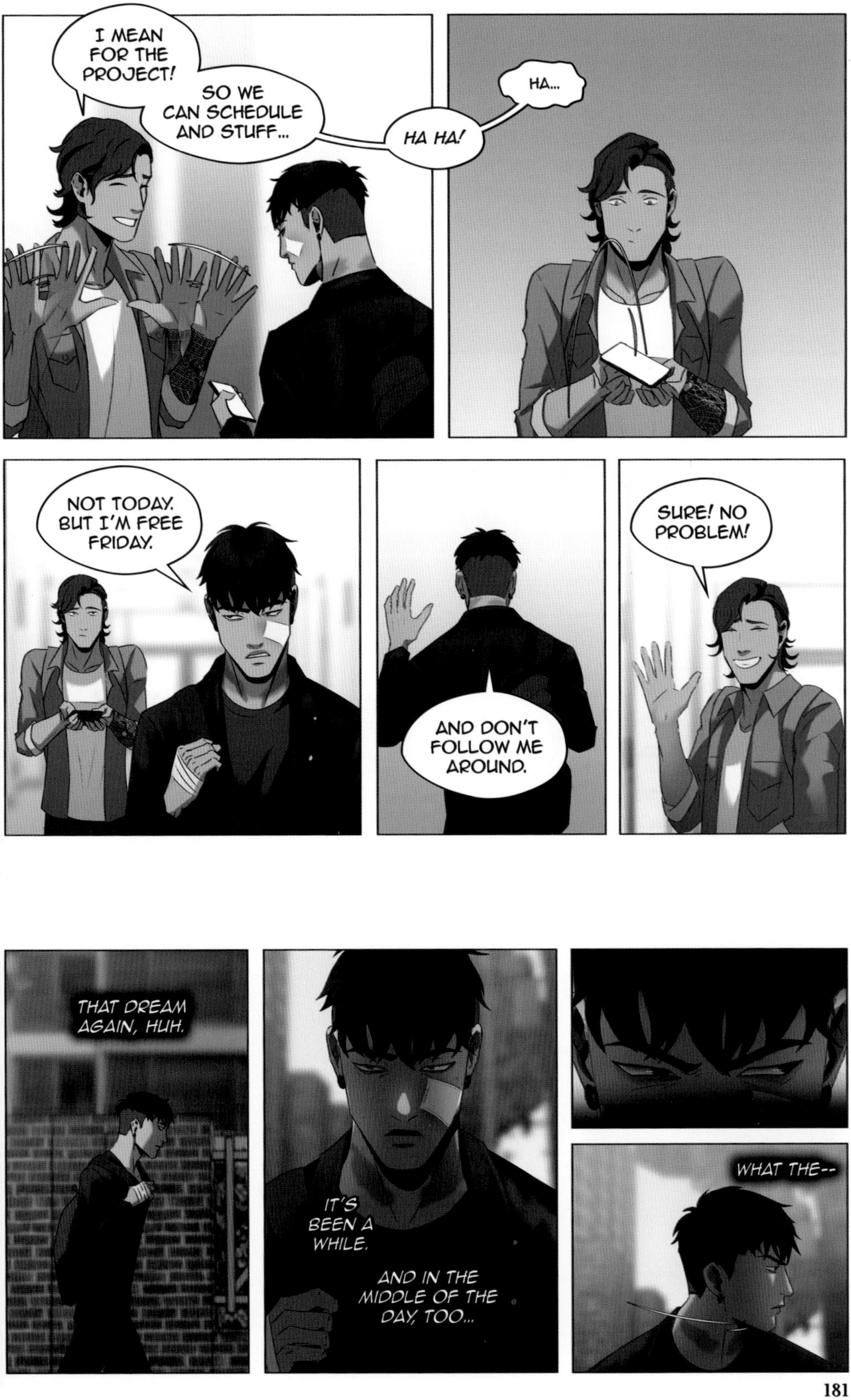
I MEAN FOR THE PROJECT!
SO WE CAN SCHEDULE AND STUFF...
HA HA!
HA...
NOT TODAY. BUT I'M FREE FRIDAY.
AND DON'T FOLLOW ME AROUND.
SURE! NO PROBLEM!
THAT DREAM AGAIN, HUH.
IT'S BEEN A WHILE.
AND IN THE MIDDLE OF THE DAY, TOO...
WHAT THE--

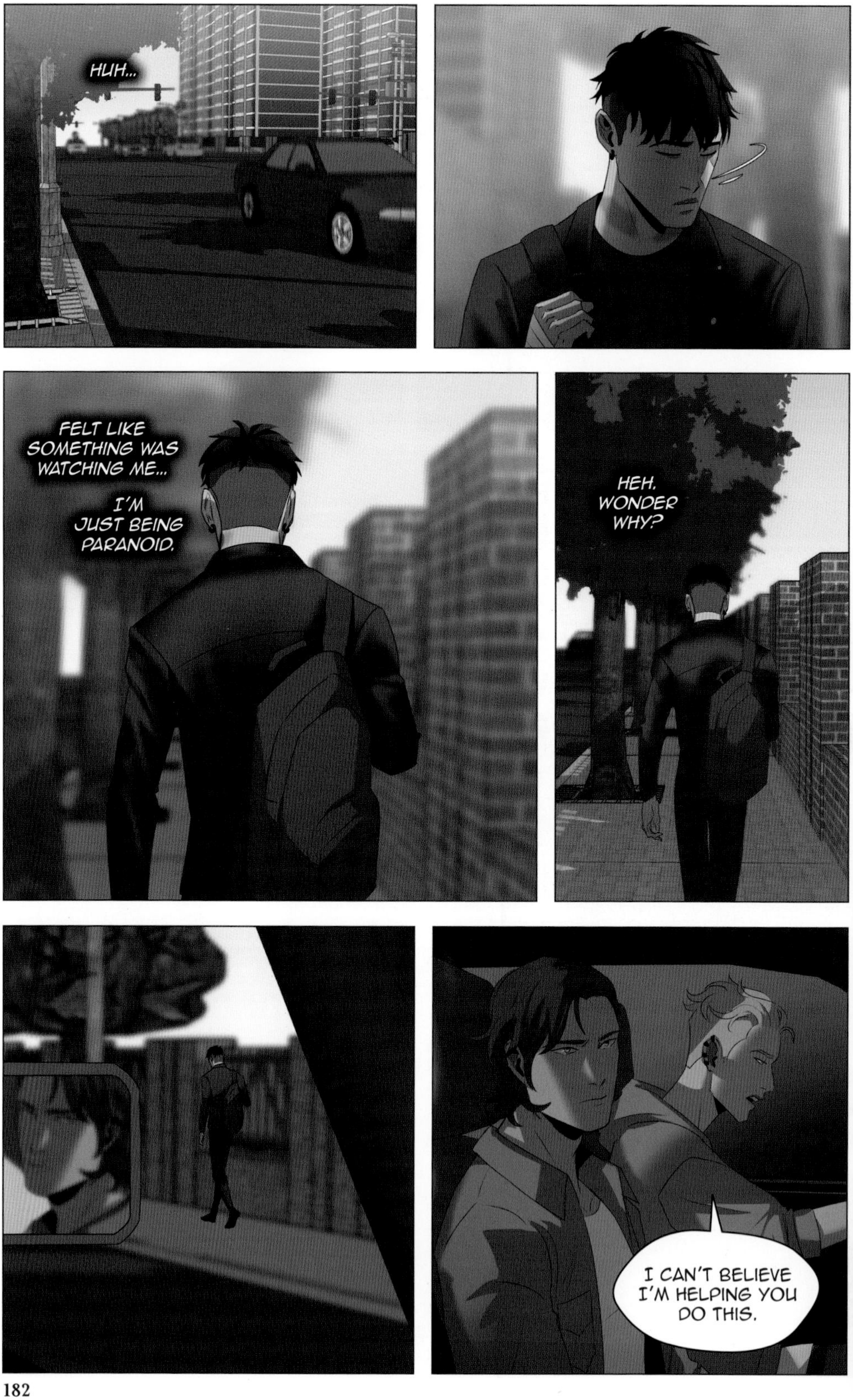
HUH...
FELT LIKE SOMETHING WAS WATCHING ME...
I'M JUST BEING PARANOID.
HEH. WONDER WHY?
I CAN'T BELIEVE I'M HELPING YOU DO THIS.

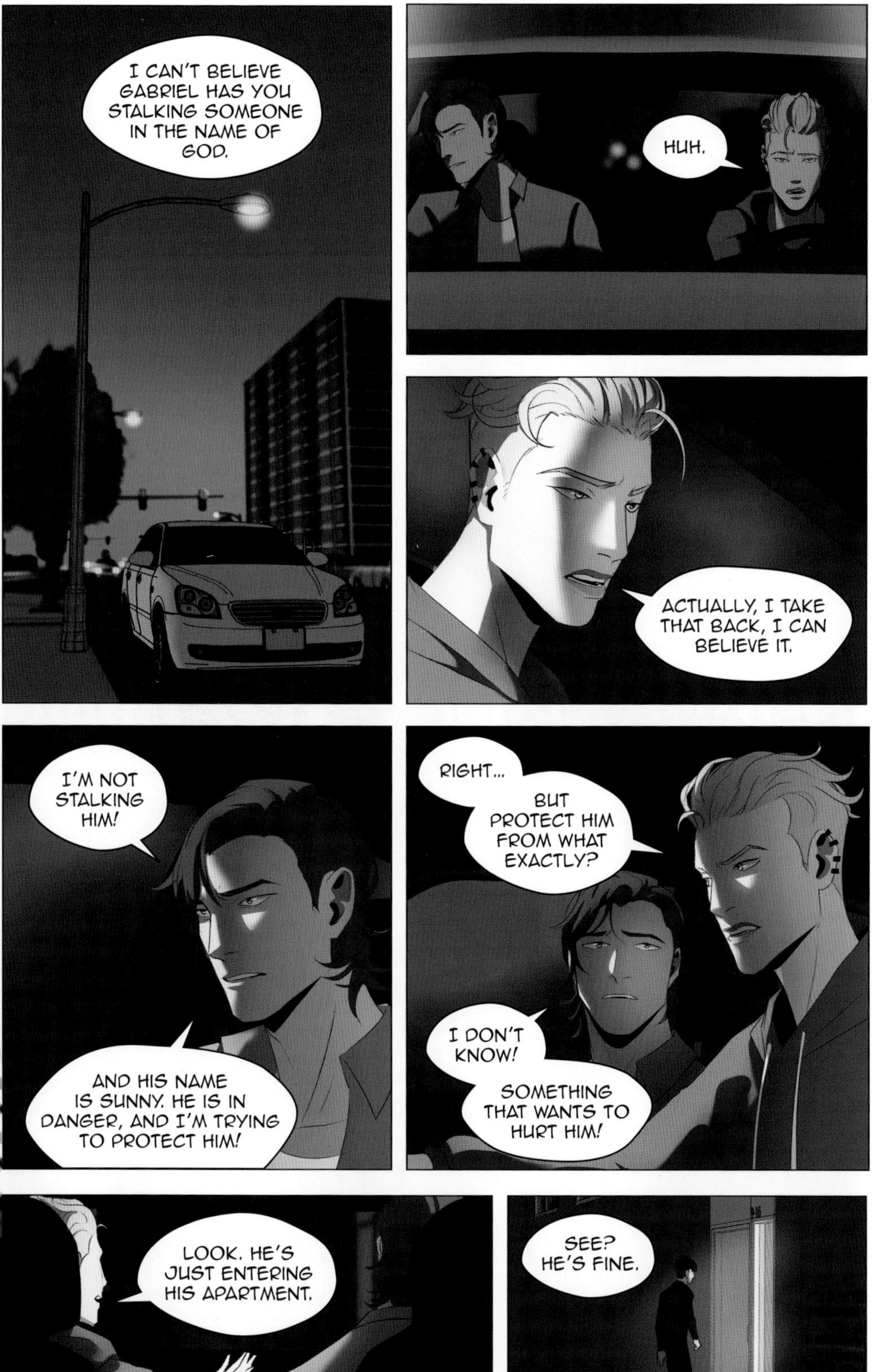
I CAN'T BELIEVE GABRIEL HAS YOU STALKING SOMEONE IN THE NAME OF GOD.
HUH.
ACTUALLY, I TAKE THAT BACK, I CAN BELIEVE IT.
I'M NOT STALKING HIM!
AND HIS NAME IS SUNNY. HE IS IN DANGER, AND I'M TRYING TO PROTECT HIM!
RIGHT...
BUT PROTECT HIM FROM WHAT EXACTLY?
I DON'T KNOW!
SOMETHING THAT WANTS TO HURT HIM!
LOOK. HE'S JUST ENTERING HIS APARTMENT.
SEE? HE'S FINE.

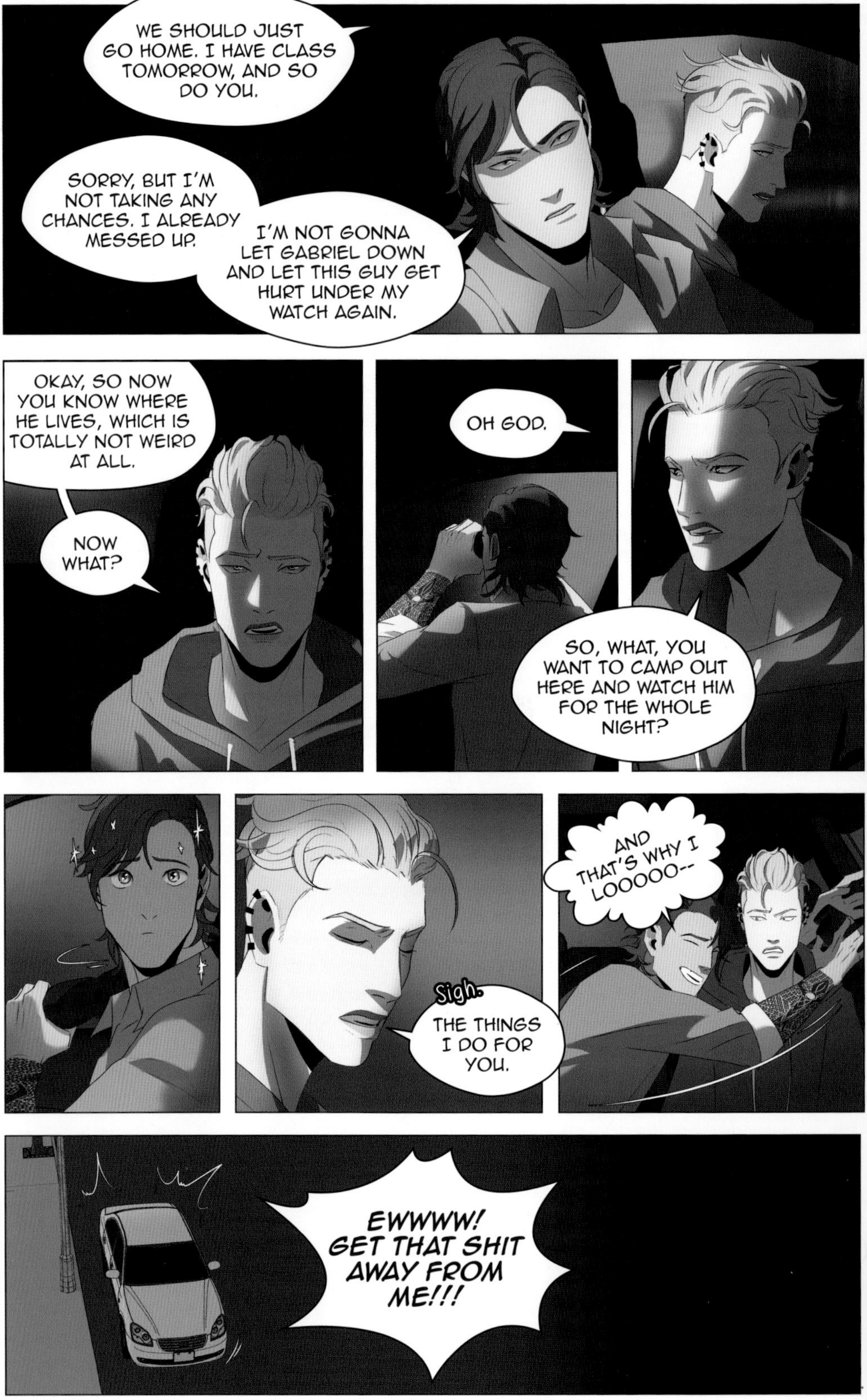
WE SHOULD JUST GO HOME. I HAVE CLASS TOMORROW, AND SO DO YOU.
SORRY, BUT I'M NOT TAKING ANY CHANCES. I ALREADY MESSED UP.
I'M NOT GONNA LET GABRIEL DOWN AND LET THIS GUY GET HURT UNDER MY WATCH AGAIN.
OKAY, SO NOW YOU KNOW WHERE HE LIVES, WHICH IS TOTALLY NOT WEIRD AT ALL.
NOW WHAT?
OH GOD.
SO, WHAT, YOU WANT TO CAMP OUT HERE AND WATCH HIM FOR THE WHOLE NIGHT?
Sigh.
THE THINGS I DO FOR YOU.
AND THAT'S WHY I LOOOOO--
EWWWW! GET THAT SHIT AWAY FROM ME!!!

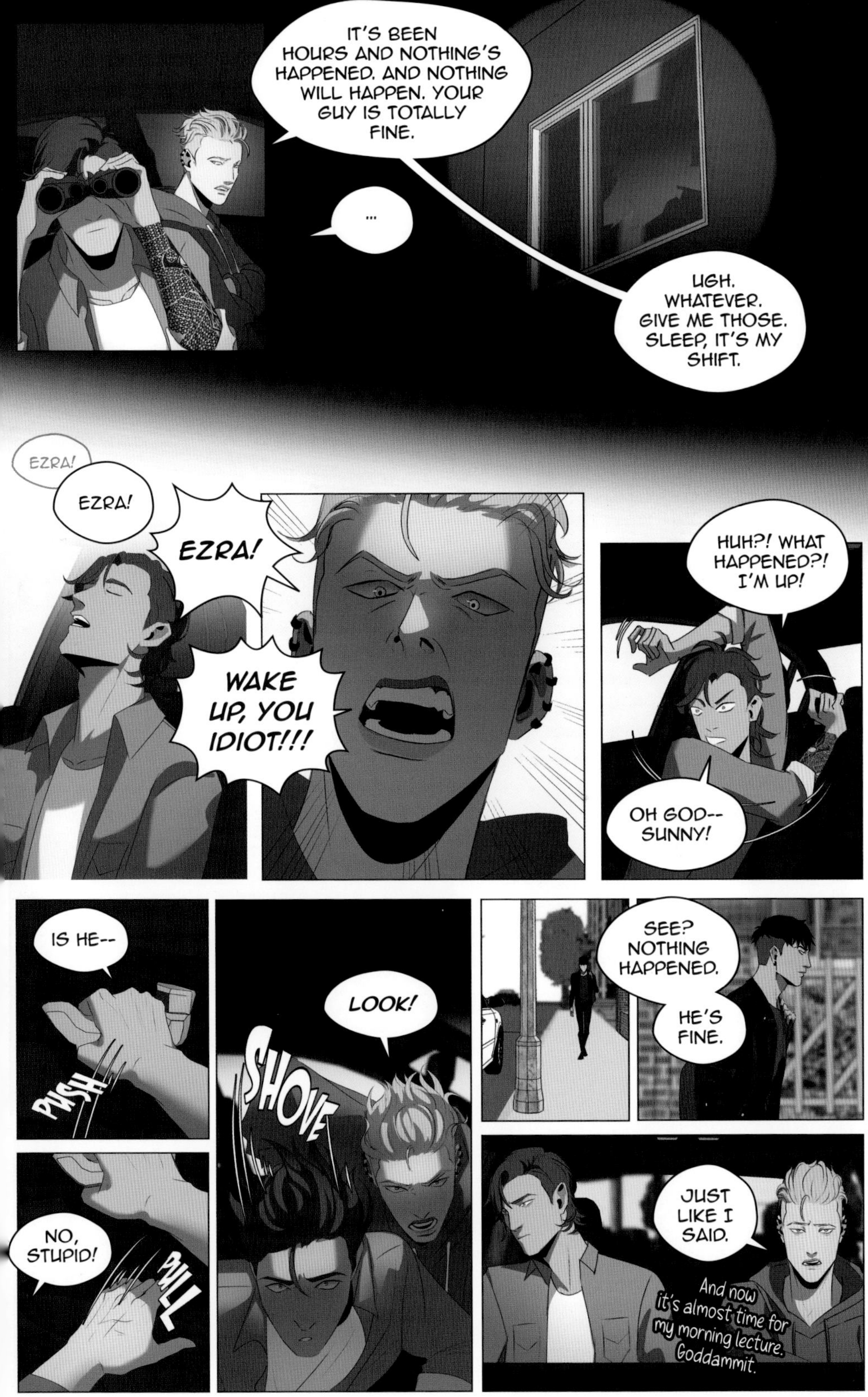
IT'S BEEN HOURS AND NOTHING'S HAPPENED. AND NOTHING WILL HAPPEN. YOUR GUY IS TOTALLY FINE.
...
UGH. WHATEVER. GIVE ME THOSE. SLEEP, IT'S MY SHIFT.
EZRA!
EZRA!
EZRA!
WAKE UP, YOU IDIOT!!!
HUH?! WHAT HAPPENED?! I'M UP!
OH GOD-- SUNNY!
IS HE--
PUSH
NO, STUPID!
PULL
LOOK!
SHOVE
SEE? NOTHING HAPPENED.
HE'S FINE.
JUST LIKE I SAID.
And now it's almost time for my morning lecture. Goddammit.

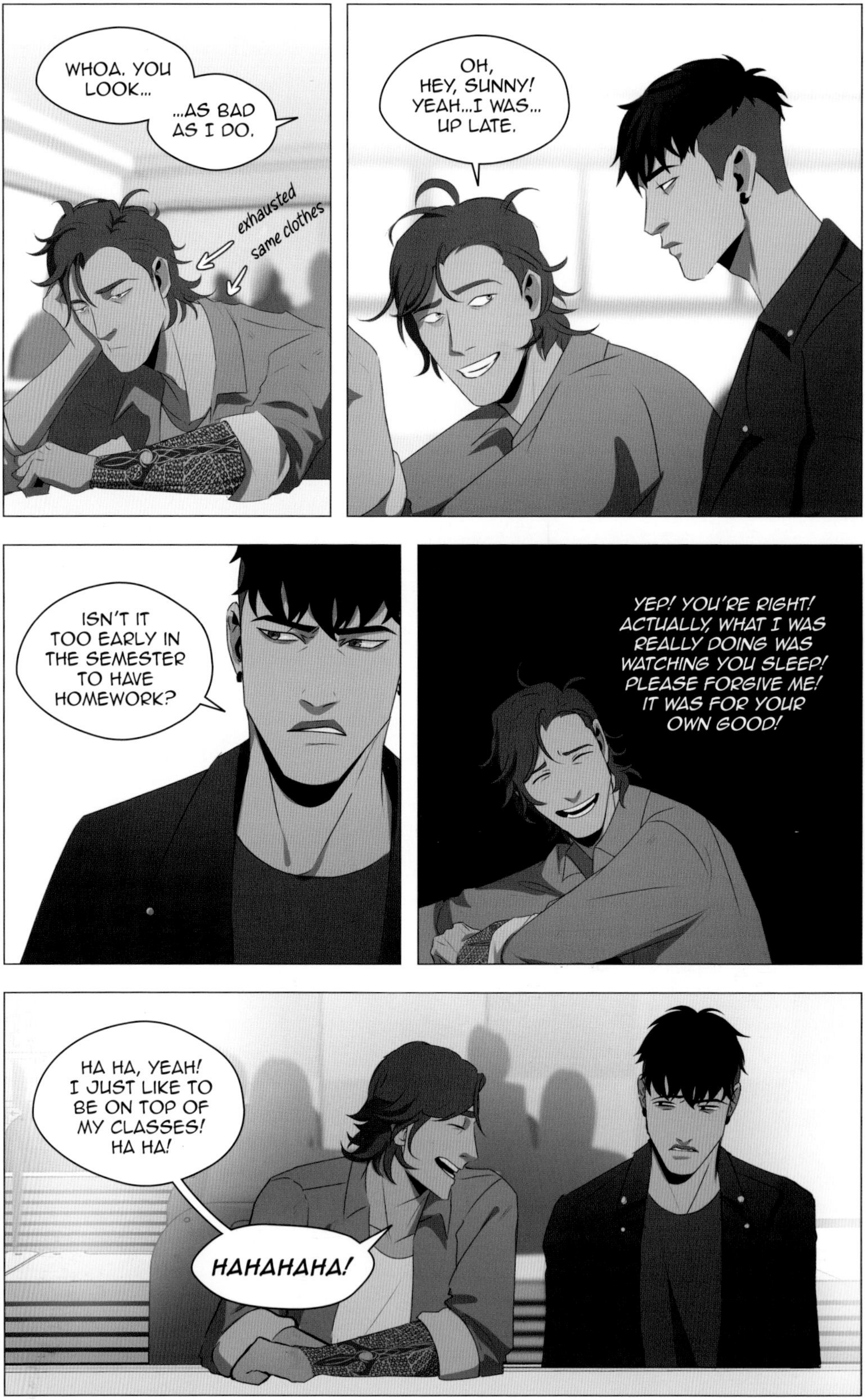
WHOA. YOU LOOK...
...AS BAD AS I DO.
exhausted
same clothes
OH, HEY, SUNNY! YEAH...I WAS... UP LATE.
ISN'T IT TOO EARLY IN THE SEMESTER TO HAVE HOMEWORK?
YEP! YOU'RE RIGHT! ACTUALLY, WHAT I WAS REALLY DOING WAS WATCHING YOU SLEEP! PLEASE FORGIVE ME! IT WAS FOR YOUR OWN GOOD!
HA HA, YEAH! I JUST LIKE TO BE ON TOP OF MY CLASSES! HA HA!
HAHAHAHA!

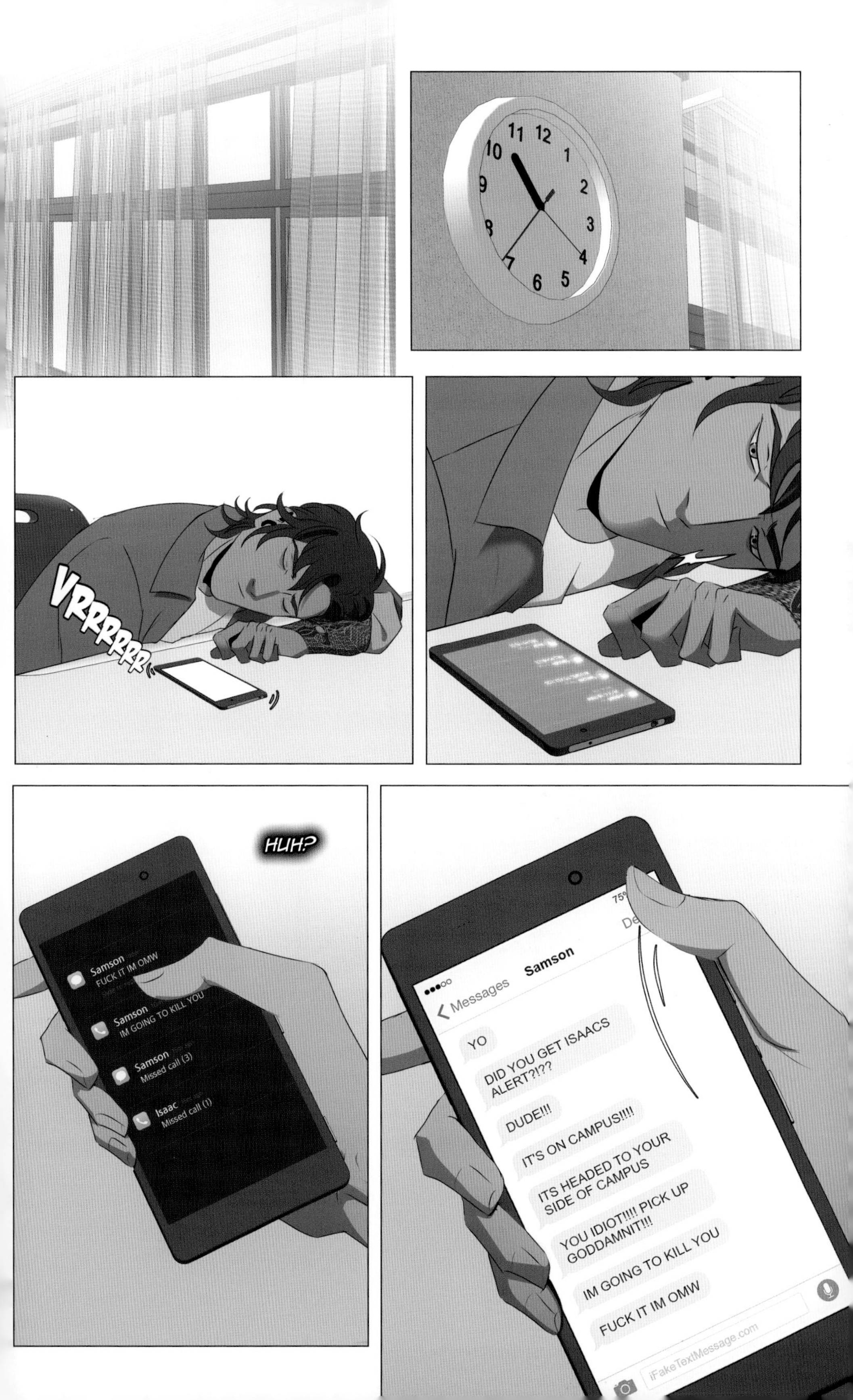
VRRRRRRR
HUH?
Samson
FUCK IT IM OMW
Samson
IM GOING TO KILL YOU
Samson
Missed call (3)
Isaac
Missed call (1)
Messages
Samson
YO
DID YOU GET ISAACS ALERT?!??
DUDE!!!
IT'S ON CAMPUS!!!!
ITS HEADED TO YOUR SIDE OF CAMPUS
YOU IDIOT!!!! PICK UP GODDAMNIT!!!
IM GOING TO KILL YOU
FUCK IT IM OMW
iFakeTextMessage.com

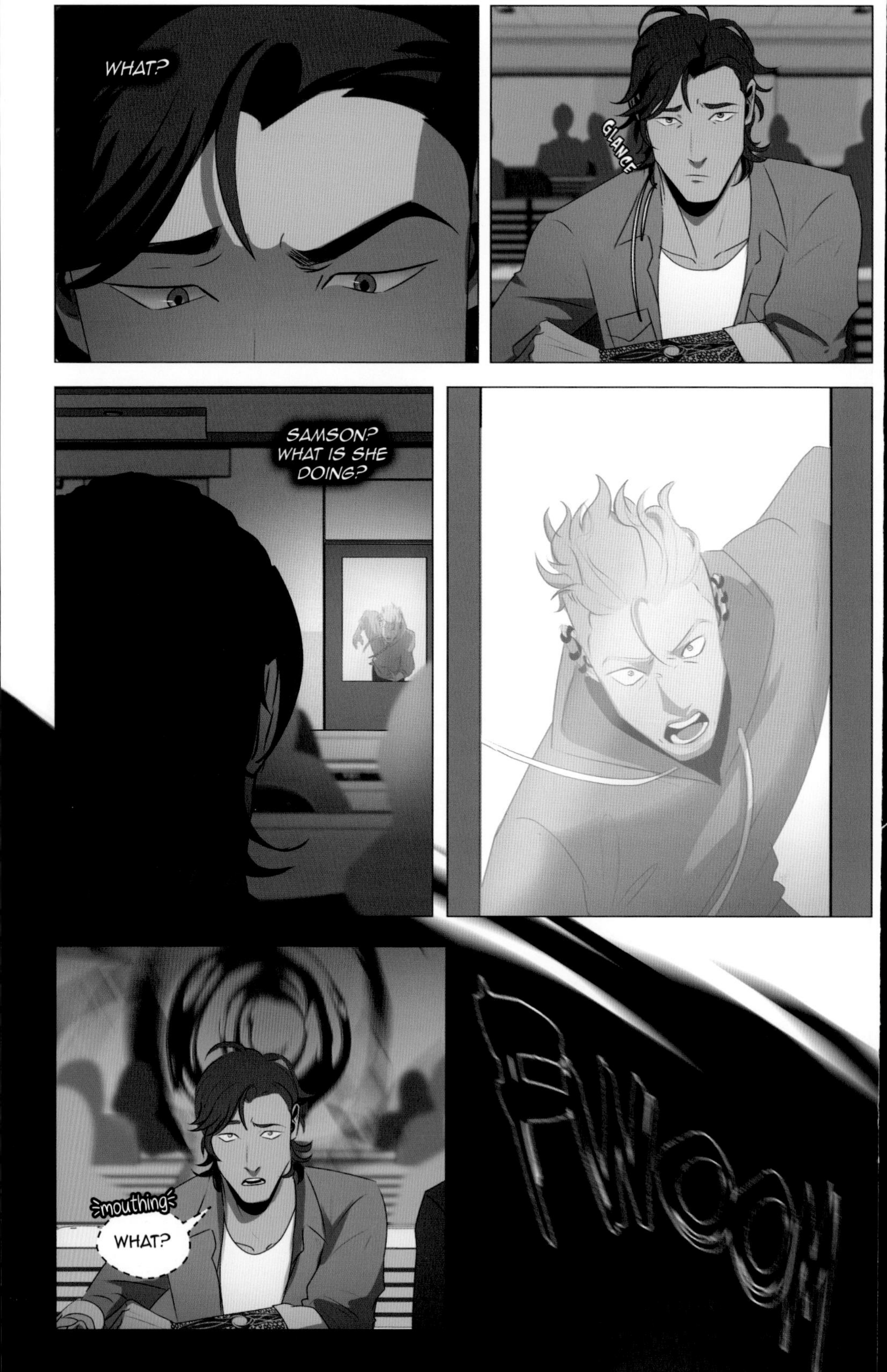
WHAT?
GLANCE
SAMSON? WHAT IS SHE DOING?
mouthing
WHAT?
FWOOOM

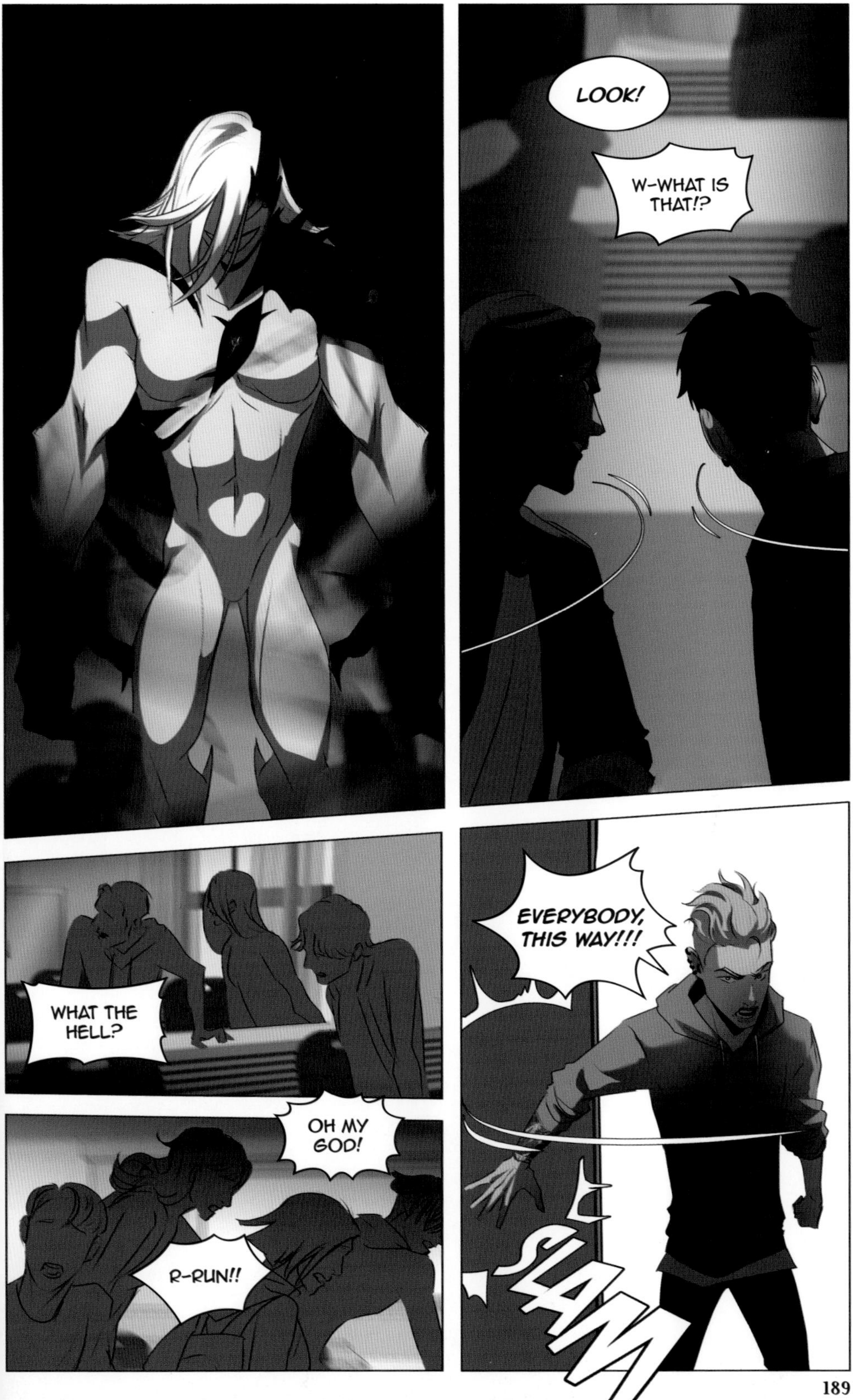
LOOK!
W-WHAT IS THAT!?
WHAT THE HELL?
OH MY GOD!
R-RUN!!
EVERYBODY, THIS WAY!!!
SLAM

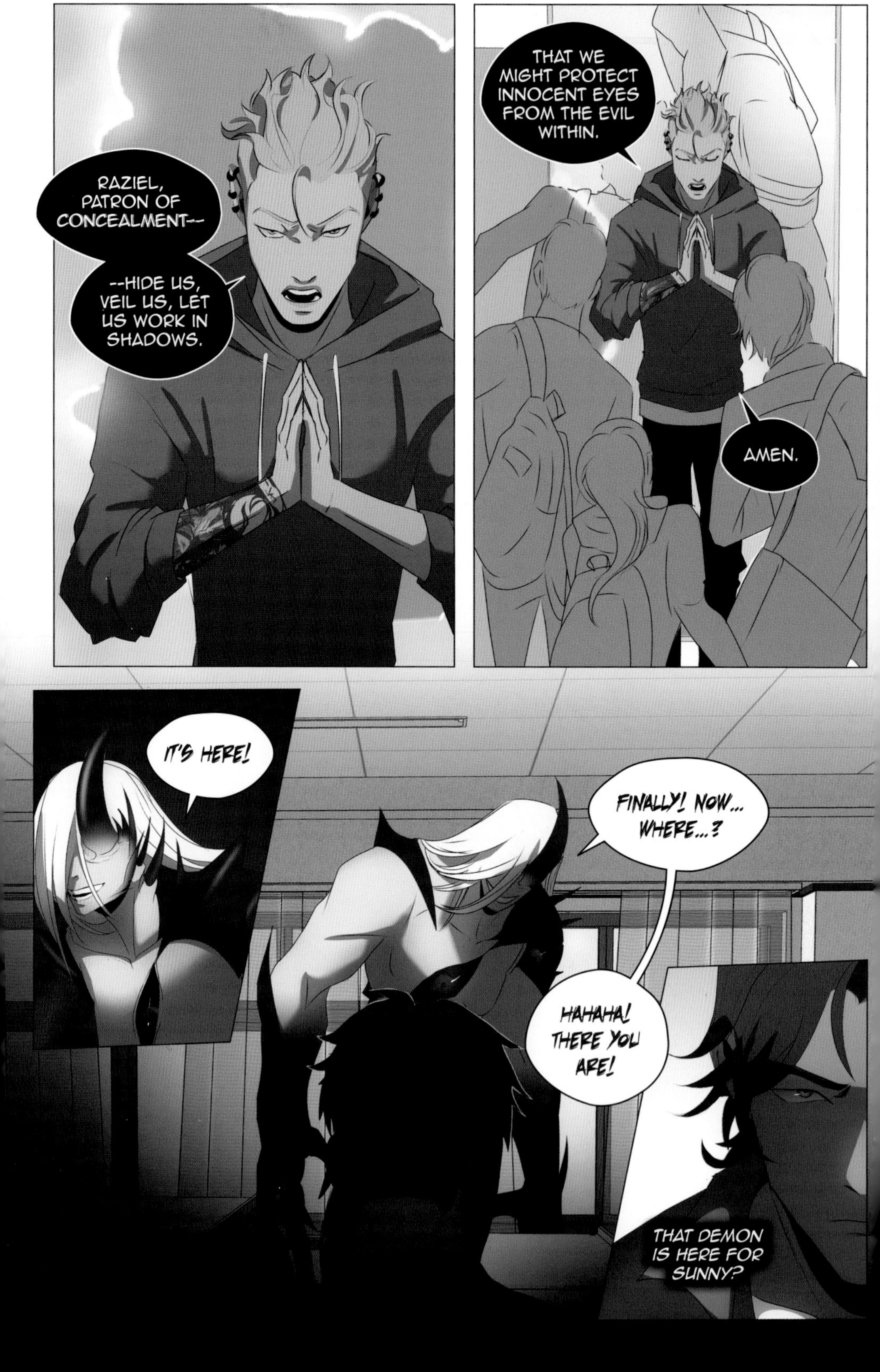
RAZIEL, PATRON OF CONCEALMENT--
--HIDE US, VEIL US, LET US WORK IN SHADOWS.
THAT WE MIGHT PROTECT INNOCENT EYES FROM THE EVIL WITHIN.
AMEN.
IT'S HERE!
FINALLY! NOW... WHERE...?
HAHAHA! THERE YOU ARE!
THAT DEMON IS HERE FOR SUNNY?

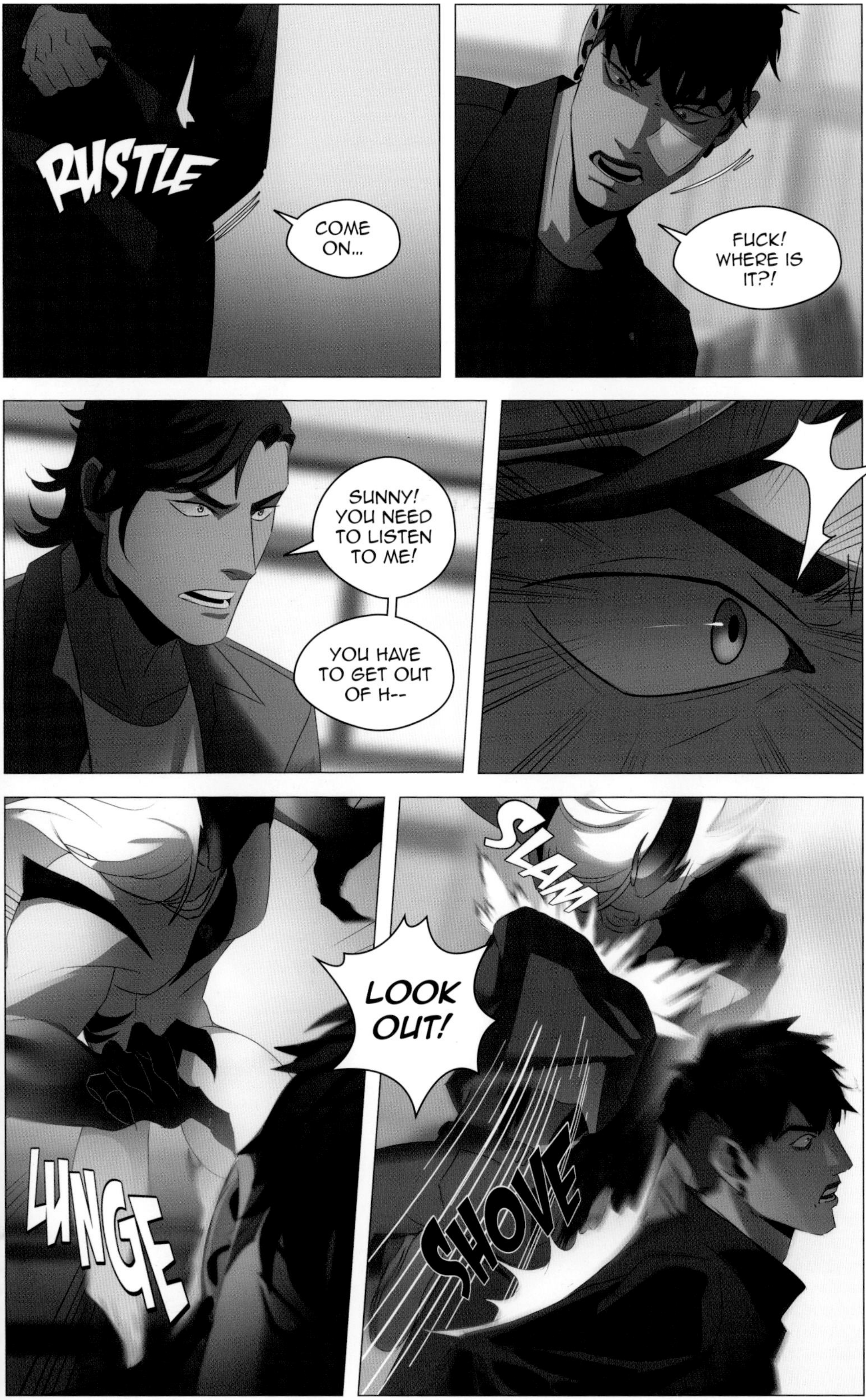
RUSTLE
COME ON...
FUCK! WHERE IS IT?!
SUNNY! YOU NEED TO LISTEN TO ME!
YOU HAVE TO GET OUT OF H--
LUNGE
SLAM
LOOK OUT!
SHOVE

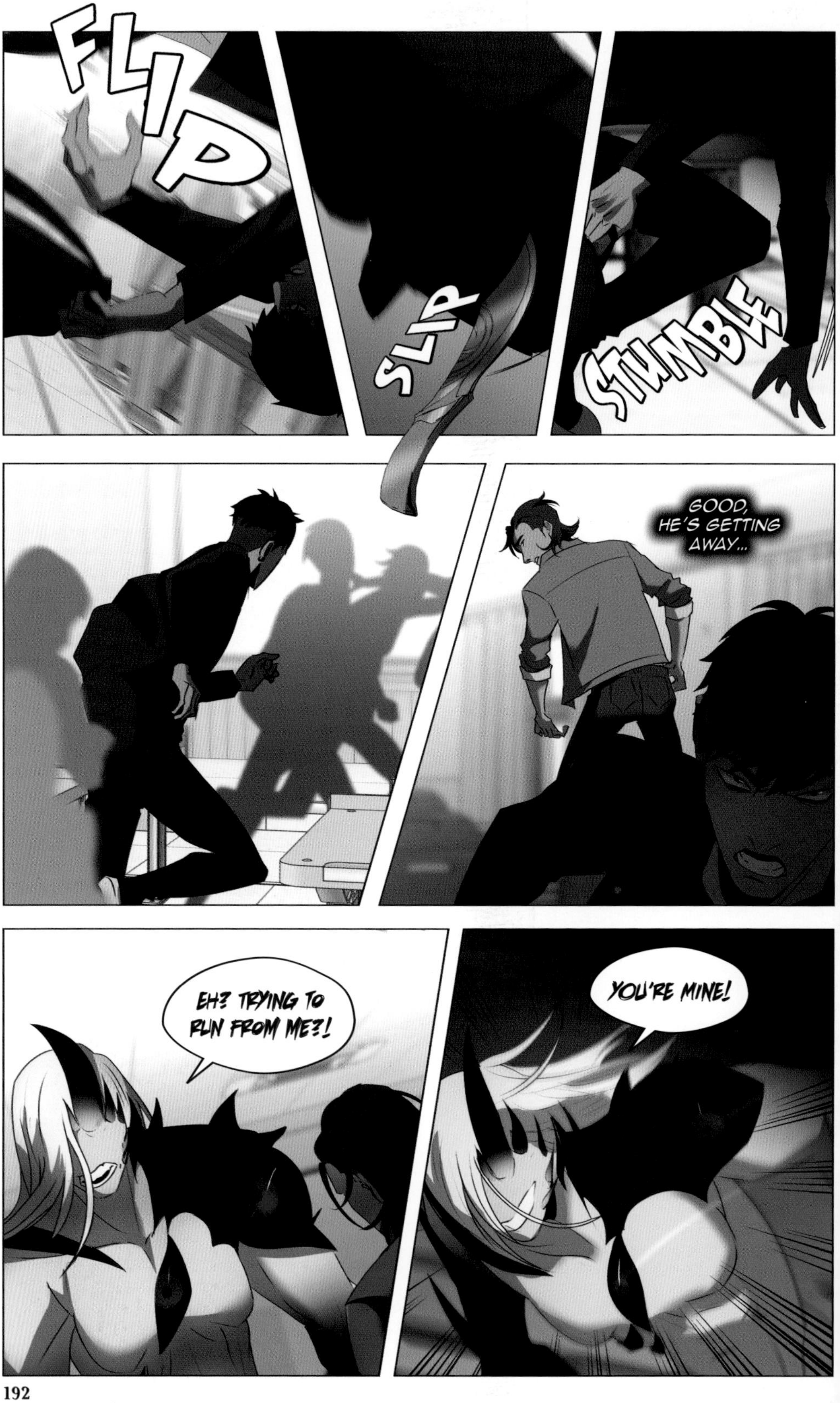
FLIP
SLIP
STUMBLE
GOOD, HE'S GETTING AWAY...
EH? TRYING TO RUN FROM ME?!
YOU'RE MINE!

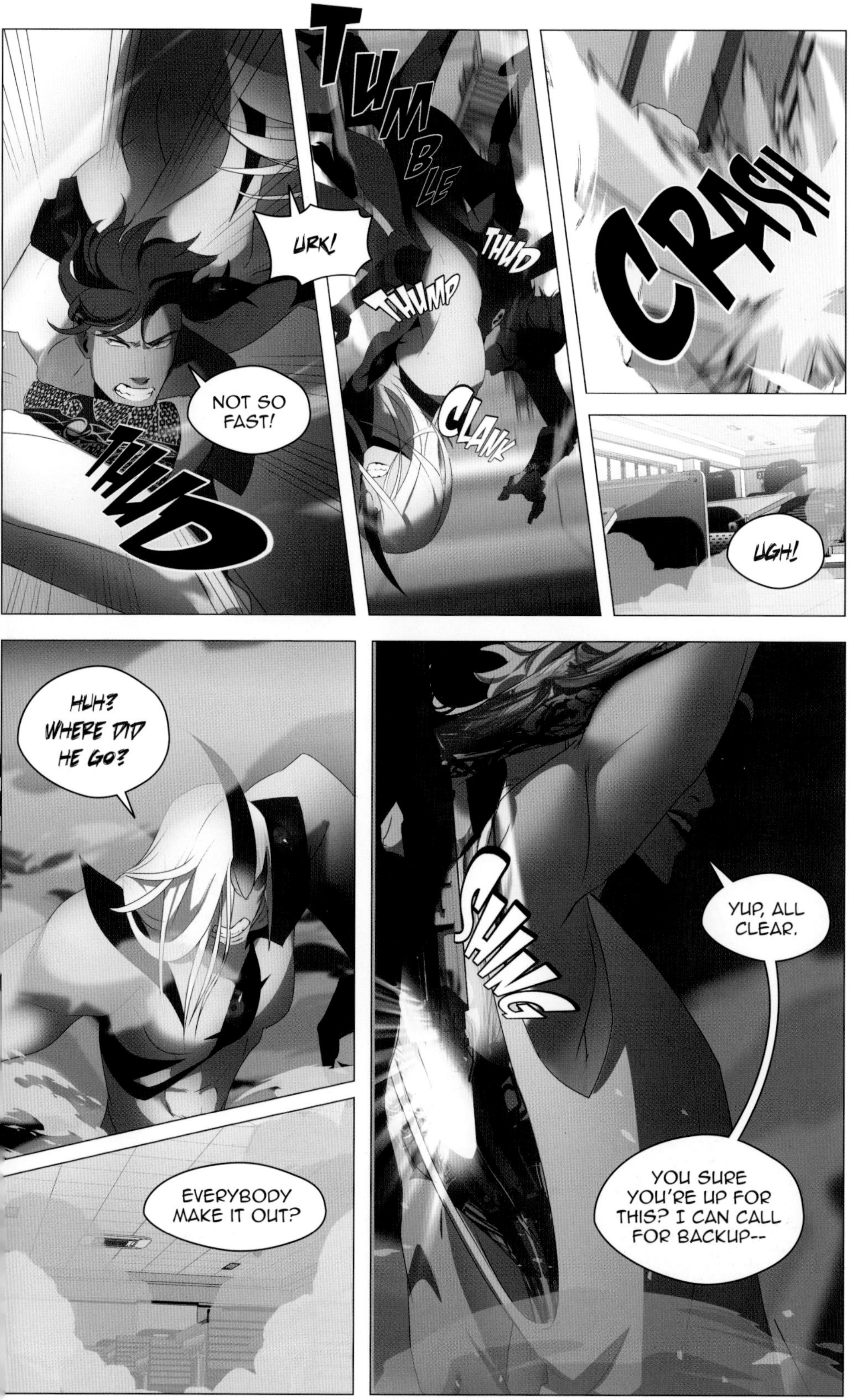
TUMBLE
URK!
THUD
THUMP
CLANK
NOT SO FAST!
THUD
CRASH
UGH!
HUH? WHERE DID HE GO?
EVERYBODY MAKE IT OUT?
SHING
YUP, ALL CLEAR.
YOU SURE YOU'RE UP FOR THIS? I CAN CALL FOR BACKUP--

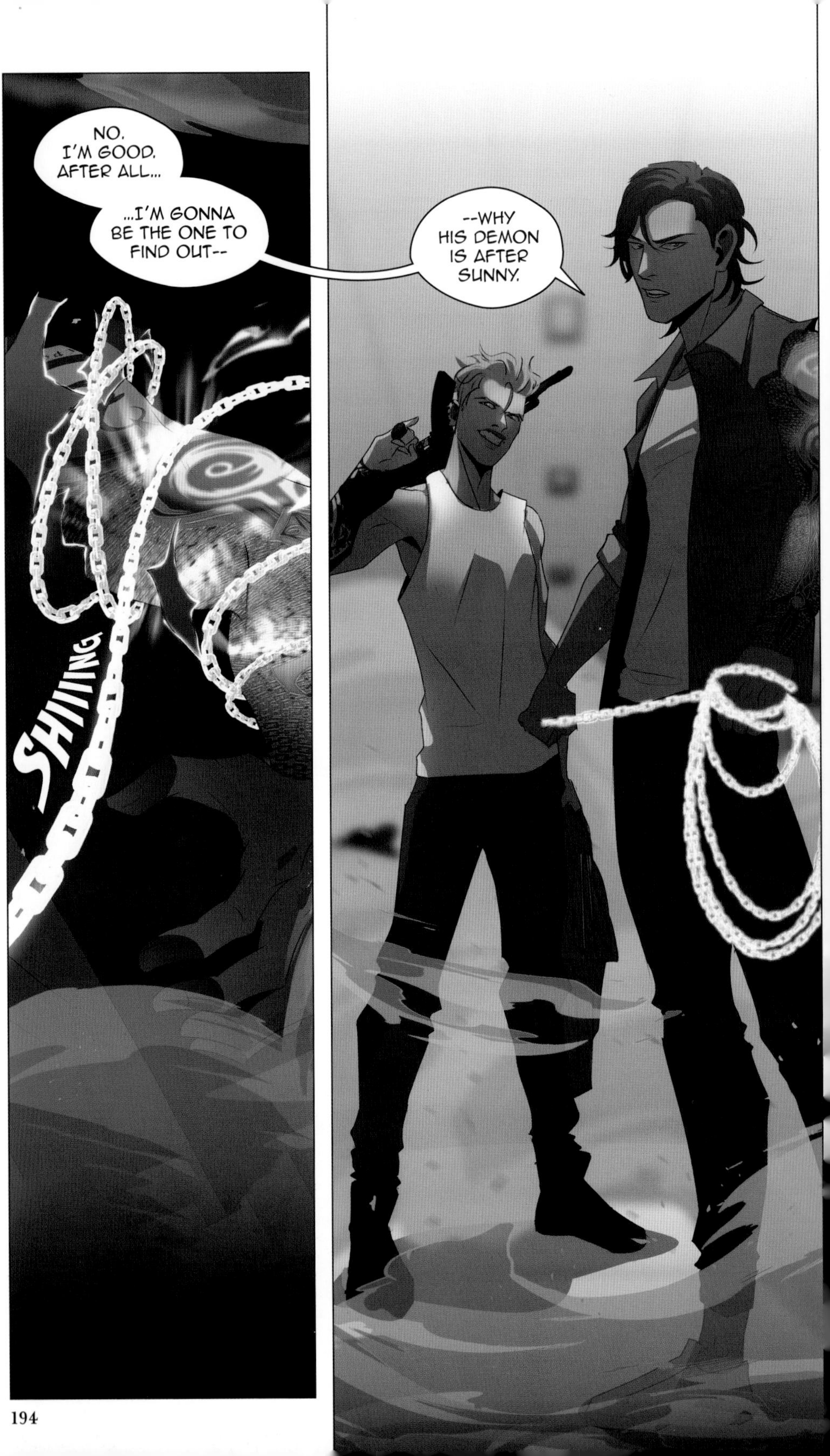
NO. I'M GOOD. AFTER ALL...
...I'M GONNA BE THE ONE TO FIND OUT--
--WHY HIS DEMON IS AFTER SUNNY.
SHIIIING

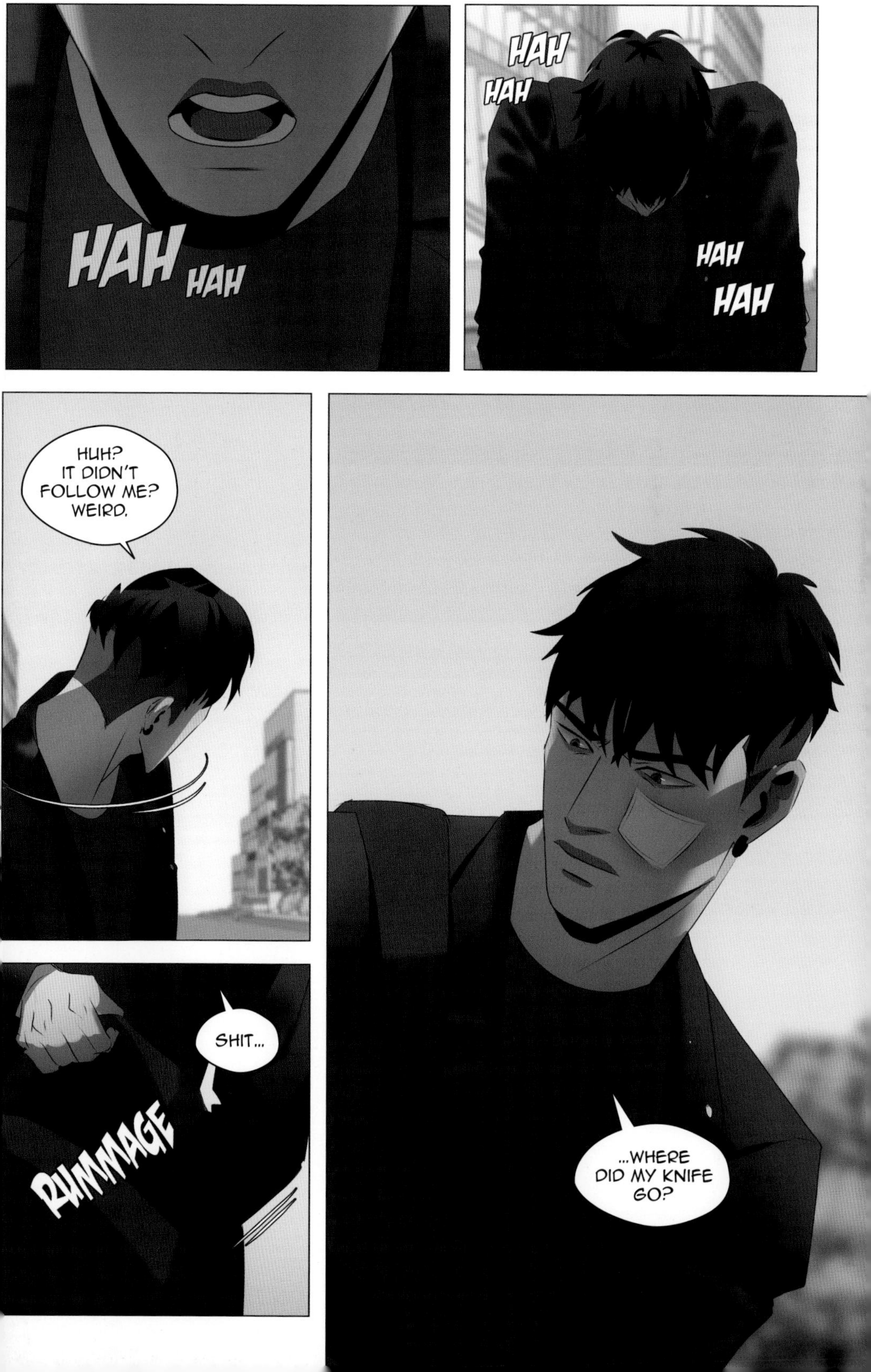
HAH HAH
HAH HAH
HAH HAH
HUH? IT DIDN'T FOLLOW ME? WEIRD.
SHIT...
RUMMAGE
...WHERE DID MY KNIFE GO?

BOOK VI

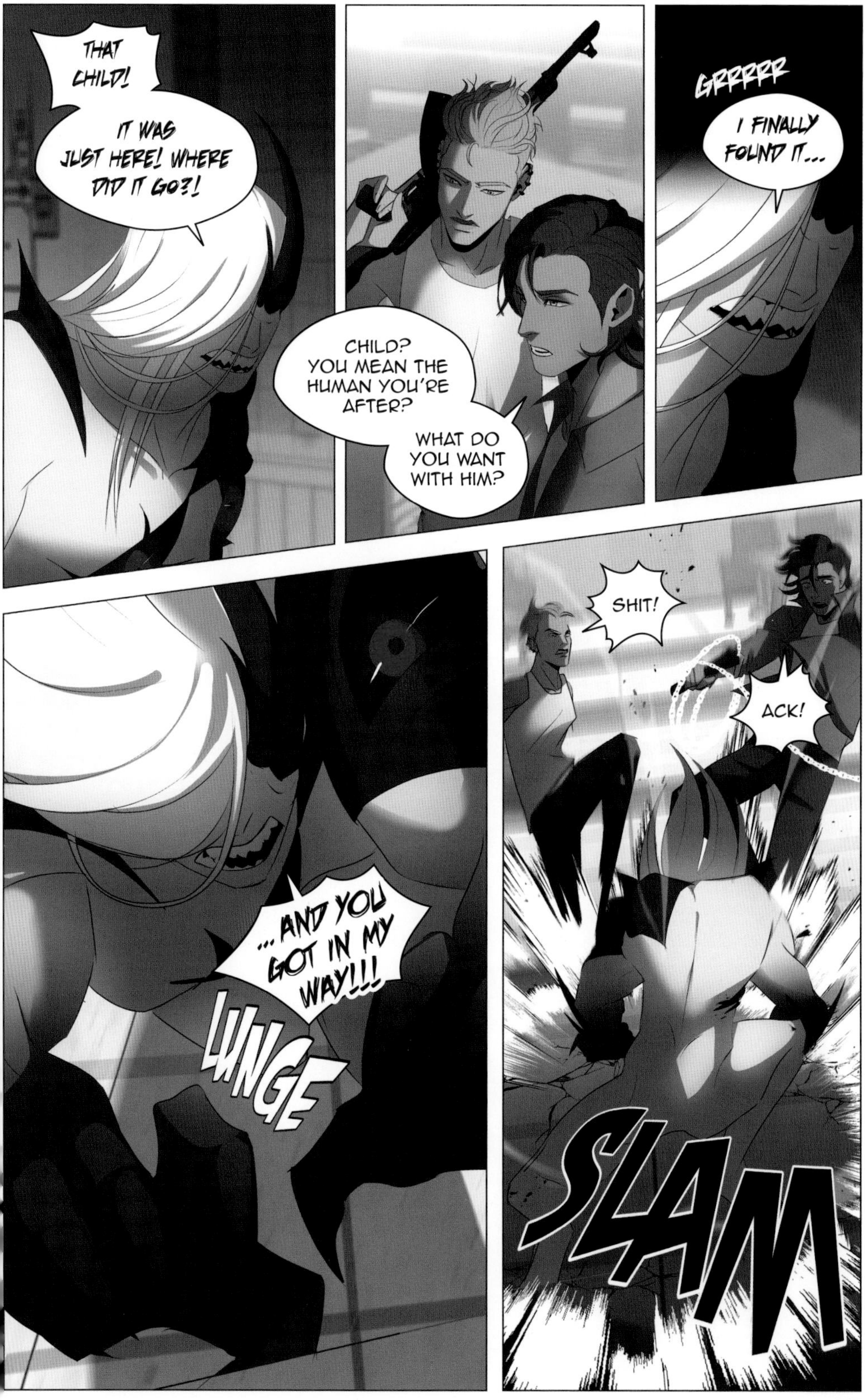
THAT CHILD!
IT WAS JUST HERE! WHERE DID IT GO?!
CHILD? YOU MEAN THE HUMAN YOU'RE AFTER?
WHAT DO YOU WANT WITH HIM?
GRRRRR
I FINALLY FOUND IT...
...AND YOU GOT IN MY WAY!!!
LUNGE
SHIT!
ACK!
SLAM

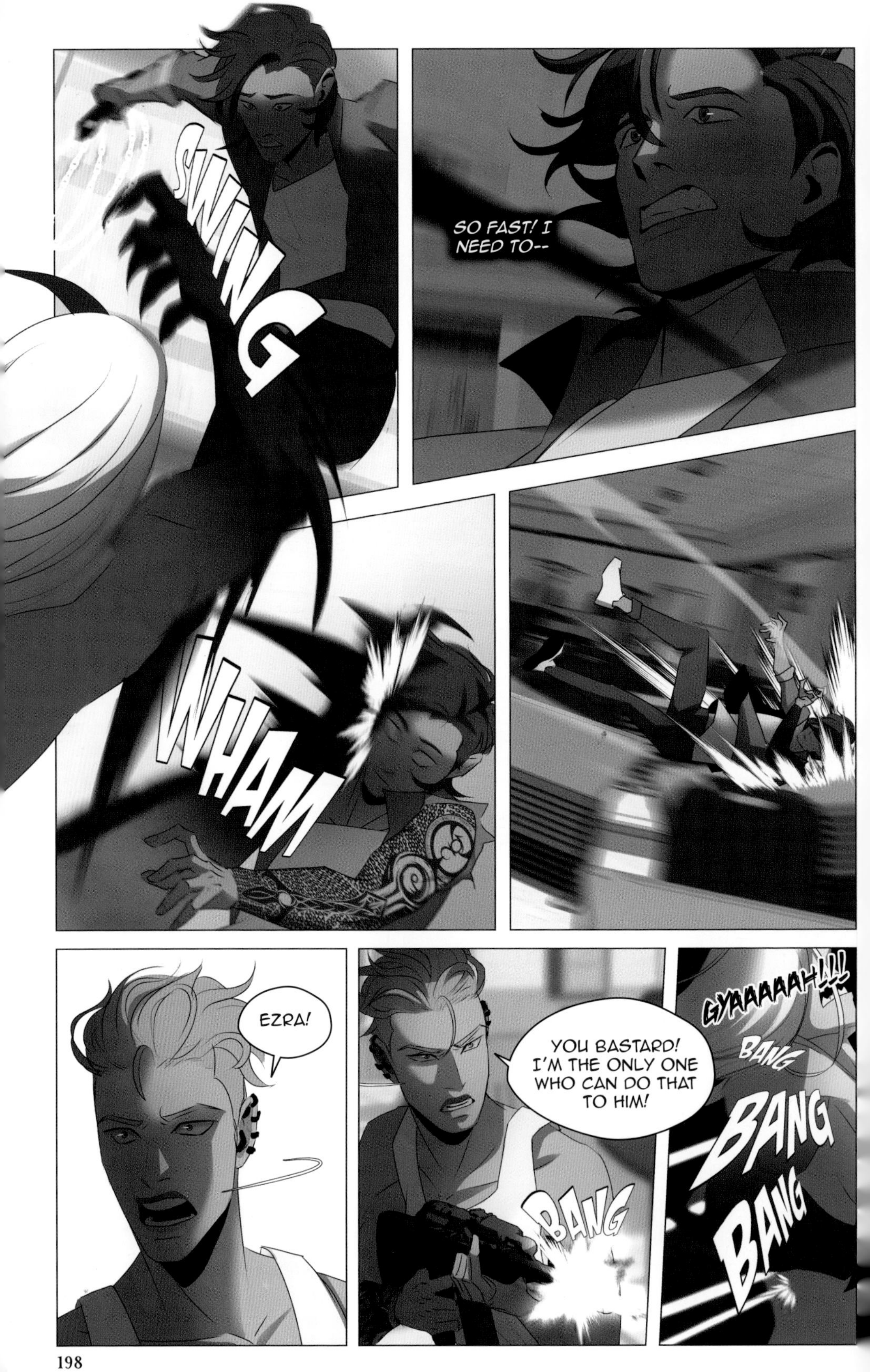
SWING
SO FAST! I NEED TO--
WHAM
EZRA!
YOU BASTARD! I'M THE ONLY ONE WHO CAN DO THAT TO HIM!
BANG
GYAAAAAH!!!
BANG
BANG
BANG

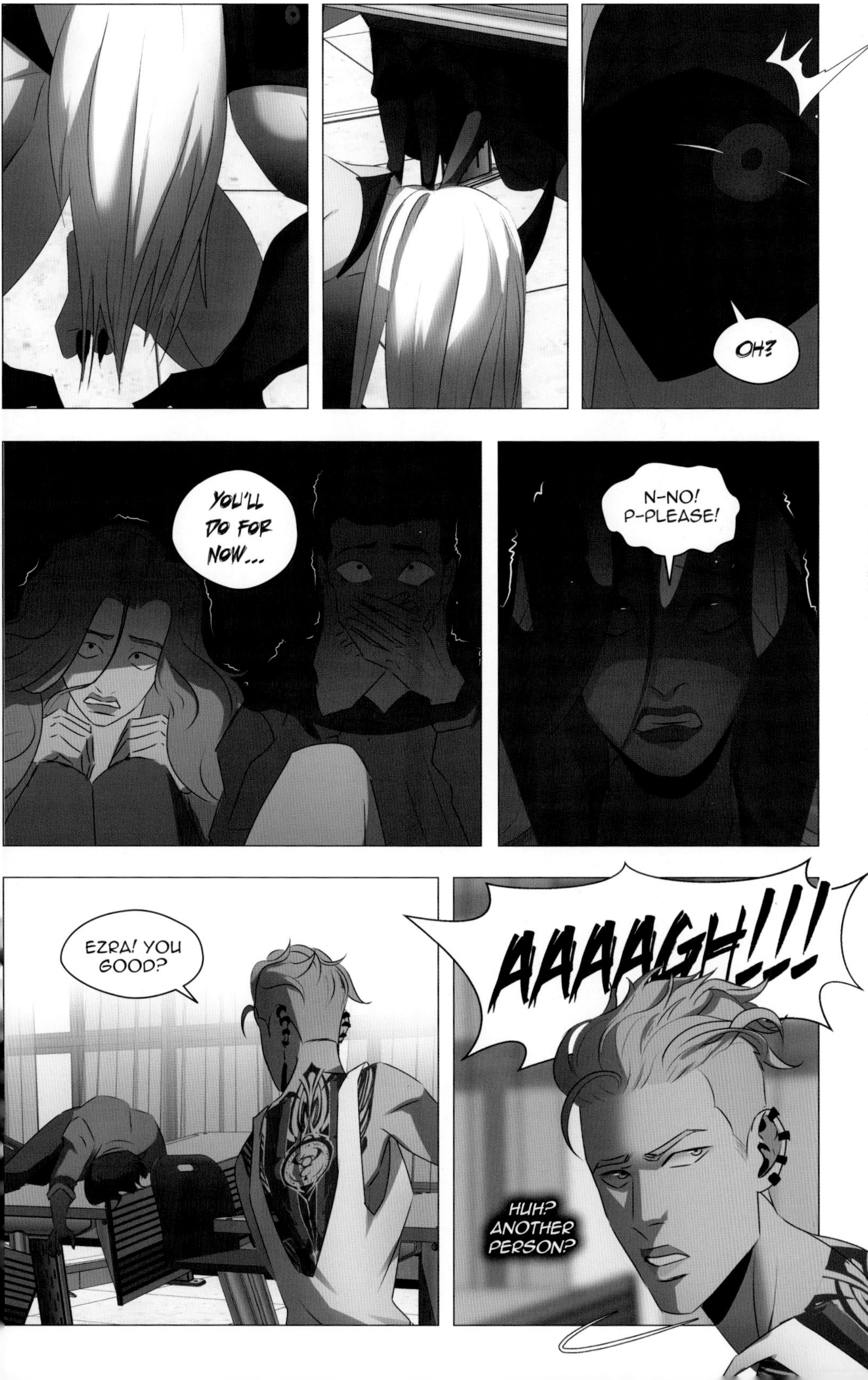
OH?
YOU'LL DO FOR NOW...
N-NO! P-PLEASE!
EZRA! YOU GOOD?
AAAAGH!!!
HUH? ANOTHER PERSON?

CLOSE
THUD
NO...

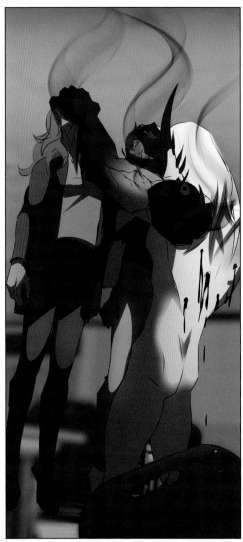

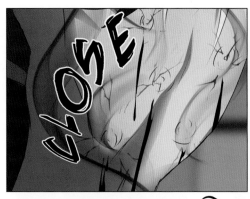

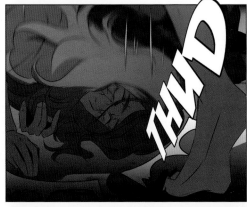

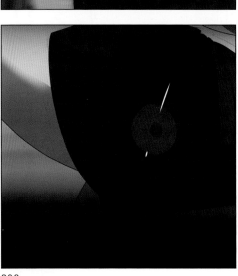

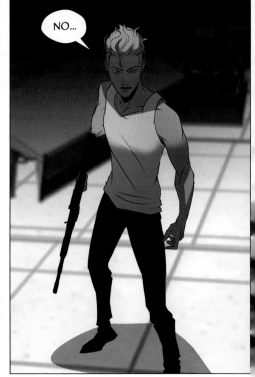

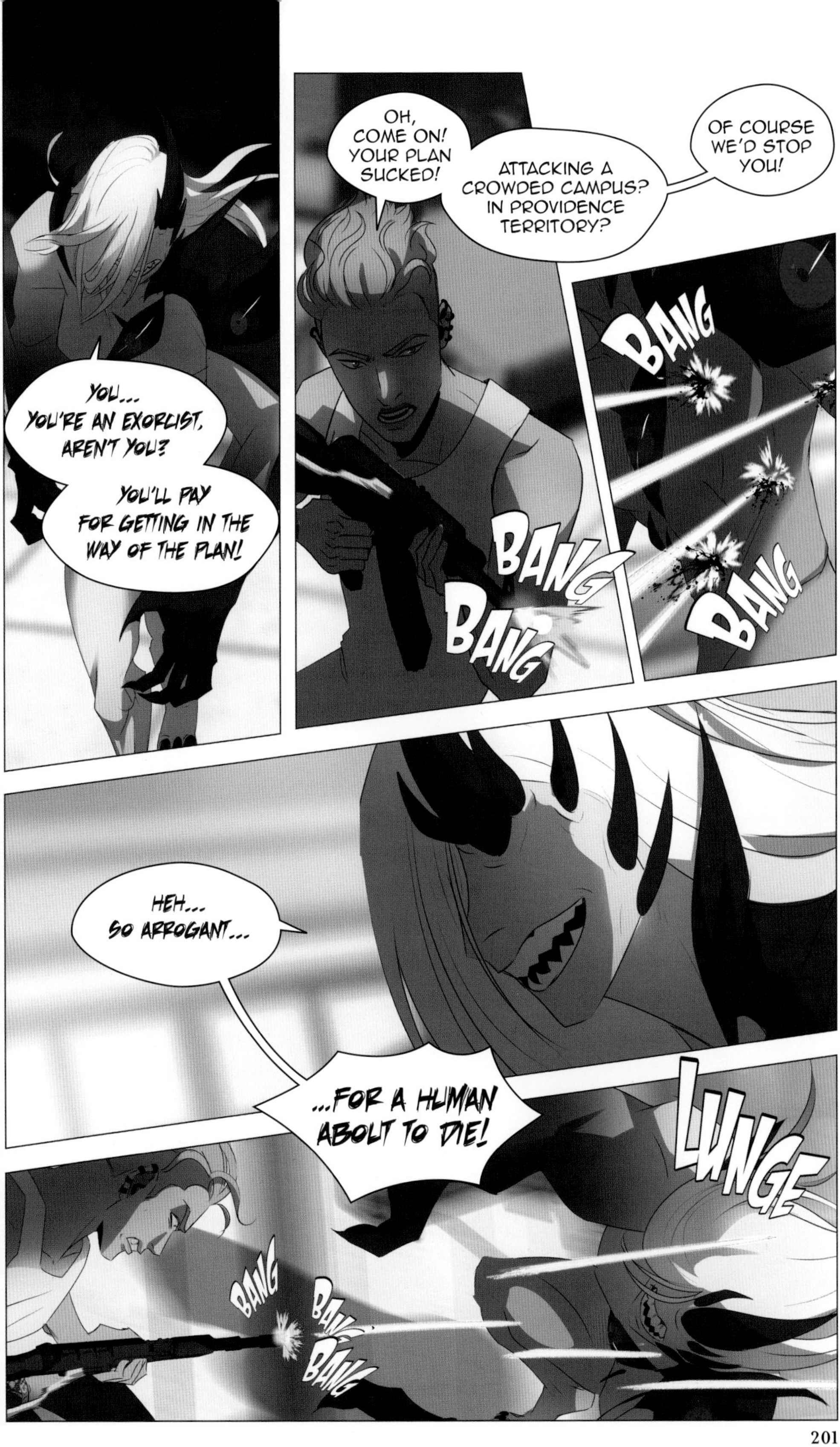
YOU... YOU'RE AN EXORCIST, AREN'T YOU?
YOU'LL PAY FOR GETTING IN THE WAY OF THE PLAN!
OH, COME ON! YOUR PLAN SUCKED!
ATTACKING A CROWDED CAMPUS? IN PROVIDENCE TERRITORY?
OF COURSE WE'D STOP YOU!
BANG
BANG
BANG
BANG
HEH... SO ARROGANT...
...FOR A HUMAN ABOUT TO DIE!
LUNGE
BANG
BANG
BANG

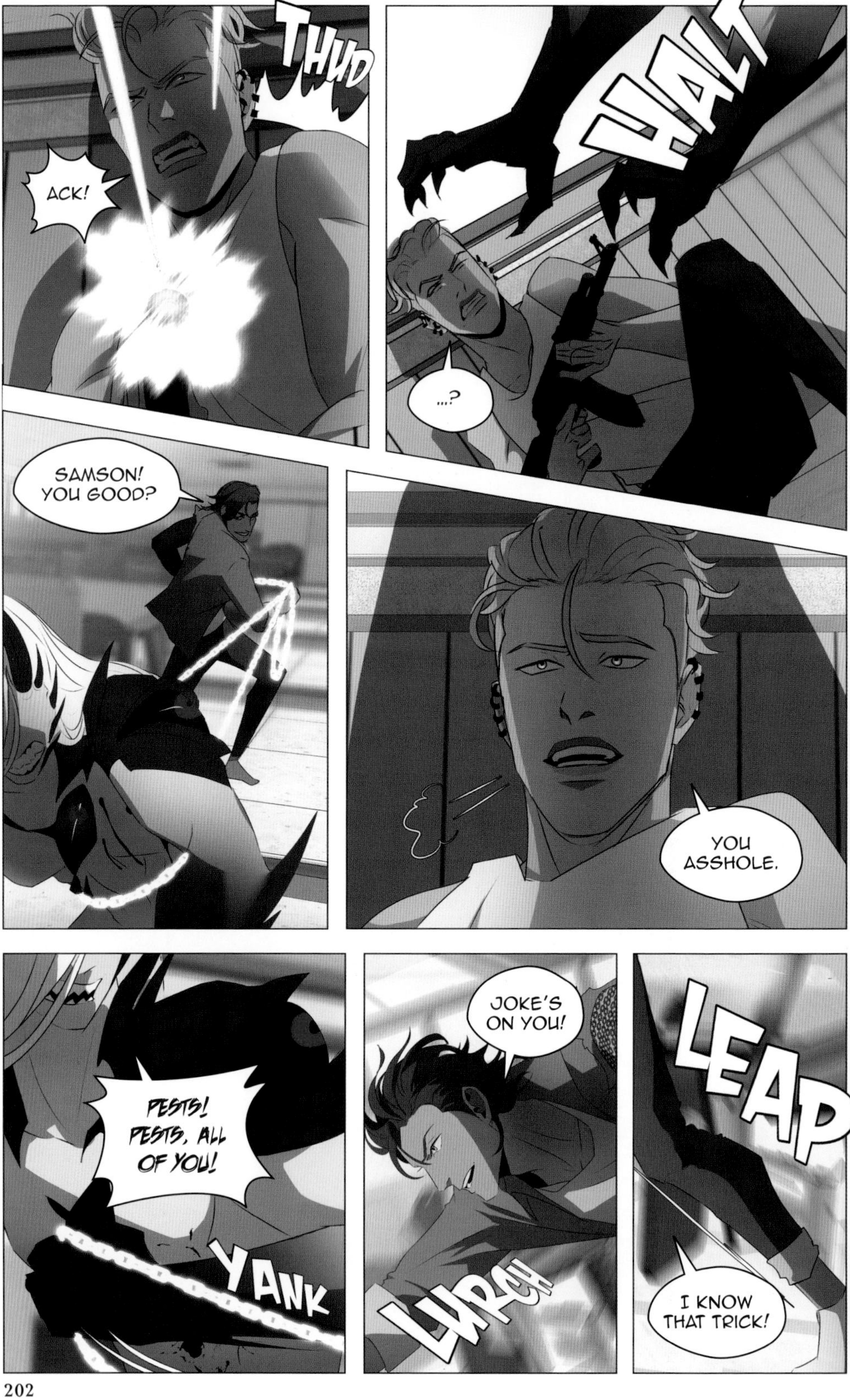
THUD
ACK!
HALT
...?
SAMSON! YOU GOOD?
YOU ASSHOLE.
PESTS! PESTS, ALL OF YOU!
YANK
JOKE'S ON YOU!
LURCH
LEAP
I KNOW THAT TRICK!

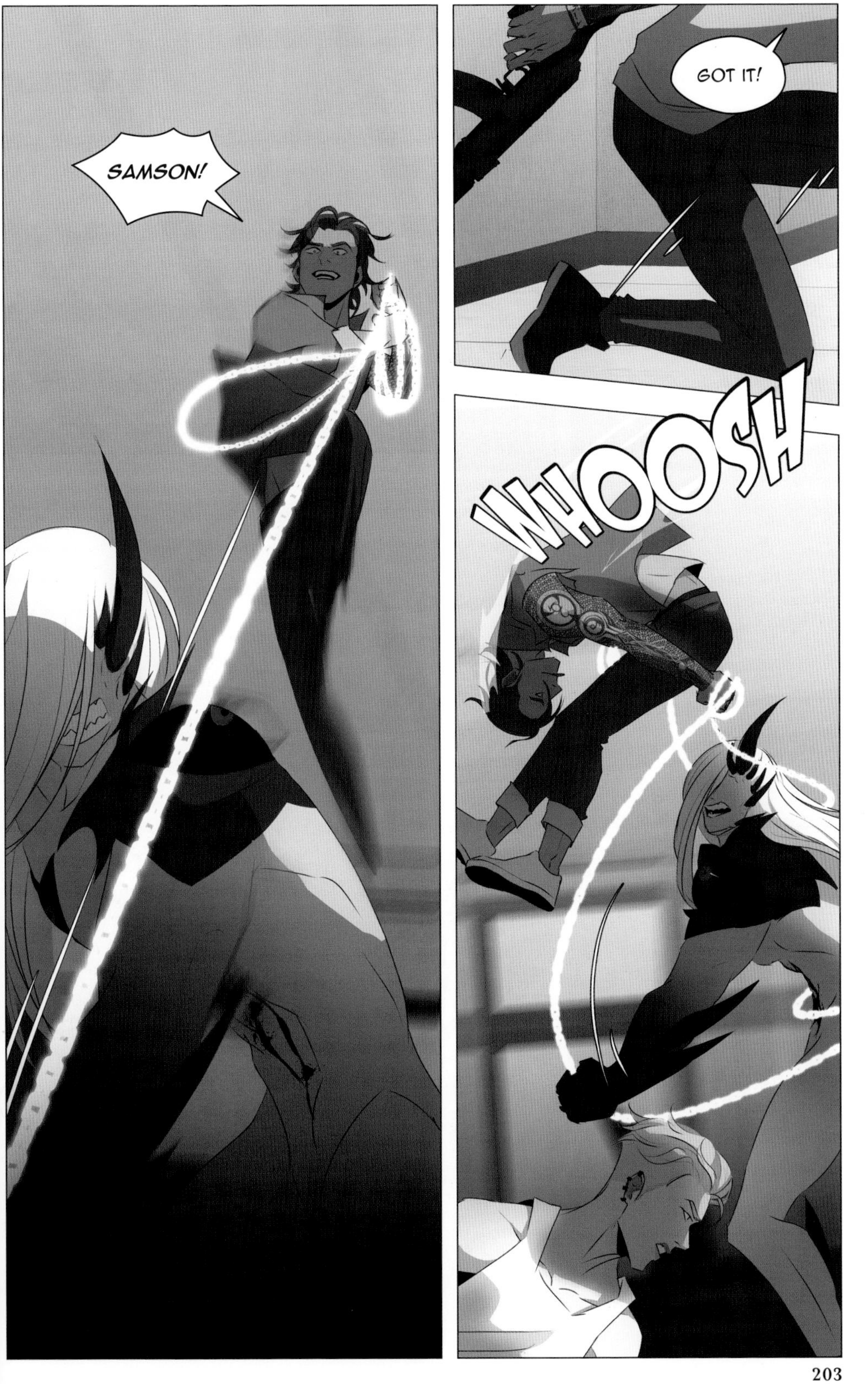
SAMSON!
GOT IT!
WHOOSH

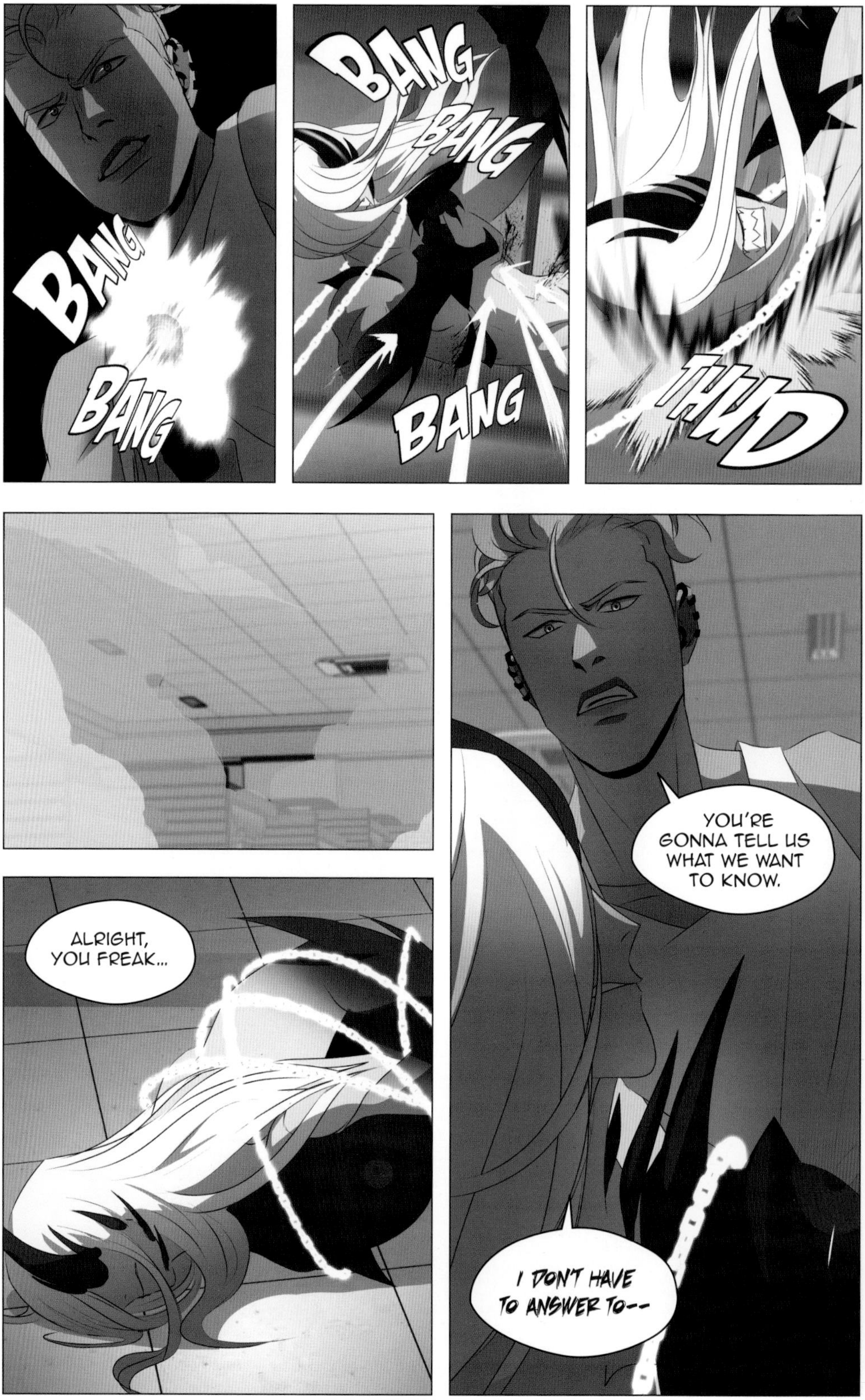
BANG
BANG
BANG
BANG
BANG
THUD
YOU'RE GONNA TELL US WHAT WE WANT TO KNOW.
ALRIGHT, YOU FREAK...
I DON'T HAVE TO ANSWER TO--

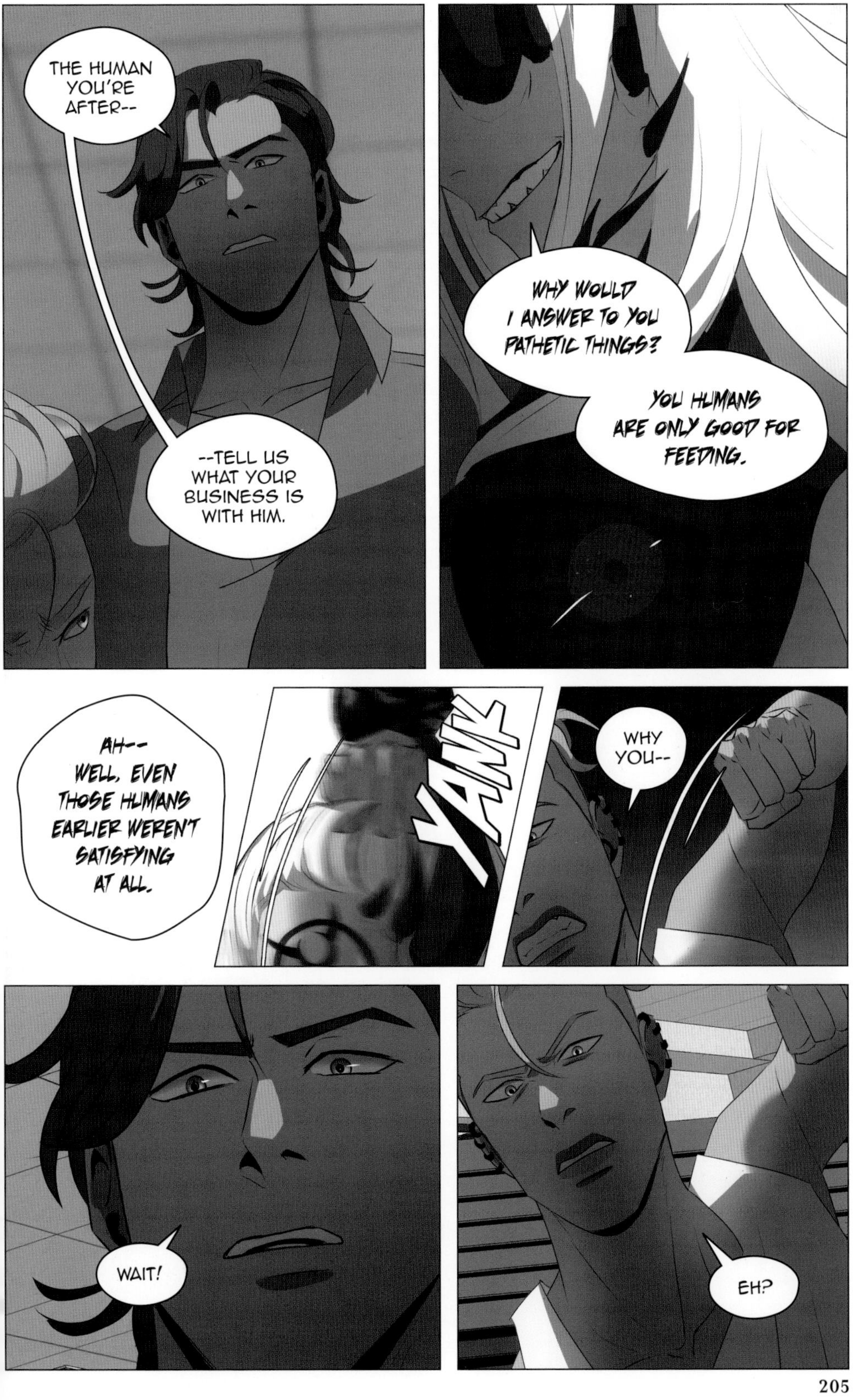
THE HUMAN YOU'RE AFTER--
--TELL US WHAT YOUR BUSINESS IS WITH HIM.
WHY WOULD I ANSWER TO YOU PATHETIC THINGS?
YOU HUMANS ARE ONLY GOOD FOR FEEDING.
AH-- WELL, EVEN THOSE HUMANS EARLIER WEREN'T SATISFYING AT ALL.
YANK
WHY YOU--
WAIT!
EH?

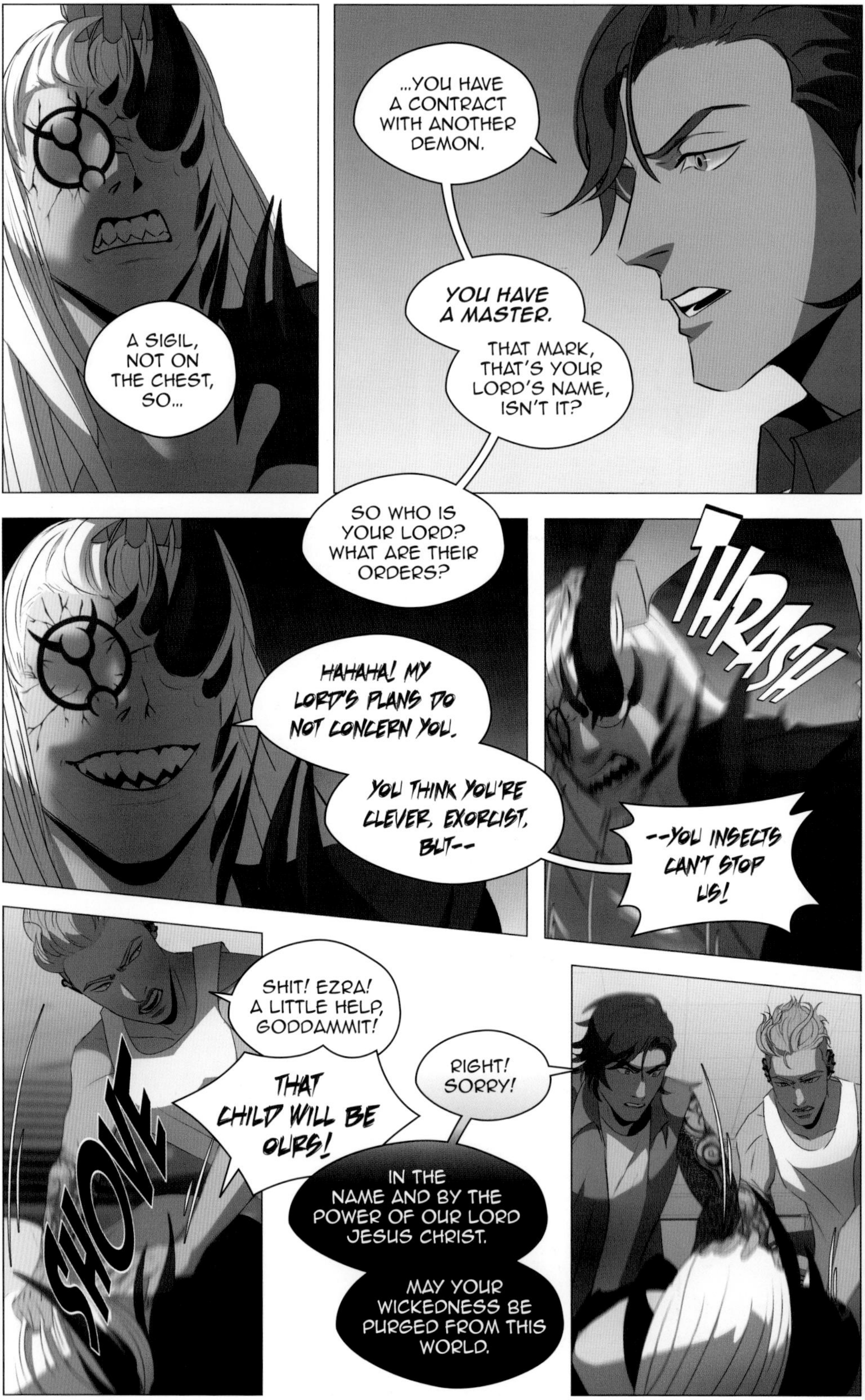
A SIGIL, NOT ON THE CHEST, SO...
...YOU HAVE A CONTRACT WITH ANOTHER DEMON.
YOU HAVE A MASTER.
THAT MARK, THAT'S YOUR LORD'S NAME, ISN'T IT?
SO WHO IS YOUR LORD? WHAT ARE THEIR ORDERS?
HAHAHA! MY LORD'S PLANS DO NOT CONCERN YOU.
YOU THINK YOU'RE CLEVER, EXORCIST, BUT--
THRASH
--YOU INSECTS CAN'T STOP US!
SHIT! EZRA! A LITTLE HELP, GODDAMMIT!
SHOVE
THAT CHILD WILL BE OURS!
RIGHT! SORRY!
IN THE NAME AND BY THE POWER OF OUR LORD JESUS CHRIST.
MAY YOUR WICKEDNESS BE PURGED FROM THIS WORLD.

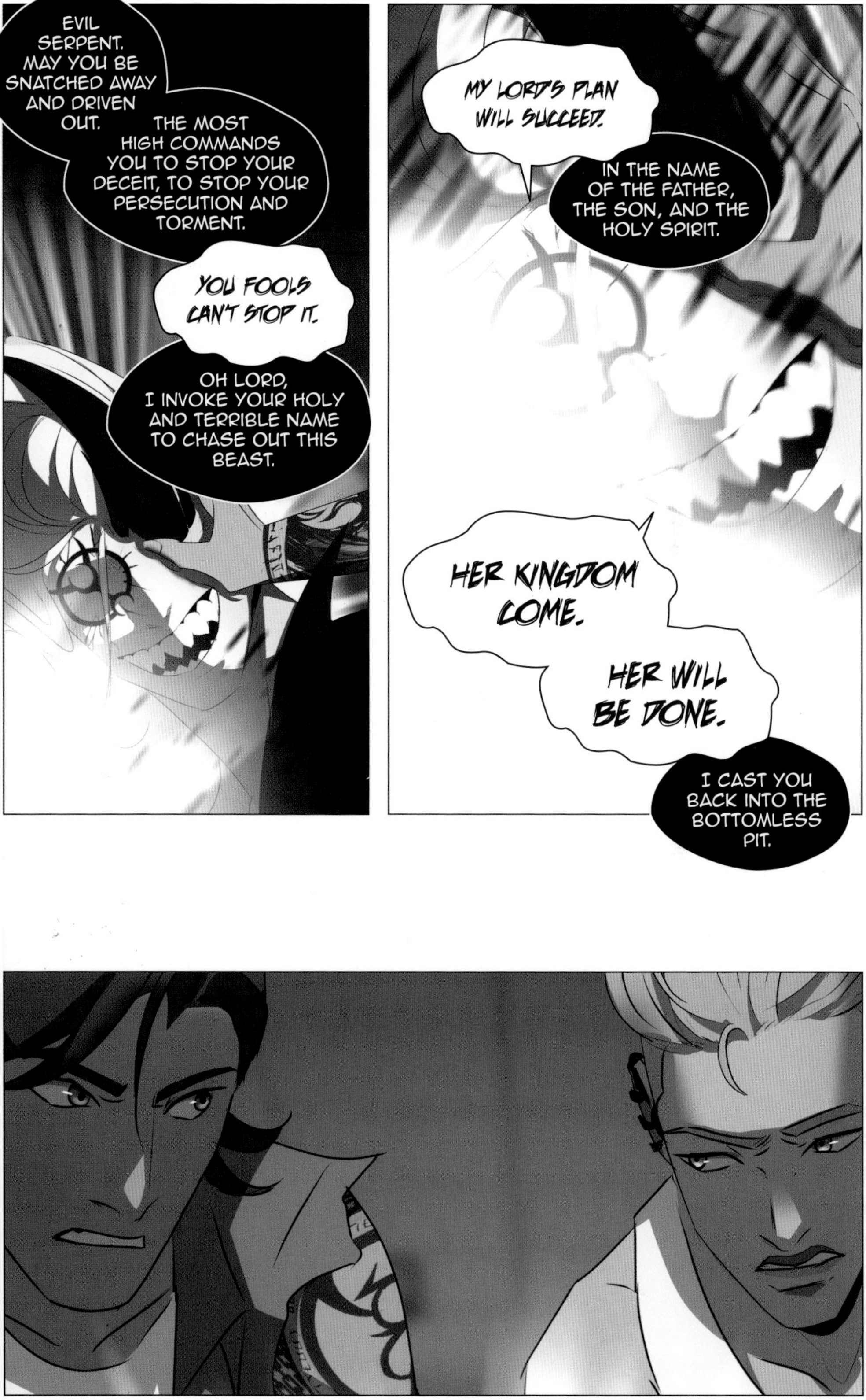
EVIL SERPENT. MAY YOU BE SNATCHED AWAY AND DRIVEN OUT.
THE MOST HIGH COMMANDS YOU TO STOP YOUR DECEIT, TO STOP YOUR PERSECUTION AND TORMENT.
YOU FOOLS CAN'T STOP IT.
OH LORD, I INVOKE YOUR HOLY AND TERRIBLE NAME TO CHASE OUT THIS BEAST.
MY LORD'S PLAN WILL SUCCEED.
IN THE NAME OF THE FATHER, THE SON, AND THE HOLY SPIRIT.
HER KINGDOM COME.
HER WILL BE DONE.
I CAST YOU BACK INTO THE BOTTOMLESS PIT.

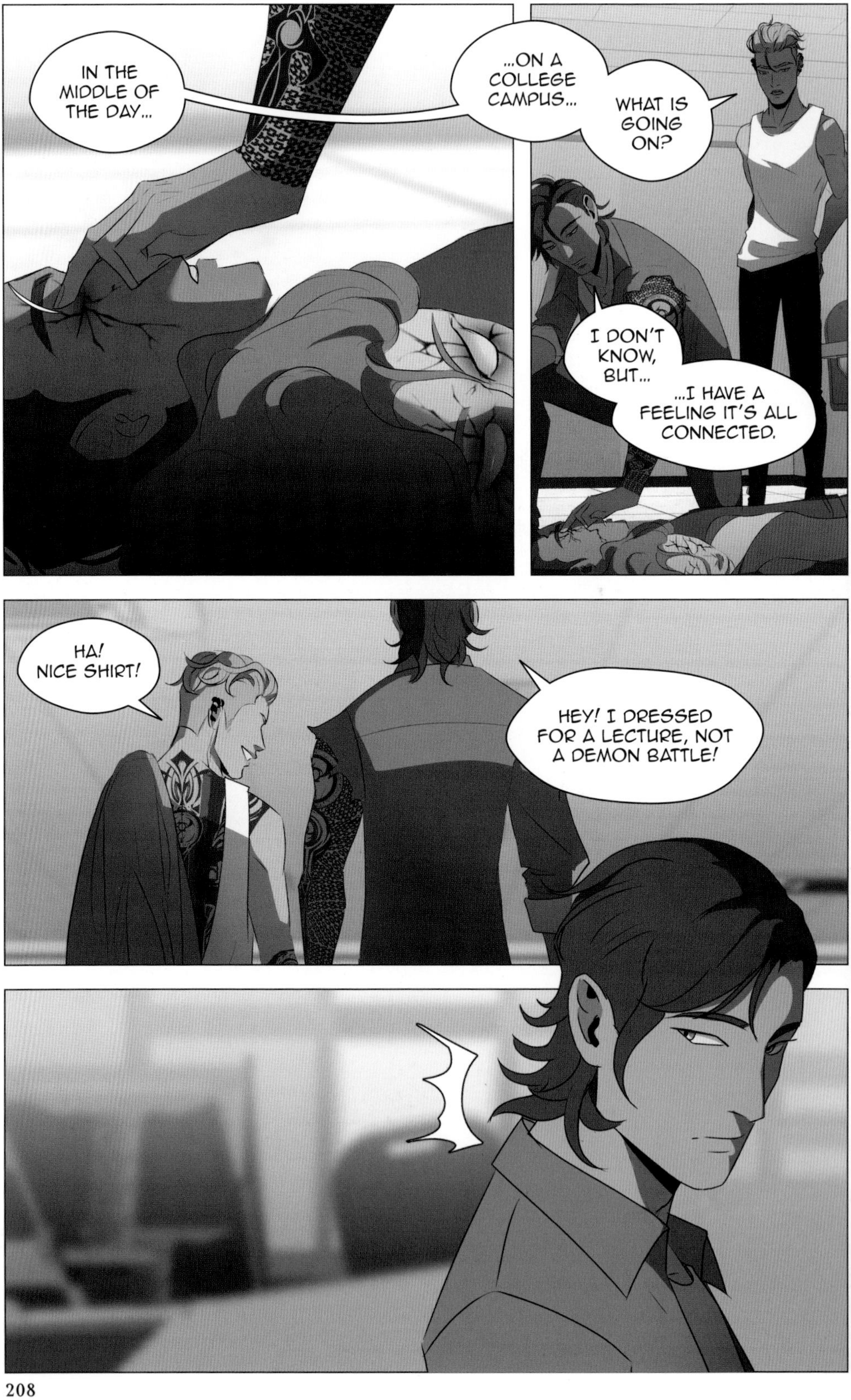
IN THE MIDDLE OF THE DAY...
...ON A COLLEGE CAMPUS...
WHAT IS GOING ON?
I DON'T KNOW, BUT...
...I HAVE A FEELING IT'S ALL CONNECTED.
HA! NICE SHIRT!
HEY! I DRESSED FOR A LECTURE, NOT A DEMON BATTLE!

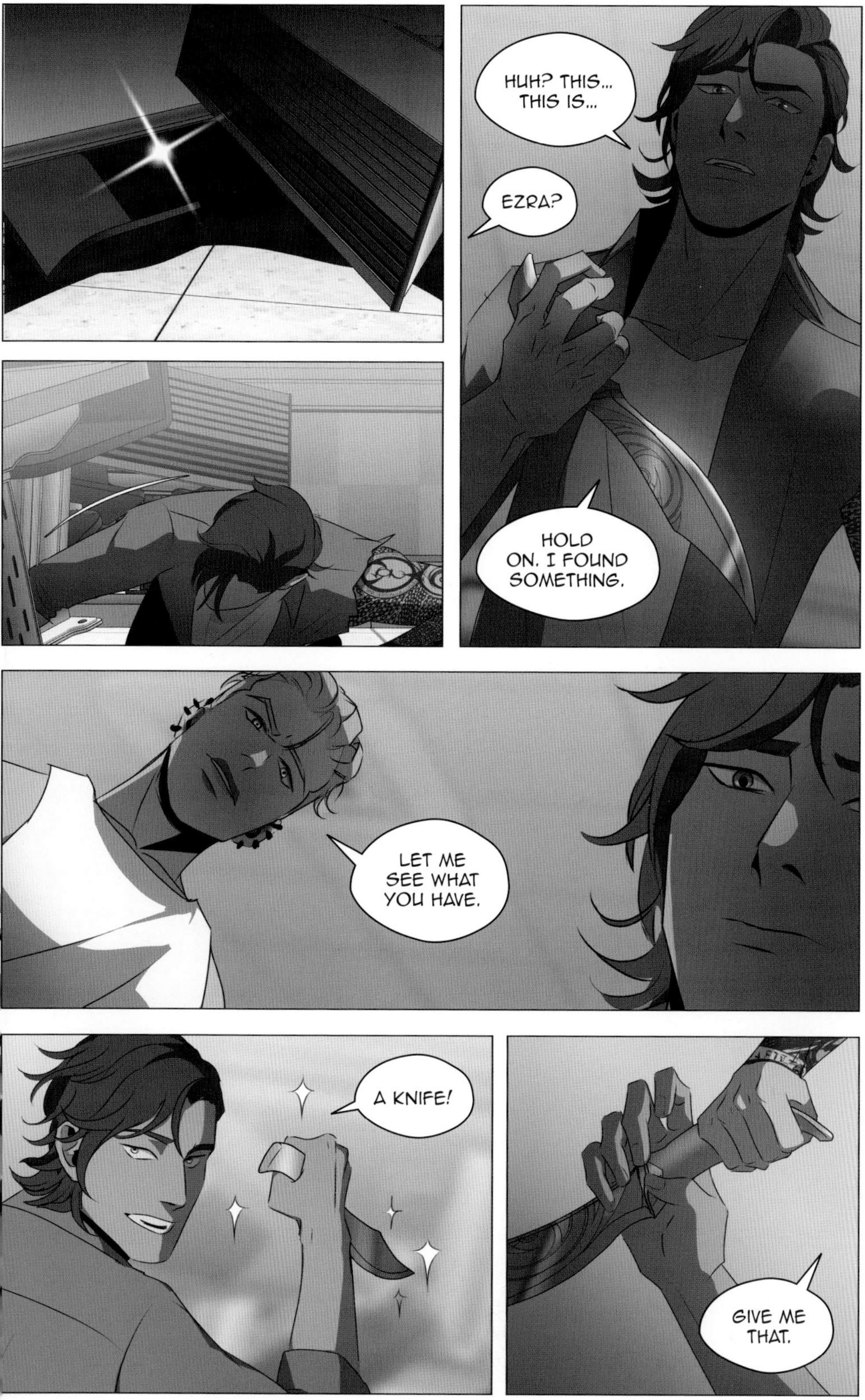
HUH? THIS...
THIS IS...
EZRA?
HOLD ON. I FOUND SOMETHING.
LET ME SEE WHAT YOU HAVE.
A KNIFE!
GIVE ME THAT.

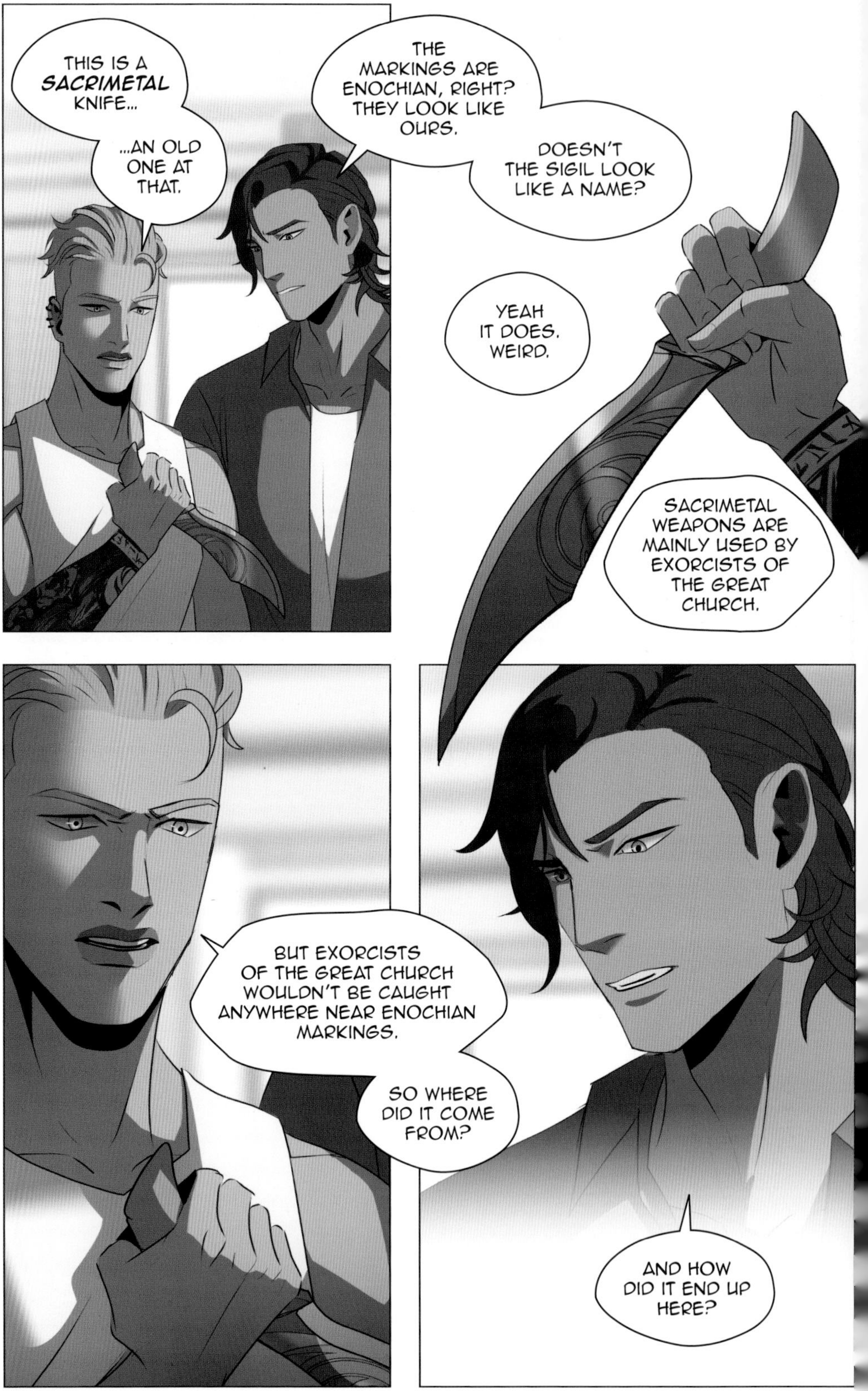
THIS IS A SACRIMETAL KNIFE...
...AN OLD ONE AT THAT.
THE MARKINGS ARE ENOCHIAN, RIGHT? THEY LOOK LIKE OURS.
DOESN'T THE SIGIL LOOK LIKE A NAME?
YEAH IT DOES. WEIRD.
SACRIMETAL WEAPONS ARE MAINLY USED BY EXORCISTS OF THE GREAT CHURCH.
BUT EXORCISTS OF THE GREAT CHURCH WOULDN'T BE CAUGHT ANYWHERE NEAR ENOCHIAN MARKINGS.
SO WHERE DID IT COME FROM?
AND HOW DID IT END UP HERE?

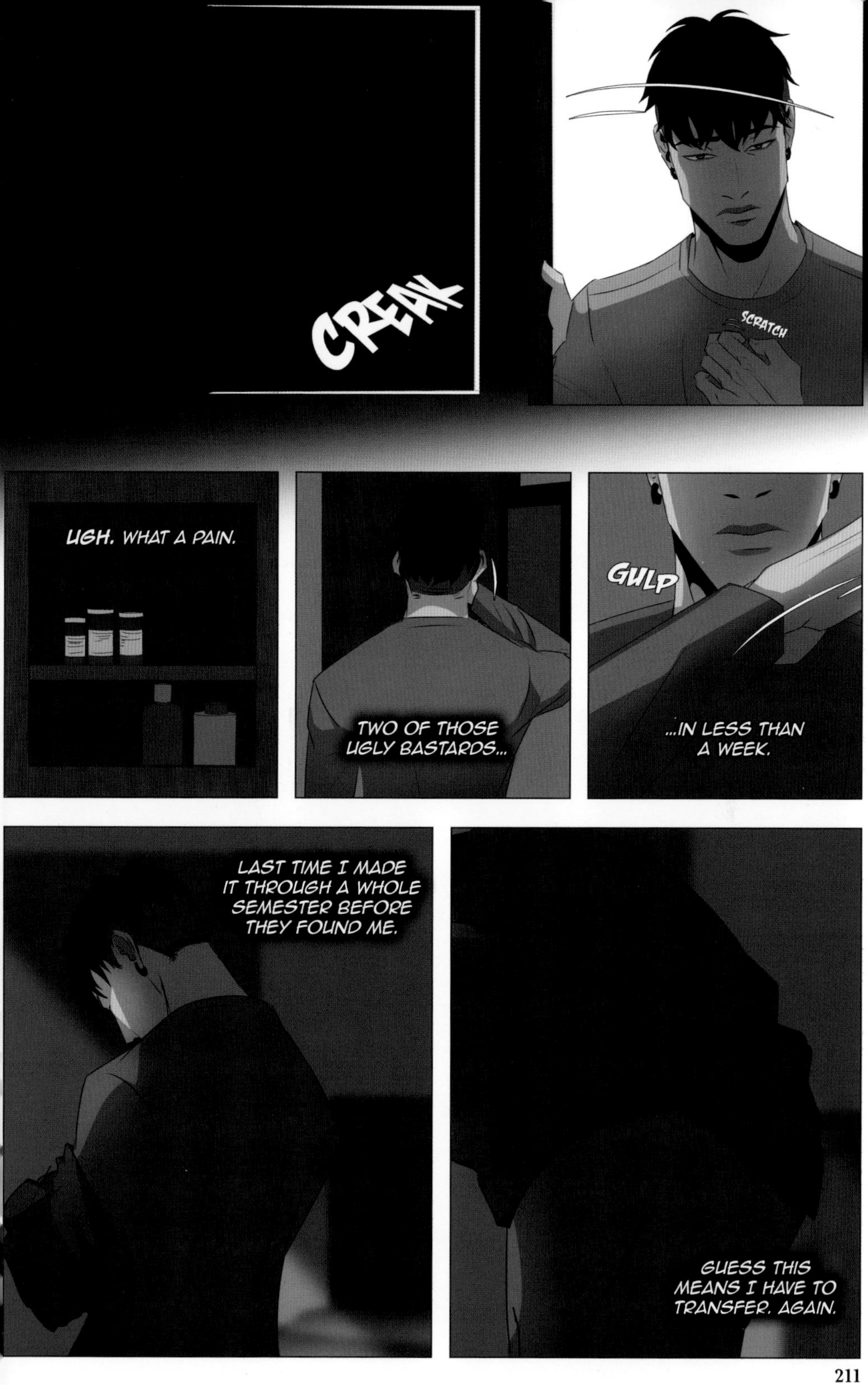
CREAK
SCRATCH
UGH. WHAT A PAIN.
TWO OF THOSE UGLY BASTARDS...
GULP
...IN LESS THAN A WEEK.
LAST TIME I MADE IT THROUGH A WHOLE SEMESTER BEFORE THEY FOUND ME.
GUESS THIS MEANS I HAVE TO TRANSFER. AGAIN.

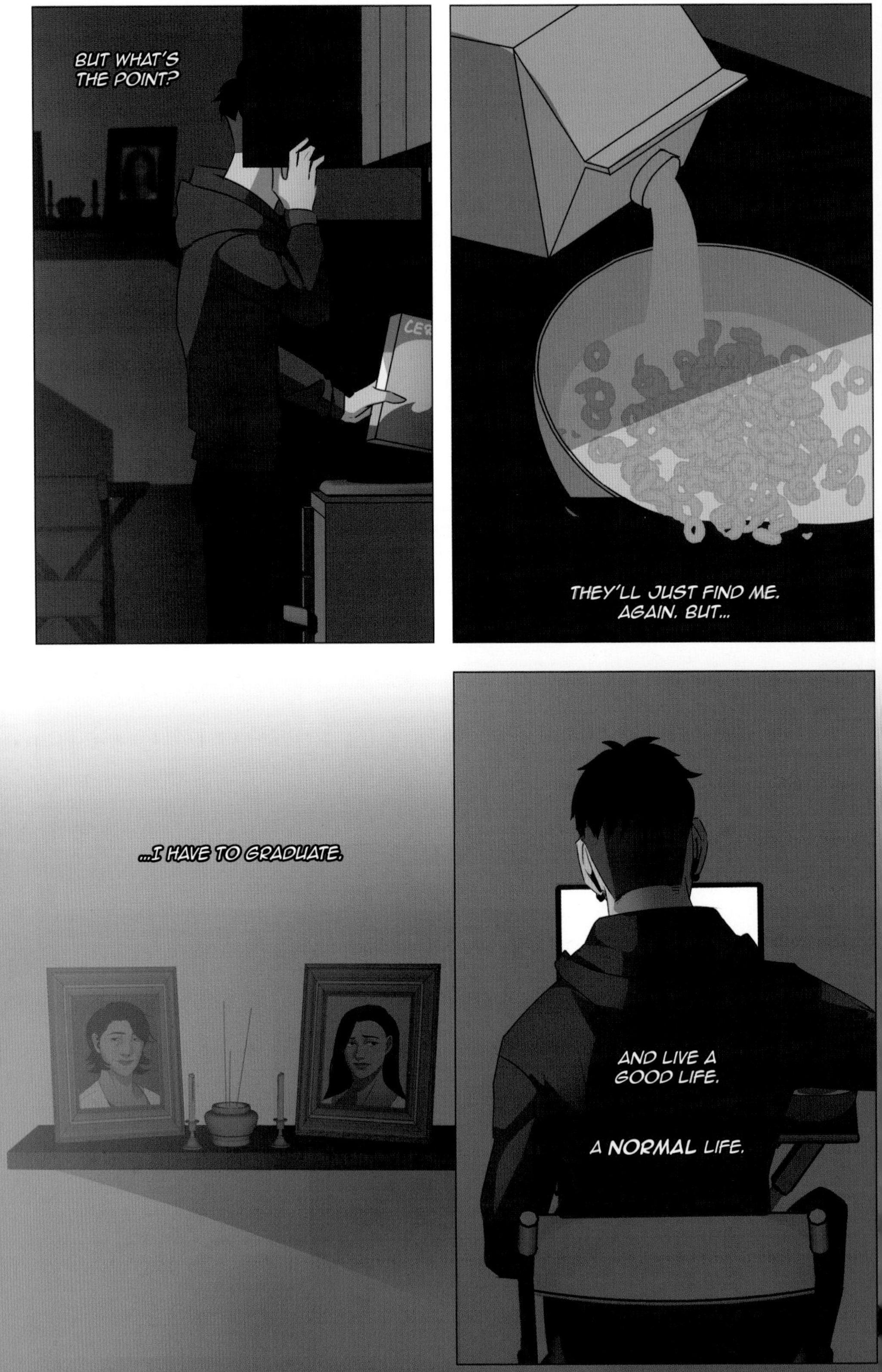
BUT WHAT'S THE POINT?
CER
THEY'LL JUST FIND ME. AGAIN. BUT...
...I HAVE TO GRADUATE.
AND LIVE A GOOD LIFE.
A **NORMAL** LIFE.

HUH?

Los Demonios Times

Two Students Killed in Building Collapse

CAUTION KEEP OUT

WAIT...

WHAT THE FUCK IS GOING ON?!

Los Demonios Tin

Two Students Killed in Building Collapse

Lorem ipsum dolor sit amet, consectetur adipiscing elit, sed do eiusmod temp et dolore magna aliqua. Quis ipsum suspendisse ultrices gravida. Risus comm accumsan lacus vel facilisis.

By Quis Ipsum | September 15, 2020 11:56 PM

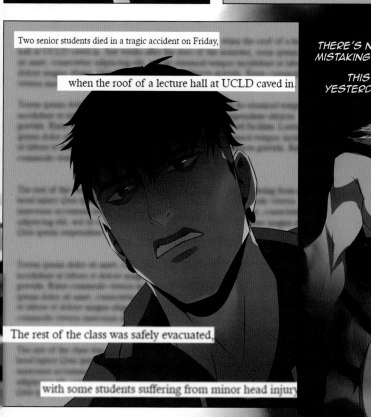

Two senior students died in a tragic accident on Friday,

when the roof of a lecture hall at UCLD caved in.

The rest of the class was safely evacuated,

with some students suffering from minor head injur

THERE'S NO MISTAKING IT.

THIS WAS YESTERDAY, BUT--

--THAT WAS NO ACCIDENT!

THAT WAS A DEMON!

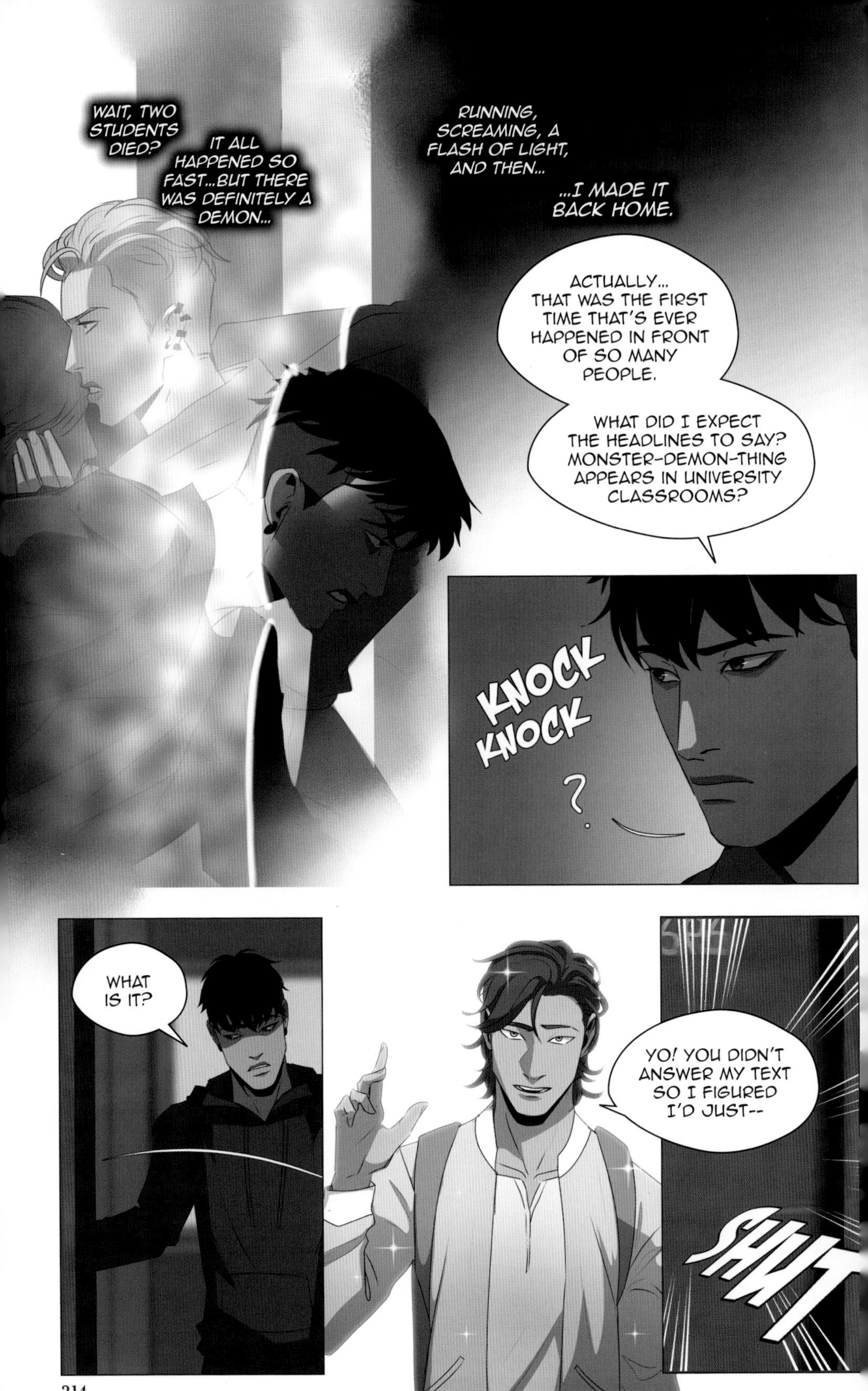
WAIT, TWO STUDENTS DIED?
IT ALL HAPPENED SO FAST...BUT THERE WAS DEFINITELY A DEMON...
RUNNING, SCREAMING, A FLASH OF LIGHT, AND THEN...
...I MADE IT BACK HOME.
ACTUALLY... THAT WAS THE FIRST TIME THAT'S EVER HAPPENED IN FRONT OF SO MANY PEOPLE.
WHAT DID I EXPECT THE HEADLINES TO SAY? MONSTER-DEMON-THING APPEARS IN UNIVERSITY CLASSROOMS?
KNOCK KNOCK
?
WHAT IS IT?
YO! YOU DIDN'T ANSWER MY TEXT SO I FIGURED I'D JUST--
SHUT

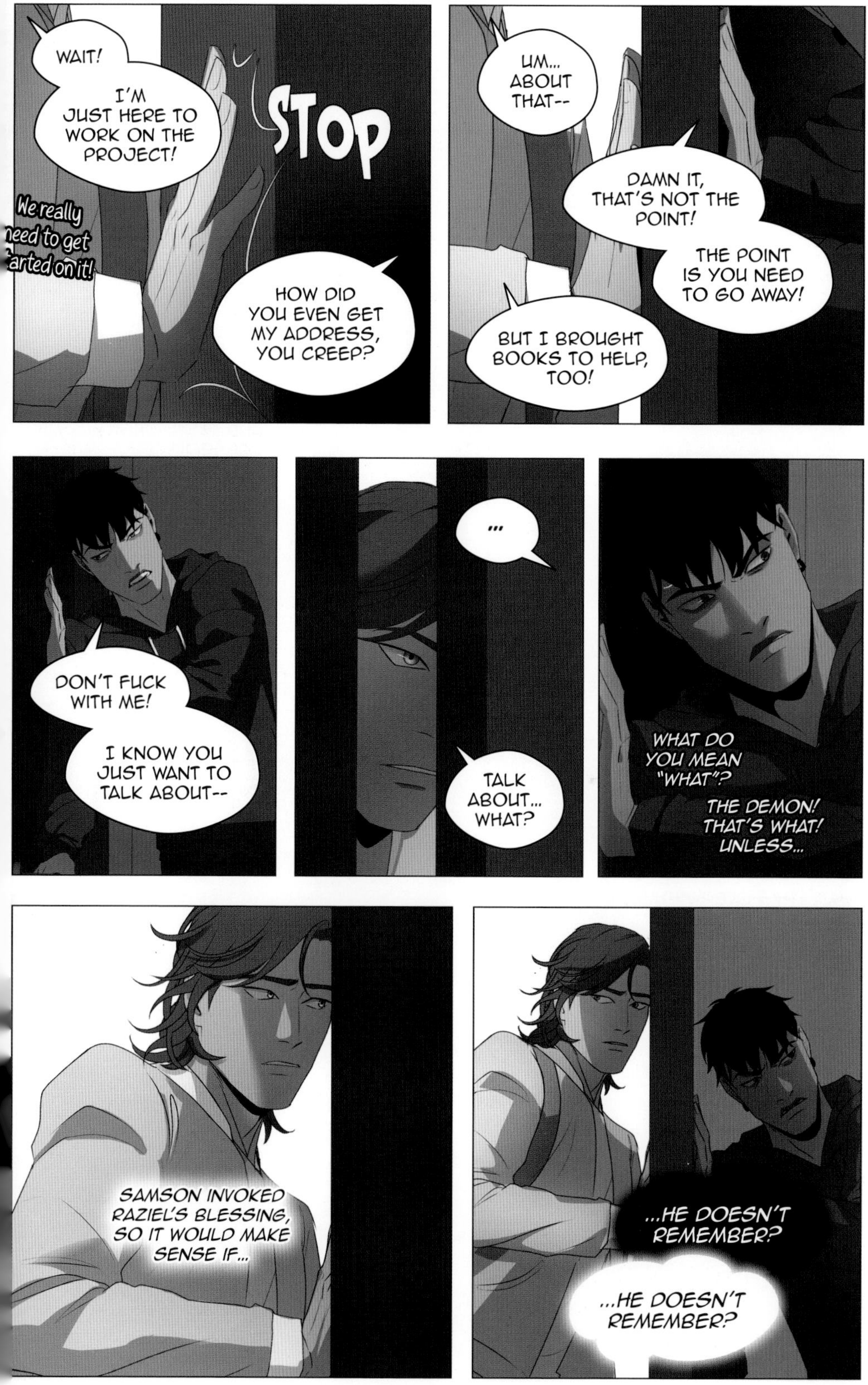
WAIT!
I'M JUST HERE TO WORK ON THE PROJECT!
STOP
We really need to get started on it!
HOW DID YOU EVEN GET MY ADDRESS, YOU CREEP?
UM... ABOUT THAT--
DAMN IT, THAT'S NOT THE POINT!
THE POINT IS YOU NEED TO GO AWAY!
BUT I BROUGHT BOOKS TO HELP, TOO!
DON'T FUCK WITH ME!
I KNOW YOU JUST WANT TO TALK ABOUT--
...
TALK ABOUT... WHAT?
WHAT DO YOU MEAN "WHAT"?
THE DEMON! THAT'S WHAT! UNLESS...
SAMSON INVOKED RAZIEL'S BLESSING, SO IT WOULD MAKE SENSE IF...
...HE DOESN'T REMEMBER?
...HE DOESN'T REMEMBER?

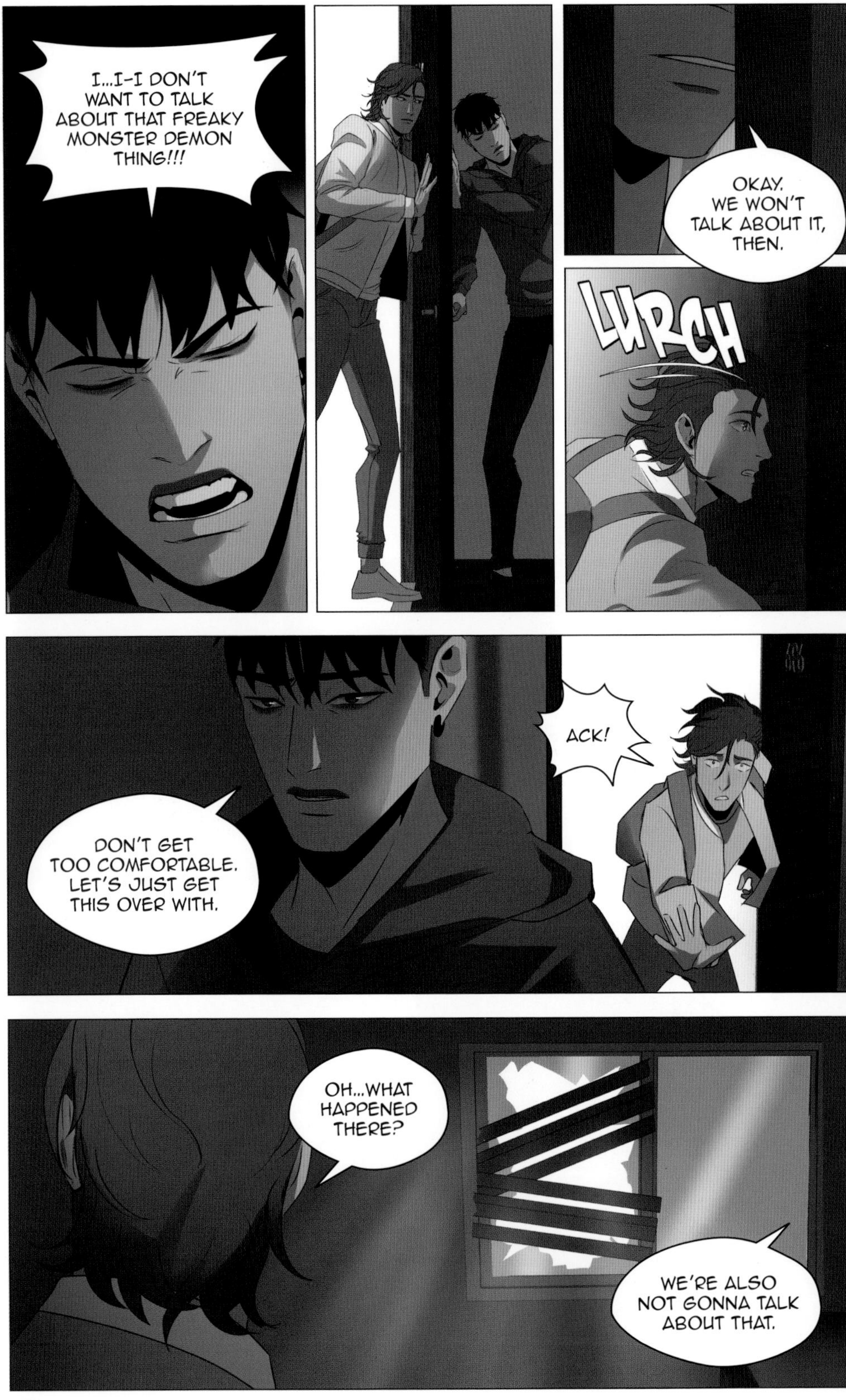
I...I-I DON'T WANT TO TALK ABOUT THAT FREAKY MONSTER DEMON THING!!!
OKAY. WE WON'T TALK ABOUT IT, THEN.
LURCH
ACK!
DON'T GET TOO COMFORTABLE. LET'S JUST GET THIS OVER WITH.
OH...WHAT HAPPENED THERE?
WE'RE ALSO NOT GONNA TALK ABOUT THAT.

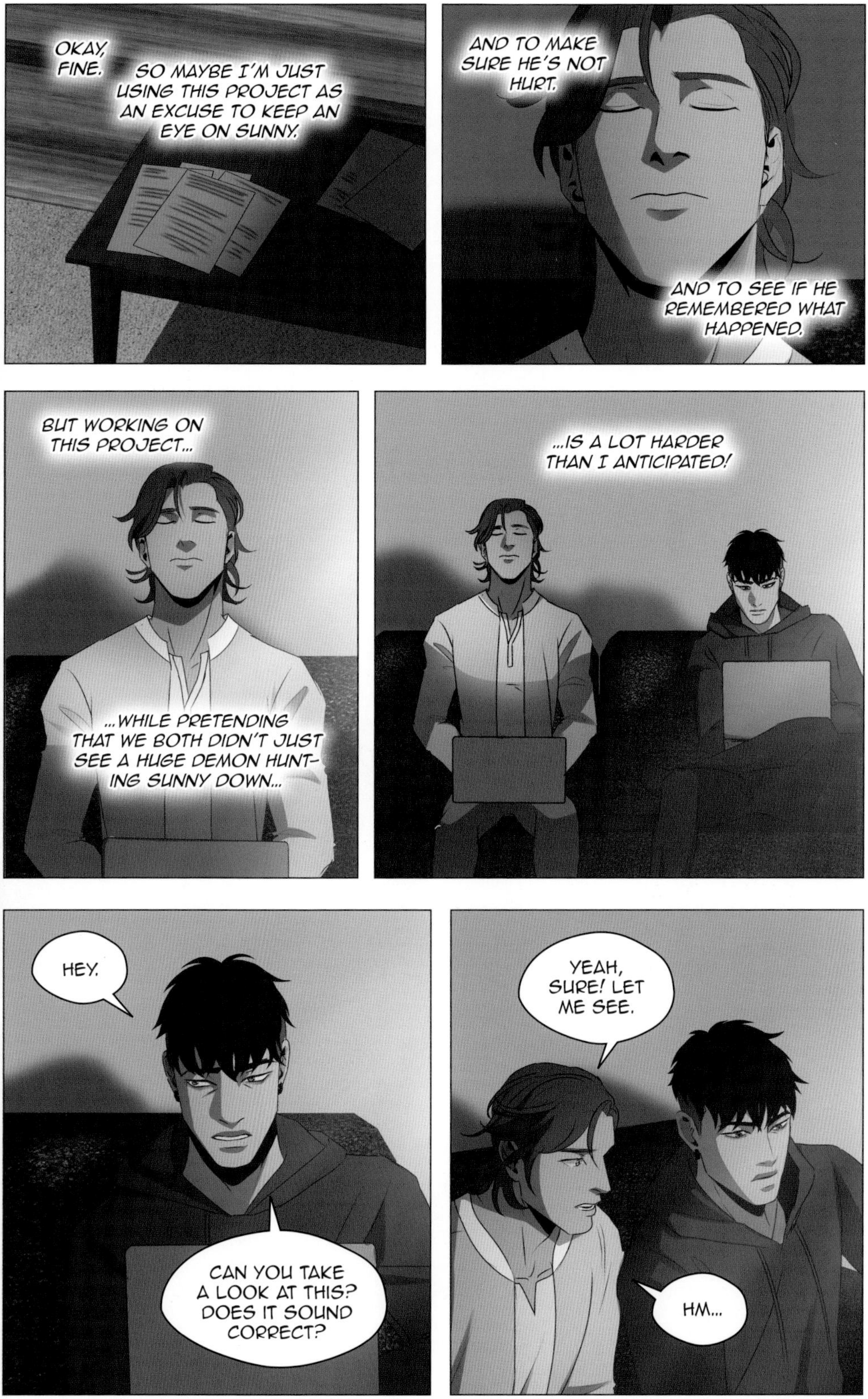
OKAY, FINE.
SO MAYBE I'M JUST USING THIS PROJECT AS AN EXCUSE TO KEEP AN EYE ON SUNNY.
AND TO MAKE SURE HE'S NOT HURT.
AND TO SEE IF HE REMEMBERED WHAT HAPPENED.
BUT WORKING ON THIS PROJECT...
...WHILE PRETENDING THAT WE BOTH DIDN'T JUST SEE A HUGE DEMON HUNT-ING SUNNY DOWN...
...IS A LOT HARDER THAN I ANTICIPATED!
HEY.
CAN YOU TAKE A LOOK AT THIS? DOES IT SOUND CORRECT?
YEAH, SURE! LET ME SEE.
HM...

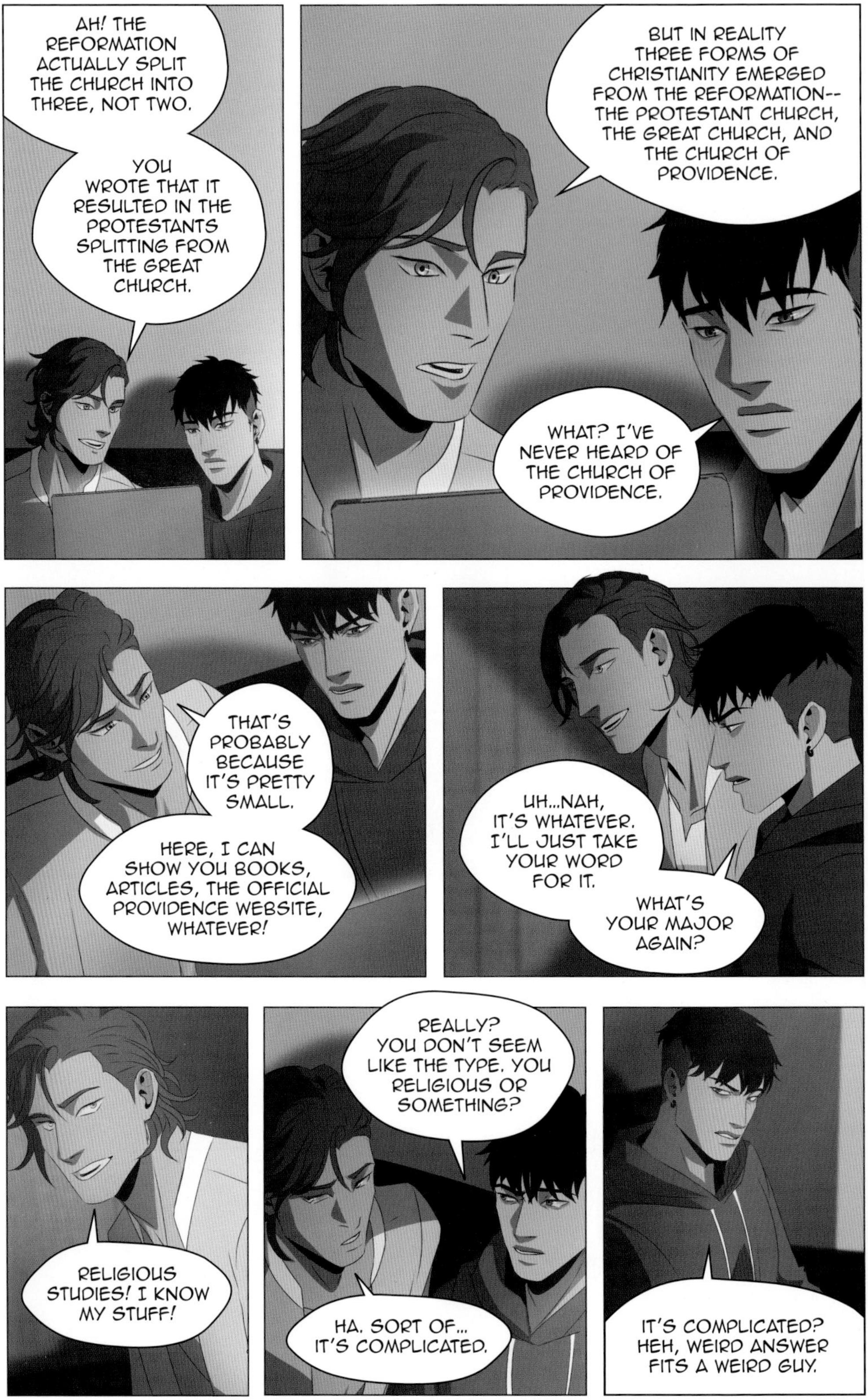
AH! THE REFORMATION ACTUALLY SPLIT THE CHURCH INTO THREE, NOT TWO.
YOU WROTE THAT IT RESULTED IN THE PROTESTANTS SPLITTING FROM THE GREAT CHURCH.
BUT IN REALITY THREE FORMS OF CHRISTIANITY EMERGED FROM THE REFORMATION-- THE PROTESTANT CHURCH, THE GREAT CHURCH, AND THE CHURCH OF PROVIDENCE.
WHAT? I'VE NEVER HEARD OF THE CHURCH OF PROVIDENCE.
THAT'S PROBABLY BECAUSE IT'S PRETTY SMALL.
HERE, I CAN SHOW YOU BOOKS, ARTICLES, THE OFFICIAL PROVIDENCE WEBSITE, WHATEVER!
UH...NAH, IT'S WHATEVER. I'LL JUST TAKE YOUR WORD FOR IT.
WHAT'S YOUR MAJOR AGAIN?
RELIGIOUS STUDIES! I KNOW MY STUFF!
REALLY? YOU DON'T SEEM LIKE THE TYPE. YOU RELIGIOUS OR SOMETHING?
HA. SORT OF... IT'S COMPLICATED.
IT'S COMPLICATED? HEH, WEIRD ANSWER FITS A WEIRD GUY.

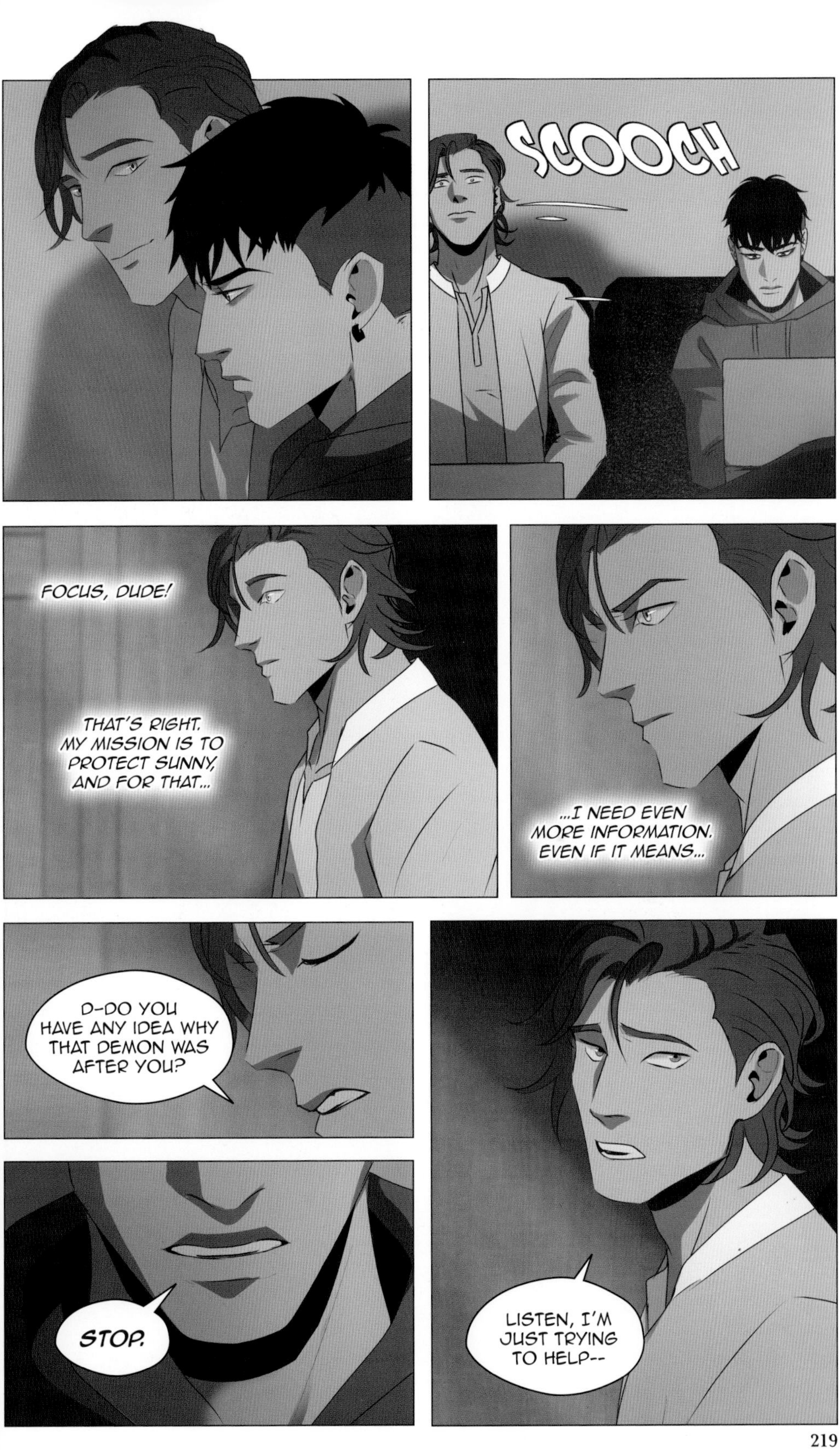
SCOOCH
FOCUS, DUDE!
THAT'S RIGHT. MY MISSION IS TO PROTECT SUNNY, AND FOR THAT...
...I NEED EVEN MORE INFORMATION. EVEN IF IT MEANS...
D-DO YOU HAVE ANY IDEA WHY THAT DEMON WAS AFTER YOU?
STOP.
LISTEN, I'M JUST TRYING TO HELP--

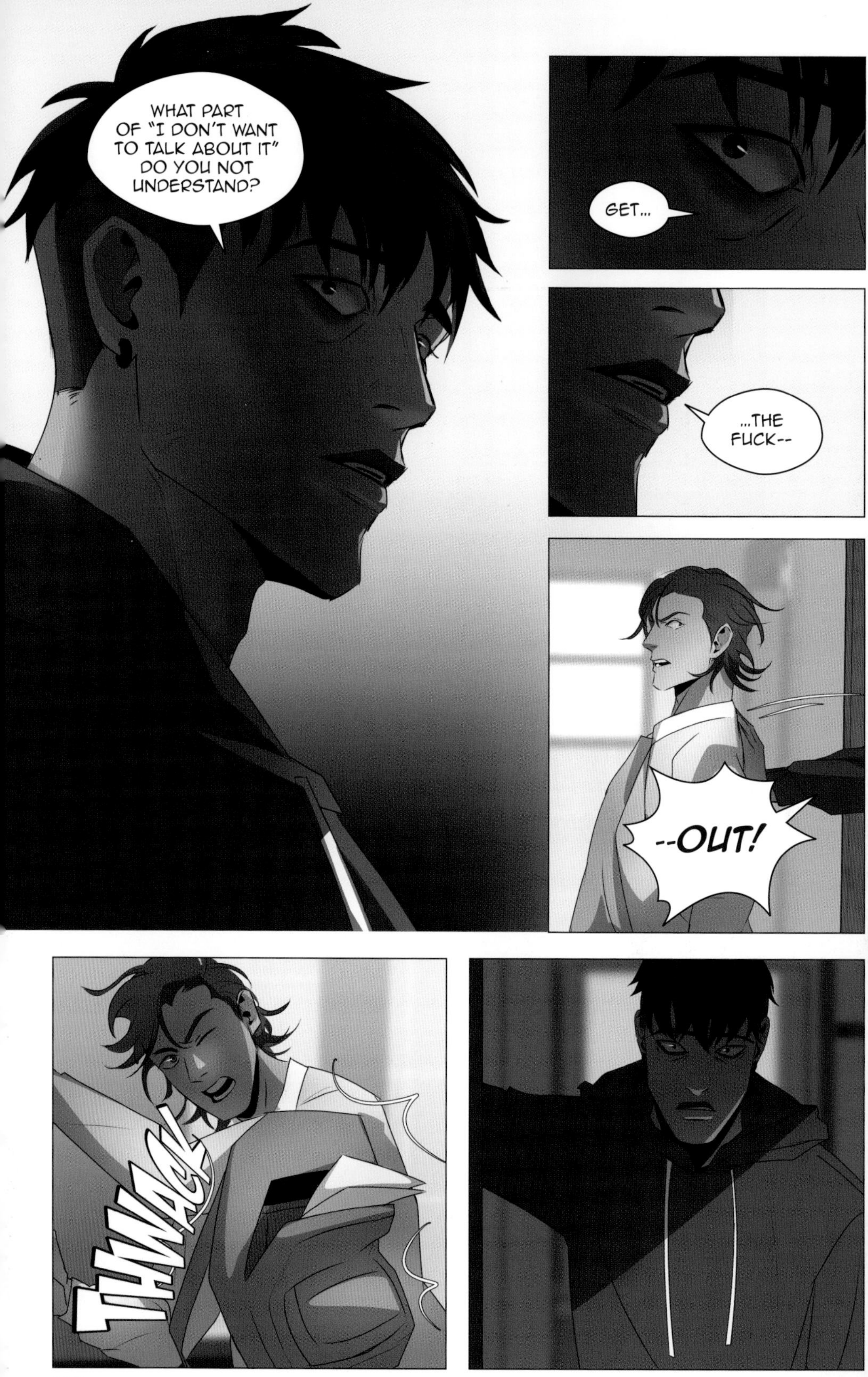
WHAT PART OF "I DON'T WANT TO TALK ABOUT IT" DO YOU NOT UNDERSTAND?
GET...
...THE FUCK--
--OUT!
THWACK

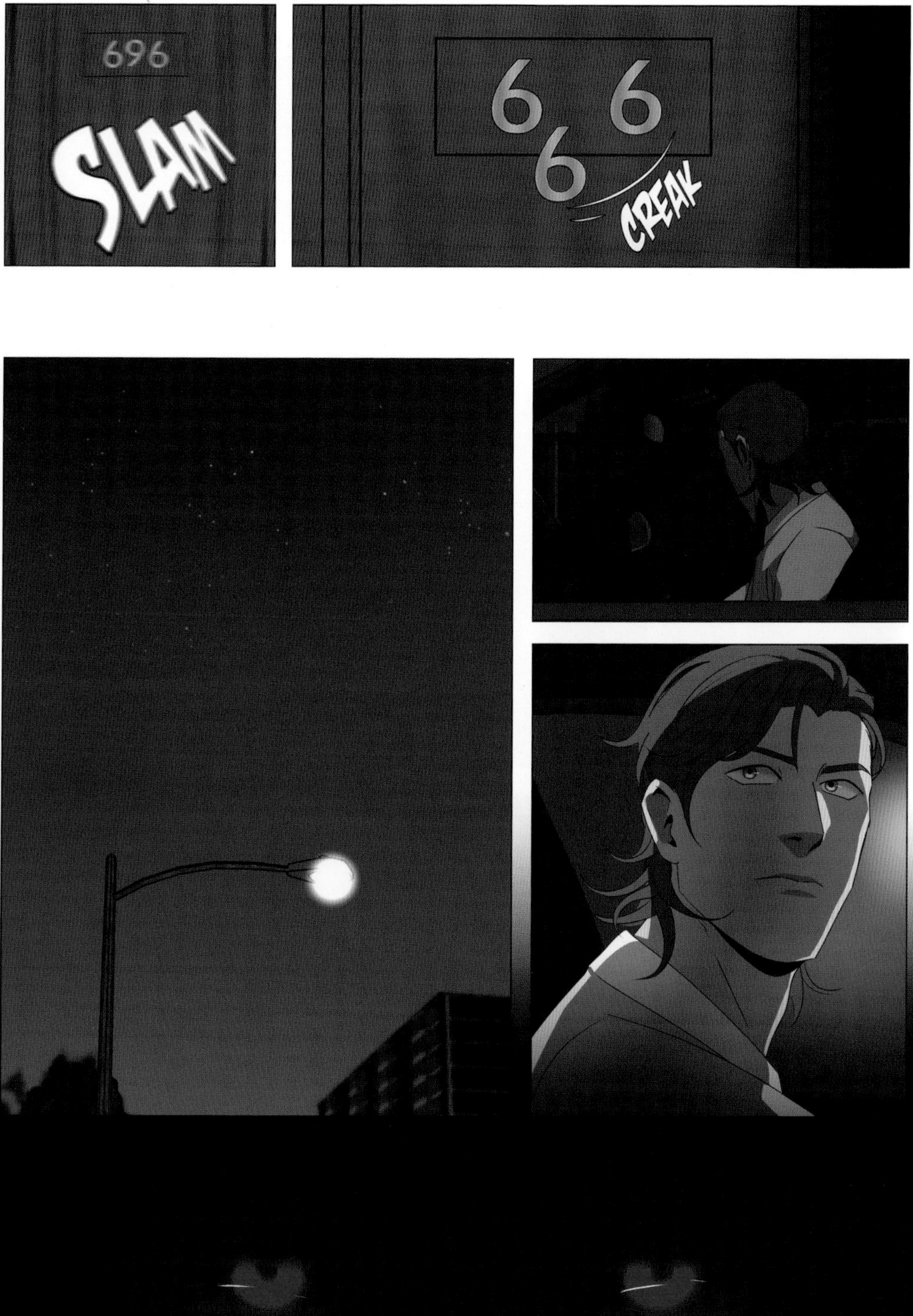
696
SLAM
666
CREAK

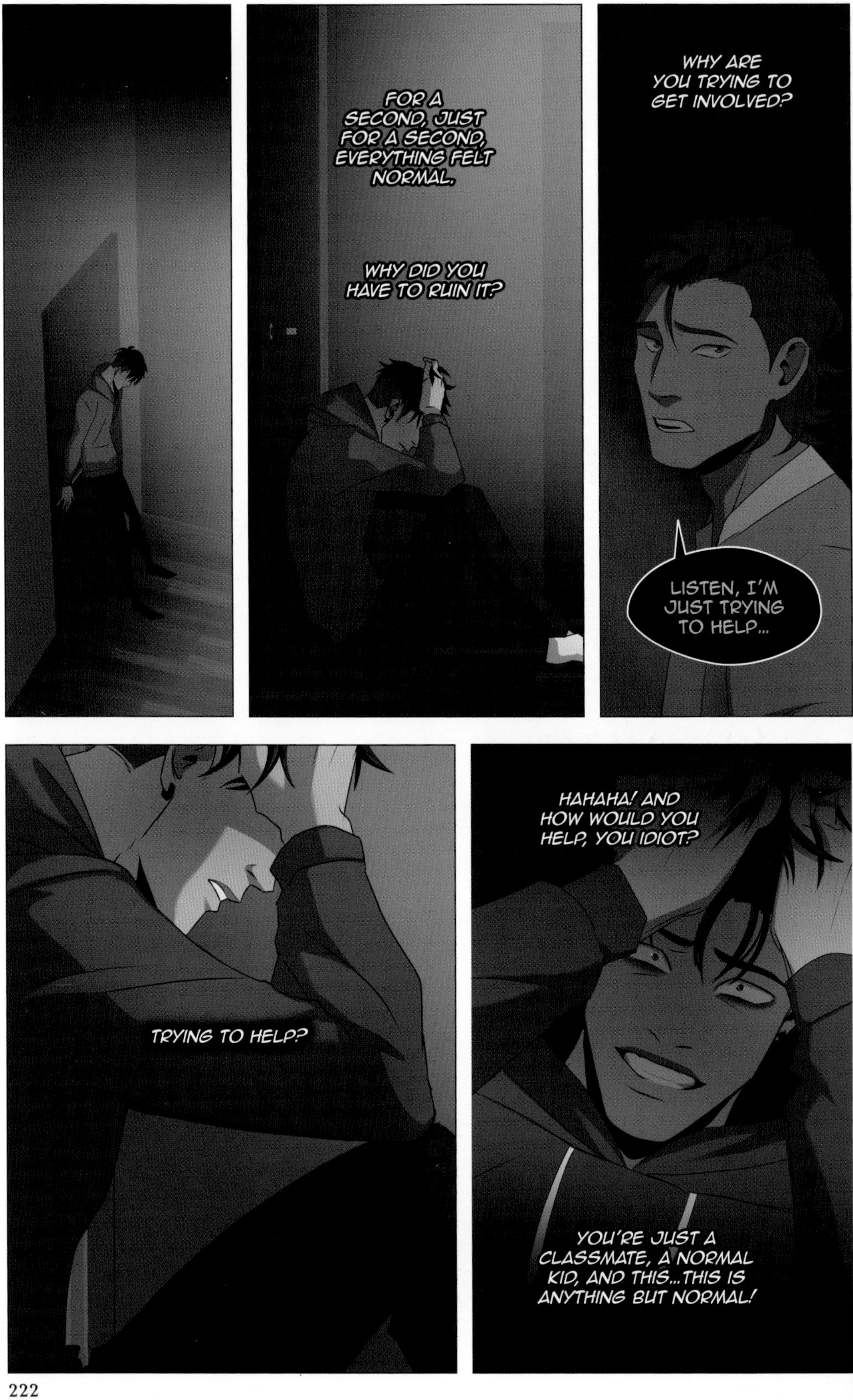
FOR A SECOND, JUST FOR A SECOND, EVERYTHING FELT NORMAL.
WHY DID YOU HAVE TO RUIN IT?
WHY ARE YOU TRYING TO GET INVOLVED?
LISTEN, I'M JUST TRYING TO HELP...
TRYING TO HELP?
HAHAHA! AND HOW WOULD YOU HELP, YOU IDIOT?
YOU'RE JUST A CLASSMATE, A NORMAL KID, AND THIS...THIS IS ANYTHING BUT NORMAL!

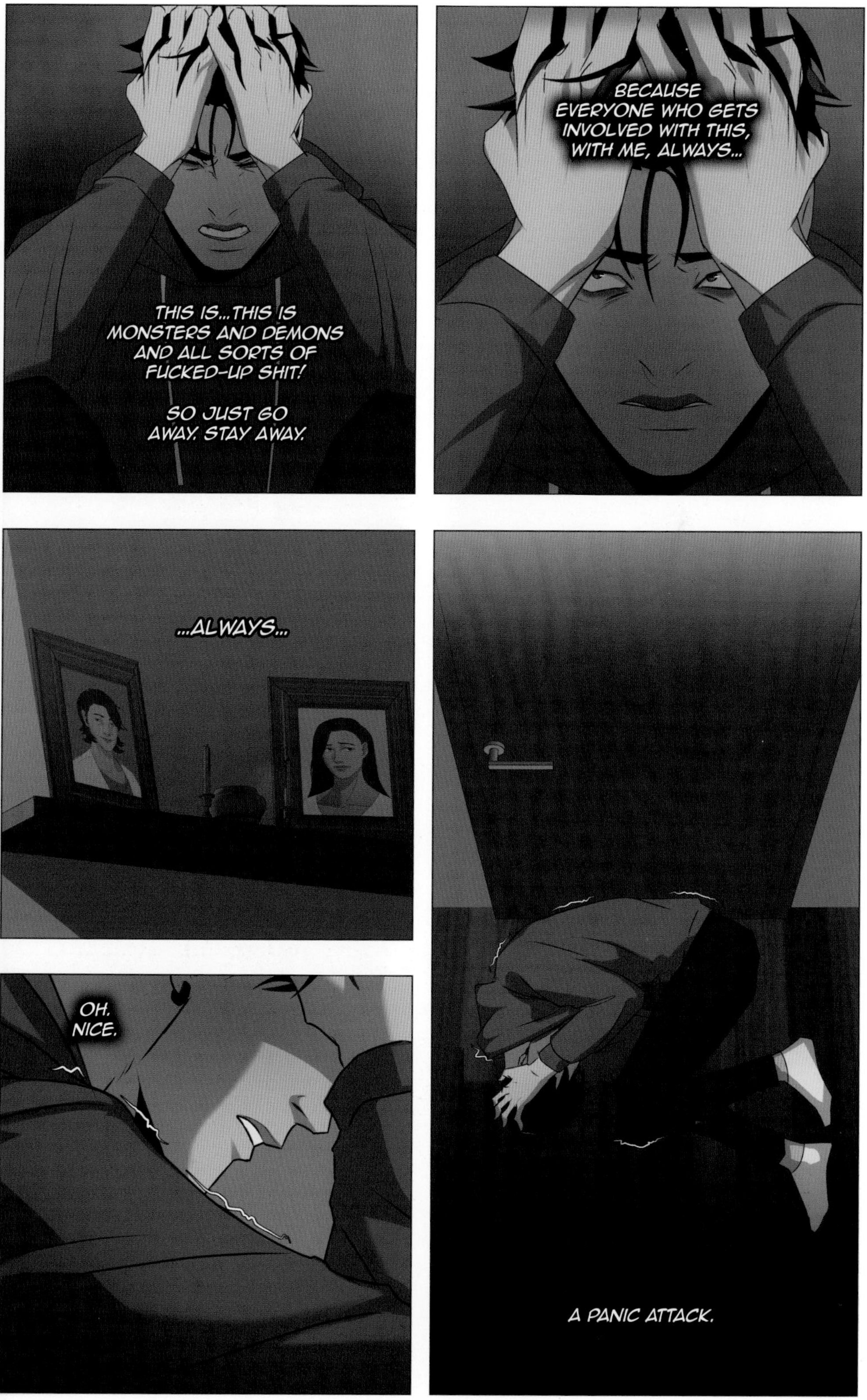
THIS IS...THIS IS MONSTERS AND DEMONS AND ALL SORTS OF FUCKED-UP SHIT!
SO JUST GO AWAY. STAY AWAY.
BECAUSE EVERYONE WHO GETS INVOLVED WITH THIS, WITH ME, ALWAYS...
...ALWAYS...
OH. NICE.
A PANIC ATTACK.

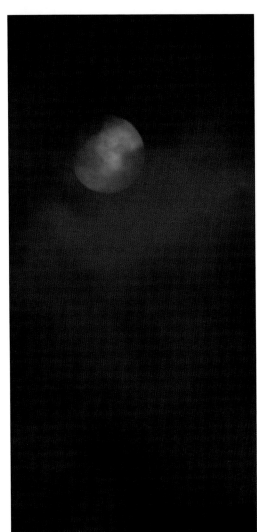

DAMN, IT'S LATE.

3:12
Sunday, September 6

WELL, THOSE ARE HOURS I'LL NEVER GET BACK.

I NEED SOME AIR.

JUST BREATHE.

YEAH, THAT'S IT.

TOMORROW I'LL START FILLING OUT TRANSFER APPLICATIONS.

THIS IS NO BIG DEAL. JUST LIKE ALL THE OTHER TIMES.

AND THEN I'LL...

WAIT. THAT FEELING AGAIN...

AS IF I'M BEING...

...FOLLOWED.

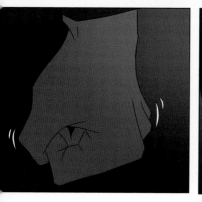

THIS MOTHERF--

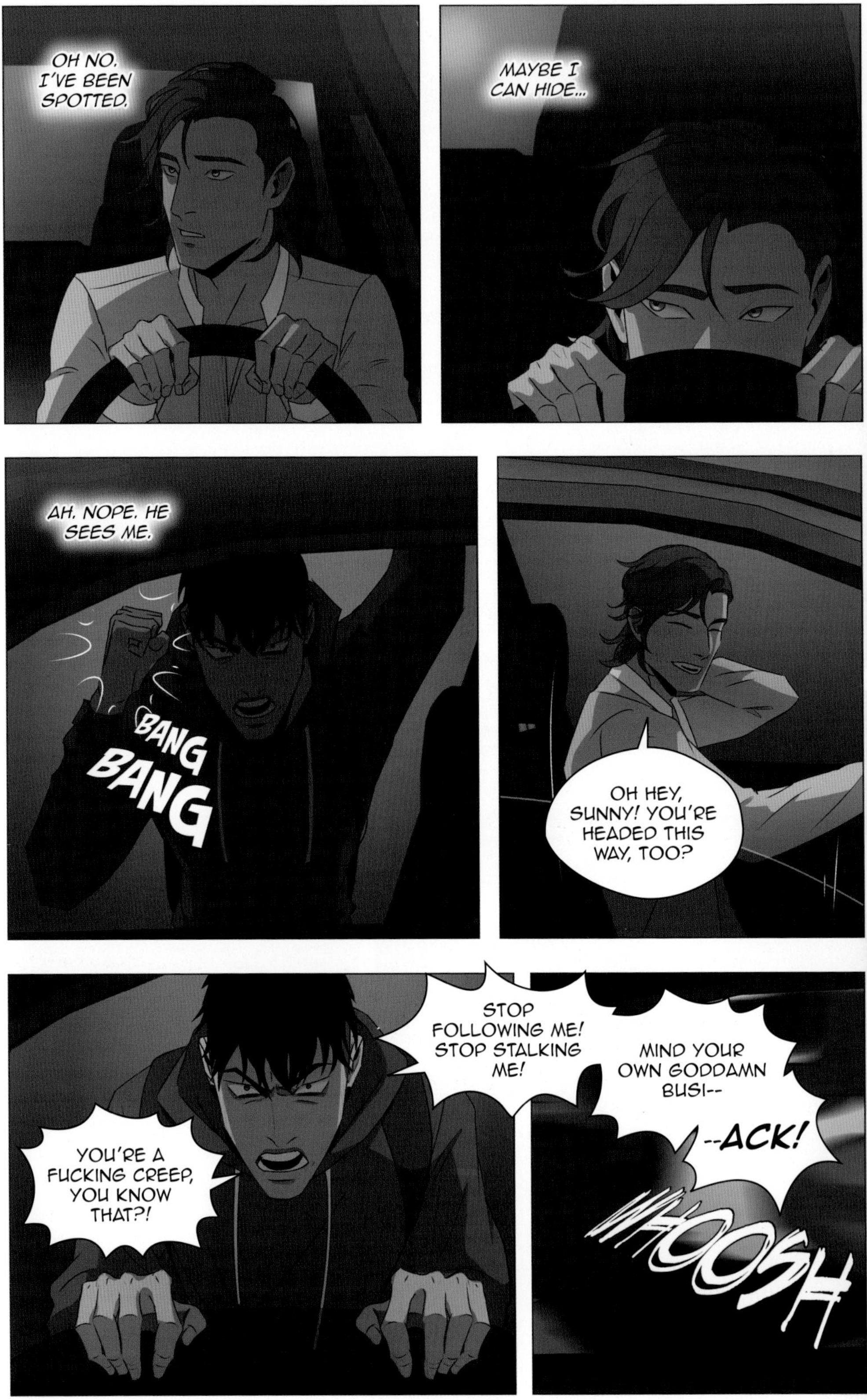
OH NO. I'VE BEEN SPOTTED.
MAYBE I CAN HIDE...
AH. NOPE. HE SEES ME.
BANG
BANG
OH HEY, SUNNY! YOU'RE HEADED THIS WAY, TOO?
STOP FOLLOWING ME! STOP STALKING ME!
YOU'RE A FUCKING CREEP, YOU KNOW THAT?!
MIND YOUR OWN GODDAMN BUSI--
--ACK!
WHOOSH

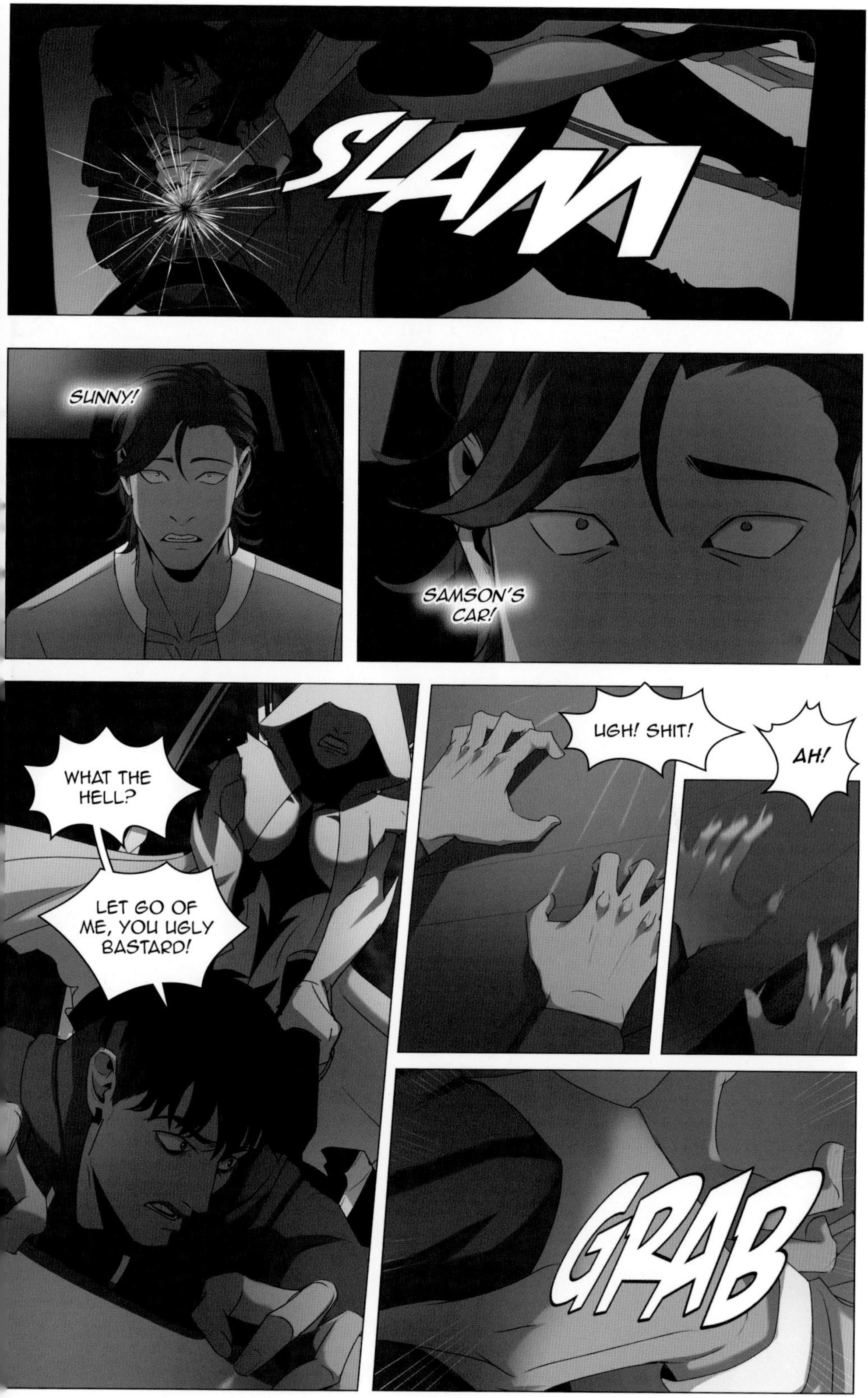
SLAM
SUNNY!
SAMSON'S CAR!
WHAT THE HELL?
LET GO OF ME, YOU UGLY BASTARD!
UGH! SHIT!
AH!
GRAB

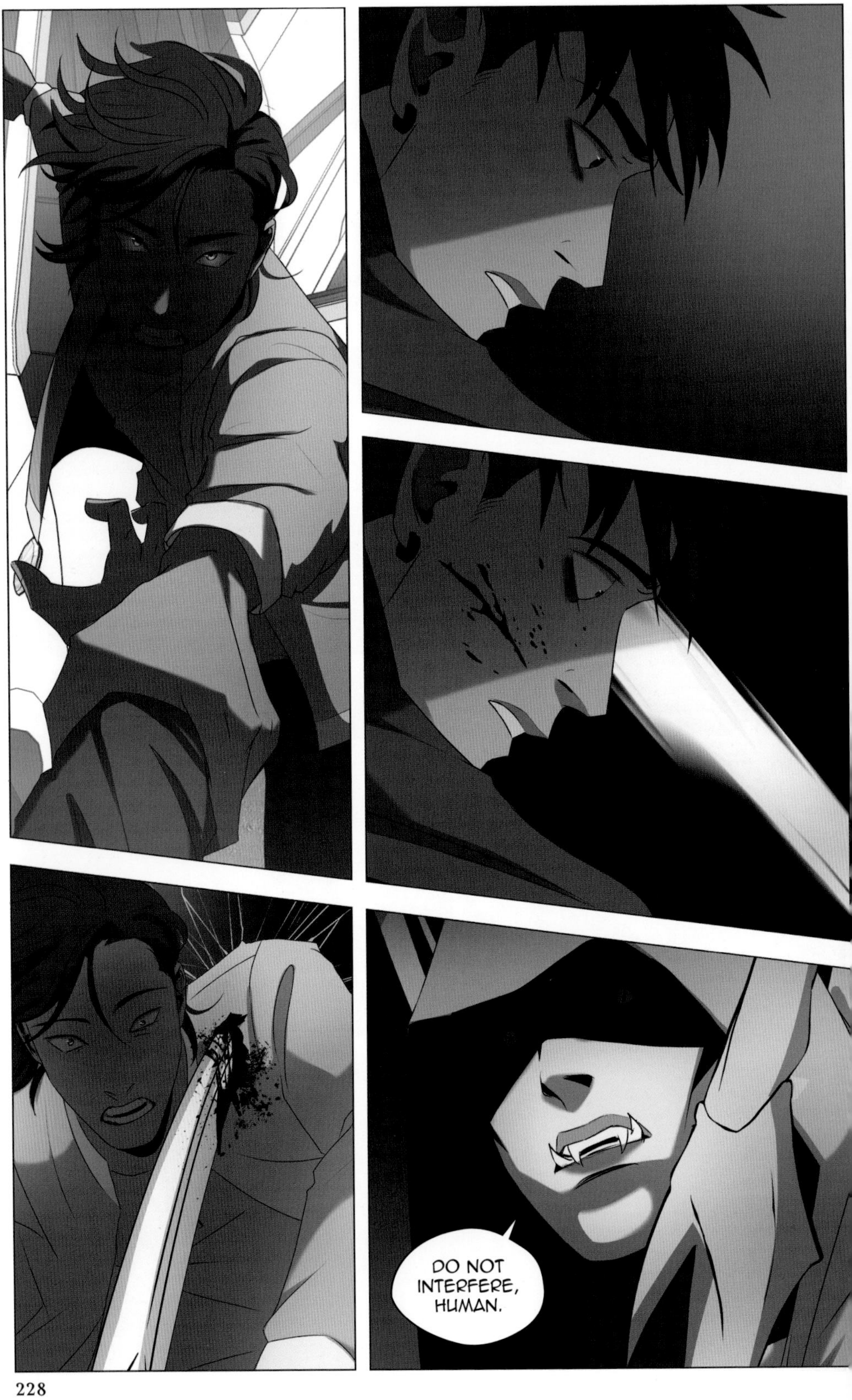
DO NOT
INTERFERE,
HUMAN.

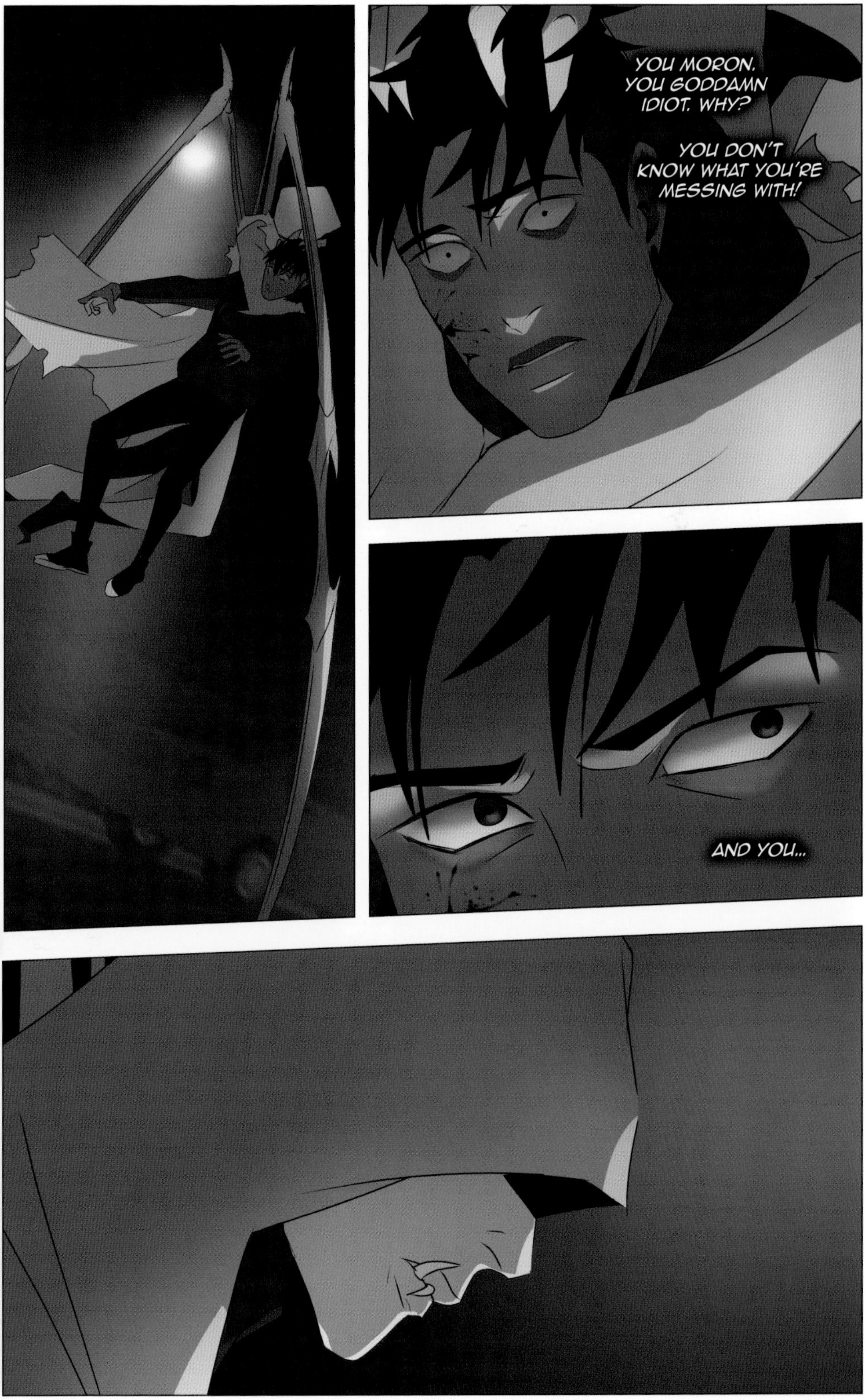
YOU MORON. YOU GODDAMN IDIOT. WHY?
YOU DON'T KNOW WHAT YOU'RE MESSING WITH!
AND YOU...

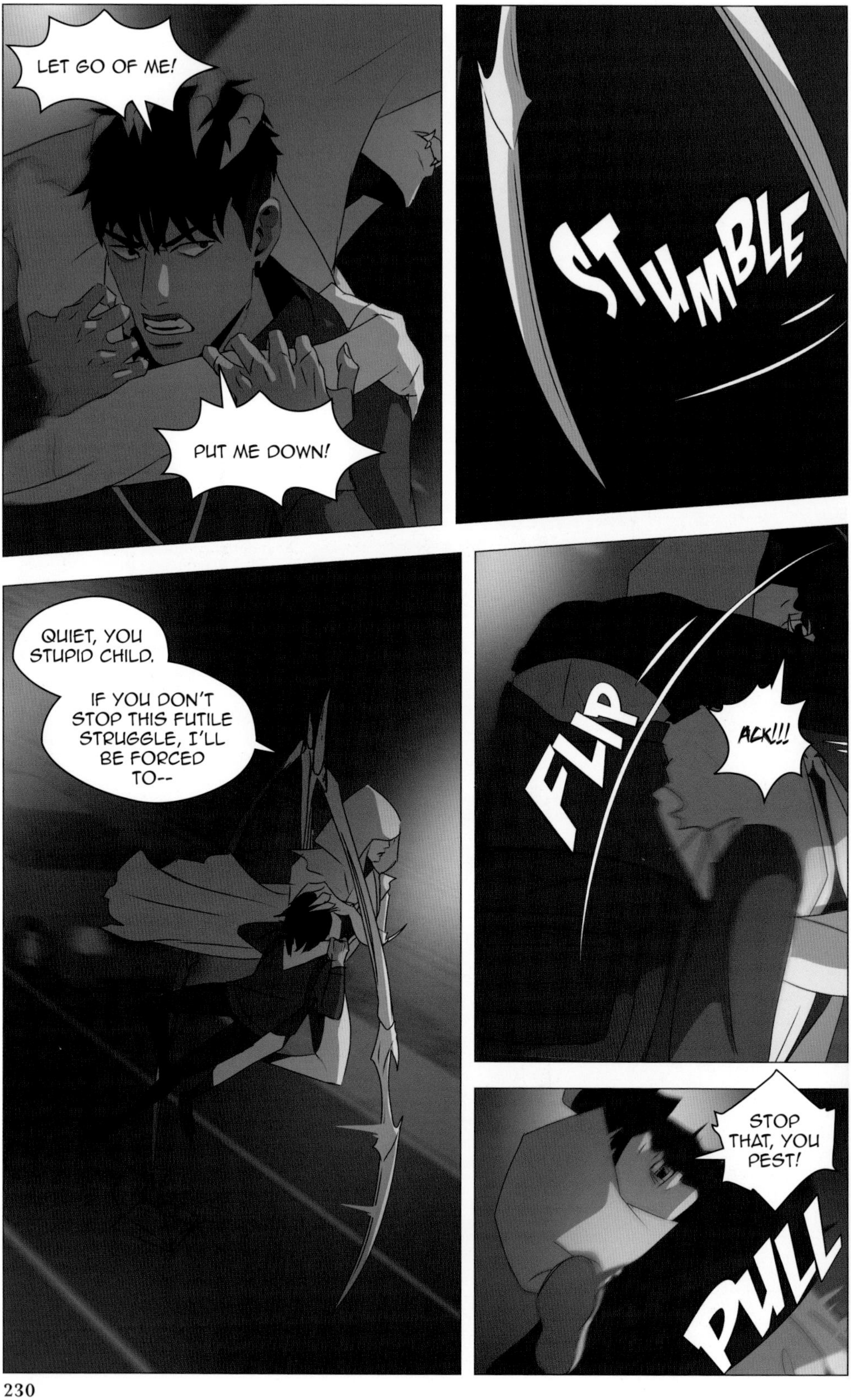
LET GO OF ME!
PUT ME DOWN!
STUMBLE
QUIET, YOU STUPID CHILD.
IF YOU DON'T STOP THIS FUTILE STRUGGLE, I'LL BE FORCED TO--
FLIP
ACK!!!
STOP THAT, YOU PEST!
PULL

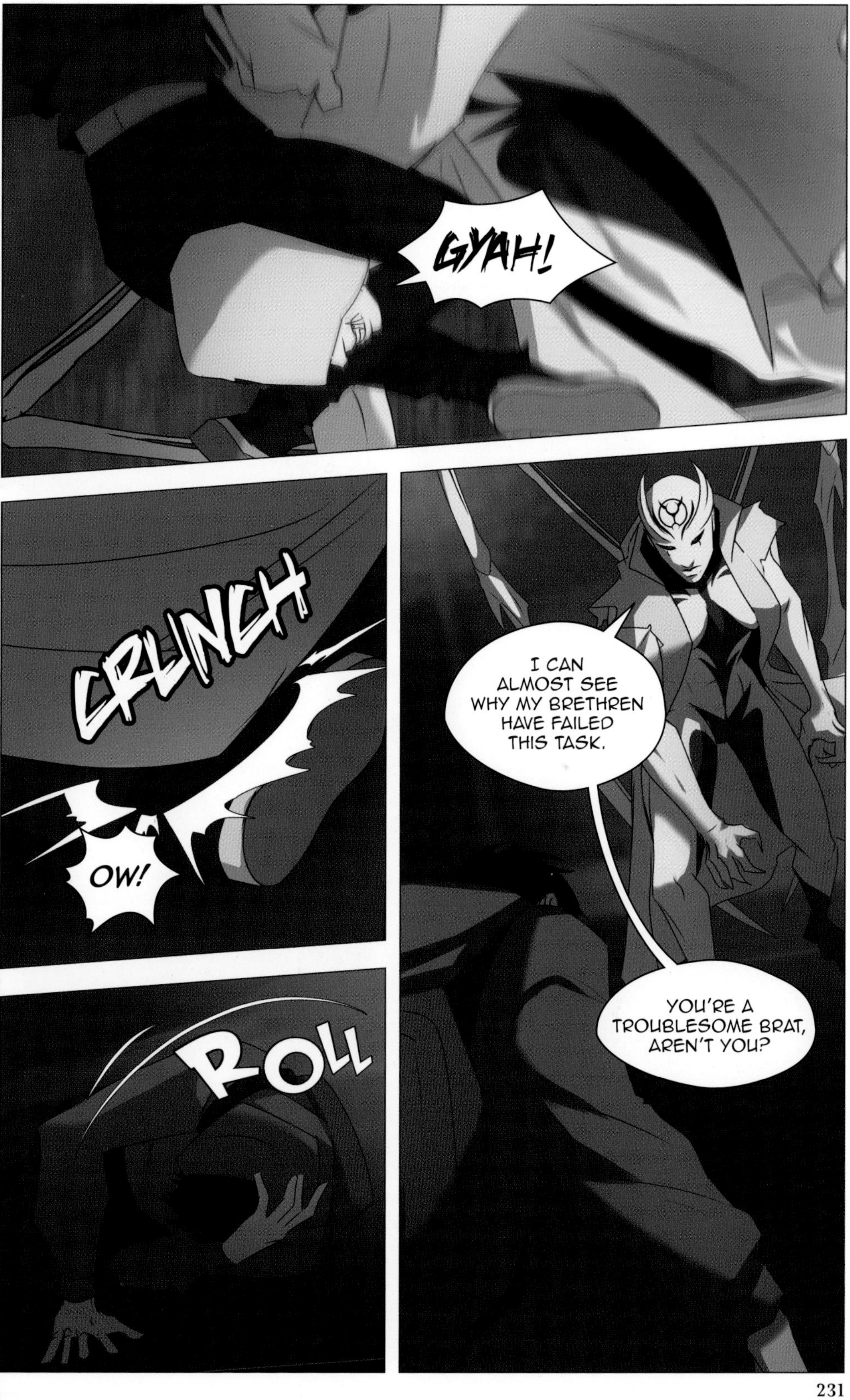
GYAH!
CRUNCH
OW!
ROLL
I CAN ALMOST SEE WHY MY BRETHREN HAVE FAILED THIS TASK.
YOU'RE A TROUBLESOME BRAT, AREN'T YOU?

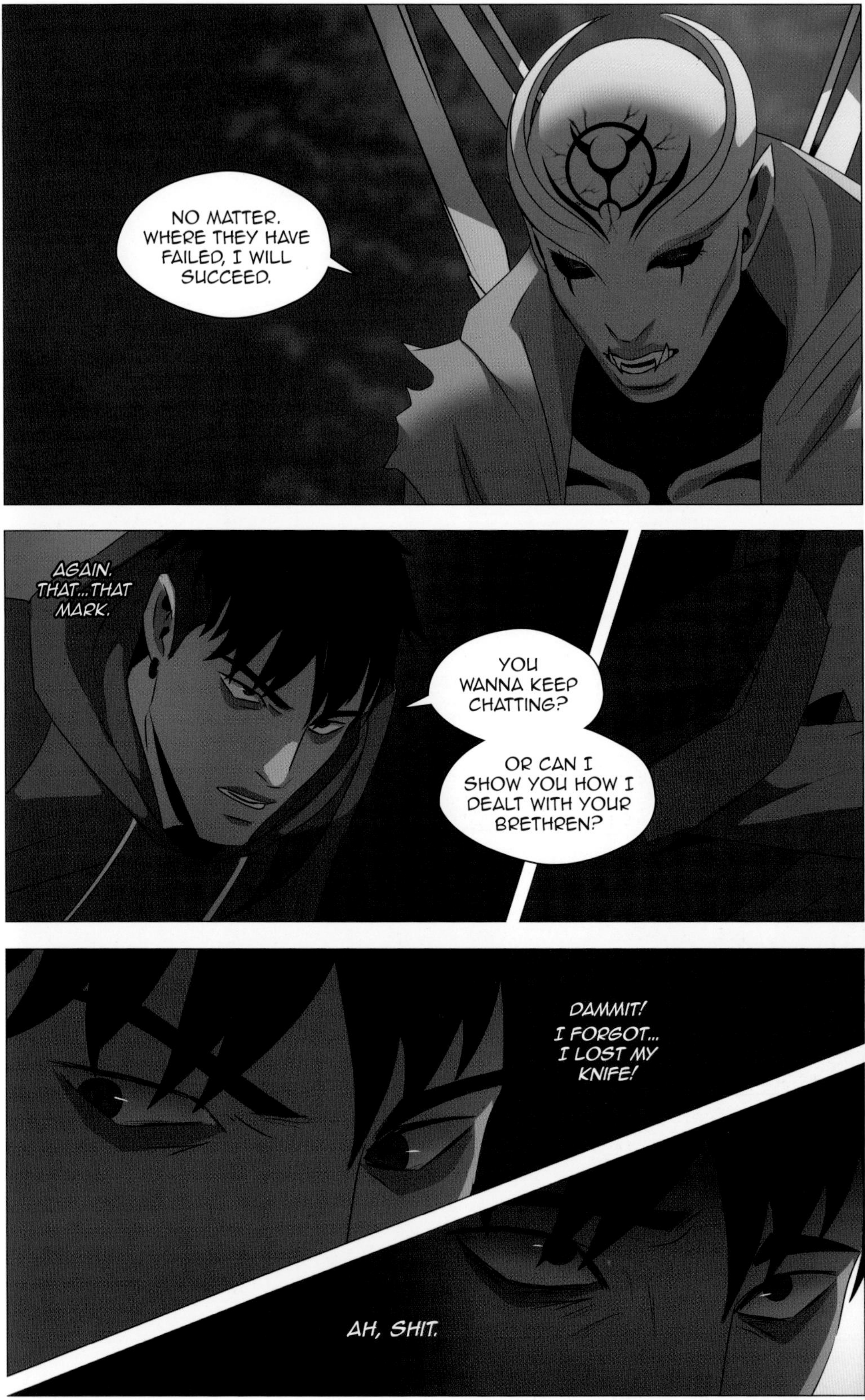
NO MATTER. WHERE THEY HAVE FAILED, I WILL SUCCEED.
AGAIN. THAT...THAT MARK.
YOU WANNA KEEP CHATTING?
OR CAN I SHOW YOU HOW I DEALT WITH YOUR BRETHREN?
DAMMIT! I FORGOT... I LOST MY KNIFE!
AH, SHIT.

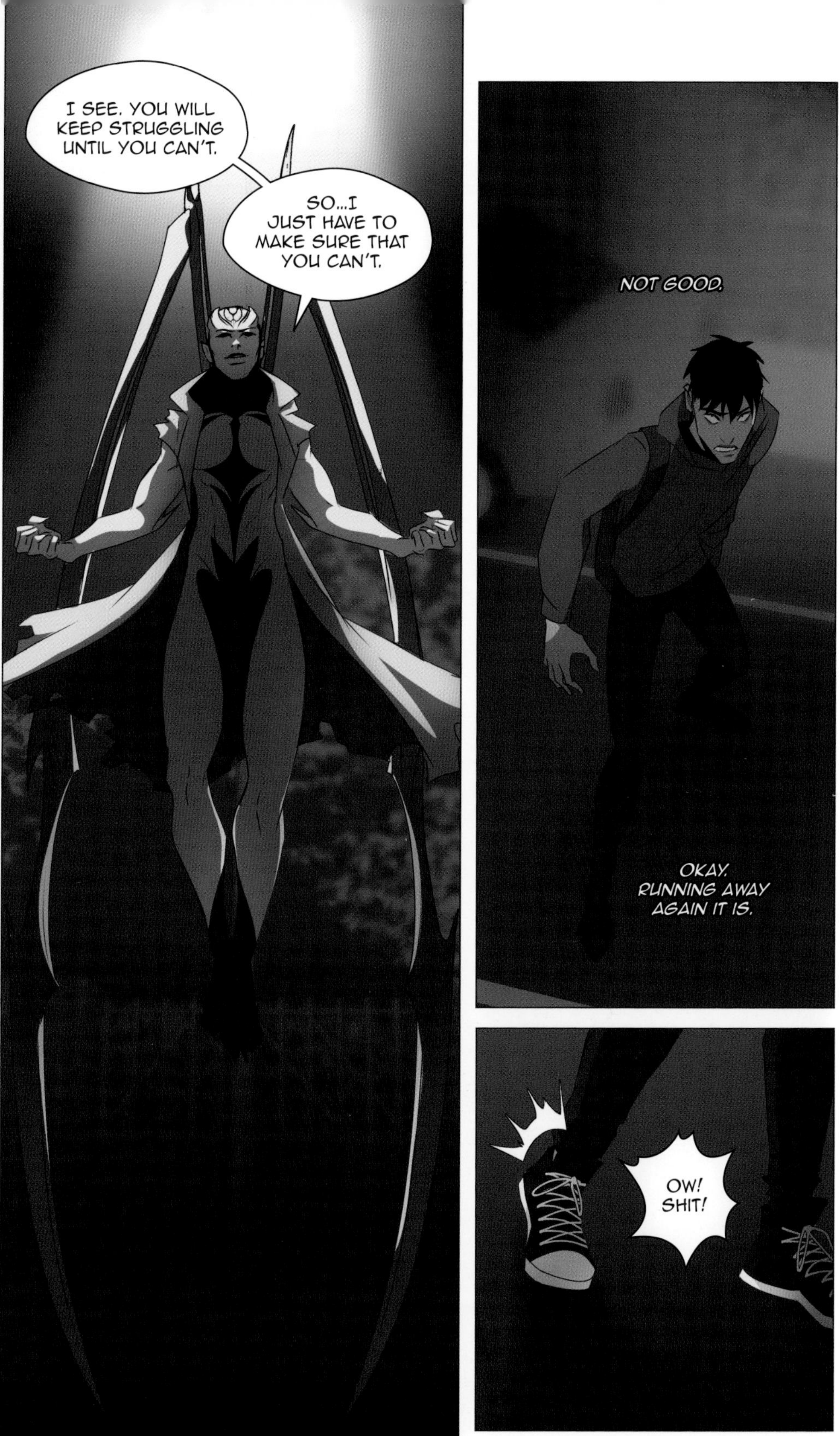
I SEE. YOU WILL KEEP STRUGGLING UNTIL YOU CAN'T.
SO...I JUST HAVE TO MAKE SURE THAT YOU CAN'T.
NOT GOOD.
OKAY. RUNNING AWAY AGAIN IT IS.
OW! SHIT!

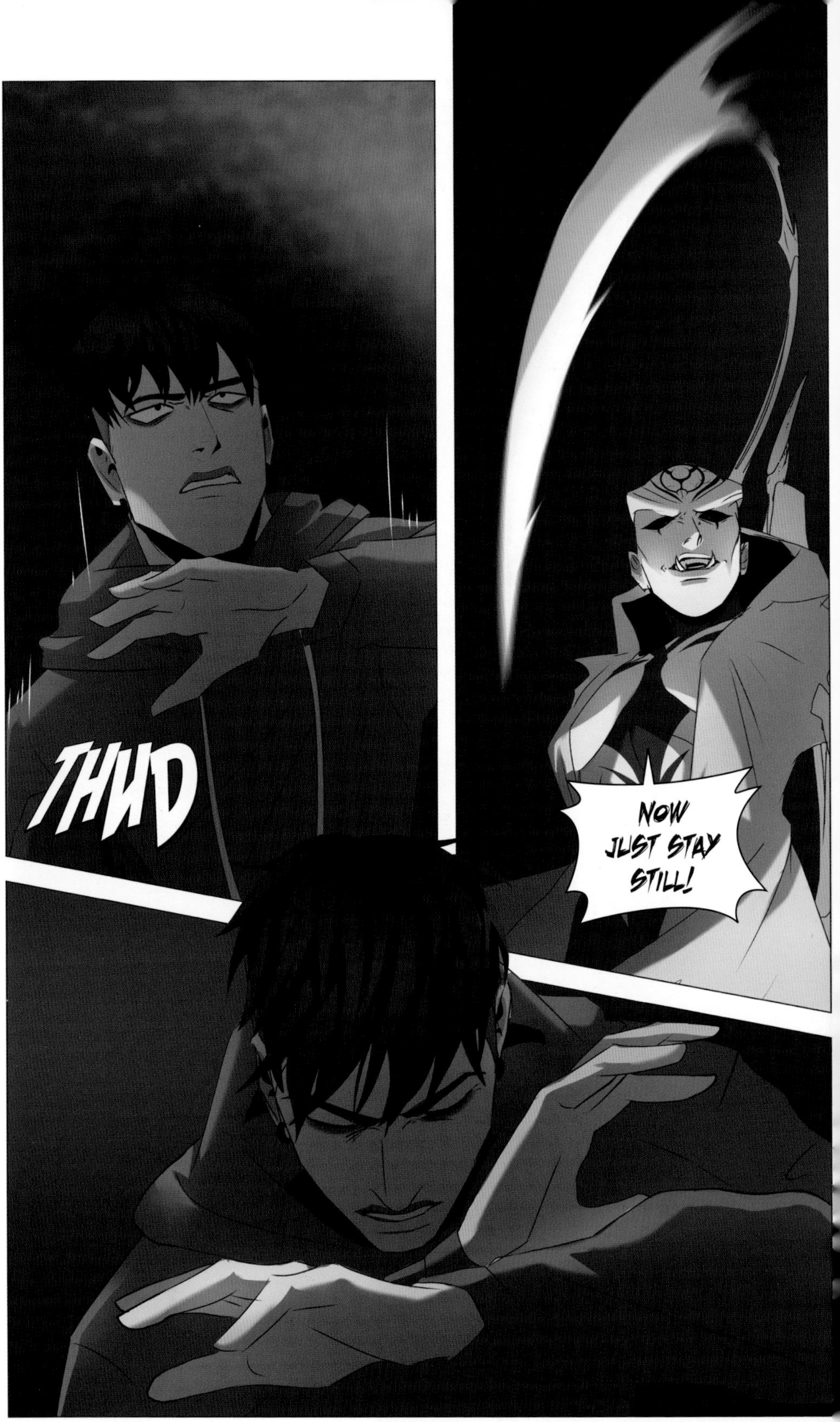
THUD
NOW JUST STAY STILL!

HUH?
WHAT THE--

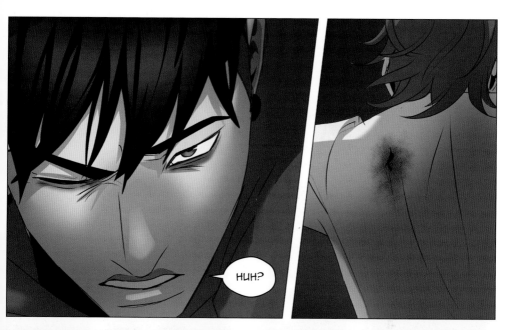

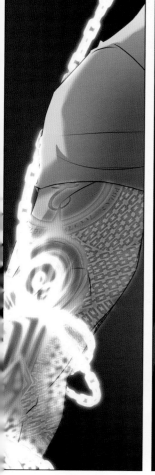

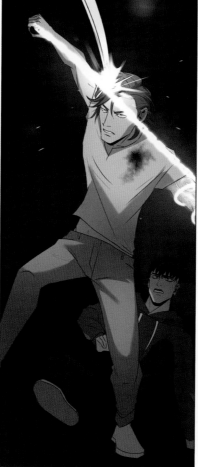

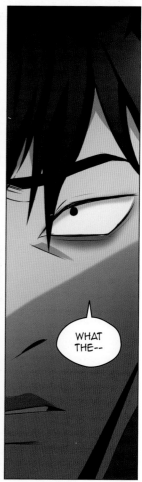

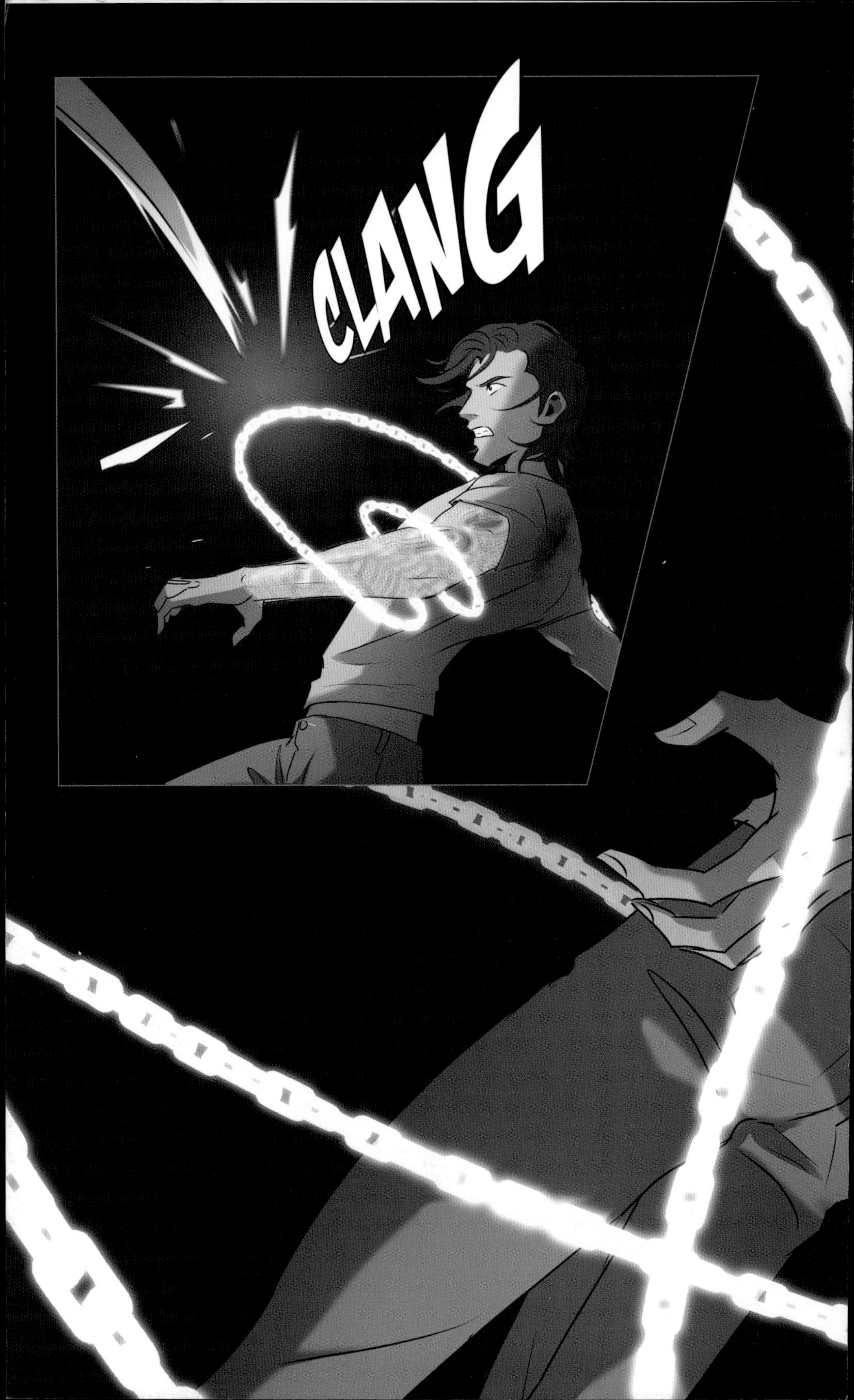
CLANG

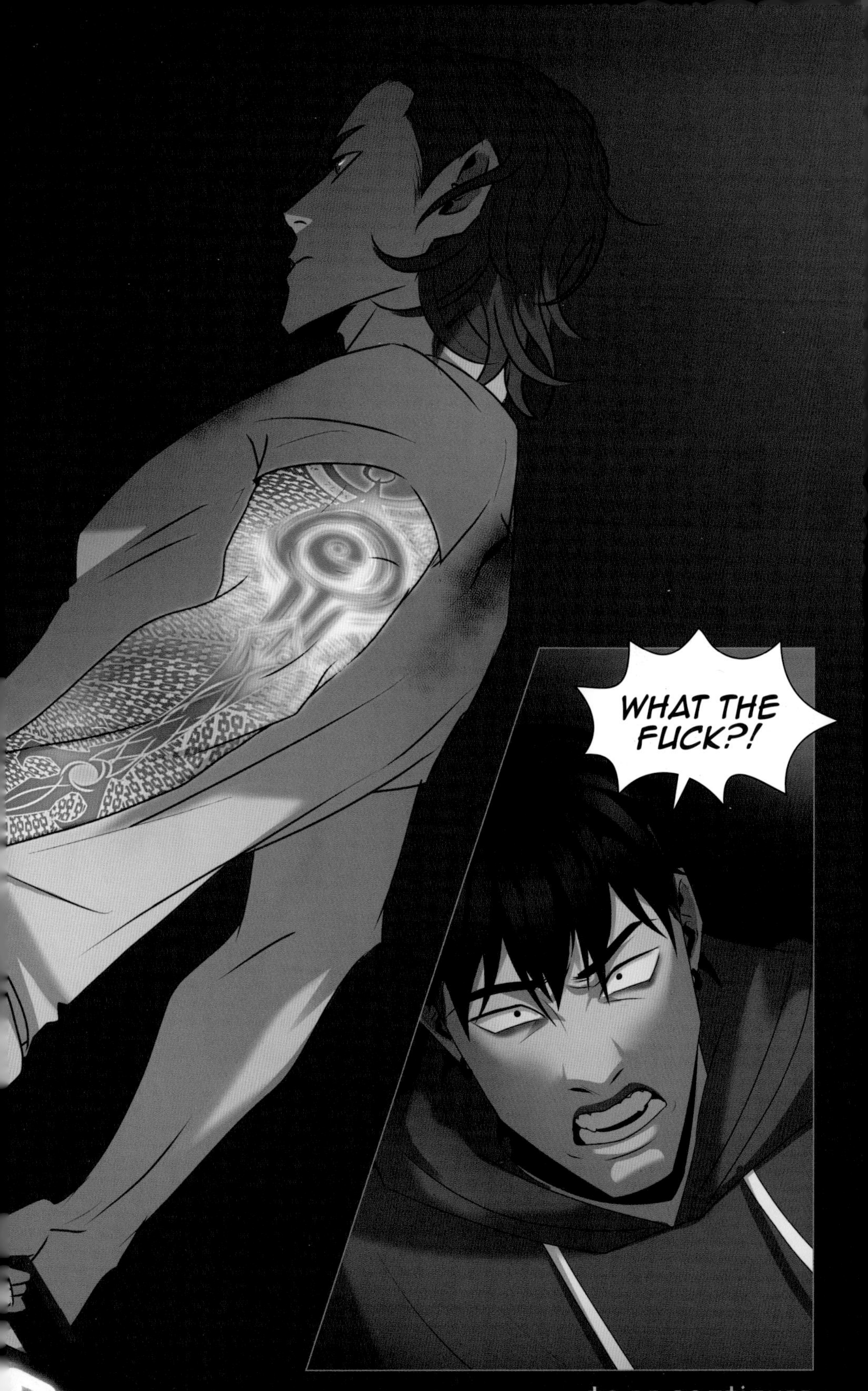
WHAT THE FUCK?!

TO BE CONTINUED...

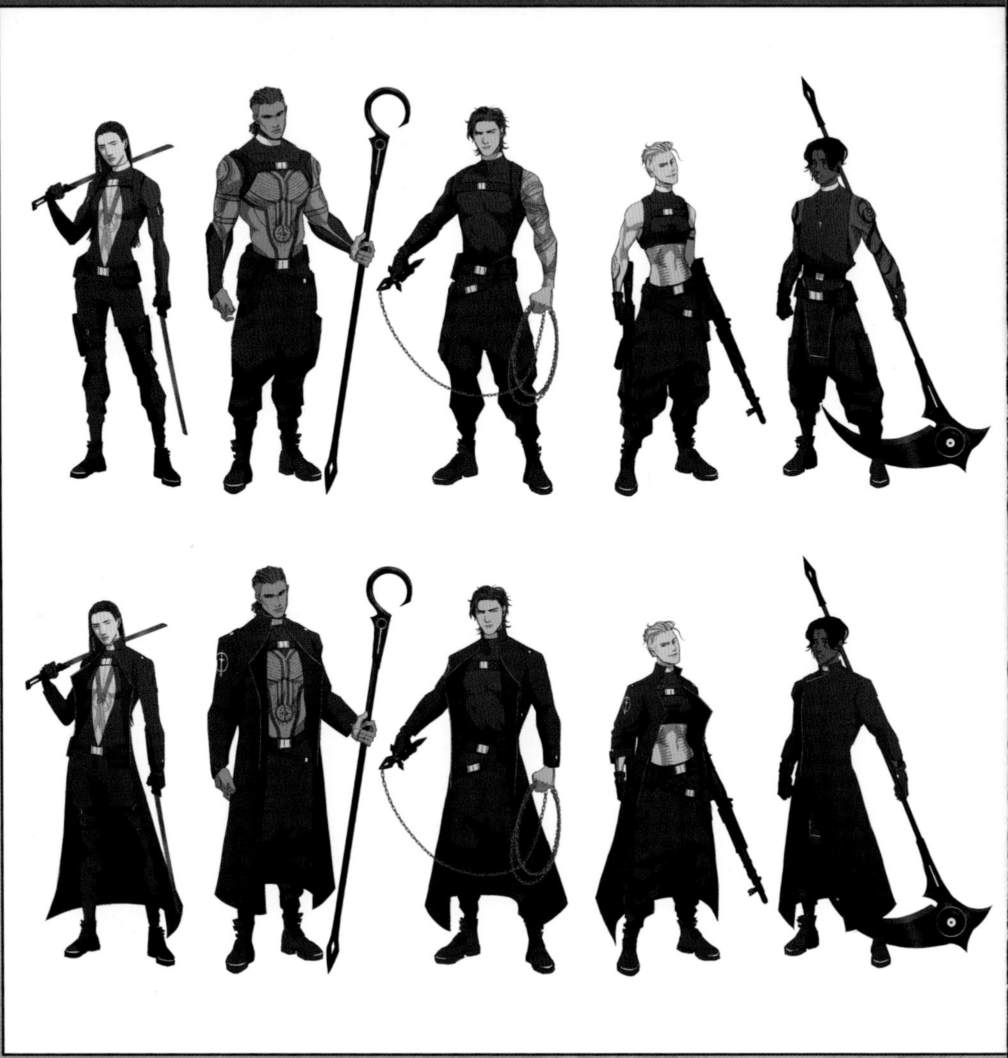

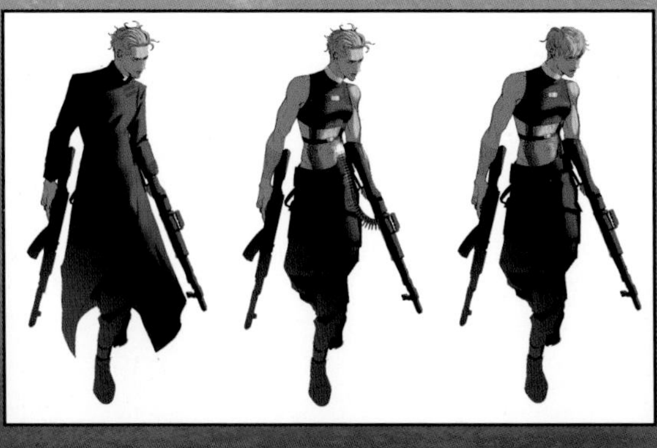

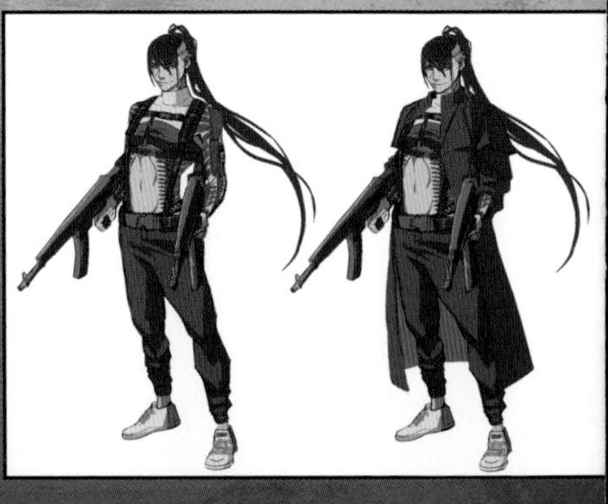

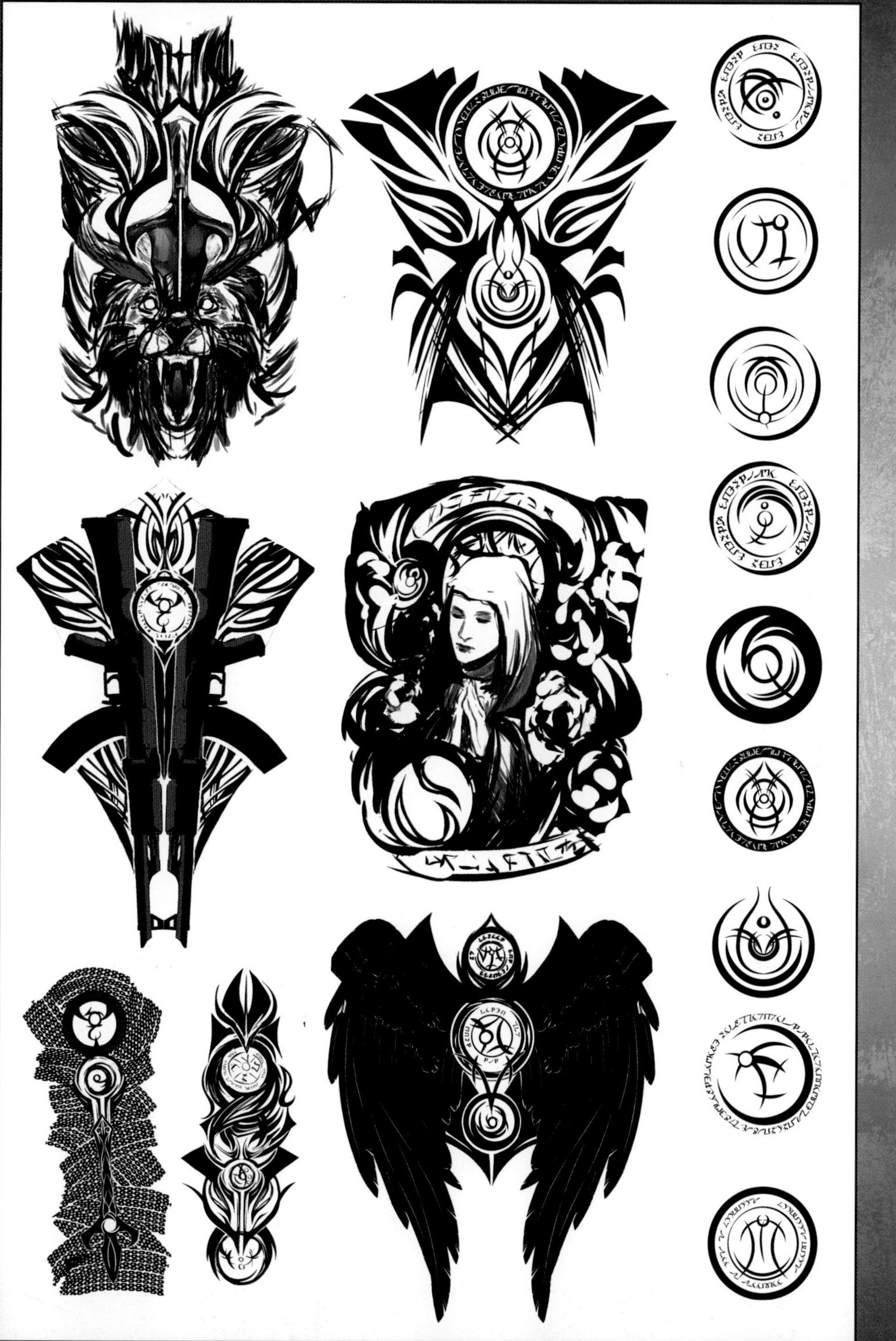